D1391560

# THE STASI FILES

**Also by Anthony Glees**

*Reinventing Germany: German Political Development Since 1945*

*The Secrets of the Service: British Intelligence and Communist Subversion, 1939–51*

*Exile Politics During the Second World War*

# THE STASI FILES

East Germany's Secret Operations
Against Britain

ANTHONY GLEES

First published in Great Britain by The Free Press in 2003
An imprint of Simon & Schuster UK Ltd
A Viacom company

1 3 5 7 9 10 8 6 4 2

Simon & Schuster UK Ltd
Africa House
64–78 Kingsway
London WC2B 6AH

Simon & Schuster Australia
Sydney

www.simonsays.co.uk

A CIP catalogue for this book is available
from the British Library.

ISBN: 0-7432-3104-X

Typeset by M Rules
Printed and bound in Great Britain by
The Bath Press, Bath

IN MEMORY OF HARRY DONIGER

1923–2001

# Contents

## CONTENTS

# Glossary

All the translations in this book are my own – my undergraduate degree was in History *and* German – and in them I have tried to recapture the peculiarities of East German officialese, which was often clumsy and opaque, while rendering its meaning clearly to the best of my ability.

In common with accepted practice today, the two German states that existed before unification on 3 October 1990 are referred to as 'the German Democratic Republic' (the GDR) or East Germany, and 'the Federal Republic of Germany' (the FRG) or West Germany. The citizens of the two states are described as 'East Germans' or 'West Germans'. What before 1990 was the GDR is termed here simply 'eastern Germany'. The current federal capital is referred to as 'Berlin'; before 1990, the capital of West Germany was Bonn and of East Germany East Berlin. The East Germans, however, always called West Berlin 'Westberlin', and East Berlin simply Berlin or 'Berlin, capital of the GDR'.

**agent of influence**: someone who secretly seeks to further the aims and ambitions of the Stasi in the knowledge that to do so will find favour with the East Germans, by using his or her influence to help establish a positive view of East Germany in the UK in order to open doors for it which would otherwise remain closed

**BfV**: *Bundesamt für Verfassungsschutz*, the West German security service

**BND**: *Bundesnachrichtendienst*, the West German secret intelligence service

**Boss**: the pre-Mandela South African secret intelligence service

**BstU**: the Stasi Archive in Berlin

**Chatham House**: the Royal Institute of International Affairs (RIIA), London

**CIA**: the Central Intelligence Agency, the main US secret intelligence service

**CND**: the British Campaign for Nuclear Disarmament

**collaborator**: a British citizen who works together with the East Germans to provide information which they seek; a British citizen who forms a confidential relationship with officials of the GDR, a state which regards Britain as its enemy; a British citizen who works together in a confidential relationship with officials of the state institutions of the GDR but is not a member of any British government agency which might formally require its members to conduct such relationships in the interests of British security

**Communist**: in an East German context, a member of the SED or any front party; in a British context, a member of the Communist Party of Great Britain (CPGB), or a supporter of Communist political beliefs; also Communist sympathiser; also fellow traveller

**co-opted worker**: in the German sense, an IM or agent who receives a salary; in the British sense, an officer who receives payment, a diplomat receiving payment for espionage, a formal source

**END**: the British European Nuclear Disarmament group

**FBI**: the Federal Bureau of Investigation, the main US security service

**FCO**: the British Foreign and Commonwealth Office

**FRG**: the Federal Republic of Germany (West Germany)

**GDR**: the German Democratic Republic (East Germany)

**go-between** (*Ermittler*): a link between a British source of intelligence and an East German officer

**HA**: *Hauptabteilung* (Main Department) – a department of the Stasi but not of the East German secret intelligence service

**HM**: *Hauptamtlicher Mitarbeiter* (member of the main office) – Stasi officer

**HVA**: *Hauptverwaltung Aufklärung* (Main Directorate Intelligence) – the East German secret intelligence service within the MfS

**IM**: *Informelle Mitarbeiter* (unofficial collaborator) – agent or co-opted worker; where used in a British context, officer, agent or co-opted worker depending on whether the IM is located in the UK or East Germany and whether salaried or not. All IMs are described by their cover-names (in inverted commas) and their real names where possible

***Kewa***: *konspirative EinwirkungsApparat* (conspiratorial unit) – a Stasi cell

**LPDP**: the East German Liberal Party

**MfS**: *Ministerium für Staatssicherheit*, the East German Ministry for State Security

**MI5**: the British Security Service, counter-espionage service, counter-intelligence service

**MI6**: the British Secret Intelligence Service, also SIS, also counter-espionage unit within MI6

**MoD**: the British Ministry of Defence

**NVA**: *Nationale Volksarmee*, the East German National People's Army

**Politburo**: the East German cabinet

***Quelle***: a source of intelligence, where source can also mean 'collector'. See **source**

**Rechtsstaat**: a state in which the rule of law is supreme

**SDI**: Strategic Defence Initiative (known as 'Star Wars')

**SDP**: the British Social Democratic Party

**SED**: the Socialist Unity Party, the East German Communist Party

**SMAD**: the Soviet Military Administration for Germany

**source** (*Quelle*): in an East German sense, any source of intelligence; in a British sense, a person or persons who gave the East Germans confidential information, in the knowledge that it might possibly, or would definitely, be passed to East German intelligence, either directly or indirectly

**SPD**: the (West) German Social Democratic Party

**spy**: in the East German sense, a source of intelligence who knows that he or she is, directly or indirectly, communicating information to the Stasi; in the British sense, someone who secretly watches, or gathers information about the activities of others and reports the results to the Stasi

**Stasi**: the East German secret service; also the East German security and intelligence service; also the Ministry for State Security; also the MfS; also the Secret Police

**Stasi agent**: in the East German sense, an IM or co-opted worker; in the British sense it can mean IM, co-opted worker, source, talent spotter or go-between. Where the Stasi is described as the institution, I use the singular. Where officers are described, I use the plural. Readers should note that the term Stasi includes both foreign intelligence-gathering as well as the secret police

**Stasi officer**: in the East German sense, *Hauptamtlicher Mitarbeiter* (member of the main office); in the British sense, any officer of the Stasi who receives a salary

**talent spotter** (*Tipper*): an identifier of British sources of intelligence

# Chronology of Events, 1979–89

During the period under discussion Margaret Thatcher was British Prime Minister, and it is more than a little significant that the issues focused on by the Stasi in London were frequently the issues that Mrs Thatcher herself regarded as the seminal ones during her premiership.[1]

## 1979

| | |
|---|---|
| 1 July | Resignation of General Alexander Haig as NATO supreme commander in protest at NATO's lack of concern about the re-arming of the Warsaw Pact |
| 12 December | NATO announces its 'twin-track' decision to deploy 572 Cruise and Pershing missiles – the former in the UK, Belgium, the Netherlands, Sicily and Germany, the latter only in Germany |

## 1980

| | |
|---|---|
| | President Carter invokes a grain embargo against the USSR and a boycott of the Moscow Olympics in protest at the Soviet invasion of Afghanistan |
| August | Polish government signs Gdansk Agreement |
| September | Polish union Solidarity formed |
| November | Ronald Reagan elected President of the USA |

## 1981

| | |
|---|---|
| 6 October | Assassination of President Anwar Sadat of Egypt |
| 13 December | Martial law declared in Poland |

## 1982

| | |
|---|---|
| 25 March | Roy Jenkins wins the Glasgow Hillhead by-election for the SDP |
| 2 April | Argentina invades the Falkland Islands |
| 5 April | The first naval units leave Portsmouth; Lord Carrington resigns as Foreign Secretary |
| 2 May | The Argentine cruiser *General Belgrano* is sunk by the Royal Navy |
| 5 June | EC summit, Versailles |
| 14 June | Argentine surrender |
| 17 September | Helmut Schmidt's government falls |
| 1 October | Helmut Kohl becomes West German Chancellor |

## 1983

| | |
|---|---|
| 23 March | President Ronald Reagan announces SDI project |
| 28 May | Williamsburg economic summit |
| 9 June | British General Election; Geoffrey Howe becomes Foreign Secretary |
| July | Martial law in Poland lifted |
| 1 September | Korean Airlines flight 007 shot down by Soviets over the Kola peninsula |
| 8 November | President Reagan delivers his 'evil empire' speech |
| 14 November | The first Cruise missiles arrive at Greenham Common |
| 22 November | Geneva arms talks break down |

## 1984

| | |
|---|---|
| 9 February | President Yuri Andropov of the Soviet Union dies |
| 8 March | The UK miners' strike begins |
| 25 June | The Fontainebleau summit settles the UK's EC budget contribution |
| 10 July | A dock strike begins in Britain |
| 12 October | The IRA Brighton bombing takes place |

6 November       Ronald Reagan is re-elected
15 December      Soviet General Secretary Mikhail Gorbachev visits
                 the UK

## 1985

20 February      Thatcher visits Washington, DC
5 March          The miners' strike ends
11 March         Gorbachev becomes Soviet leader
2 May            G-7 summit, Bonn
16 October       South Africa discussed at the Commonwealth
                 Heads of Government meeting
15 November      The Hillsborough Anglo-Irish agreement is signed

## 1986

9 January        Michael Heseltine resigns over the Westland Affair
15 April         The USA attacks Libya
6 May            G-7 summit, Tokyo
3 August         Special Commonwealth Conference on South Africa
24 October       Britain breaks off diplomatic relations with Syria
15 November      Thatcher–Reagan summit at Camp David
5 December       London EC Council

## 1987

28 March         Thatcher visits the Soviet Union
8 June           G-7 summit, Venice
11 June          British General Election
17 July          Thatcher visits Washington
7 December       Gorbachev meets Thatcher at RAF Brize Norton
8 December       INF Treaty signed in Washington, DC

## 1988

March            NATO summit, Brussels
19 June          G-7 summit, Toronto
2 November       Thatcher begins three-day visit to Poland
8 November       George Bush elected President of the USA
21 December      Bombing of PanAm flight 208 over Lockerbie

## 1989

| | |
|---|---|
| 5 April | Gorbachev begins three-day visit to the UK |
| 29 May | Fortieth anniversary of NATO |
| 3 June | Tiananmen Square massacre, Beijing |
| 9 November | East Germany opens the Berlin Wall |
| 10 December | End of Communist rule in Czechoslovakia |
| 22 December | Romanian President Ceauçescu overthrown |

# Introduction

This is the history of the UK operations of the East German secret service, the *Ministerium für Staatssicherheit*, or Ministry for State Security. Today it is called simply 'the Stasi', but before being wound up in early 1990 it was known in the German Democratic Republic by a variety of other names, usually 'the firm' (*die Firma*). This book is based on unique unpublished documentary evidence, chiefly from the Stasi files in Berlin, as well as on interviews with some of those who were involved, in one way or another, with the Stasi's espionage in Britain.

It is the first such study to have virtually open access to the Stasi files, and, because of a German court ruling in March 2002, will probably be the last. It aims to make a contribution to contemporary history and to the history of intelligence during a period which ended a little over ten years ago. Looked at in one way this book is about spying, but it is also about British–German relations – or to be precise, British–*East* German relations – from 1973 (when Britain recognised the existence of the GDR) to 1990 (when Germany was reunified). The analysis of that intelligence activity does not merely illuminate 'the missing dimension' in that relationship.[1] It demonstrates that the very essence of the relationship, from the East German viewpoint, was always espionage and rarely diplomacy, with an element of trade policy thrown in.

Unlike Britain's intelligence services which exist in at least five quite distinct institutional forms (the Security Service, MI5; the Secret Intelligence Service, MI6; the Government Communications Headquarters, GCHQ; the Defence Intelligence Staff, DIS; and the Assessments Staff and Joint Intelligence Secretariat), East German intelligence was a unitary body – the 'Ministry' – which comprised both a security service and a secret foreign intelligence service called the HVA (*Hauptverwaltung Aufklärung*, or Main Directorate Intelligence). By the end of 1989 the service consisted of more than 90,000 official personnel and as many as 150–170,000 agents, who came to be known as IMs, or co-opted workers, as MI5 terms them, which most accurately describes their true role in the UK.[2] The HVA was the largest single unit within the Stasi and worked almost exclusively in the West. It had 3,819 officers, led until 1986 by Markus Wolf and then by Werner Grossmann. In addition, the Stasi (like any intelligence service) could rely on its contacts, or persons of trust – who, in the case of Britain, were British.

Despite its Communist goals, the entire service was run on what might best be called Prussian authoritarian lines. It was centrally controlled, with Erich Mielke – Politburo member, government minister, but styled *Armeegeneral*, and salaried accordingly – presiding at the top and ready to intervene at every level beneath him. All within the Ministry (apart from the small numbers who defected to the West) obediently followed his instructions and those of the 'Centre' (generally referred to by the Stasi as *die Zentrale*) in Stasi headquarters in East Berlin's Normannenstrasse. To fail to do so was a heinous crime which could even lead to execution, a solution for some major misdemeanours favoured by Mielke himself.

It was a highly professional secret service, often said to be the best in the Soviet bloc. It dedicated itself to the 'Chekist' principles of 'aggression through conspiracy for the protection of the Communist cause' established by Lenin and his own Mielke, Felix Dzerzhinsky (statues of whom abounded in the headquarters in Normannenstrasse).[3] What this meant was that at home the Stasi attacked and persecuted all internal opposition to Communism, often displaying great cruelty and genuine sadism in order to neutralise it. Abroad, it collected intelligence as a means of bolstering the state and its Communist rulers. The 'Ministry' called itself, and *was*, 'the sword and the shield' of East German Communism. It never wavered in its belief that 'to be forewarned' was 'to be fore-armed'. This drove its unquenchable thirst for secret intelligence.

All in all, the 'Ministry' was one and a half times the size of the East German army. It was vast. It doubled in size between 1972 and 1989, increasing the numbers who worked for the Stasi by about 3,000 each year.[4] Its size provides some clue as to the extent of the repression it sustained. In Hitler's Third Reich, the Gestapo consisted of 13,500 officers.[5] By 1938 this meant that there was one officer to every 4,800 inhabitants. In the German Democratic Republic there was one officer to 180 inhabitants. If we add the number of IMs to the officers, we get an even more astonishing figure: one Stasi member to every seventy people. At the height of Stalin's terror in the 1930s, there was one KGB officer to every 5,830 inhabitants – eighty-three times fewer KGB than Stasi members per head of population.[6] In the 1980s, there was one KGB officer to 595 Soviet citizens.[7] By 1989 some two million individuals – almost 12 per cent of the East German population – had collaborated with the Stasi in some way or other.[8]

Not surprisingly, this book is one that the Stasi intended should never be written. Because of their terrible record of criminal abuses and to safeguard the secrets of their spies, the Stasi, and the HVA in particular, embarked on an orgy of file destruction following the collapse of German Communism in 1989–90. Millions of documents were shredded because they told the truth, both about the system of repression that the Stasi upheld and about the extent and power that came from the intelligence the Stasi had collected.

The East German Embassy at 34 Belgrave Square was the London base for several Stasi officers. At the same time it was also the HVA's Residency 201, and home, too, for the military intelligence unit of the National People's Army, the NVA. Both were discrete secret groupings, though firmly under Mielke's overall control, and, like all the other Stasi officers and agents in London, they were there illegally, in direct contravention of international law.

Not all the documents which dealt with British operations were in fact destroyed. Some were missed, some turned up in peculiar places –

the desks of former Politburo members, the garages of former officers – and some could be reconstituted by specialist teams. Successful 'aggression through conspiracy' demanded adherence to a strict system of record keeping, but some files and shreds and shards of paper remained. Even though the evidence we possess today is still frequently in fragmentary form, we are able now, thanks to painstaking detective work, to know enough to paint a comprehensive picture of what the Stasi was doing in Britain during the 1980s.

In Britain, the Stasi's goals were, first, to gain secrets about British military and political strategy; second, to spy on, and try to steer those British organisations which had an influence on internal GDR affairs; and, third, to obtain secret intelligence which would assist in repressing the GDR's domestic dissidents. This required the Stasi carefully to target specific individuals with special knowledge of the matters which concerned it, and to manipulate a wide range of British individuals and institutions, from MPs to university dons, for the same purposes. After the clampdown on the KGB in Britain in the early 1970s, in addition to its own East German concerns, the Stasi, always wholly within the KGB's orbit, increasingly became its surrogate, with some 50 per cent of HVA intelligence going to the Soviet Union.[9] It is reasonable to believe that its work for the Soviets was further intensified after the 1985 defection of Oleg Gordievsky.

The story of the Stasi's intelligence operations can be told in a concrete and coherent way not just because these operations were reflected in the documentation, however fragmented, which exists today, but also because all of them were focused on concrete and coherent political ends. There was more than a hint of classic German efficiency in the way the Stasi went after intelligence in such a single-minded way. Its was not a broad-brush approach; it did not seek to know something about everything. Rather, it sought to know everything about just a few things. Within this focus, pieces of intelligence were collected by Stasi officers and then used by the 'Centre' to construct, layer upon layer, a product which could be given to policy makers as a comprehensive final intelligence digest or as an instrument of punishment and control.

That product and the processes by which it was constructed were recorded. As a result, readers of this book can rely on documentary evidence of its existence (a very rare commodity in the field of intelligence studies). The purpose behind the Stasi's operations, however complex some of them may have been, is always crystal clear.

It is important to differentiate between intelligence officers, agents and sources as is discussed later on in greater detail. MI5 refers to all its human sources of information as 'agents' (unlike the FBI, where its 'agents' are the officers). These were the people who had access to the information that MI5 required and they were run by their intelligence officers. The Stasi's system was more elaborate and consisted of 'officers', and then 'agents' or IMs run by the officers. However, where these agents operated in Britain under legal cover (as diplomats, journalists or academics) they were invariably what we in Britain would actually call 'officers', because they drew an official monthly salary from the Stasi. This is why the term 'co-opted workers' is sensible when applied to so-called 'legalists' because these spies had nominal or part-time posts outside intelligence, but were themselves asked to recruit further agents (and were therefore acting as officers in a British sense). *Their* agents or sources, however, were the Stasi's British assets. Where the Stasi planted 'illegals' in Britain, they were straightforward agents, also called IMs, run by paid co-opted workers and officers in East Germany. This elaborate structure – conspiratorial and fluid, and therefore always hard to detect – was designed to generate effective intelligence while maximising the security of all those involved.

To add to the complexity, the 'legalist' (East German) co-opted workers were often described in the Stasi files as 'sources' (*Quellen*). This was plainly not always an entirely accurate description of what they did since the files show that their British agents were the actual sources of much of the intelligence they gained (and from time to time were also, and confusingly, called *Quellen*). In effect, in Britain, East German officers controlled agents in London, under legal cover, who were co-opted workers who themselves ran further agents, variously called 'sources' or simply 'persons of trust' in what schematically resembled a pyramid. Where no legal cover existed, the same pyramid was to be found, although all controllers were based in East Germany (and, as far as we can tell, almost always in Leipzig).

While everyone who provided secrets to the Stasi would have had a cover-name, neither we nor they may necessarily know what it was. The distance between the provider of intelligence and those who collected it and passed it on formed a safety net (or so it was thought) to protect officers and sources from the force of the Official Secrets Act and the stigma of assisting the work of an East European secret police. The Stasi was able to increase that distance, where required, by employing talent spotters (*Tipper*) and go-betweens (*Ermittler*). This makes it possible that some of the Stasi's British agents genuinely did not know that they were passing information to East German intelligence officers. But virtually all of those described in this book did know and, to their credit, do not dispute this aspect of the matter. What they do take issue with is whether this did any damage to anyone, a delicate topic which deserves, and receives, further investigation. Some of the Stasi's sources understood plainly that the East Germans with whom they had contact were intelligence officers. Others were sure only that whatever they said would ultimately reach the ears of East German intelligence. From the Stasi's perspective what counted was the collection of intelligence. From their source's standpoint, however, what counted were their own political attitudes towards East Germany, their consciences and their common sense, or the lack of them.

Some of those examined here were straightforward spies who sold British secrets to the HVA for cash, or who secretly gathered information about the activities of people or groups in whom the Stasi took an interest, and reported the results. We have their cover-names, a description of the secrets they sold, and, sometimes, an account of the secrets themselves. We also have a record of some of the cash they received.

Others looked at in this book, however, were agents of conviction who wanted to fight for Communism (or, as it seemed easier to formulate it, 'against Fascism') and for whom money was not a factor. The Stasi invariably exploited a certain sort of person, ready to collaborate because they sympathised with the goals of East German

Communism. Dr Robin Pearson of Hull and Fiona Houlding of Manchester came into this second category, as did 'Lissy' and 'Jaguar' (who lived near Oxford), agents we know only by their cover-names. So, too, did Irene Fick, almost certainly the source code-named 'Freundin', who gave counsel to certain East Germans, who she knew would report her views to the Stasi if they were not members of it themselves. She may also have passed on to them the names of others who would help them. As a member of the British Communist Party, she felt a strong bond with East Germany. Like Barbara Einhorn, a Sussex University sociologist, equally drawn to the GDR, she did not exactly ignore the fact that the East Germans took political prisoners, but never let it get in the way of her own working relationship with them. Einhorn herself was actually imprisoned for a while by the Stasi in their central interrogation jail at Hohenschönhausen in Berlin, thanks to a tip-off the Stasi received from London. Yet this experience, awful though it must have been, did not alienate her from the GDR. As she herself recounts, she continued to deal with its diplomats and at least one military intelligence officer right up to the fall of the Berlin Wall in 1989.

Men like Canon Paul Oestreicher of Coventry Cathedral, a former general secretary of the British section of Amnesty International and then a senior Church diplomat working for the then Archbishop of Canterbury, or his friend, John Sandford of Reading University, who met privately with Stasi members, believing, so they say today, that they would in some way be able to convince the East German Politburo that rigid repression of human rights activists there might end up undermining the success of Communism in Germany. In Oestreicher's case this involved, on at least one occasion, handing over to the Stasi a list of political prisoners in whose fate he took an interest (this simply annoyed them). Sandford thought his hidden discussions with the Stasi would assist the East German opposition in less well-defined ways which he is today not prepared to discuss. Although both men wanted the GDR to gain a more 'human face', they did not, they affirm, want Communism itself to disappear. They stubbornly refused to accept the fact, proven many times over in the 1970s and 1980s and before, that Communism and liberty were incompatible for the simple reason that the former could not exist unless the latter was denied.

Others sourced the Stasi for entirely different reasons. Lord Roper became an agent of influence, or as he puts it, a possible source – though one, he says, who gave absolutely nothing away – in the belief that to deal directly with the Stasi served the high policy interests of the United Kingdom and that British intelligence would protect and watch over him. Détente – and the removal of possible causes of nuclear conflagration between West and East – was seen by many at the time, including Roper himself, as the best means of securing world peace and alleviating the lot of all Eastern Europeans. In his view (and it was a view widely held, especially by the West Germans) you could convince the Communists you meant peace only if you spoke to them as equals. The Stasi files, however, show that, unlike others who took this line, Lord Roper let this idea run away with him, putting himself at considerable risk.

In 1987 Lord Roper can be found in the Stasi files discussing strategic policy with a number of East Germans – some of whom, he says, he knew were Stasi intelligence officers. By June 1989 he was proposing to offer the same set of people an opportunity to – in the East Germans' own words – 'develop contacts in the security policy and military sphere', which they rated – again in their own words – 'as an exceptionally effective measure in support of foreign information gathering'. The files also reveal that the Stasi, in the person of 'Eckhart' (shown here to be a young East German intelligence officer) and Lord Roper had shared very similar concerns in aspects of British politics and international affairs for several years before 1989. Had the Stasi devised some secret means of picking Roper's brains since the early 1980s? Was he, unknowingly, its London 'consultant'? There is convincing circumstantial evidence to indicate that he, and his special areas of expertise, were the objects of Stasi attention long before 1987 – even if the techniques used by the Stasi to pull off this astonishing coup remain a matter of speculation.

The Stasi could rely on two other sorts of British assets. The first was a group of British military intelligence spies, who worked for them on arms technology issues and on the British peace movement (CND and its associated group, END). These spies were all run and recruited by the military intelligence officers serving in London, and included traitors who betrayed this country and its values. These officers did their own independent targeting, and the files disclose the real names of two of those on whom work was done: Bill Bowring, a Lambeth councillor, and Derek Furze, a journalist, neither of whom may have understood the final purpose of the contact they had with the East Germans. There is no evidence to suggest that either betrayed the interests of the UK. Nor is there any reason at all to believe that, if they possessed any secrets, they would have passed them to the East Germans. However, if they did not know that dealing with the East Germans was highly dangerous, they ought to have done. Few at this time could have escaped exposure to what John le Carré was writing.

The Stasi could also count on one last group of assets – a potpourri of various men and women who, for one reason or another, were able to illuminate specific issues on which the Stasi wanted enlightenment and who saw no harm in telling them certain things of use to the East Germans, and helping in other ways too. They were misguided, and we may deprecate what they did, but these people were not traitors, for they possessed no state secrets. Among them we find Bruce Kent, the CND leader, and a prominent Quaker, Peter Jarman, as well as a host of other players including Lex Hornsby, Ian Mikardo, Clive Jenkins, Burnaby Drayson, then Tory MP for Skipton, and Professor Vic Allen, then at Leeds University. Mostly, where they are still alive to do so, all these people accept that they knowingly assisted the Stasi or those reporting to them. They point out that they broke no law and that their status as sources emanates only from the Stasi's perception of those it regarded as intelligence assets. This is indeed the case. The record of the files is the record of what the Stasi believed and the fact that they believed a thing does not mean that it was always the truth; nor does the conviction that they were making a gain in any particular area mean that Britain or the West was actually being damaged, still less that their sources intended to do Britain and our interests any harm.

Everyone – whether German, British or of any other nationality – who knowingly or even half-knowingly worked for the Stasi, as officer or source, was serving an organisation committed to upholding

Communism in East Germany with an armoury of repressive weapons which could gravely abuse the human rights of anyone regarded by the Stasi as a threat to the regime. Furthermore, they were serving a state which – as the Stasi files show – saw Britain as 'the enemy', one against whom the Stasi was (as Mielke frequently put it) 'at war'.[10] Each and every one of these people was to a greater or lesser extent collaborating with the East German regime. They chose to work together with its representatives in confidential relationships but they were not members of formal British agencies who might be authorised to maintain such contacts for the purposes of Britain's national security. That they may have done so to try to improve the quality of the East German regime, and that they were themselves spied on by the Stasi – its victims as well as its sources – does not make their actions less questionable. It merely emphasises their naivety in trying to collaborate with the representatives of a wicked police state.

Former HVA officers may claim today, as its former chief Markus Wolf has also done, that the HVA was not quite as wicked as its domestic colleagues in the Ministry for State Security. In fact, the HVA had its people working within every East German Stasi office and they were every bit as implicated in the abuses as their Stasi colleagues.[11]

This book names many of the individuals who, the Stasi files show, attracted the Stasi's interest as well as those who helped it in secret. Strong evidence is provided to permit identification of at least some of the hundred Stasi agents said in 1999 by the then Home Secretary, Jack Straw, to have operated in Britain.[12] As is discussed below, it seems probable that the only complete record of the true identities of the Stasi's Western spies is now held by the CIA, which may or may not choose to make it public at some time in the future. Sources close to the CIA insist that the names will never be made public because there is an 'operational aspect' to possessing them.[13] What this means is that the CIA may see some use in the people concerned, perhaps as double agents, in the future.

This book shows that the huge manpower and resources concentrated on the Stasi impacted directly on its operations in the UK.

Britain, and especially London, were riddled with Stasi spies of one kind or another. The Stasi were highly opportunistic and fed on their British sources like locusts, frequently relying on what one Stasi officer has termed 'Comrade Chance' to further their prospects. They rarely, if ever, went for individuals who were at the time major figures in public life, opting instead for significant members of the 'second division' who might pass on what their superiors were saying and writing down in private, extracting the maximum intelligence with the minimum risk. The Stasi called this 'washing the bear without getting it wet', a good description for many of its operations in Britain.

It is hardly surprising that what followed constituted a serious breach of national security. Stasi spymasters in London included at least one very senior arms expert with special training in explosives, chemical and nuclear weapons. Evidence from the Stasi files suggests that London was used by the Stasi as a clearing house for arms deals, not least with terrorist groups in the Middle East.

MI5, whose job it is to investigate and counter covertly organised threats to the UK such as espionage, has been formally presented with some of the evidence contained in this book in a series of meetings which took place between 2000 and 2002.[14] Although there is no doubt that it appears to take the facts in the Stasi files very seriously, at the time of writing MI5 has apparently interviewed only one of those identifiable as officers or sources. Despite having its own, privileged access to the archives, it is plain that a number of the individuals examined here were as unknown to the Security Service after 1990 as they had been before. Because of facts like these, the Stasi records do more than show how the Stasi operated: they also provide a fascinating slant on British political life at this time and on our own secret services, MI5 and MI6.[15]

Stella Rimington has very recently claimed (but without any documentary evidence to support this, and not mentioning the Stasi once by name), that MI5 'watched the Soviet and East European embassies very carefully indeed; we interviewed as many of their contacts as we could to find out what was going on. We ran double agents against them.' MI5, she says, even fed them false information ('chicken feed') and tried to recruit them to the British side.

How far Ms Rimington's recollections reflect the full truth is open to conjecture. We cannot be sure precisely what MI5 did or did not know about the Stasi's UK operations. To her credit, she acknowledges the extent of the problems which MI5 had to address as a result of the use to which the Russians and their East European allies had put their London embassies:

> Among all those people had been a large number of officers of their civilian and military intelligence services, present in Britain for the sole purpose of spying on us and our allies and spreading propaganda and disruption. In April 1971 the Government, acting on advice from MI5 and the Foreign Office, had expelled from the country 105 Soviet intelligence officers in what was known as Operation Foot, which effectively damaged the Soviet intelligence operation in this country for some time. In the five years since Operation Foot, Soviet intelligence officers had begun to creep back into some of their old positions in the embassy and trade delegation, and into some new ones in other Soviet organisations too. The Warsaw Pact countries' intelligence services were also well represented in London under various covers.[16]

She also recognises – implicitly – what she doubtless regards as MI5's inevitable inability to properly address these problems, noting that 'their massive assault on the West had its successes, not surprisingly'.

At the end of the day, however, she insists that the 'exclusions policy' of careful vetting of diplomats' visas allowed MI5 to prevent anyone 'firmly identified as an intelligence officer' from coming to the UK so that 'many hostile intelligence officers were negated in this way before they ever arrived' and any who slipped through the net would be systematically monitored in the UK to prevent them causing damage.

It is sobering to contrast her reassuring view with the evidence of the Stasi files, which present a very different picture of secret activity in the UK. If MI5 were quite as successful as she claims, it is certainly remarkable that only one East German 'diplomat' (exposed by a defector) was forced to leave London, that it only ever caught two out of the hundred or so Stasi agents who had been active in the

UK (both exposed by West German counter-intelligence), and that by 1989 the Stasi could still muster British sources to gain the secrets it required. Yet the effectiveness of the Stasi's UK operations should not lead one to conclude that a liberal democracy like Britain can do without a strong and ever-watchful security service. This book takes the very opposite line. A security service which fails fully to track and act against a hostile agency like the Stasi is not a reason for believing that good security is not necessary. It is an argument for demanding one which is properly effective.

Now, more than ever, the free Western democracies need the best security and intelligence services they can afford. If there is a question about MI5 and MI6 today in the aftermath of the destruction of the World Trade Center on 11 September 2001, it is how to make them even more effective. To think otherwise is, in the context of an increasingly fissile world, highly dangerous. Sources close to MI5 claim, with undoubted sincerity, that the Security Service's record against the Stasi was 'pretty good'. But they also concede that the Stasi were also 'pretty good' while adding that it was impossible at that time for MI5 to have known everything. It is possible to accept this judgement without ignoring the evidence in this book – that to have done reasonably well is not to have done well enough.

This book raises serious questions about how a society which prides itself on being open and generally transparent – as Britain was in the 1980s and is today – can protect itself from hostile secret services which mean to do it harm. The Stasi files show that Britain's openness was used by the Stasi as a weapon against it. They deployed it with skill, and the free-speaking habits of our political class allowed the Stasi to derive much benefit for their own ends, assisted frequently by a willing band of GDR sympathisers. Furthermore, the behaviour of some in MI5 and MI6 in the 1970s and 1980s, and the political repercussions of their antics (which led many to conclude that much of security and intelligence work was a costly and rather poor joke) made life much easier for the Stasi in Britain than should have been the case. The thinking public in the 1970s and 1980s became distinctly edgy whenever the word 'conspiracy' was mentioned. The fact that not every conspiracy was genuine was often used to argue, wrongly and perilously, that *no* conspiracy was genuine. Yet the word 'conspiracy' aptly described the Stasi, not least because it was the one they used to describe themselves.

It is clear that, long before 11 September 2001, the various opportunities that Western states unknowingly offered their enemies were exploited by many other hostile groups, of which al-Qaeda is but one. They flourished in areas where security services feared to tread – often at the heart of the communities of the very Western states whose libertarian values they despised with such deadly loathing. Those seeking to defend the great democracies could do worse than study carefully the ways in which the Stasi was able to thrive in London in the 1980s, and not just because of the Stasi's connections to terrorism in Arab lands.

Bizarrely, this book also shows that the 1989 Official Secrets Act (which, it seems, was rewritten then primarily to stop former British intelligence officers from writing their memoirs) is probably useless when it comes to prosecuting some, if not all, of the Stasi's agents and sources.[17] This begs an important question as to whether the Act can protect Britain's homeland security adequately. It is true that in February 2002 a security guard at British Aerospace who stole some of Britain's and NATO's defence secrets and attempted to sell them to the Russians was jailed for eleven years. Stasi spying in Britain, however, generated similar damage to our safety, but no convictions have occurred and no attempt has been made to gain any sort of compensation for it – whether from the Federal Republic of Germany (the successor state to the GDR in international law), from the officers (who broke the conditions of the diplomatic immunity accorded them) or from their many UK agents. Not everything that the Stasi collected was as damaging to Britain's interests as the Aerospace secrets. However, as is explored in the following chapters, virtually everything the Stasi picked up did sustain the interests of Communist East Germany. A Stasi spy like Robin Pearson, whose career is examined in detail later on, worked for the Stasi in the 1980s in Edinburgh, Leeds, London, York and Hull. He did not, it seems certain, betray major defence secrets – but only because he did not get access to any, despite getting dangerously close to some by 1989. Even so, it is not hard to see why MI5 argued in 1998–9 that Pearson ought to be prosecuted if similar sorts of people were to be turned away from undertaking similar commissions for states which today regard the UK as their enemy. Contrary to some press reports, sources close to MI5 say that its officials did indeed seek Pearson's prosecution but were told 'it was not their call'.

Here, then, for the first time, the files and the excerpts of files on Britain are laid open. Part I of the book sets out the background to East German espionage operations in the UK. It describes East Germany's appalling record of human rights abuses and the pivotal position in them taken by the Stasi. It examines the nature of the relationship between Britain and East Germany, making use of some of the best scholarly writing on the subject as well as eyewitness accounts and contemporary East German texts. Readers who want to know only about the espionage, sample its fruits and confront the puzzle of identification, should turn at once to the second and third parts of this book; in doing so, however, they will miss a vital aspect of the plot: the very background to the spying.

Part II tells the story of the fruits of the Stasi's operations, presenting actual documents to reveal the work of a security and intelligence service that saw Britain as its bitter enemy. The examples of what was collected, passed on and processed, include reports on British–American relations, on conflicts inside the Conservative government and the Labour Party, advances in weapons technology and strategic thinking, and on the IRA on whom the Stasi kept a close watch. (They regarded the IRA with much sympathy but believed that Britain's careful monitoring of IRA activities could endanger their own interests in this sort of terrorism.)

Part III shows how the Stasi was constantly on the alert for any MI5 or MI6 activity which might affect the GDR in some way. Traces of this can be found in these pages. It also identifies many of the East German intelligence officers and 'co-opted workers' operating in London, both for the HVA and for the military intelligence unit. With one exception, none of these people has ever been identified before – and none has been called to account for espionage against this country. Here too we see how difficult it is to make the files reveal the names of the East German spymasters who plotted against Britain; but, with hard work, firm conclusions about who they were – and are – can today be drawn. The spy code-named 'Eckhart' receives special investigation, for the story surrounding his espionage is particularly compelling – and disturbing.

Part IV deals with the Stasi's British assets. Although we now know the cover-names of the Stasi's spies in the military and technology spheres, we still do not know their actual identities. They are, perhaps, the most dangerous of the Stasi's British agents: they have spied once for a hostile intelligence service and could well do so again. They are plainly open to blackmail. We have more information about the HVA's British sources. While gaining secrets from Britain in fields it deemed crucial, the Stasi infiltrated and tried to steer British institutions, all of which are listed here for the first time – including CND, END and various university departments of German and East European studies. We learn how the Stasi officers went about collecting secret intelligence and recruiting new agents and people they could trust. Evidently this trust was reciprocated because, until now, none of these persons has ever revealed their exact connection with the Stasi. Here, too, at the heart of the British peace movement, is the documentary trail of what the Stasi called 'subversion' (*Zersetzung*). MI6 terms it 'disruptive action' – the undermining and overthrowing from within of those regarded as enemies of Communism. Some of the material on this is dense and detailed, for these were very complex operations. Once again, the documents and scraps of documents are allowed to speak, although here they are fleshed out by interviews, frankly – and generously – given by many of those named in them.

The Stasi spying may have stopped in 1990, but the consequences of East German espionage and infiltration are still with us now. Many of those who worked for the Stasi are still at large. The Stasi's links to certain intelligence services in the Arab and Latin American worlds are a matter of record, and Britain's security today would appear to warrant the uncovering of all espionage networks – even those considered to have become inactive a decade ago – if only to rule out any involvement in current intelligence activity.

A former, very senior British secret intelligence officer has spoken recently of his astonishment at the extent of Stasi spying in London, as revealed by the Stasi files. He added: 'We did know that the Stasi were very, very good; they had loads of money; the KGB gave them a free hand and they were German. As the Hungarians liked to joke, "the Germans can make everything work, including Communism": that is why we feared them.'[18]

## The Context of the Story

This account of the Stasi's secret activities in Britain before 1989–90 is set in the context of the curious relationship between the UK and East Germany that had emerged after the creation of the GDR in 1949. From then until the early 1970s, Britain – a main player in NATO and a liberal democracy – quite reasonably regarded East Germany as no more than a Communist dictatorship, an artefact of the Cold War and a Soviet satellite. As such it was denied formal recognition, as a result of which the gaining of such recognition became the East Germans' main diplomatic aim, pursued both overtly and in secret throughout the 1950s and 1960s. Following the American and West German lead, Britain then changed its tack and recognised East Germany in 1973. Some Britons – usually (but not always) on the left of the political spectrum, and including more than a sprinkling of academics – now welcomed the GDR as the state which had 'come in from the cold'; several preferred it to the Federal Republic, casting a blind eye to its horrors. The British government, however, remained consistently cool towards the GDR. Indeed, NATO's rearmament after 1979 led to growing tension between Britain and East Germany, and consequently to a huge extension of the Stasi's interest in Britain.

While West Germany and the United States remained the main enemies of the GDR, Britain was a close ally of both and still a major world player. Britain was also home to a burgeoning peace movement, represented by the Campaign for Nuclear Disarmament (CND), which had seen a massive revival of its political fortunes and was at the height of its powers. CND attitudes dominated large areas of the British Labour Party and its leadership. The East Germans had every wish to help CND prosper, and to see the Labour Party, led by Michael Foot and then Neil Kinnock (both deeply committed supporters of unilateral nuclear disarmament), trounce Mrs Thatcher at the polls. In addition Britain had by now become a base of active assistance to an enormous array of Eastern European and Russian dissidents, ranging from Poland's Solidarity to Church groups throughout the Soviet bloc.

There was indeed much to occupy the Stasi in Britain, and it was small wonder that the organisation was so heavily involved in certain aspects of British life and believed there was much here to fight for.

In the event fortune did not smile on the Stasi: Margaret Thatcher won a second term of office in 1983 and the impact of her victory compounded President Reagan's decision in the early 1980s to put the Soviet system (the 'evil empire') under increasing pressure. By no means only military in nature, the policy of both Thatcher and Reagan also emphasised the importance of civil and human rights, and the strong Western attachment to them. In this way, Britain and America hoped to nurture anti-Soviet feeling behind the Iron Curtain in the hope that, one day, Soviet totalitarianism would be forced to yield to these basic values. Margaret Thatcher, for example, went out of her way to support the dissidents behind the Iron Curtain. Surprisingly, perhaps, after 1985, under Gorbachev's direction (or arguably the lack of it) both the Soviet Union and its satellites found themselves taken more speedily down this path than had seemed imaginable. In the case of East Germany, but unbeknownst to the East German leadership and the Stasi, by the summer of 1989 the Russians decided that they would no longer fight to sustain Communism in the GDR. The Berlin Wall fell, and with it the East German regime and its most important prop, the Stasi. The GDR Embassy and Residency 201 in London were wound up, files were burned in the back yard of 34 Belgrave Square – and East German spying ceased.

This is the background to this book's examination of the varied aspects of the secret intelligence war waged by the East Germans in the UK, behind the 'invisible front', as they called it. The years from

1979 to 1989 are explored with particular care, for these were the years when the GDR knew itself to be most seriously threatened by what was happening in the West and set the greatest weight on intelligence collection as its best means of striking back, short of any suicidal military action.

## The Stasi Archive in Berlin

The Stasi Archive – or to give it its full name, the Archives of the Office of the Federal Commissioner for the Files of the Former East German State Security Service – opened for business in January 1992, acting in accordance with a federal German law (finalised in the Federal Law of 20 December 1996). When Germany had become a single nation again in October 1990, ownership of the Stasi materials had passed to it.[19]

The Berlin Archive was constructed from documentary material left behind, as it were, by the Ministry for State Security, the MfS, in 1990. There was, however, a big gap in it. In order to bring about a peaceful transition from Communism to democracy, special permission had been given to the HVA by the transitional East German government in the first months of 1990 to 'dissolve itself'. The Ministry as a whole was able to destroy many of its records and the HVA managed to destroy almost all its files, in particular its ultra-sensitive list of agents, sources, contacts and persons of trust.

However, it was not fully successful in this. For one thing, the HVA had believed that the indexes to its archives, which had been encoded and stored on magnetic tape, would be indecipherable, and these were put to one side pending future destruction; this never happened. For another, some HVA outstations, most notably the Leipzig one, which had a special responsibility for running agents in the West, did not follow instructions fully (the bulging files on both Robin Pearson and Fiona Houlding emanate from the Leipzig outstation). Finally, a certain amount of HVA material had been distributed to the GDR leadership on a regular basis, in the form of intelligence digests. Not every leader had returned the material as requested and what was not returned was collected by the Berlin Archive. Fragments of other files appear to have escaped the shredders by chance. The names of several of the Stasi's British sources and their case officers were hereby conserved. Where only one or two references to individuals can be found in these fragments, it is safe to assume that in their original state the files contained many more.

The Archive has today been augmented by means of various retrieval processes which have re-created files which had been shredded. Experts have also decoded the magnetic tapes containing lists of pieces of intelligence stored in the Stasi's central registry (but not the actual contents of this intelligence). The material extracted from these magnetic tapes is known as SIRA. It forms the basis for Chapters 6 and 7 and Appendix 5; it gives us not only an idea of what the Stasi was after, but a clue as to who supplied it. Even now, new documents are continually reappearing and a number have been included in this book.

The fundamental authenticity of these documents has never been called into question but, from time to time, doubts have been raised about their veracity, motivated by legal and frequently political considerations. The German courts after 1990 were not proactive in seeking to punish the GDR's and the Stasi's human rights abusers. Often appearing to place 'social peace' (that is, turning a blind eye to Stasi crimes in order to avoid bitter public conflicts) above retribution and restitution through legal process, the courts have more than once raised doubts about the truthfulness of the Stasi's files as a convenient excuse to sidestep legal action. Precise figures are still hard to ascertain, but it is plain that only a minute proportion of GDR human rights abusers has ever been brought to justice, and only about 3 per cent of those directly involved in Stasi activities paid even the relatively mild penalty of having to relinquish their jobs, where they were publicly funded.[20] The new Federal Republic seems set to repeat the mistakes the old one made in respect of the bringing to justice of Nazi abusers, ignoring Martin Luther King's admonition that 'social peace is not the absence of conflict but the presence of justice'.[21]

To date, the veracity of the evaluations reached in the files by the 'Centre' (as opposed to the motley views of informants in the field) has never been found wanting. Numerous individuals identified in them as Stasi sources or co-opted workers claimed that they were framed and have initially received a sympathetic hearing. But further research by the archivists who manage the files has invariably revealed that the files tell the truth. While not everyone who was given a cover-name by the Stasi went on to be signed up as a co-opted worker – or as a formal agent – no one recorded as providing information to the Stasi of their own free will has been able to show that the allegation was false. What would have been the purpose of making false records in files never intended to become public property?

The Berlin archivists emphasise today that the Stasi were demonstrably not merely very proud of their organisation but wanted it to succeed at all times. The idea that they would be helped in this by keeping false records and faked files for their own internal use is, the archivists point out, absurd. The Stasi had every interest in ensuring that, at the 'Centre', their reports, digests and documents were as truthful as it was possible to make them.[22] The noted American scholar Jim McAdams quotes one former Stasi officer as explaining this in the following terms:

> It was a basic precondition, as everyone who worked with the information knows, that the [files] had to be reliable. It would not have been valuable at all to recruit someone who was a blowhard [fantasist or liar]. The things we needed had to hold water; they had to be interesting [for operational purposes]. It was the rule for us to compare and contrast different sources of information. In scholarship, the truth content of every piece of information has to be chewed over; you are a capable scholar if you use proven information to come to the right conclusions. This was the way we conducted our work [in the Stasi] as well.[23]

It is, of course, vital to distinguish between the various pieces of intelligence passed to East Berlin (which may, like all items of 'humint', contain distortions and untruths) and the data gleaned from the intelligence by those charged with evaluating it, often called 'facts'. Great care was taken to exclude lies and disinformation in internal evaluations or conclusions. Not to have done so would have been extremely dangerous and would have undermined the very basis of focused intelligence gathering. Correspondingly, no Stasi-inspired disinformation is to be found masquerading as 'fact' in their collection of core, central files. What is more, the files provide a record of continued intelligence contacts with those the Stasi regarded as reliable while indicating when contacts were not pursued because their reliability was suspect. While there is no complete record of the Stasi's central conclusions (all of which were prime candidates for the shredding machine), enough survive to show that a central evaluation of a 'fact' was invariably a statement of the truth.

The Stasi Archive had become the only security and intelligence service archive in the world that was now entirely open to scholars. Its 180 kilometres of files, listing vast numbers of operations, were accessible as photocopies, the originals being at all times retained by the Archive. Dotted around the files were the real names of certain intelligence officers, but mostly only the codenames of agents, contacts and some of the sources. A number of sources appeared under their real names, others could be unearthed by referring back to the incomplete registers still extant. The names of public figures mentioned in the files were not blacked out on the copies. Names of individuals deemed to have no public political identity were blacked out, however, but not always particularly thoroughly.

Although it is the duty of archivists to conceal information they believe should not go into the public domain, it is the duty of historians to see if they can, by legitimate means, circumvent that process, using other, open, sources. This has been done here.

Before March 2002 the Stasi Archive was a unique gold mine for serious objective research into intelligence. US Freedom of Information legislation has revealed *some* American intelligence documentation, at least in part (for even here sensitive material has been expunged). Although the Thirty Year Rule by which the UK's public records are brought into the public domain specifically *excludes* documents relating to intelligence and security issues, from time to time documentary evidence relating to the work of the British secret services is made public. Yet when this happens, it does so only with the full agreement of those services. This means not merely that the material concerned is at least fifty years old but that its sensitivity and therefore its usefulness are likely to be strictly limited. The Stasi Archive, quite patently, is in a different league altogether.

The German government had agreed to the release of these documents chiefly because it believed the files would establish the truth about the nature of East German Communism and offer convincing explanations for its hold on power for forty years. It also believed that the process of unification, which it saw, in part, as consisting of East Germans coming to terms with the traumas that they had undergone before 1990, demanded that those East Germans who had been victims of the Stasi should know that this had been the case and that, where appropriate and possible, they should be enabled to seek retribution for the wrongs that had been done them.

The suggestion that to release such documents would be to open a Pandora's box was dismissed in the mid-1990s with the much more weighty argument that a failure to tell the truth about the past would be more damaging still. In order to assuage the objections (particularly of the Americans) that to disclose details of how secret services operate, and to open documents which might contain the names of Western intelligence agents, would damage the interests of Western intelligence as a whole, the German government agreed that these interests should be protected and that names of agents and of alleged agents should be blacked out. Historians can accept this ruling without difficulty. By December 1996 some 830,000 people had visited the Archive and more than one million applications had been received, the vast majority to read their own files.

Ironically, what the German government could not have realised was that some of the documentary evidence related not merely to its own secret activities but also to the illegal actions of some of its major political figures, including (most famously) Helmut Kohl, whose phone calls were tapped and transcribed in thousands of reports. This was the result of atrocious (West) German counter-intelligence (in preventing the Stasi from spying on the German Chancellor) as well as appalling domestic security (by being unaware that Dr Kohl had been behaving corruptly).

The German government – thanks again to its own poor intelligence services – also failed to discover that sometime in mid-December 1989 a Stasi officer named Rainer Hemmann had passed to a KGB officer named Prinzipalov various secret intelligence files, microfilmed in 1988. Prinzipalov (who died under mysterious circumstances in 1997) was a double agent for the CIA, to whom he sold his material for a reputed million dollars. The CIA then spirited the files (now known by their codename 'Rosewood') to their headquarters in Langley, Virginia. These files included the cover- or codenames of the HVA agents and their real, or 'clear', names.

Some of those who had undertaken secret intelligence work for the Stasi against the United States – such as the Clark Ring or David Sheldon Boone – were quickly brought to justice and sentenced (members of the former receiving seventeen to twenty-one years' imprisonment, the latter twenty-four). Others, however, appear to have been recruited as American double agents and kept in their posts. This, together with the refusal by the US government to return its Rosewood material to the Stasi Archive in Berlin (a refusal now apparently rescinded but to no discernible effect), has naturally caused much friction between the US and German governments.

The world of international scholarship, fruitfully beavering away at the material in Berlin, was dealt a major and probably mortal blow on 6 March 2002, when the head of the Stasi Archive ordered that, pending new legislation, the Archive would henceforward be closed to most, if not all, scholarly investigation. This was the result of a surprising injunction against the Archive by the former Chancellor of Germany Dr Helmut Kohl, supported, bizarrely, by his party political opponent, the Social Democrat German Minister of the Interior, Otto Schily.

As German Chancellor and chairman of the Christian Democratic Union at the time of unity in 1990, Kohl (who was himself a historian by training) seems to have been instrumental in framing the original public records law in respect of the Stasi material, believing that the new Germany could only benefit from understanding the terrible history of the East German secret police. By the turn of the new century, however, he was speaking about the 'totally evil stench of the Stasi files'.[24] Yet the fact that the intelligence on him and the Social Democrats gained (wrongly) by the Stasi is a severe embarrassment confirms, rather than undermines, the claim that this is an archive of major historical significance.

At the moment, however, the previous degree of access, in particular the absence of any blacking out of the names of 'persons in contemporary history', has been rescinded in its entirety. The Stasi Archive is effectively being closed down for historical research – it has proved too hot for the Germans (and perhaps not just the Germans) to handle. The court's ruling will lead to new legislation being passed by Parliament and, until this is done, no new materials will be released. Currently, the federal parliament is considering proposals for new legislation, but drafts indicate a major curtailment of access, with real research by any individuals not personally affected by Stasi espionage becoming impossible. The unique significance of the Stasi Archive in its pre-March 2002 guise can hardly be exaggerated. It has allowed the story of the Stasi's operations in the UK to be told, with comprehensive footnotes, in the Stasi's own words.

# PART I

# PRELUDE TO ESPIONAGE

# 1

# The Secret Police State

The Stasi jail at Hohenschönhausen (literally, 'high, pretty houses') – which was the central investigation prison for the German Democratic Republic – is situated in the north-east of Berlin. It will never be the most obvious starting point for the visitor to the new Germany and its sprawling capital. But if you want to understand the Stasi and its legacy for German political culture, particularly in the east of the country, or if you want to understand German contemporary history, there is no better place to start.

To reach it, if you are coming from the old western part of the city you have to drive through the Brandenburg Gate from what used to be the western and free sector of the city. You carry on down Unter den Linden, once one of East Germany's best-known avenues, then past the Palast der Republik – the People's Palace – whose northern side, facing the Berliner Dom, was home to the Volkskammer, or the People's Chamber, of the GDR. Its bronzed glass windows were once seen as the height of modernity. Going towards Friedrichsstrasse railway station, you pass gigantic statues of Karl Marx and Friedrich Engels in the Marx–Engels Forum before coming to the vast and impersonal concreted spaces of the Alexanderplatz (not built to be user-friendly), with its fancy clock that tells people rushing to their trains the time in Havana, Moscow, Delhi, Beijing and Cairo as well as in Berlin. Behind you stands the huge concrete TV and radio tower built by the Communists to cock a snook at the

West. It soon became a landmark in both parts of the city; bizarrely, its tiled spherical dome gathers the sunlight and reflects it in the form of a crucifix. The Communist leadership, committed atheists, became very fed up with this unwanted (and unintended) by-product of its architect's fancy.

The road turns into a broad highway, still called Karl Marx Allee (before that it was Stalin Allee). It was here that the big set-piece military parades of the old German Democratic Republic took place. You can still sense their presence: the endless rows of tanks churning past; the rocket launchers with their assorted missiles, the grey columns of National People's Army soldiers, goose-stepping effortlessly as they approach the tribune 'of honour' on which the East German leadership is perched, waiting to salute them. Behind the soldiers come the 'armed workers' brigades', ready and trained to defend the revolution, and then tens of thousands of Free German Youth members, identikit young Communists in blue shirts, followed by the red-scarfed Young Pioneers, all grinning a touch inanely, then waving as they heave into the view of First Secretary Erich Honecker and his intended successor Egon Krenz (like his boss, a former Youth leader). They stream past the ranks of the rest of the Politburo, some smiling, others impassive, among them Erich Mielke, the long-serving Minister for State Security. He uses his Stasi to run the East German police state for his party.

The Allee is empty now, of course. Renovation is transforming the run-down flats which look down upon it (this part of the Allee has become a listed site). Driving further north-east, you pass row upon row of tall, anonymous buildings and the road soon becomes an urban autobahn. On the left you can find Normannenstrasse. It does not seem that unusual: old pre-war houses on one side and several newer blocks on the other. On closer inspection these newer blocks can be seen to form an immense compound which fills the entire northern part of the road. Some of the buildings seem to be standard modern plate-glass offices, but, less usually perhaps, there is also an inner set of buildings. Once you could only reach them by passing through a barrier. Today it has gone, and there are no longer armed guards to check your identity. To one side there is what looks like (and once was) a large clinic. In front of you, a peculiar bricked screen conceals what you then realise must be the entrance to the real centre of this curious kingdom.

This is the headquarters of the Stasi, '*die Zentrale*', the 'Centre'. Behind these walls worked Erich Mielke and his many men. Some of them ran the vast network of intelligence officers and agents which reached across the globe. Some ran the chain of jails and torture chambers which kept the Communists in their positions of power. The plate-glass windowed buildings housed the various registries, the files kept on countries and their leading figures as well as the records of millions of intelligence intercepts, 'humint' (human intelligence) and 'sigint' (signals intelligence). Inside, to the left, is a large red marble statue of Felix Dzerzhinsky, the founder of the Cheka – Lenin's notorious secret police. Immediately ahead is the paternoster lift which carried the staff to the various floors.

On the third floor, the 'Comrade Minister' – Erich Mielke, general in the National People's Army – had his suite of offices. They included a large armour-plated safe, and his personal office with an array of coloured telephones, one of which carried a direct line to the First Secretary, Honecker. A switch allowed him to record worthwhile conversations (the tape recorder was concealed in a tasteful cabinet of German oak). Leading out of this office there was, on one side, a large conference room. A panelled cupboard hid a large sheaf of maps, mounted horizontally; maps of all the countries in the world where the Stasi conducted its secret intelligence and security operations. Some, such as that of the United Kingdom, carried little flagged pins, which denoted sites of particular interest.

On a low cabinet stood a highly polished head of Lenin. Next door, there was a bedroom, with a bathroom and small kitchen: when things were difficult for the regime, Mielke would sleep here. When the German revolution of 1989–90 forced Mielke out of his headquarters, three British intelligence officers were reported to have visited this suite, and the East German dissidents guarding the building were more than a little surprised to find them predominantly interested in the bathroom. One sat on the lavatory, the other in the bath, while the third photographed them for the office album. None of them could ever, in their wildest dreams, have imagined that one day they would be fooling around in the bathroom of the East German spy supremo.

From Normannenstrasse to Hohenschönhausen jail is only a few minutes further north-east. Tucked away, at the end of Genslerstrasse, nestling among 1930s suburban villas (many of them clad in the yellowish-grey concrete used widely in the Third Reich) a watchtower can be made out. As you approach it you still see high walls, barbed wire, warnings to keep away. Here is a prison, in the very heart of Berlin, bang in the middle of a leafy bourgeois district, overlooked by endless flats (some used by ordinary working people, others by middle-ranking party *Nomenklatura*, or cadres, as well as the Stasi officers who worked nearby). Before 1989, the building did not appear on maps of East Berlin. On paper, it simply did not exist. They hid it not by tucking it away in some distant, isolated part of the country, but by the simple expedient of not recording its presence, right there, in the heart of Berlin, convenient for the employees of the Stasi. It was normal for them to work where they lived.

Their presence was never far from the minds of the East German people. In East Germany, the state and the Stasi who sustained it lived side by side; they coexisted in daily contact. It was no mere coincidence that Erich Mielke lived out his final days a few steps away from one of his worst jails. He and his coterie of former officers (who guarded his every step) saw no incongruity in choosing homes so close to the places in which they had imposed their terror on the most recalcitrant opponents of the regime.

Protected by the barbed wire perimeter fences, a 4.25 metre wall and watchtowers on the outside, the guts of this prison contained more than one hundred special punishment cells, and, worst of all, regulation torture chambers. A visitor might be forgiven for thinking he or she had stumbled upon a Nazi concentration camp. Although the Russian and East German secret police did use former concentration camps, this is not one of them. In the Third Reich it served as a canteen for workers.

Visitors to the *west* of the city in search of historical sites are often unsettled by a trip to a pretty villa at Wannsee. It was once owned by the SS and used by Reinhard Heydrich, head of the SD, the Nazi security police. It was here, in January 1942, that agreement was reached on how to conduct the extermination of more than six million

European Jews. It is a beautiful spot, overlooking a picturesque lake; yet within the well-appointed and prosperous villa, the execution of a terrible plan had been agreed upon. The villa and its secret seem far removed from each other. Here was the villa at Wannsee; there were the killing fields and charnel houses of the East.

In the case of the German Democratic Republic, attitudes were rather different. The regime did not plan a racial war; its use of terror became less murderous and more psychological as the years passed. Yet the GDR was a wicked police state for all that. What is more, Hohenschönhausen jail was only one of twenty-two sites on which terror was actually carried out.

This was a state which pretended to be a new sort of Germany, a better Germany, a far cry from the Nazi Germany which preceded it. This was a Germany which could boast friends and admirers in the West – men and women who chose not to think too deeply about the true anatomy of this country. Did they know about Hohenschönhausen and its twenty-one clones? In fact, the existence of terror was not really a secret. It was there if you wanted to see it.

Today, Hohenschönhausen has been turned into a memorial and a museum. Its director is Hubertus Knabe, one of Germany's most perceptive – and persistent – historians of the East German secret police state. He presides over a ghostly and shocking site. When East German Communism collapsed in 1989–90, the Stasi was able to remove most of its paperwork from here. But it could not take away the physical evidence of its work.

Offices, interrogation rooms and rows of cells were constructed on the three floors above ground level. Until 1989 the jail had been run by Colonel Siegfried Rataizick who today, despite being seventy, still cuts a menacing, somewhat fanatical figure, with wild, hard eyes and a readiness to tell anyone who wants to listen that he was proud of what he did, and, given half a chance, would do the same again.[1] Prisoners would be taken to his jail, usually at night, in an unmarked van through the 'garage entrance'. They would be greeted by a guard whom inmates learned to call 'Major Arsekicker', and by the bright beams of more than twenty floodlights. The Stasi guards regarded the prisoners as 'belonging to a different biological strain',

Rataizick attested, and in need of 'extensive re-education'. Rataizick was paid a large salary of almost 47,000 Ostmarks and had a chauffeur-driven Fiat at his disposal: Mielke rated him highly.

Some rooms in his prison had built-in, concealed X-ray machines; whether to check that prisoners carried no weapons or to irradiate them in order to weaken their resistance (as some believe) is still uncertain. But the worst horror was hidden away in the cellars, known to inmates as the 'U-boat', the submarine. It was here that the punishment cells were located – rooms with no natural light, no water, no lavatories. Prisoners were forced to soil themselves or squat on a tin can which was passed from cell to cell at infrequent and irregular intervals. One room contained a Russian-designed water-torture device. Prisoners would be trussed up on a wooden frame and bent forward with their faces a few centimetres from a pan of water. Water would trickle down specially constructed grooves in the tin sheets which covered the walls of the chamber. Their naked feet were immersed in a pan of water. During interrogation, the Stasi officer could dunk the prisoner's head in the pan if he felt he was not getting the right answers. Inmates were kept in this cell for days on end; their feet rotting, their minds also sodden and their ears assailed by the constant dripping of water as it percolated down the walls of the cell. Another set of rooms were kitted out for a different sort of torture. These were cells lined from ceiling to floor with thick black rubber. Entirely soundproof, it was here that prisoners could be subjected to very special treatments and suffer the most appalling indignities and cruelties.

Sigrid Paul has personal knowledge of the rubber cells. In 1964, as a prisoner she was regularly forced to remove blood and excrement after the interrogations had been completed.[2] The crime of these prisoners? That of opposing the totalitarian rule of the Socialist Unity Party, the East German Communists.

The prisoners are no longer there; the cells are now clean and empty. But the presence of inmates seems concrete enough, and ex-prisoners themselves believe that at least part of them has never left. Indeed, if you go to Hohenschönhausen, you are likely to be shown around by one of several former inmates who believe that they can live with what they suffered only by showing the site of their suffering to others. Many thousands have shared their first-hand experience of Communist terror. Some had been deemed 'antisocial', and beaten for teenage follies; others, like Bernd Lippmann, were believed to be opposition ringleaders. He was arrested for distributing photocopies of *Animal Farm* to his friends. Repeatedly abused, he was eventually 'bought free' by the West Germans.

Other former prisoners have recorded messages for those who visit Hohenschönhausen. These are on display as you enter the building. Horst Jänichen has written, 'My whole life has been stamped by my time in jail here.' Manio Röllig wrote, 'During the day you have to be strong; but at night time you can weep.' Sigrid Paul, now sixty-six, has noted, 'I am opposed to the idea that we should forget what happened to us, against the "Oh, it wasn't that bad really." You see: the Berlin Wall ran through my heart.'

## Introducing the GDR

How did East Germany like to portray itself? How was it really governed? How much did people in the West know what it was like? How far could they find out?

East Germany – or, to give it its proper name, the German Democratic Republic – was a German state which existed for forty-one years, from 1949 to 1990. The precise reason for its demise during 1990 (the state itself ceased to be on 3 October 1990) remains a matter of debate.

By the mid-1980s the GDR's economy was no longer functioning properly, but was sustained only by vast quantities of hard Western cash generously poured into the country by its wealthy West German counterpart, the Federal Republic. The money, it was hoped, would not only improve the lot of ordinary East Germans (which it hardly did: large amounts of it went straight into the pockets of the Communist leadership, the Stasi and the SED) but would also keep alive the idea of a special German relationship between the two Germanies. Apart from the failure of the East German economy to deliver the goods, the regime also had to contend with a small but determined internal opposition. Its members wanted an end to repression. But the very repression they opposed was effective and ruthless enough to keep them down.

Probably the biggest single cause of East German collapse in 1989–90 was an external one, over which the regime had no influence (and on which it had no intelligence – a point returned to at the end of this book). It stemmed directly from the policies of Mikhail Gorbachev, who became leader of the Soviet Union in 1985. The fateful decision he ultimately took – that Soviet forces would no longer be prepared to fight to maintain Communism in Germany (as they had done there in 1953, in Hungary in 1956 and in Czechoslovakia in 1968), nor even to allow the East German forces to fight for this purpose – robbed the East German Communist leaders of their ultimate line of defence and, indeed, their very *raison d'être*. Without Gorbachev and without the Soviet Union, East Germany was finished. Paradoxically, had Gorbachev decided otherwise, East Germany, like the People's Republic of China, would almost certainly still exist today, with the Stasi implementing the Tiananmen Square solution to the East German dissident problem.

East Germany may now be dead but it is not entirely buried. The state itself, with all the institutions and paraphernalia of statehood (armed forces, youth movements, national anthem and so forth) has long since gone, but parts of the old country survive as the new five eastern Federal *Länder* of the new Berlin Republic, still unsteady and uneasy pieces in this vast new state. The old East German Communist party allegedly reinvented itself in 1990 before unification, but many of its rank-and-file members were old Communists, and its financial reserves (taken over from the SED) make it probably Germany's richest single political party and have bought it an apparently fixed place in the eastern parts of the new Germany's political system. Many of the Germans who believed they had flourished in the old East Germany, and believed in it and its Communist values, continue to peddle what they claim were its basic 'values'. They do not mean the terror, of course.

It is revealing to see how East Germany liked to present itself to the West. In 1971 Erich Honecker became the new East German leader, although his title at this time was simply 'First Secretary' (of the ruling Communist Party) – just another term in the jumble of verbiage and obfuscation which the East Germans (like other Communists) used to disguise the 'objective reality' of the actual facts. Apart from their Soviet occupiers (or 'our friends', as the parlance had it), the East Germans had, from 1949 until then, only ever known one ruler, the hardline Stalinist Walter Ulbricht. (As things turned out there were only ever to be two leaders of Communist East Germany in its forty-year history.)

To celebrate Honecker's arrival, and to present the GDR, quite mendaciously, as a vibrant alternative to West Germany, the regime commissioned *Introducing the GDR*.[3] In it we read that East Germany comprised 108,178 square kilometres (about 41,700 square miles). To the north it was bounded by the Baltic Sea. Its frontier to the west with the Federal Republic of Germany was 1,381 kilometres long; to the south it bordered on what was then the Czechoslovak People's Republic, and to the east the People's Republic of Poland. Going south from the Baltic lowlands – part of the vast Central European plain – East Germany turned from flat-land into the mountainous regions of the Harz, the vast forests of Thuringia, the Erzgebirge and the high hills of 'Swiss' Saxony, as it was termed. Its chief mineral resources were lignite, or brown coal (burned everywhere as fuel and responsible not only for the distinctive sour smell which pervaded the GDR but also for wide-spread environmental damage), potash and rock salts, some oil and natural gas and iron ore.

East Germany's population topped seventeen million, of whom more than half (nine million) were women. It was a source of pride, we learn from the book, that more than 8.2 million East Germans were in 'gainful employment'. (It was perfectly true that everyone had a job of sorts, but, as East Germans liked to quip, 'We pretend to work – and they pretend to pay us.') Almost exactly one-third of the population was retired, the result, the introduction says, of the population losses suffered in two world wars.

Moving on through the text, the reader is soon confronted by a full-page photograph of the country's leader, Erich Honecker. From both the position of the picture and its iconic nature there is no doubt that he is boss. He is introduced as the 'First Secretary of the

Central Committee of the Socialist Unity Party of Germany'; dressed in an immaculate brown lounge suit, with a brown tie and a round party badge in his lapel, he can be seen peering incisively, if slightly quizzically, straight at the reader, his small alert eyes framed by what were at the time (and are once again today), a vaguely chic and modern pair of small, square black-framed spectacles. He could not look less like a man of destiny; he could easily be mistaken for a senior clerk somewhere, or possibly a head teacher, perhaps of a technical college. He has a mean, severe face and his lips are thin and cruel.

Alongside him we find the famous German humanists Goethe, Schiller and Beethoven, all members, it is said, of the 'progressive bourgeoisie'. The book then reminds us of Germany's first 'revolutionary party, the Communist League, led by Marx and Engels', adding helpfully that 'the slogan of this party, "All Germany shall be a unified, indivisible republic", fully corresponds to the interests of the people and the nation'. The East German authorities wanted their country to be perceived as a *German* state, founded on *German* traditions – and supporting the idea of German unity.

While the West German government, once Helmut Kohl became Chancellor in 1982, did not rule out – in public, at any rate – the possibility of some sort of union or confederation of the two German states, by 1989 most Western observers reckoned that in practice, if not on paper, there were now two quite distinct German nations – a West German one and the GDR. The East Germans had long since given up the idea of any kind of union (indeed East Germans had never called their country Ostdeutschland – East Germany – but preferred *die DDR*, or *deutsche demokratische Republik*, and referred to themselves as *Bürger der DDR* – citizens of the GDR, the initials *DDR* becoming by the 1980s a substitute for the word 'German').

Nevertheless, the book continues, not all German traditions were good ones. 'Foreign imperialist powers', we learn, 'especially the USA', supported 1930s Nazism, 'using it as a spearhead against the Soviet Union.' But, we further learn, 'German imperialism had lost the war even before having started it'. 'The people's struggle for independence and democracy' was stronger and the 'socialist order of the Soviet Union was far superior to the fascist–imperialist policy of conquest'. Thanks to Soviet efforts (no mention is made of Britain's or America's role in the war) 'Hitler–Germany' was defeated.

Now, the history continues, came the time to build a new Germany; although 'in 1945 many Germans had not yet become fully conscious of this'. Luckily, however – we are told – 'the Communist Party of Germany, the party which under the fascist dictatorship had made the heaviest sacrifices of blood, proved equal to the task facing society'. Correspondingly, on 7 October 1949 the GDR was established 'as an expression of the bitter struggle going on between the forces of imperialism, war and reaction on the one hand, and the forces of peace, democracy and socialism on the other'. 'For the first time in German history,' the book says, 'a truly peace-loving, democratic state was created, a state in which fascism, militarism, revanchism and racial hatred [would be] eradicated for all time.'

Economic and industrial construction, it relates, were now the order of the day and (in the eyes of its official propagandists at any rate) the GDR was moving forward by leaps and bounds. While the Americans, with their massive support of West Germany, were claimed to be making 'huge profits', the SED created the 'conditions for the systematic and proportional development of the national economy'.

The book insists, obviously enough, that this was all a huge success: the 'victory of the socialist relations of production and the consolidation of the socialist state power' was made possible 'only through the ever broader involvement of the citizens in directing and managing all spheres of social life'. Yet there were, it says, clouds on the horizon: learning that the West Germans were planning to 'incorporate' the GDR by military aggression, 'on 13 August 1961 the GDR safeguarded its frontiers and saved peace in Europe' (a mealy-mouthed reference to the building of the Berlin Wall).

The book goes on to tell us that the GDR is a 'workers' and peasants' state'. Whatever this might mean in reality, it soon becomes clear that understanding its governance is going to be extremely complicated. It is, we are told, a state committed to democracy and human rights, values sustained by its entire political system: 'doing everything for the wellbeing of man, and the happiness of the people and the road marked out by the SED has

proved to be correct and successful'. Socialist state power, we
learn, is 'exercised by the working people through democratically
elected people's representative bodies which form the foundation of
the state organs'. These bodies feed into five political parties
(including Christian Democrats and Liberals) 'each of which is
independent' although the 'leading party' is the SED (formed in
1946 by the merger of Socialists and Communists). These parties
and other institutions form the 'National Front of democratic
Germany' which, together with the 'Democratic Bloc', puts forward
candidates for elections, some 335,000 in all.

Alongside an account of the 'organs' already described, a 'simplified' diagram was then provided to show how the 'People's Chamber'
(of five hundred deputies) is the 'democratic' pinnacle of a structure
based first on 186,233 deputies of the 'Community representative
bodies', then of 16,949 deputies of the 'District Assemblies', leading to 2,840 deputies of the 'County Assemblies'. Alongside all of
them is a vast series of committees and permanent commissions and
the 'Council of State', the 'Council of Ministers', the 'County
Councils', the 'District Councils' and the 'Community Councils'.

Readers will find these various organs (the National Front, the
councils, congresses, democratic blocs, people's chambers, councils
of states, of ministers) confusing enough, but they make up only half
the story. Alongside these organs of state there exist the organs of
the Communist Party – the cadres (or members at every level), the
'Central Committee' and the 'Politburo', which met once a week,
the leading roles within it being taken by the nine or so 'secretaries'
who ran departments. On paper, this was a state run from the
bottom up.

Parallel to the Politburo there existed the 'Council of State', in
theory the most important organ of government, which had about
twenty members (of whom a majority were SED members), and the
'Council of Ministers', which had about forty members (the vast
majority of whom were SED members). Western scholars spent a
great deal of time puzzling over which of these three bodies was *the*
East German government, and by looking carefully at who was 'in'
and who was 'out', who visited Moscow or Warsaw or who was left at
home, they attempted to read the runes and come up with an answer

as to what was actually happening in the GDR. Beneath the Council of Ministers there was a parliament, the Volkskammer.

In its propaganda, the GDR insisted it was not a one-party state but a democracy in which political decisions were executed by the state organs, under the political control of the majority party – the 'majority' party because in 'free elections' it gained a plurality of the votes.[4]

One thing is certain today – in reality the ruling Socialist Unity Party, the SED, and its flip side, the Stasi, controlled everything. Not surprisingly perhaps, *Introducing the GDR* makes no mention at all of any secret police; there is nothing here about Mielke and his Ministry for State Security, not even in the index. There is no hint that this was a dictatorship run by a clique of corrupt Communist bosses who sought and gained for themselves and their families the very standard of living they gladly denied their compatriots. In the large government compound of Wandlitz, the East German *Nomenklatura* owned Neff ovens, Miele washing machines and dishwashers, and watched West German pornographic videos on televisions also made in West Germany. They did not even drive East German or Russian cars – Volvos were their chosen make.[5]

Some British and American observers chose to put the best face on East Germany. They happily listened to East German leaders saying things like *'Frieden ist das erste Menschenrecht* – Peace is the first human right'; since the GDR was dedicated to peace, this was taken to mean that human rights were in safe hands.[6] To prove this a special issue of the government's own *GDR Review* carried pictures of a fracas in West Berlin in December 1980 which, under the heading 'What Human Rights Really Mean Under Capitalism', purported to show a 'police attack on defenceless demonstrators. Even women and children were beaten up.'[7]

Writing in 1977, Jonathan Steele, a noted British journalist, stated that 'Ulbricht was not unlike Konrad Adenauer'; Ulbricht's former personal secretary was quoted (without comment) as claiming 'we have created a state which is clean and decent, where orderliness reigns and people are hard working' and Stefan Heym, a leading East German intellectual, commented that 'all the GDR lacked was sparkle'.[8] Kurt Sontheimer and Wilhelm Bleek, authors of *The Government and Politics of East Germany*, a standard text on the GDR, make no reference to repressive measures or those who enacted them. Klaus von Beyme's 1984 book on the GDR makes no mention of Mielke, and only one quite indistinct one of the Stasi.[9] Hermann Weber's 1988 book contains only two one-line references to him. Generally, there was not much quality research carried out on the GDR prior to 1978.[10]

Yet anyone who visited East Germany and kept their eyes and ears open could tell that it was a police state; experts on East Germany knew this better than anyone else. Even in 1989 the experience of travelling to the eastern sector of Berlin was a genuinely frightening one. In their jackboots and jodhpurs, the East German People's Police reminded everyone of the SS. What must it have been like to be in thrall to them all the time, not just for a couple of hours? It is easy today, moving effortlessly from the western to the eastern part of Berlin, to forget that before 1990 this same journey was a menacing one, which took the individual from a free world into Communist totalitarianism.

What was also very apparent, even by 1989, was the economic misery of East Germany. Those who could only visit East Berlin (special permits were needed to travel more extensively) could see for themselves the destitution in this part of the city. Yet this was the capital of the GDR, its showpiece; if it looked like this here, what on earth was the rest of the country like? People were dowdy and grim. Men in heavy raincoats stood around, endlessly staring. There were few cars and most of those were miserable Trabants, made largely out of plastic, powered by two-stroke engines. In 1989 many buildings in the government quarter still bore the scars of wartime damage. Modern buildings invariably looked tacky; railway stations were sordid even by British standards. In the big supermarket near the Alexanderplatz it was clear that consumer goods were not simply shoddy and in short supply but also horrendously expensive. Washing machines, for example, were on special offer – but for more than the equivalent of £1,500 in 1989 prices, with monthly pay a small fraction of that.

But far more important than material deprivation was that of human rights. We should not baulk at applying this yardstick since it was, ironically, one used by the GDR itself. The ruling Communists always claimed that in the GDR there was full, constitutionally assured liberty and democracy, and a wide range of codified human rights upon which people could rely. Individuals detained by the East German authorities were forbidden from mentioning their experiences in detention, something that only leaving the GDR, or the collapse of the state, could expunge.[11] In official statements about itself, the regime presented itself as one committed to lawfulness, governed by the rule of law (the German term for such a state is *Rechtsstaat*): 'The human rights aspired to by the working people for centuries have become reality in the GDR. These rights are not comparable with the customary basic rights of citizens in capitalist countries and are guaranteed politically by the power of the working people, materially by socialist ownership, and juridically by the socialist legal system. The constitutional provisions on the basic rights are direct valid law . . . The observance of the basic rights of all citizens is a social necessity.'[12]

'Every citizen has the right to state his opinion freely and publicly. Free expression of opinion in word, writing and pictures forms part of the liberty of citizens, consciously to give shape to their own social life. The freedom of the press, radio and television is guaranteed. It corresponds to the humanist character of the socialist social system of the GDR that the right of the free expression of opinion may not be misused for purposes of militarist and revanchist propaganda, warmongering and proclamations of religious, racial and national hatred . . .'[13]

'The GDR is not merely a lawful state,' the regime insisted, 'it is the only lawful German state . . . in the GDR the important lessons of the past have been learned.'[14] 'The development of the GDR stands in harmony with the democratic principles of the law of peoples [*Völkerrecht*]; its policies correspond to those of the UN Charter. It is different with the FRG . . . there the same forces hold power who supported the Hitler regime.'[15]

'Are the citizens of the GDR allowed to state their opinions openly and freely?' the authors of this work ask. 'Yes,' they reply. 'It is unthinkable that in the GDR a citizen who criticises the work of a government minister, who finds shortcomings in an institution or administration, would lose his position, or even be arrested. But more than this, citizens do not just have the right to state their opinion, they have the duty to do so. There is only one qualification: expressions of opinion, and meetings, must serve democracy and peace. Attacks on the democratic state are banned in article 6 of the Constitution.'[16] 'Who is punished under law? Particularly severe is the way in which courts require agents to face their responsibilities: those who serve foreign, hostile secret organisations, or by spying or sabotage seek to disturb the process of building socialism in the GDR.'[17]

It is revealing that the GDR made such generous use of concepts like democracy, human rights and freedom of speech. It did not merely claim to be a lawful state (indeed, the only lawful German state) but a model state in terms of its upholding of the rule of dem-ocratically generated law. The abuses of human rights perpetrated by the Stasi were not simply abuses *per se*, but also abuses within the framework of the legal description that the GDR used about itself, but only ever on paper.

As far as the GDR itself was concerned, this sinister waffle not only indicates that the regime was wholly cynical in its treatment of its dissident citizens, but that it would be comprehended as such by its subjects. They knew that 'spying . . . sabotage . . . disturb[ing] the process of building socialism' were not words with specific meanings, but catch-all indictments which gave terror a free rein. To have laws guaranteeing dissent, criticism and free emigration, and to persecute those who sought to make use of these laws, was plainly intended to make to their subjects a very basic point about the will and nature of the regime, and its total determination to exercise power.[18]

One of the very few pre-1990 British books which gave real weight to the existence of political prisoners in East Germany was Timothy Garton Ash's excellent study of the GDR. Yet even he grossly underestimated the numbers involved, claiming that the GDR had fewer than 7,000 political prisoners and that none was taken after 1979 (which was not the case).[19] In 1996 it was estimated that from 1949 to 1989, some 250,000 people were imprisoned for political offences. Twenty-five thousand of these died in jail. The true number of those punished by the regime was therefore thirty-six times greater than one of its most perceptive observers had allowed in 1981.[20] From 1963 until 1989, 33,755 political prisoners had literally been bought free by West Germany, a fact which might have been better digested.[21] Western ignorance or indifference to the human rights abuses of the Stasi in the GDR helped to institutionalise them.

Most scholars certainly thought the GDR was an enduring feature on the European political landscape. As the leading West German scholar on the GDR, Hermann Weber, wrote in 1988: 'The GDR has existed for forty years, much longer than the fourteen years of Weimar, or the twelve of the Third Reich. This proves that the GDR, like the FRG, is one of the historically most stable states in recent German history.'[22] Weber's chief researcher turned out to be a Stasi spy.

Many, if not most, studies of the GDR produced since the 1960s had in fact stressed what was regarded as its impressive economic strength, and more than one spoke of an 'economic miracle' which it was claimed had occurred in East Germany during the late 1950s and 1960s.[23] David Childs, for example, a prominent British observer of East German affairs writing in 1966 approvingly quoted a *Times* report stating that the East German economic success story was 'more miraculous' than the West German one. He conceded that up to 1966 expansion was not as strong as it had been in the 1950s but argued that that was at least 'partly due to temporary factors such as the crisis of 1961' (by which he meant the building of the Berlin Wall).[24]

Charles S. Maier hits the mark with his conclusion that, 'By the late 1980s, many observers held [the GDR] to be a Communist "success story".'[25] Yet barely a year later, he continues, 'its economic residue was perceived in terms of second-rate machines, crumbling housing, cardboard cars, and an atmosphere choked by industrial fumes and lignite dust'.

Why did scholars not fully realise this? Maier puts forward an intriguing explanation: that many Western, in particular West German, political and business leaders had, in promoting closer ties with the

GDR, generated straightforward self-deception. 'The most disastrous consequences were concealed because Western policy makers, intellectuals and businessmen decided that their interest lay in stabilising the eastern blocs.'[26]

It would be disingenuous to expect every academic to have known a great deal about the Stasi before 1989–90 since much of its activity was secret, but enough *was* known to have given it priority in any serious study: books by K. W. Fricke and reports compiled by the SPD's Ostburo were widely available.[27] There was also witness testimony from the 3.1 million East German refugees. But Fricke and the refugees did not always find it easy to get a hearing.[28] The significance of both the Stasi and human rights violations in the GDR *was* understood (and reported) by Amnesty International after 1962.[29]

Why did repression in the GDR receive less attention than it deserved? Norman Naimark argues that before 1989 it was considered 'politically inappropriate for West German scholars in particular to dwell on the totalitarianism of the East and the mechanisms of repression that the East German citizens were forced to endure'.[30] This explanation may, however, hold water for all Western scholars, not just German ones. Others may have been sympathetic to what they regarded as the genuine achievements of East German Communism, or believed the positive aspects of the GDR outweighed its negative ones, which were, consequently, not worth stressing. Bias is always an enemy of good social science. Since 1990, however, scholars have been greatly helped in understanding the essential nature of the GDR thanks to the Bundestag Commission of Enquiry, more witness testimony and, perhaps most importantly, the Stasi Archive.[31]

One early, very public pointer to the Stasi's essential role came with Markus Wolf's November 1989 plea to the East German people not to give up 'real, existing Socialism' – the leadership's phrase for Communism. Although he had stepped down as deputy leader of the Stasi, his public role now made it obvious that there was a firm link between the secret police and political rulers (something that ordinary East Germans had known only too well).[32] The close bonds between SED and Stasi leaders were first described by Joachim Gauck, using evidence from the East German archives which made it clear that insufficient attention had been paid to the role of the secret police in controlling life in eastern Germany after 1945.[33] As Naimark observed in 1994, 'The Stasi formed the backbone of the GDR and permeated the country's every aspect, an integral part of the historical emergence of the country. The Soviets and the SED did not create the Stasi as an afterthought for securing East Germany . . . rather from the very beginning security concerns helped create an East German state that was inseparable from its internal police function.'[34]

All told, more than 200,000 eastern Germans died either directly or indirectly as a result of Communist policies carried out between 1945 and 1989; that is 1 per cent of the total population of East Germany.[35] Of these the vast majority, some 170,000, perished during the first and most cruel wave of Sovietisation, which lasted until 1953. At least 90,000 people were executed by the Communists as opponents of the regime, or died as a result of a policy of deliberate starvation and inhuman treatment. Seventy thousand died in camps in East Germany and some 20,000 in Soviet gulags. Some two million East German women were raped by the Soviet troops; one estimate suggests that more than 200,000 women died as a result of such violation.[36]

From 1945 until 1950, 122,671 people (some of whom were Nazis but others simply anti-Communist) were interned at Sachsenhausen and Buchenwald concentration camps.[37] At the end of the war, Buchenwald was out of operation for only eighty-nine days before being reopened by the Soviets, Sachsenhausen scarcely longer.

The above figures indicate only the number of deaths officially recorded. Experts believe that the numbers of those executed, and disposed of without trace, will cause these figures to be revised upwards. Political victims of the first phase of Stalinist persecution provide a testimony of almost unbelievable horror which firmly links the behaviour of the two totalitarian German regimes.[38] Other victims of this era have experiences of similar suffering.[39]

But, as current research shows, serious abuses did *not* stop when Soviet occupation formally ceased in 1949; indeed, they continued unabated right up until the fall of the Wall. Significant numbers of people were imprisoned and systematically tortured by the state throughout the 1980s. The children of parents intent on fleeing to the West were kidnapped and given up for adoption to more reliable citizens.[40] The rigging of votes and the administration of harmful performance-enhancing drugs to young athletes without their knowledge are further examples of commonplace abuse committed by the state on its citizens.[41]

As the GDR became more established, deaths in prison and political executions (though never out of the equation) gave way to other, often psychological, forms of terror. Falco Werkentin writes, 'Estimates made today of some 200,000 to 250,000 people imprisoned in the years *1949–89* [my italics] are realistic.' From 1958 to 1966, 63,949 people were arrested for trying to flee the GDR (the German word for this is *Republikflucht*). From 1964 to 1970, 20,820 people were given prison sentences for this offence. In the Honecker years (1971–89), 64,091 people were arrested for attempting to flee – on average 3,000 per annum until 1987 (when 5,696 were arrested). In 1988 the number was 9,169. There are no figures for 1989. The number of people jailed during the period 1979–89 totalled 23,368. In 1988, 2,337 were imprisoned; in 1989, 2,569.

The Stasi was given five prisons of its own in East Berlin and another seventeen throughout the GDR added to the full complement of normal prisons. Many of those imprisoned wished simply to exercise their human rights and flee the GDR. In the 1980s, however, the GDR's tradition of persecution was faced with a new threat: organised dissent based on a demand for peace and civil rights (powerful because these were values the GDR claimed as its own). The Stasi sought to terrorise dissidents and use Western support for them as evidence that they were traitors to the GDR.

Today, the German Federal Ministry of the Interior estimates that from 1949 to 1989–90 some 25,000 died in GDR prisons – either deliberately murdered or through neglect – 170 were executed for political crimes and 127 people killed in connection with the 1953 uprising.[42] Other sources claim that 75,000 escapers were jailed (averaging seven a day).[43] Their ages ranged from one to eighty-six. The last border death occurred on 23 September 1989. More than forty of these were children or youths; thirty victims were women.

The museum at Checkpoint Charlie believes that 943 people were killed while fleeing to the West, that more than one million East Germans spent periods in prison for political offences (which may have included trying to escape) and that from 1948 to 1988 some 2,901,000 refugees fled from the GDR to the West.[44]

Falco Werkentin notes that 'the GDR always refused to give figures of its political prisoners'; as early as 1950 the Ministry of Justice forbade the use of the term 'political prisoners'. Yet the government itself wished to know how many political prisoners there were. In the 1950s 'the press reported political trials and there were show trials'. Some 30,000 to 35,000 were imprisoned after the 1953 revolt. By May 1953 some 67,000 people were in jail, of whom 40–50 per cent were political prisoners. The high number of people arrested in the final years of the GDR's life may be explained in terms of those who sought to flee to the Federal Republic. Despite the fact that article 10 of the 1949 Constitution declared that every citizen had the right to leave the GDR, thousands were imprisoned every year for doing just this. The 1979 legal code stipulated a maximum eight-year sentence.[45]

It is instructive to note not just the uniformity of the methods of abuse that were employed, nor the consistency of their application since 1945, but how closely they reflect the account given of them by Arthur Koestler in his novel *Darkness at Noon*.

The prison at Bautzen, formerly a Nazi camp, was an accepted symbol of terror in Communist Germany; the implications of being sent there were generally known.[46] Detainees were kept either in barracks or large rooms containing some 400 people, rooms containing forty, or single cells of up to six people. Detainees were incarcerated with ordinary criminals and former Nazi war criminals. Prisoners were often beaten by the NKVD or the Volkspolizei. There was neither lavatory paper nor sanitary towels. Testimony from another prisoner taken in 1948 corroborates this picture.[47]

It is not possible to devote more than a few lines to the vast number of heartrending testimonies to death, torture and widespread human rights abuses that have emerged since 1990.[48] Two young Social Democrats, Hermann Kreutzer and his girlfriend, committed opponents of fusion between the SPD and the SED, were

sentenced to twenty-five years each in 1947 at the request of the
SED and were tortured, beaten and deprived of sleep. One was sent
to Bautzen, the other to Sachsenhausen. They were released in
1956. A West Berlin reporter was kidnapped in 1950 by the Soviets,
beaten repeatedly over seven months to extract a confession, then
sentenced to twenty-five years at Workuta in the Arctic Circle.[49] A
young student arrested by the Stasi in 1961 for trying to persuade
American servicemen in East Berlin to take him with them to the
West was offered his freedom in return for spying for them. When he
refused, he was kept in solitary confinement for 203 days, where he
contracted dysentery. He was given no medical help, and suffered
appallingly. Such people today make no secret of their suffering
under Communism but too few are minded to listen to them. One
of the best-known stories was that of Margret Bechler. By 1997,
her book revealing her experiences had run into eighteen editions.
Supported by documentary evidence in the form of letters and scraps
collected over the years, it told a horrifying tale of the inhumanity
of the Soviet and East German Communist states.[50]

Conditions did improve marginally for political prisoners after
1949 and then again after 1968, when a new, milder legal code was
promulgated. A new law of 7 April 1977 said that, in line with 'the
humane nature of the Socialist State', efforts to 're-educate prisoners should be made'. In fact, this was nothing more than forced
indoctrination. Prisoners who resisted were treated with the utmost
brutality. Nor was there any general improvement in prison conditions. There was, however, a trend in the GDR as well as in other
states to decrease the numbers of individuals given custodial sentences. Yet even so in the GDR there were 180–200 prisoners per
100,000 inhabitants, whereas in West Germany there were only
eighty-seven – two and a half times fewer.[51] Many dissident women
suffered severe abuse after 1973, especially in Hoheneck jail.

A recent collection of testimonies proves that abuses persisted in
*kind* if not in number until 1989.[52] In 1974 a doctor was arrested
with his wife and child while attempting to escape to the West. The
doctor's wife was taken to another room with their child. He did not
see her again for four and a half years, but heard her scream as their
child was taken from her. The child – since freed – was placed in an

orphanage in Erfurt. In another case, a dentist arrested on 5 October 1976 and taken to the investigation prison of the MfS at Schwerin was confined to his cell for several weeks for refusing to sign a confession, then sentenced to four years and transferred to Cottbus. Here he refused to work, and from September 1977 until May 1978 was locked in the 'tiger's cage', roughly two metres square, with opaque glass in the window, with no lavatory. The cell was not heated and during the day he was not permitted to lie on his bunk. Freed after almost two years, he fled to the West. Another man arrested for political offences on 15 November 1988 was kept with six others in a four-by-four-metre cell; four of them had been arrested trying to flee. Another political prisoner, taken on 25 October 1988, was held at Cottbus. 'I was confronted by the worst guard there. He ordered punishment exercises, standing still during the free hour; I twice saw how he beat up prisoners without reason.'

Josef Kneifel, the so-called 'Panzer detonator' who had blown up a tank monument to the Red Army in March 1980 (no one had been hurt in the explosion), was arrested with his wife. Refusing to work, and referring to himself as a 'prisoner of the Communists', he was repeatedly beaten. The punishments increased after February 1984 when he was sent to Bautzen I. He still refused to work. On 2 January 1987 he was chained to a steel net, on his back, unable to move, to torture him into agreeing to be 're-educated'. He was kept on the net for four days and only removed when he appeared to be close to death. He was bought free in the summer of 1987 following the intervention of a number of West German institutions. Another Cottbus political prisoner recalled that on 6 January 1978 he and three others were ordered to clear snow and ice in the bitter cold. They refused and five men, led by the 'Red Terror' (a guard called Schulze who was convicted after 1990), ordered a so-called 'canon-ade': ten to fifteen men proceeded to beat the four prisoners into submission.

It may in any case be argued that the *numbers* of those who were killed, died or were abused is, in one sense, irrelevant. From the point of view of the victim, persecution by a government for political beliefs peacefully held, and lawfully communicated, is in itself a valid 'performance indicator' of the behaviour of that government, quite irrespective of the numbers involved. Yet the vast numbers involved indicate the *extent* to which persecution was used to exert control, and to intimidate society as a whole.

Furthermore, persecution has, and was intended to have, a long shelf life.[53] It is sometimes suggested that the worst abuses of human rights took place under the Soviet occupation, and that this cannot be laid at the door of the East German Communists. While it is certainly the case that the worst abuses, chiefly in terms of numbers killed and possibly in the brutality of the treatment, took place before 1953, and especially from 1945 to 1949, it was the GDR that was the 'beneficiary' of this legacy. Brutality thus served as a 'bottom-line' warning to dissidents throughout the period of Communist rule in Germany. Indeed, it seems unwise to differentiate between Soviet and German Communism when ascribing guilt for human rights abuses.[54] The damage done to individuals since 1945 persists to the present day.

The truth, therefore, was that the reality of political life in the GDR was very different from the way in which the regime presented itself to the world. This was a state which lacked any genuine constitutional protection of civil rights. Some analysts of East Germany preferred it to the Federal Republic which they – quite wrongly – regarded as revanchist and neo-Nazi. But the Federal Republic was always a constitutional state; the GDR was at base a brutal and repressive state. Plainly, the parallels that existed between Nazi Germany and the GDR – as well as the significant differences – will continue to be debated for many years to come and how the German authorities have dealt with the GDR period will doubtless have consequences no less far-reaching, in their own way, than those that stemmed from earlier failures in respect of the Third Reich. James McAdams, who had stressed the differences between the two regimes, nevertheless emphasises that the 'Communist states [of Europe] were more like their fascist contemporaries than their defenders would ever admit, aiming to gain and maintain complete control over their subject populations'. He quotes a leading German view that the Nazi 'campaign of destruction against "Marxists and alien peoples" had its parallels in the Communist struggle against the "class enemy"; the one group disregarded human rights from the standpoint of race . . . the other from class'.[55] One defining characteristic of Nazi terror was certainly its obsession with race, another the vast numbers murdered because of it. But state-run terror is still terror and to its victims it matters not a jot whether they are one of thousands or one of millions.

## The Secret Police State: The Stasi and the GDR in 1989

> We know that a wrongdoer can infiltrate our ranks. We do realise this. Were I to discover someone like this, he would not be alive tomorrow morning. I'd have a very short hearing, of course, because I'm humane. That is why I take this line. But let us be clear about why we have to be so hard. Some say 'don't execute, no death sentences'. All this is absurd, Comrades. They are swine. Execute them. Without laws, without legal trials and procedures and so forth.
>
> – Erich Mielke, taped speech, 19 February 1982

Let us, for a moment, go back in time to East Berlin, basking in the warm sun of the summer of 1989. This particular summer is a very important time for East Germany, for it is celebrating its fortieth birthday. One of the GDR's chief guests of honour at the fortieth-anniversary jamboree is Yasser Arafat, the leader of the Palestine Liberation Organization and the mastermind of the massacre of the Israeli athletes at the Munich Olympics of 1972. He is a popular if somewhat outlandish figure, adding a touch of exoticism with his fedayeen headdress and three-day beard. What his presence in East Berlin implies, though no one dares say so, is that there exists a direct connection between the East German Politburo, the Stasi and the violence in the Middle East, a sinister and frightening aspect of the Stasi's place in GDR diplomacy.

The Stasi, and the HVA within it, do not merely work as a security and secret intelligence service. They also set up security and intelligence services for those in the Islamic world who are prepared to benefit from their expertise. At the Stasi's college in Potsdam, their leaders learn about Marxism and the methods and organisation of security and intelligence activity. At the top-secret Springsee complex in Beeskow outside Berlin, as well as in the dismal camps of the Middle East, Stasi weapons specialists train large numbers of special forces (or terrorists, depending on one's point of view) in explosives, chemical weapons and even nuclear devices.[56]

But there are whispers in the summer of 1989: things are not quite as happy as the East German Politburo insists. Behind the propaganda and set-piece rallies, there are one or two signs of serious discontent in East Germany. Thousands are trying to flee to the West through Hungary; dissidents seem edgy and increasingly aware that Gorbachev's Soviet experiment may change things for ever. Even so, the regime seems well in control. The Stasi does what it is paid to do and does it well.

Its 85,000 officers are busy. In 1989 the Stasi possesses 1,819 official, sports and health premises, 836 other premises and 18,000 flats. It has 838 'conspiratorial' premises, usually held under false names, as well as 5,503 flats, used for 'security purposes' and containing 'special equipment'. It owns 12,000 cars and 5,456 customised vehicles, with various types of weapons and surveillance equipment attached. This year it has already spent 45 million Ostmarks (some £1 million) on updating its organisation. It has 9,200 officers in internal counter-espionage, 'securing the economy' (that is, watching over the workers and rigging the economic data) and fighting the dissidents.

In 1989 the Stasi can be found using 2,171 East Germans to open letters, 1,486 to tap telephones, 4,000 on various intelligence operations and counter-intelligence operations against NATO powers from inside the GDR. It employs 8,426 in electronic intelligence gathering, 4,876 in protecting various luminaries and state institutions. The Stasi uses 2,244 individuals as interrogators, 1,284 to gather facts; 10,559 Stasi members work in the district or regional offices of the Stasi in the GDR. Twelve thousand are on border control duty, 13,254 in adjunct security (site services, financial, personal, medical and organisational security) and 16,000 working within guard and security units.[57]

Those dissidents who are thinking of actively spoiling the

anniversary fun are also well catered for. Mielke has, in his *Panzerschrank*, the large safe in his office in Normannenstrasse, a file marked 'Plan for Day X' (code for the day before Communist rule begins to disintegrate).[58] These are the procedures to be followed should a 'counter-revolutionary situation' occur. The file contains a list of 85,939 East Germans to be arrested by 211 of Mielke's special elite corps, the 'officers for special duties', or *OibEs*, at a rate of 840 people every two hours. On 8 October 1989 he actually orders the first stage to be put into effect.

Some of those believed to be capable of causing trouble will be required to visit the psychiatric clinic at Waldheim (there is also a Stasi jail nearby). Enemies of the regime, he reasons, are probably temporarily insane and may learn to value 'real existing Socialism' after a stay at the clinic. They will be 'looked after' by Professor Wilhelm Poppe (aged fifty-seven in 1989), an executive committee member of the GDR Society for Psychiatric Medicine, who is in charge.[59] He is a strong believer in the benefits of a drug called apomorphin to treat 'temporary insanity' (it causes continuous retching over long periods). After 1990, Poppe said that he had simply been helping the sick: 'one met a lot of people in those days', he explained, 'who seemed perfectly normal but were, in fact, insane and believed they were persecuted by the Stasi'.

He did concede that several of his nursing staff were Stasi officials. Former inmates told a different story. One of them, a thirty-five-year-old worker, was taken to Waldheim in order to 'provide' information about his brother in the West who worked for Daimler-Benz. He was left naked for five days on straw to encourage him to enter 'giving mode'. Werner Janasek (aged forty-three), who had sent a letter to President Reagan, was sent to Poppe's clinic for a twenty-four-day course of treatment. A thirty-two-year-old woman, believed by her family to be dead, was found in a locked cell in Waldheim in 1990; there were no papers explaining the reasons for her imprisonment and those files on her that did exist contained obvious forgeries. According to a porter at the 'clinic', 'therapies' carried out there included burning the soles of inmates' feet and spraying foam into their eyes. For many hours female detainees were immersed up to their waists in water; at night some would be raped. Perhaps not surprisingly in the circumstances, Professor Poppe immediately fled following revelations about his 'clinic'. Today, his whereabouts are unknown. Like so many of his Stasi comrades, he has been able to slip into the shadows, leaving only the scars of his handiwork behind him.

# 2

# Britain and the Germans in the East

This is a book about Stasi intelligence operations against the United Kingdom as revealed by the Stasi files, but precisely because it is about the Stasi and the UK it is also a book about British–GDR relations. Most people regard the relationship between states as a diplomatic one, in which each state respects the sovereignty of the other and where each agrees to conduct its dealings with the other on the basis of the 1961 Vienna Convention, which regulates diplomatic relations. In fact the true basis of East Germany's relations with the UK relied far more on the Stasi's secret and illegal activity in the UK than on any above-board association. In this sense, British–GDR relations were, from the East German viewpoint, more about the Stasi than anything else.

Curiously, perhaps, most academics have completely ignored this dimension to British–East German relations. Two of the most recent studies of British–GDR relations do not even mention the Stasi interest in Britain. One might be forgiven for thinking that culture and trade were all that concerned the East German diplomats in London. Even so, and tellingly perhaps, neither study sees fit to give the name of a single East German diplomat working in London.[1] The inference to be taken from this is that no GDR diplomat in London ever did anything sufficiently diplomatic to merit inclusion in a book. And so it was.

Indeed, none of the diplomats at 34 Belgrave Square played a key

role in overt British–GDR relations. As Bert Becker rightly suggests, in the areas of economic relations between Britain and East
Germany recognition changed virtually nothing in what seemed a
downbeat diplomatic relationship.[2] That assessment is perfectly
correct if we exclude the secret dimension. Indeed, the East
Germans were so keen to get their spy ring up and running once
they were finally recognised, and so completely uninterested in the
formal niceties of diplomatic life, that the East German ambassador
never even bothered to present his credentials to HM The Queen.[3]
To anyone who observed the East Germans in Britain after their
arrival in 1973, it was clear that, however much interest they pro-
fessed to have in trade and culture, they could not really have cared
less about any genuine expansion in these fields.

Normal diplomatic relations never took off. More than one scholar
has noted that it seemed paradoxical that, having spent so much
energy on gaining diplomatic recognition, the East Germans then
appeared to do very little with what they were given.[4] Britain was
never visited by Honecker. The explanation is that the GDR was
able to get all it wanted from its relationship with the UK from the
use of its diplomatic cover to engage in secret intelligence activity
against the UK.

The core role played by the Stasi in all East German affairs should
not surprise us. Not only did the Stasi's brief extend throughout the
entire remit of government, including foreign affairs – the Stasi files
show that Mielke personally checked and approved all international
treaties and agreements signed by East Germany – but the most
vital measures taken by the government were usually Stasi ones.[5] A
folder in the Stasi files, dated 11 August 1961 and inscribed simply
'Operation "Rose"', shows that the construction of the Berlin Wall,
the most infamous symbol of the East German regime, was an early
Stasi task.

Joachim Gauck, Germany's leading researcher on the Stasi and
the first guardian of the Stasi records, offers evidence for this provided by the East Germans themselves: 'The Ministry for State
Security was established to be the executive organ of the dictatorship of the proletariat. As such it organises its activity under the
leadership of the Socialist Unity Party, on the basis of the decision

of that Party'. This statement of what the Stasi did comes from the Stasi's 'Law College' (Juristische Hochschule) at Potsdam. In explaining it, Gauck writes: 'The actual question of who controlled whom was never asked. The state apparatus and the security apparatus were forged into one single interactive unit.'[6] When we speak of the East German leadership, we are therefore also speaking of the Stasi. Behind the policies of the Socialist Unity Party, whether at home or abroad, we always find the Stasi. Similarly, Stasi officers were always members of the party.[7] The Stasi was East German Communism in action.

In the eighteenth century, the French Revolutionary politician, the Comte de Mirabeau, remarked that Prussia was not 'a state with an army, but an army with a state'. In much the same way the GDR was not a state with a security and intelligence service, but a security and intelligence service with a state. Nor is it, for this reason, correct to call the Stasi a 'state within a state' as is sometimes done.[8] As one of Mielke's most trusted colleagues, General Dr Siegfried Gehlert, head of the Karl-Marx-Stadt Stasi, put it succinctly: 'There could be no German Democratic Republic without a Stasi since it was the Stasi's job to ensure that peace, order and security existed for the citizens.' Confusing peace, order and security with the repression of a police state was, of course, wholly in the tradition of Third Reich double-speak, where 'law and order' meant utter contempt for the rights of the individual and 'justified' the brutal repression of whoever was deemed 'the enemy'.

As far as Britain was concerned, the East German leadership believed that secret intelligence on British affairs would help it to sustain its position of power. Britain was not the most important single target – that was the Federal Republic, closely followed by the United States of America. It was, however, a significant target, possibly more so than France. As we have seen, there were specific aspects of Britain's political life in the 1980s in which the East Germans plainly took a great interest. This chapter describes the mechanisms the East Germans deployed in order to achieve their initial goal of establishing a base in London from which to conduct espionage against Britain.

They wanted to know all they could about the mindset of British policy makers and agenda setters. They wanted information on the precise nature of the policies that were being made, especially if they were secret, were concerned with defence and arms, or in some way impacted on the internal affairs of East Germany. They wanted to find out who was making policy and what their motives were, to collect data on the leading politicians, and, given their understandable preoccupation with the West Germans, were always desperate for up-to-date material on the nature of the British–West German relationship. Finally, they were consistently interested in knowing about any Britons who had interests, economic or political, in East Germany, and who might be giving secret support to anyone inside the German Democratic Republic regarded as their enemies. In short, they wanted to secure Communism in East Germany for the imaginable future and this meant neutralising its opponents.

The East Germans' intelligence work was 'defensive', in that it was not intended to destabilise Britain as a whole, but it was also invasive and subversive. They certainly attempted to penetrate organisations which they saw as especially threatening, and either to undermine or to destabilise individuals within them if the Stasi was told they were dangerous. The Stasi did not want to trigger an armed conflict with any Western power, but it was without doubt a *hostile* intelligence and security service, one which always regarded the West and the United Kingdom as its enemy. In order to achieve its aims in the UK, the Stasi knew it needed to get as close as possible to the political class (those who took an active interest in politics and helped determine its course) and its institutions (those responsible for shaping and delivering policy). This explains its emphasis on 'humint'; 'sigint', which is chiefly concerned with military intelligence, cannot deliver such information.

In theory, there were two main methods of running agents in Britain. The first, and most fruitful, was to construct a network of relationships based on open or semi-secret diplomatic ones upon which, in time, a secret intelligence framework, based on recruited agents, could be superimposed. This has long been an example of classic spycraft: all secret intelligence services exploit the possibilities presented by diplomatic activity. For many years, MI6, for example, has used posts in British embassies throughout the world as a cover for their officers. Yet precisely because this strategy was so well known it had a downside: it had to be assumed that security services were always alert to the possibilities of such activity. In the case of Britain, the Stasi was obliged to assume that MI5 would always suspect its diplomats of espionage and, if it caught them, would use the time-honoured means of dealing with such a problem – the arrest or expulsion of such 'diplomats' so as to neutralise secret work.

The second, and most hazardous, way of spying on a hostile state was to construct a network of 'illegals' – penetration agents and spies who could operate independently of diplomatic cover.

As far as the first, safer, option was concerned, for the first twenty years of its existence (from the early 1950s to the early 1970s) the Stasi faced a major and apparently intractable obstacle to working fully in the UK. This was the British government's steadfast refusal to recognise the GDR as a state, thereby refusing to enter into a diplomatic relationship with it and denying it an embassy in London (and failing, in turn, to acquire a British embassy in East Berlin). As a consequence, there could be no diplomatic cover for the Stasi in the UK. It meant that secret intelligence work against the UK had to rely on illegals (posing as journalists, for example), on overt Communists and on fellow travellers (who might be expected to sympathise with the GDR's aims) as well as German refugees from the Third Reich who might have been Communists or sympathetic to them.

Britain's policy of non-recognition was partly the outcome of the often unrelenting stance adopted towards Soviet and Eastern European Communism in the early 1950s but partly also – and increasingly into the 1960s – the outcome of the British readiness to defer to their West German NATO allies when it came to dealing with the East Germans. Marianne Howarth, an expert on this issue, states quite clearly that she believes Britain's national interest in fact demanded neither recognition nor non-recognition.[9] It made little difference to the amount of trade that was conducted, or to the cultural ties that had been developed. Rather, Britain's policy towards the GDR was an adjunct to its far more important policy towards West Germany.

Without an embassy, the East Germans had to tap its illegal sources. There were long-standing links between many East German Communists and Britain. It is worthwhile noting that a significant number of members of the East German elite had such links: the current edition of *Who Was Who in the GDR*,[10] published by the Stasi Archive, lists at least 151 leading East Germans with such a connection, many of whom lived and worked in the United Kingdom in the late 1930s and in the 1940s, returning to eastern Germany after 1947. Of these, a large number were politically active in the German Communist Party in exile in London, in the 'Free German Youth Movement' or the 'German Trade Union Association' in Britain. Oldrich Cerny, the former (post-Communist) chief of the Czech secret intelligence service, has confirmed that the Communist Czech secret service had a small number of British sources, all of whom had been recruited as agents during, and in the aftermath of, the Second World War.[11]

The German Communist Party, the KPD, had established an office and a network in London in the mid-1930s. Several extremely prominent German Communists spent the war in London including Robert and Jürgen Kuczynski, the latter an academic at the London School of Economics. Robert's daughter, code-named 'Sonja', had been the radio operator for the Red Orchestra spy network and in Britain was the courier for atom spy Klaus Fuchs. She had been in the UK since 1942. She was, however, a secret Communist and ordered to keep away from the party organisation, and MI5 seemed unaware of her activities, in Oxford and then Great Rollright, in the Cotswolds. She fled to East Berlin in 1950, just before Fuchs's arrest. In 1969 she was awarded the Order of the Red Banner of the Red Army and her autobiography, *Sonja's Rapport*, became an East German classic.[12] Wilhelm Koenen (a leading figure in the official UK–GDR relationship), Margarete Wittkowski (later head of the state bank), Hans Herzfelder (head of Western broadcasting in the GDR), Horst Brasch (head of the 'League for Friendship between Peoples') and Kurt Hager (the GDR's leading ideologue) were major examples of prominent GDR leaders who had spent the war years in the UK. Brasch and Hager were both very senior SED members.[13]

There was, however, an obvious additional risk inherent in the situation facing the GDR because of non-recognition. Everyone, especially the Stasi, knew that MI5 and the Foreign Office had kept close tabs on German Communist exiles in the United Kingdom.[14] Known Communists, whether Britons or émigré Germans, were carefully registered and therefore identifiable. While East German illegals masquerading as West Germans could enter the UK more or less freely, East Germans with East German passports could never do so. The visa requirement was never abolished.

The Stasi's best bet therefore was to try to gain recognition while seeking, in the meantime, to infiltrate its agents into the UK as West Germans. Since, technically speaking, none of them were ever caught, we cannot know how many people we are dealing with here. Several spies, sometimes believed to have been East German, were actually not spying for East Germany: Klaus Fuchs, for example, went to *East* Germany on his release from jail. But like 'Sonja', he had spied for Soviet military intelligence (the GRU), not the Stasi. The Krogers were, despite their name, South African rather than German. In the 1980s, a West German tip-off caused Special Branch to arrest Sonja and Reinhardt Schulze; they became the *only* two Stasi 'illegals' in the UK ever to be caught. Both were HVA agents (but carrying Swiss passports).[15] The Stasi files do, however, contain evidence of successful espionage in the UK prior to 1973.

Whatever else it may have meant to the East Germans, gaining diplomatic recognition meant in particular the establishment of a more secure spy base in Britain. It was therefore an overriding goal for them. Indeed, because the Stasi's job was to realise the political desires of the regime, a vital part of its illegal work in the UK even before recognition in 1973 was directed towards precisely this end. Secret intelligence became the means of opening up more opportunities for – secret intelligence. Dismantling the policy of non-recognition became a Stasi concern.

Before 1973 there did exist a few official East German organisations in the UK concerned with trade and culture. But before then they were either staffed by British citizens or by East Germans residing in the UK with permits which had to be renewed twice a year. Some of these individuals may have been agents for East

German intelligence, but it was highly risky to use such people as spies. While the GDR had a strong interest in making contact with British citizens who might help it to press its claim for recognition, it had little interest in using people too strongly associated with it in public as its spies.

As we shall see when we come to examine specific cases of Stasi spying in the UK, steps were usually taken to distance its secret agents from any link with East Germany or East German institutions. Once the relationship had been secured, any overt links had to be severed or at least cut back to what might be considered by the British authorities as a normal level of contact with a country in which one had a legitimate interest. The British Foreign Office believed that in the 1960s, especially on the left of the political spectrum, Britain was 'particularly favourable ground' for East German Communist propaganda.[16] Anyone seen to be too close to the GDR could all too easily become a liability to the Stasi rather than an asset.

Britain regarded the East German regime with suspicion and considered it a straightforward Soviet satellite, a state given life and form by the Soviet Union itself. Yet to many Britons it was understandable that the Soviets believed that they had a duty to 'sort' the Germans once and for all, now that history had given them a unique opportunity to do so. Twice during the twentieth century Germany had tried to destroy Russia, most brutally and murderously after 1941. Even if there had been periods when Soviets and Germans seemed to be as one, the German onslaught on the Soviet Union on the night of 21–22 June 1941, code-named Barbarossa, unleashed such appalling terror on the Russian people that many agreed with the Soviets that Germany should never again be in a position to attack their country. Some 13.6 million Russian soldiers and seven million Russian civilians were killed by the Germans between 1941 and 1945.

Soviet leaders obviously believed that the best way of preventing future German supremacy was to convert Germany into a Communist state. To do so would abolish once and for all the German threat, at the same time ensuring that the interests of the Soviet Union could be established firmly on the soil of Central and perhaps, from this base, of Western Europe as well. No Russian could be under any illusions as to the difficulty of such a task, least of all Stalin, who once allegedly complained: 'To impose Communism on a German is like putting a saddle on a cow.'[17]

In order to consolidate their hold on power, initially at any rate in the eastern part of Germany, the Communists worked on three distinct areas. The first, and most important, was the use of Soviet armed and secret police to impose Communism on the people themselves. The Russians had 300,000 troops in eastern Germany, augmented by 20,000 'security troops'.[18] The second and third elements were both concerned with disguising what was being done: the Communists appealed to the Social Democrats in the Eastern Zone to unite with them to form a single working-class party and they developed the fiction that East Germany was to be a pluralist state, under 'Socialist' leadership but with non-Communist parties apparently being allowed to work in freedom. Communists immediately suggested a fusion of the KPD and the SPD to form the 'Socialist Unity Party', the Sozialistische Einheitspartei, or SED. By 1946 this had taken place, partly as the result of Communist pressure, partly because some Social Democrats believed it to be the right thing to do, and partly because the majority of Social Democrats who did not like it at all were powerless to prevent it.

From the outset, the British authorities were not unaware of Communist intentions and had taken every opportunity of encouraging eastern Social Democrats to resist the Communist embrace. By May 1946 Ernest Bevin, Britain's Labour Party Foreign Secretary, was telling his Cabinet – in a memo marked Top Secret – that there now existed a 'Communist threat' in East Germany and that the Western powers might have to accept that two German states would come into existence.[19] Significantly, he likened the Communist abuse of power to that of Hitler and the Nazis ('What was done in Brown is now being done in Red') and, now that the SPD had been 'practically eliminated and forced into fusion with the Communists', the creation of a new totalitarian German state in the East was simply a matter of time.

The East German Communists seem to have established their own security service in the summer of 1946. Although this has been described as 'independent', it is inconceivable that it was created without Russian support and approval.[20] The Russians had initially deployed their own security service but by 1947 the secret East German political police force was already in action. It was later to become the Stasi, using Department K-5 of the German criminal police and the intelligence and information section of the administration for the interior as its base.[21] Norman Naimark notes that 'not only Nazis but significant numbers of former SS and SA members found their way into the police', of whom the later Stasi chief, Erich Mielke, was a Communist member. In November 1947 he was given his own 'department for intelligence and information' whose aims were 'disinformation, spying and intelligence' and 'influencing public opinion by sponsoring the writing and planting of articles, reports and news in the press in order to inspire the population to think positively about the government and the SED'.[22]

In the event that positive thoughts were not forthcoming, the Soviet secret police and then the Stasi resorted to their tried and tested alternative: terror. As we have seen, they reopened some of the Third Reich's most notorious concentration camps, at Sachsenhausen and Buchenwald, as well as in Bautzen.[23] A large number of these victims of Soviet brutality were 'rehabilitated' (declared innocent of any wrongdoing, including neo-Nazi activity) by the Russian Federation in 1995.[24]

On 12 March 1947, in an address to Congress, President Harry S. Truman made it plain that the United States and its Western allies would do all they could to resist further Communist takeovers. It was too late, of course, to save East Germany or any of the other Soviet satellites, and to unleash a nuclear attack on the Soviet Union (the only other option) was unthinkable. The Cold War was beginning to divide Europe, and within Europe the division of Germany was almost complete. On 24 June 1948 the Warsaw Pact was set up. Almost at once, to show the West that they would not be contained the Soviets decided to try to force the Americans, the British and the French out of West Berlin and to detach this part of the city from the Western world. What they did not entirely bargain for was the Western response in the shape of the Berlin Airlift, which demonstrated most effectively the resolve of the West to counter Communism with all the means at its disposal – short of war.

# 3

# Recognising East Germany

While Stalin's ultimate aim had almost certainly been a single Communist German nation, he preferred a Communist part-Germany to a non-Communist united Germany (just as the West preferred a democratic West Germany to one German nation under Communist control). The East German state, the GDR, was duly established on 7 October 1949, a little while after the creation of the West German part-nation. Otto Grotewohl, as SED leader, was given the task of creating a government. On 25 October Georg Dertinger became the first GDR foreign minister and immediately sought to establish diplomatic relations with any state prepared to reciprocate. In the event, only the Soviets and the 'people's democracies' of Eastern Europe and Asia obliged.

As early as 7 October 1949 the West German Chancellor Konrad Adenauer had declared that the East German government did not represent the East German people and should therefore not be recognised. The Allied High Commission agreed: 'the so-called government of the German Democratic Republic', it stated, 'is an artificial creation, devoid of any legal basis and has no title to represent Eastern Germany . . .' Non-recognition became high policy and any idea of exchanging ambassadors with the GDR was deemed 'repugnant'.[1] The Americans underwrote this.[2] Britain decided it would not even have economic contact with the GDR, although trade could be conducted by private individuals or through the Soviet Union.

Seeing in this an advantage for themselves, the East Germans continued to demand German unity, and for this reason Adenauer did everything he could, short of precipitating an armed conflict between West and East Germany (which would have meant nuclear war), to stifle the East German regime and counter its nationalist line. The West German government insisted in its so-called Hallstein Doctrine of 1955 (named after the diplomat who formulated it) that it would break off relations with any state which recognised the GDR.[3] It also declared that under no circumstances would it renounce its claim to represent all German citizens whether they were citizens of West or East Germany.[4] The Hallstein Doctrine was loyally adhered to by the Federal Republic's Western allies and by none more firmly than the United Kingdom.

The East Germans' response to this was to try to get recognition as quickly as possible from the West.[5] They rehearsed endlessly what they insisted were the advantages the world would derive from recognising them: were they to be admitted to the community of nations they promised to work for peace and, as far as the UK was concerned, to promote British–East German trade and German culture in Great Britain. It made good sense for the GDR to win friends in British politics, public life and academe, especially in the field of German studies. Being able to show Britons that the GDR shared the German cultural heritage would sustain those scholars sympathetic to East Germany and give them a more powerful voice. The Politburo saw, too, that recognition could serve a very different end. By letting the East German people see that the GDR was now accepted as an independent German state, the regime's stranglehold over them would be even harder to break.

Even so, the East Germans understood that recognition by the West would be a collective decision, with the lead taken by the United States, in tandem with the Federal Republic of Germany, the Western country most immediately affected by the impact of a legally recognised second German state. Yet British support was vital too, not least because Britain, as one of the victorious nations in the Second World War, had important German interests and rights, especially in Berlin. By getting its supporters and sympathisers in the UK to emphasise the supposed advantages of recognition at every opportunity, the East German leaders believed that at best the British government would be forced to go with the flow.

The East Germans quickly grasped, given the prevalence in some quarters of anti-(West) German feeling in Britain, that it would make sense for their work in the UK to contrast the 'peace-loving and anti-Fascist' stance of the GDR with the 'revanchist neo-Nazi ambitions' of the Federal Republic. It would be especially effective in the UK, which had a strong peace lobby. In 1949 the Soviet Union had set up a 'World Peace Council' which had a British Peace Committee affiliated to it. It was in essence a Communist-fronted organisation, exploiting shamelessly the idea of 'peace' as a means of strengthening Communism throughout the world. The East Germans had their own Peace Council and this became a primary focus for influencing British opinion formers.[6] The Communist Party of Great Britain was, at first, the chosen conduit for their messages. As early as 1950 Harry Pollitt, the British Communist boss, had sent a message to the East German leader, Wilhelm Pieck, which spelt out the position very clearly: 'there are two Germanys, that of the Hitler supporters – the Germany of Adenauer and Schumacher . . . and the Germany of Pieck and Ulbricht which wants to live in peace with the people of Britain, France and the Soviet Union'.[7]

In April 1953, the East German Volkskammer made a formal 'appeal' to the Westminster Parliament in the form of a 'warning against the imperialism and militarism' which, not surprisingly, it claimed to detect in the policies of the Bonn government but, oddly, failed to discover in itself. Like all other official communications from the GDR, this appeal was not answered: all notes and memoranda from the GDR were always returned 'unread', and sometimes literally torn up in the presence of the East Germans who had handed them over. The GDR had to content itself with pointing out that it had taken the United States sixteen years to recognise the Soviet Union. Recognition, it seemed, was simply a matter of time. The anti-Communist uprising of 16 and 17 June 1953, brutally suppressed by Soviet tanks, naturally detracted somewhat from the East German pitch. Its leaders had to wait until Western memories of the uprising subsided, as they were confident they ultimately would.

In 1955 an 'inter-parliamentary group' was set up in East Berlin, headed by Wilhelm Koenen, who had been a leading Communist in London during the Second World War, to bring Western parliamentarians to the GDR; the first visit, which included British MPs, took place in 1957. In February 1959 forty-eight Labour MPs called for the *de facto* recognition of East Germany; between February and May of that year ten Labour MPs had trooped off to East Berlin where they were granted audiences with Walter Ulbricht.

As far as the idea of expanding trade with the UK was concerned, this, too, was chiefly conceived as a device to further the claim for recognition (the trade was fairly minimal in any case).[8] From 1955 to 1958 imports from the UK doubled (from a very low base) and, because of the foreign currency problems that the East Germans had by virtue of their place in the Communist trading bloc, trade never amounted to very much in a global sense, even if some people got very rich from the trade that they did do.[9]

The GDR could not afford to buy anything from the West that was not essential to its economy, but it was interested in Western technology, to which trade gave it access. The West, on the other hand, was always prepared to buy cheap goods to sell on. Machinery and machine tools were the most important items but there was trade, too, in raw materials. Of special significance was the import of East German potash and other chemical fertilisers, but East German radios, furniture, cameras, shoes, toys and musical instruments came to be well established in British markets. Yet, because of the non-convertibility of the Ostmark, bilateral trade had to be very carefully regulated. The GDR had a foreign trade chamber which was given a British section in 1970 to oversee dealings with the CBI and the London Chamber of Commerce. In addition, the Leipzig trade fair had its own office. Indeed, the Leipzig fair was the jewel in the crown of the GDR's trade system.

It was, therefore, no surprise that the annual Leipzig fairs were the chosen forum for delivering the initial message which would then, it was hoped, be picked up and taken back to the UK. The first post-war fair had been held as early as 1946 and subsequent fairs were regularly attended not just by British industrialists but also by MPs.[10] From the early 1950s, some British businessmen, notably Sir

Rudy Sternberg, who was to become a friend and supporter of Harold Wilson, had pursued trade with the GDR. Even so, trading relationships were not allowed to transcend the strictures of non-recognition, a fact frequently bemoaned by several leading parliamentarians. Major British companies which regularly exhibited at Leipzig included Rolls-Royce, Massey Ferguson and Standard Motors. There was, of course, nothing untoward about any of this in principle but any contact with the East Germans carried the potential danger that it might be subverted by them.

The East Germans devoted considerable resources to persuading MPs – by various means – of the advantages of recognition. The GDR could rely on a coalition composed of Conservative MPs who had, or claimed to have, financial interests in trade with East Germany, Labour MPs with trade interests and left-wing Labour MPs who supported the GDR for ideological reasons. Although the last group had their uses, their potential was limited since everyone knew that their motivation was political. The MPs with trade interests were, however, a different matter: they were seen as being extremely helpful to the East German cause. The East Germans were aware of the impact on policy and on public opinion that MPs could make by asking Parliamentary Questions, and it was relatively easy to build bridges to such MPs, particularly when what they were being asked to support were things widely deemed to be beneficial to British interests, such as requests for more trade (or improved security in Europe). MPs offered a real chance of a quick return on the time and expense that was devoted to cultivating them. Time, expense and care were, indeed, devoted in considerable measure by the East German planners to creating a parliamentary lobby for the recognition of East Germany for trade reasons. By the mid-1960s this lobby included two Conservative MPs: Burnaby Drayson, MP for Skipton (who had visited the 1953 Leipzig fair), and Brigadier Terence Clarke, MP for Portsmouth West. Drayson is listed in the Stasi files as a firm HVA contact, and also has an entry in the F16 index of persons of interest to the HVA.

Labour MPs with a special concern for the GDR included Ian Mikardo, Renee Short, Will Owen and Arthur Lewis and, most importantly, Harold Wilson, who became leader of the Labour Party

and then Prime Minister. Will Owen, the MP for Morpeth, was a specially noteworthy character. As Chapman Pincher first revealed in
1982, Owen was a Czech spy code-named 'Lee', allegedly earning
£500 per month for his espionage against Britain.[11] Christopher
Andrew and Oleg Gordievsky add that Owen was the 'most enthusiastic' agent run in the UK by the Czech Secret Intelligence
Service, the StB.[12] Owen had been recruited shortly after his election in 1954 by an officer working under diplomatic cover as second
secretary. Although his official cover-name was 'Lee', he was known
within the residency as 'Greedy Bastard' – for obvious reasons.
Despite his hefty 'fee', he demanded free holidays for himself in
Czechoslovakia. Andrew and Gordievsky write, 'though only a backbencher, Owen became a member of the Commons Defence
Estimates Committee and provided "top secret material of the highest value" on the British Army of the Rhine and the British
contribution to NATO'. He was uncovered in 1970 following the
defection of Josef Frolik, who had also served in the London residency and had seen some of his material. Tried for espionage, Owen
was subsequently acquitted because, perhaps somewhat bizarrely,
the prosecution failed to prove that the material he had handed
over was classified.

Following his acquittal, Andrew and Gordievsky state that Owen
made a full confession to MI5 in return for a guarantee of immunity
from further prosecution. They do not, however, mention his links
with the East Germans. It is safe to assume that, since the StB had
no conceivable interest in paying Owen to promote the recognition
of the GDR, Owen was actually paid by the Stasi.

Ian Mikardo, MP for Tower Hamlets and a ferocious left-winger
who was for many years on the National Executive of the Labour
Party, had visited the Leipzig fairs in the early 1930s. Despite his
left-wing views, he ran his own upmarket consultancy company
('Ian Mikardo Ltd') with the equally left-wing Jo Richardson (at that
time his personal assistant but subsequently also an MP) as a fellow
director.[13] Mikardo's name has so far not shown up anywhere in the
Stasi files. Given his strong support for the GDR over many years,
this may mean that the HVA successfully destroyed all traces of its
dealings with him, or, perhaps more probably, that his contacts with

East European intelligence were all handled by the intelligence service of a state other than East Germany.

Several of the others, however, were organised to support East German claims, and then developed a personal interest in East German trade afterwards.[14] They were undoubtedly part of a proto-type 'perks for questions' lobby, with the difference that they were paid not by a powerful individual or firm but by an East European police state. Some of them were paid cash to become East Germany's lobbyists, while others received the more dubious perk of free trips to the GDR. Even at the time, the behaviour of this lobby caused public disquiet. In the late 1950s, using Brigadier Clarke MP, the East Germans approached a British PR company, Notley's Advertising Ltd, asking for help in promoting their trade campaign with the UK. Their account was handled by one Lex Hornsby, who had been a public relations consultant with the Ministry of Labour.

Hornsby very quickly became the most important person working for East Germany in the UK. As Marianne Howarth has discovered, he played a decisive role in transforming the public perception of the GDR in the UK and became an indispensable asset to the GDR, working for it in a highly professional and dedicated manner. He set about identifying and bankrolling MPs whom he thought would be sympathetic to the idea of an increase in trade with East Germany. Within nine months, two board members of Notley's had resigned because of the growing importance of the firm's links with East Germany. One of them accused Hornsby's MPs of 'going to Germany to ingratiate themselves with the East German government in the hope of getting contracts and agencies'.[15] Neither Hornsby nor his MP friends were in the least put out by this. Indeed, the reverse was the case: Hornsby expanded his activities. In the 1960s, for example, he was paid £20,000 by the East Germans, a very considerable sum, and had 'a monopoly position' in the representation of the GDR in British public life.[16]

When Notley died in 1966, Hornsby set up his own company with Burnaby Drayson and Brigadier Clarke as paid consultants for the East German account. He moved into several different areas, all of which supported the GDR's wish for recognition from a variety of angles. He helped the East Germans to set up at least four different offices in London. In 1959 they opened one dealing with trade (which became the chamber of foreign trade), and in 1971, at the East Germans' behest, took very grand offices in Belgrave Square, close to the West German Embassy, which subsequently became the location of the East German Embassy. Another became the London office of the East German news agency ADN, run by Dr Franz Krahl, a former Communist exile in London. When Krahl's residence permit was not renewed in 1961, following Western outrage at the building of the Berlin Wall, several MPs, including Burnaby Drayson, spoke up in Parliament on his behalf.[17]

In 1960 Hornsby helped to set up Berolina Travel Ltd, a company specialising in travel to East Germany which had the monopoly on all official group travel to the GDR. Since most travel was in fact officially sponsored, the company did well (after 1989 it was privatised; the company trading today under the same name has no links with the pre-1990 firm). In 1964 Hornsby arranged for Will Owen MP to become chairman of Berolina, for which he received an annual sweetener of £500.

Hornsby also arranged visits for MPs and prominent British men and women to the GDR (using Berolina Travel). In 1961 Sir Leslie Plummer, the head of the Greater London Council, visited East Berlin together with Mikardo. In 1962 William Callow, the Lord Mayor of Coventry, also visited the GDR. Later he wrote, 'for sixteen hours a day we were busy finding out whether there is any truth in the charges that undemocratic methods are employed in the GDR. We established that these charges are completely false. We found no evidence of suppression or absence of democracy in Weimar, Dresden or East Berlin. The delegation had not been able to find any justification for the contention that elections take place under police supervision or that people are afraid to criticise the authorities.' This statement must have caused the East Germans considerable satisfaction: here was evidence of money very well spent.[18] Not every MP invited to the GDR was taken in by the experience, however. After one such visit, Bob Mellish MP, for example, referred to the GDR as being run like a 'puppet government not worth tuppence'.[19] George Brown MP, later a Labour Foreign Secretary, liked to insist that the German Democratic Republic may have been German but was absolutely not democratic.

In 1965 Hornsby arranged the founding of an 'All-Party British–GDR Parliamentary Group', whose chair was Will Owen and which had Renee Short as a deputy chair. It could muster forty MPs with Eric Lubbock (now Lord Avebury) for the Liberals – and Burnaby Drayson representing the Conservatives – and pressed for the recognition of the GDR.[20] Hornsby also handled the publication of *The GDR Review*, a well-produced example of Communist propaganda which mixed political, social and economic 'facts' and interviews with prominent and 'ordinary' East Germans and pictures of the GDR's sightlier aspects.[21]

Working with Harraps, the well-known publisher, Hornsby commissioned a book entitled *Profile of East Germany*, which purported to be a genuine and objective British study of the GDR by several commentators, including two British academics, David Childs and David Johnston. Another contributor, Denis Hayes, is also listed, with Drayson, as an HVA contact.[22] What was not made clear to its readers was that not only were the book's authors paid for their contributions by the East Germans (who were also able to provide the authors with information if required and ensure that the text suited their requirements) but the book itself was actually printed in East Germany. Read today with this knowledge, it is clear that it is a straightforward, if refined, piece of propaganda and whitewash.[23] In 1966, when the book was published, it underwrote the view that the GDR was a vibrant state with which the UK ought to do business.

A glance at *Hansard* shows that from 1954, no MP ever raised in the Chamber the question of human rights abuses in the GDR or mentioned that it was a police state (although in May 1957 the West German Social Democrat Franz Neumann had written to Hugh Gaitskell to ask his help in gaining the release of 1,500 political prisoners in East Germany and suggesting that he visit the two jails at Bautzen and Waldheim. Gaitskell did pursue this matter but outside Parliament).

Harold Wilson was one very prominent supporter of recognition, while making it plain that he regarded the Berlin Wall as an 'affront' to democratic Socialists in Britain. In December 1961 he made it clear he wished to see the GDR recognised quickly. Speaking in Parliament, he declared 'recognition exists for some [of us] as a fact' (albeit, he said, one to be granted only in return for an agreement on Berlin). In July 1962 he once more demanded 'some measure of recognition' for the East Germans. On 22 February 1962, as newly elected Leader of the Opposition, he said that if he were Prime Minister he would offer *de facto* recognition of the GDR in return for securing access to Berlin and an acceptance of Germany's eastern borders. Not surprisingly, Labour's 1964 election victory, which saw Wilson become Prime Minister, was seen in East Berlin as the real start of change in respect of British policy towards the GDR. Yet, rather to the amazement of the East Germans, once in power Wilson did nothing about the matter, although he did not drop his personal enthusiasm for it. Recently released government papers show that Wilson wanted to press forward with recognition and was irked by what he regarded as the obstructiveness of the Americans and the West Germans.

It is revealing to look at the efforts of the 'East German lobby' in Parliament during this period as reflected in *Hansard*. One important example is provided by the major debate on trade with East Germany in 1958 initiated by Ian Mikardo. With his customary rhetorical skill, Mikardo claimed that, although the reasons why recognition mattered (or so he claimed) were economic rather than political, the decision not to recognise East Germany was a purely political one, and the outcome of pressure from the United States and the Federal Republic. Mikardo did his level best to undermine the West German case: 'We don't recognise East Germany but neither do the West Germans. Yet they do trade whilst putting their allies under the utmost pressure not to recognise the GDR.' It was intriguing that a Labour MP was putting economic arguments ahead of moral and political ones, and accusing the British government of base motives when it put moral and political arguments ahead of alleged economic ones.

'Big Mick' then gave chapter and verse of what he claimed was political pressure being put on British exporters. From June to July 1957 a trade delegation from the GDR Chamber of Foreign Trade visited London and the Federation of British Industry and invitations were issued for further talks. In October, however, Mikardo explained that the Federation had suddenly cancelled the invitation;

this had to be the result of government intervention. Inter-German trade was now worth £153 million, he stated, adding, 'I go to West Germany a good deal not just as a tourist but because I have some industrial and business connections there. I get a good look at what is going on there and the West Germans are laughing at us fit to burst.'[24]

Surprisingly – or so it seemed at the time – he was strongly supported by the Conservative backbencher Burnaby Drayson. He did not mention his own business connections with the GDR, nor his contacts with people who might be East German intelligence officers. A government minister responded by saying Mikardo's statistics were 'quite unrelated' to those he had and that Britain 'could not conclude a trade agreement with East Germany because we do not recognise the authorities as a government'.

The building of the Berlin Wall in August 1961 was a major, if temporary, obstacle to the trading relationship. In February 1962 Edward Heath, then Lord Privy Seal, made it plain that the East German regime was one which abused its people. He declared, 'at the present time contacts with East Germany can be used to give the impression, wrongly, that this country condones the continuing illegal and inhuman stoppage of free movement in Berlin by the East German regime as well as the continued Communist threat to the freedom and security of West Berlin'. He advised Britons to think twice before visiting East Germany for trade or any other reasons.[25]

In December 1965 another Labour MP, Renee Short – who visited East Germany with a party of MPs every year – decided the time was ripe to take up the cudgels again. Largely thanks to her, in November 1967 thirty-one Labour MPs put down a motion asking that the GDR be recognised. She liked to emphasise neo-Nazi activity in the Federal Republic (which today we know was sustained by the Stasi) as a way of pressuring the government into recognition.[26] Her questions plainly had an impact. By 1968 *Hansard* stopped referring to the GDR as 'East Germany' or 'Germany: Eastern Germany' and began to call it 'the German Democratic Republic'. By 1970 Sir Alec Douglas-Home, the Foreign Secretary, could be heard in the House talking about 'normalisation' between the UK and East Germany, and in the summer of the same year Lex Hornsby managed to persuade Beattie (Lady) Plummer of Topplesfield, a friend of Harold Wilson, the composer Malcolm Arnold, the industrialist Sir Rudy Sternberg (later Lord Plurenden) and the well-known journalist James Cameron to form a committee for the recognition of the GDR.[27] Becker relates that in May 1971 a meeting took place in a London hotel attended by several prominent British citizens who were supporters of the GDR's wish to gain recognition. They included Richard Crossman, D. N. Pritt, Paul Oestreicher and John Peet, a Communist journalist.[28] Peet, a former West Berlin Reuters chief who had defected to East Berlin in 1950, was an East German fellow traveller par excellence, and wrote a fortnightly 'newsletter' called the *Democratic German Report*. Read with more attention than it deserved by certain leading lights on the left of British politics, journalists and academics (for whom Peet was a source of 'statistics' about the GDR),[29] it had modest success before being wound up in 1975. Clive Jenkins, increasingly seen as a leading trade unionist, was another keen pro-GDR lobbyist. He, too, was an HVA contact and his name shows up on its index.[30]

On the cultural front, the East Germans decided in 1965 to set up a 'Potsdam Discussion Group', intended as a counterweight to the influential Königswinter conferences with West Germans. Concurrently, an early British–East German 'Friendship Society', called Bridge, was established, with Gordon Schaffer, a British Communist, as its first secretary. Labour Party members were forbidden to join it as it was a proscribed Communist front organisation. After recognition, it was relaunched in 1974 as the Britain–GDR Friendship Society and opened to the Labour Party. Indeed, in 1975 Ron Hayward, the general secretary of the Labour Party, visited East Berlin to formalise the official link between Labour and the SED, which recognition had also made possible. He was subjected to close scrutiny by the Stasi during this visit.[31] By 1972 Bridge had some 2,000 people on its mailing list and from 1 January 1976 its new secretary, Sheila Taylor, was paid a good salary, equivalent to a teacher's annual income.[32] Sheila Taylor was also of particular interest to the East Germans, as is explored below.

In September 1967 a further Potsdam Discussion was held on the theme of European Security and the GDR, but the repression which followed the Prague Spring of 1968 temporarily ended any chance of bringing leading British figures to the GDR and the Potsdam Discussions were abandoned. One notable success was scored in October 1969 when the GDR managed to propagandise a visit to East Germany by the well-known author Nancy Mitford, although her actual verdict was a touch ambiguous. She wrote afterwards: 'the journey was simply amazing . . . they were all so nice . . . East Germany fascinated me. As for present living conditions, by our standards they are poor but of course that makes touring more agreeable. No motors on the roads. East Berlin is very shabby and badly lit but there are no advertisements, all the pretty old buildings are there more or less restored . . . Except for the tyranny and terror of which one got an occasional glimpse, I would much rather live in the Eastern part . . .'[33]

What the East Germans were after was not just pressure for recognition. University lecturers, school teachers and artists of various kinds were all seen by the East Germans as possible conduits who might convey the GDR's political message to the political class. The fact that (quite falsely) the GDR could present itself as the 'better' German state, and therefore the home of a 'good' German culture ('better' than that of the 'Fascist' Federal Republic), as well as projecting an image of itself as a contemporary culturally refined state, was seen as something likely to attract those interested in culture in Britain (and other Western states). Significant numbers of British academics undoubtedly had some sympathy for this view of the GDR (although they were often ignorant of the real political purpose behind this image).

## The Road to Recognition

It is plain that, with the passage of time, the East German efforts were beginning to have an effect on Western governments. Rather more importantly, however, the realisation that the Cold War could all too easily become a hot one and the growing American interest in détente implied a reconsideration of Western policy towards the

GDR.[34] Recognition could be seen as a necessary consequence of a policy of détente based on the complete acceptance of the status quo in Europe.

On 26 February 1966 Ulbricht made the first of several formal requests for the GDR to join the United Nations, rejected a month later by the West but strongly supported, not surprisingly, by the Soviet Union and its satellites. The East Germans did not, however, give up: it was during these years that they developed 'friendship associations' and 'recognition committees' in various states.

During the early 1960s, the Hallstein Doctrine came to be regarded by West Germany's opposition SPD and its chief ally, the USA, as increasingly problematic. For one thing, the building of the Berlin Wall in 1961 indicated that non-recognition was not stifling the GDR. If anything, it was becoming more self-confident. For another, the new US President, John F. Kennedy, was genuinely afraid that any future quarrel between the two German states could quickly escalate into a nuclear holocaust (a view shared by Harold Macmillan, the British Prime Minister).[35] Adenauer himself stood fast, but such was the importance to the West German political establishment of staying in step with the United States that by 1963 he found himself forced to leave office, to be replaced by someone keener to fall into line with the Americans. This in turn strengthened the hand of the SPD (who joined the West German government in 1966) and of Willy Brandt, the Social Democratic leader and Governing Mayor of West Berlin (who was particularly close to the Americans). He saw that for many reasons West Germany would have to change its policy towards the GDR and the whole of Eastern Europe and the Soviet Union – a wholly new Eastern policy, or Ostpolitik, was needed in order to promote détente. When Brandt became West German foreign minister, before becoming Chancellor in 1969, a radical rethink of intra-German relations was undertaken.

Ostpolitik could now gain momentum. By successfully convincing West German voters of the hard truth that Germany had been divided into two separate states, relations with the Soviet Union could be improved. That, in turn, led the East Germans to propose that they be recognised in full as a sovereign German state, and that the interzonal boundary between the two Germanies would be the GDR's state frontier to the west. In addition, it insisted on the abandonment of the West German claim to sole representation for Germany at international level, the complete detachment of West Berlin from West Germany, and seats for both German states in the UN. Negotiations were to be pursued through the Soviet Union.

In February 1970 the GDR indicated its interest in discussing Brandt's ideas. However, the East German Politburo knew from its many agents in Bonn how badly Brandt wanted a deal, and it took every opportunity of raising the stakes in the certainty that a package including recognition would be agreed. The Soviets appeared to signal their own wish to move forward when, in May 1971, the old Stalinist Ulbricht was replaced by the younger Erich Honecker. On 3 September, agreement was clinched. The final obstacle was the West German Parliament. Faced with the possibility of failing to gain ratification, when the vote was taken it emerged that two opposition members had voted for Brandt. They had been bribed by the Stasi.[36]

The treaties were passed by the Bundestag on 17 May 1972. On 3 June a four-power agreement on Berlin was signed. The Basic Treaty governing relations between West Germany and the GDR was signed in East Berlin on 21 December 1972. It stated that neither German state could act in the name of the other, and that each accepted the other's independence. Both states were to seek membership of the United Nations, which was accorded in September 1973. Permanent representative missions (but not embassies) were to be set up in Bonn and East Berlin.

The Communists had clearly got what they wanted. For the first fifteen or so years following the Basic Treaty with the GDR, there seems no doubt that the West Germans assisted substantially the bolstering of the Communists, both by political means and by credits. To the ordinary East German, however, the fact that the West Germans had ceased to be adversaries radically altered the way in which they perceived their Western cousins, generating grass-roots changes among the East German population which, in the end, helped to overthrow the regime. This was not something the West Germans had either wanted or foreseen.

The Conservative government which had come to power in 1970 in the UK made it plain that it supported Brandt's policies of détente, including his attempt to come to what Sir Alec Douglas-Home, the Foreign Secretary, referred to as a 'modus vivendi with the GDR'. The agreements signed in 1972 between East and West Germany on transit arrangements and, above all, the Basic Treaty of December 1972, triggered the first formal meetings between British and East German diplomats. In November Foreign Office officials had held a meeting with the deputy GDR foreign minister although he was received simply as a private individual. By the end of December, however, Douglas-Home was ready to negotiate with Otto Winzer, his East German opposite number. Negotiations started on 23 January 1973 and were concluded on 8 February when diplomatic relations started up. The British Embassy in Unter den Linden was opened in April and, in return, the Foreign Office arranged for the East Germans to be given the very site in London they had already identified as their heart's desire – 34 Belgrave Square, so close to the location of their mortal enemy, the Federal Republic, at number 22.

The UK had recognised the existence of two German states. The GDR had got what it wanted. Non-recognition had been justified by the GDR's lack of democracy and its policies of repression. To reverse the policy could be taken to imply that these major flaws had been addressed or that Britain no longer cared about the human rights abuses that had consistently been the hallmark of East Germany. In the event, the 1975 Helsinki Final Act, with its stress on human rights, restated in a more general (but by no means worthless) statement on the normative moral values which recognition had appeared to downgrade.[37] It is true, however, that the West Germans were far more interested in working together with the East German regime and making it easier for German families, divided by the Wall, to have contact with each other than in stressing the inherent human rights conflicts between the free and the Communist systems. Given the West German mood, and the British need to follow suit, it is a depressing fact that, until Margaret Thatcher became Prime Minister in 1979, British politicians on both the left and right found it easier to turn a blind eye to what the East German regime was doing to its people. Thatcher's passionate line on human rights in Eastern Europe was always regarded with suspicion by the West Germans in their own dealings with the East German regime. However understandable, this was not to their credit.

# PART II

# THE FRUITS OF STASI ESPIONAGE

# 4

# Spying in the West

The East Germans now had their embassy and, by 1974, they were ready to exploit it. What use did they – or, more accurately, the Stasi – actually make of it? One answer can be gleaned from the internal structural alterations undertaken to make the building secure. When the Embassy of the Federal Republic took it over after unification in 1990, officials noticed that the internal dimensions of various rooms were far smaller than their external dimensions suggested. Extensive and sophisticated cladding had been installed to make the rooms impervious to penetration by any external listening devices.[1] The Stasi meant business.

Recently, when told I was working on a book on the Stasi's operations in the UK, one of the most senior figures in British intelligence quipped, 'So it will be a short book, then.'[2] I replied that the fact that he, and some of his colleagues, should think so was a measure of the Stasi's success. Its record in London, as revealed by the Stasi files, was patently far more substantial than he seemed to realise even today. Yet his comment highlights a more general problem facing all analysts of intelligence. How can we identify and measure 'success' (or 'failure') in secret intelligence collection and analysis? Intelligence chiefs often say – with ample justification – that some of their best successes have consisted of ensuring that things do *not* happen.[3]

What they mean is that the intelligence failures of the other side may often be the result of unseen successes on the part of our intelligence services. This is reasonable enough – but it must then follow that the unseen successes of the other side may frequently be the result of blatant failures by British intelligence. Things are more complicated where the absence of obvious covert (or overt) trouble from an unfriendly power is taken to mean 'British intelligence must have done its job'. A lack of evidence of spying may indicate that there was none – but it can also indicate it was executed with such great skill that British security was ignorant about it.

The fact that East Germany has disappeared may make our intelligence failings in respect of the Stasi seem less unsettling than they deserve to be. There are clearly those within the British government who take such a line. As Home Secretary Jack Straw plainly thought this was the case, supported by various intelligence chiefs in MI5, including two director-generals, Stella Rimington and Stephen Lander, as well as others in other parts of the community who cannot be named. The existence of the Stasi files proves that the truth is very different. They show that there was a high level of hostile intelligence-gathering in Britain. That being so, the Stasi's unseen successes must be rated a failure on our part. MI5 certainly did know about some of the Stasi's activities. However, as we will see in the next few chapters, although the Stasi did not get away with everything, the vast majority of East German officers and sources operating in Britain were not known about, and did get away with much of what they set out to achieve. The Stasi files show, beyond any serious doubt, as MI5 now accepts, that most of the Stasi's assets and operations in Britain during the 1980s were well concealed from MI5 (and MI6). The extent of the Stasi's success in Britain is a chilling indictment of the complacency of some senior members within British intelligence.

From the viewpoint of British intelligence, the only enemy worth any serious attention seems to have been the KGB. Frequently, the other Communist intelligence services were, if not dismissed, at least relegated to the wings as small players. Peter Wright, who left MI5 in January 1976, two years after East German recognition, famously claimed to have 'bugged and burgled' his way through Communist embassies in London, but the fruits of his and his successors' labours were plainly meagre. In almost forty years of East German spying in Britain, British intelligence caught only three Stasi members, all of them in the 1980s. One officer, Heinz Knobbe – apparently the deputy ambassador – was expelled (having been named by an East German defector in 1983) and two illegals, both HVA spies, were caught in August 1985 (thanks to evidence supplied by West German intelligence, but not by Peter Wright).[4] Their trial was the first successful espionage prosecution in twenty-five years but at least one major British newspaper, the *Guardian*, was told they had been spying for the Russians, which in fact they had not (the Stasi files describe them clearly as 'the HVA couple').[5] Neither the Stasi nor any East German officer or spy features in the index to Wright's book, not the only aspect of his book shared with Stella Rimington's vain history of MI5 in the 1980s.[6]

The 1980s were, of course, critical years when the entire security of the West was at stake – and therefore precisely the sort of time when high-grade counter-intelligence work was the *sine qua non* of successful policy-making. It was an era of seismic shifts in the relationship between the two nuclear superpowers, the USA and the USSR. In the late 1970s it became clear that, under Brezhnev, the Soviets were developing a new range of missiles which seemed to call their commitment to détente into serious question.[7] In 1979, under pressure from James Callaghan and Helmut Schmidt, NATO began a programme of extensive rearmament. Then, with the onset of Reagan's presidency in 1980, pressure on the Soviet Union increased, culminating in Gorbachev's decision to give up his European empire in 1989–90. The changing dynamics of superpower relations formed the context of the secret struggle between the Communist bloc and the West.

These years saw a decisive struggle for mastery not only between the West and the Soviets, but also between those who held power in the Soviet bloc states (the various Communist leaders) and the dissidents in those states who wanted to wrest it from them. Because the issues that lay at the heart of superpower relations were always to do with human rights, peace and war, they were issues that mattered more to the people of the Soviet bloc than to anyone else. As long as these issues were on the international agenda, they could

not do other than cause internal ferment – and probable trouble –
for all Communist regimes. As a result, every Communist intelligence and security service – including the Stasi – was obliged to
develop strategies to protect Communism and to seek to overcome
the tide of dissidence beginning to sweep Europe. Unless successfully managed, it could risk the very future of Communism in the
continent. Of course, the Stasi, like its fellow secret services, was in
no doubt that, with good intelligence, it would be possible for policy
makers in East Germany to protect themselves and their country. In
the 1980s, therefore, the Stasi redoubled its efforts to discover what
Western leaders thought, by finding out what their plans were, and
by developing timely counter-measures to be able to continue to
hold down their subjects behind the Iron Curtain. This, then, was
the Stasi's task – and the reason why Western counter-intelligence
needed to be highly alert at all times.

What the Stasi was ordered to uncover in the UK, in the focused
and targeted way set out for it, was secret intelligence which might
shed light on the British attitude towards the dissidents of Eastern
Europe, which perplexed the East German leadership no less
gravely than it did their Soviet comrades. In addition, of course, they
were also concerned to uncover the UK's defence secrets in the
aftermath of the 1979 twin-track NATO rearmament programme,
and other UK secret policy intentions. The Stasi wanted to know
the private views of Britain's leading personalities, to penetrate the
British peace movement (which also involved an element of steering
on the part of the Stasi), to investigate the condition of the British
Labour and Conservative parties and, in the early 1980s, to examine carefully the emerging split in the ranks of the British Labour
Party which led to the formation of a breakaway party, the SDP.
The HVA, and the Stasi more generally, were charged with gaining
intelligence in these areas, although the UK's defence secrets were
also targeted by a military intelligence unit established in 34
Belgrave Square in 1974. (A military spy code-named 'Hampel'
had been in London since 1970 – four years before the embassy was
opened – thanks to Lex Hornsby.)

All these subjects (with the exception of the emphasis on the SDP)
correspond clearly with the things that concerned Western intelligence

during the latter Cold War period, very much as Doug McEachin, a former, very senior, CIA officer, has described them from the CIA's point of view.[8] There was no doubting their importance. What the East Germans were after was material of specific importance to the GDR, but also of wider concern to the entire Eastern bloc, including the Soviet Union. This was because since 1971, when more than a hundred Soviet 'diplomats' had been expelled by the then Foreign Secretary, Sir Alec Douglas-Home, the Russians believed their East German comrades might stand a better chance of spying in the UK than they themselves did. If British counter-intelligence continued to concentrate on the KGB rather than the Stasi, this may be one explanation for the latter's achievements. Equally, certain prominent British people might have found it easier to talk to East Germans than to Russians – and sometimes they might even have thought those East Germans were West Germans (and therefore our NATO allies, which the Soviets never were).

This intelligence about the realities – usually the *secret* realities – of British policy was, as far as we can tell today, to be gained chiefly by 'humint' – by the use of agents to collect secret information, preferably as documents but also, and more frequently, as reports to the Stasi. 'Humint' was not highly rated by British intelligence chiefs. Since the beginning of the Second World War they had tended to concentrate on signals intelligence ('sigint'). There were many reasons for this. The Enigma codebreakers of the Second World War working for MI6 could offer government a steady and extremely reliable source of intelligence without resorting to foreign agents or even leaving the country; 'humint', on the other hand, had suffered a catastrophic blow even before the war had broken out when two MI6 officers were captured by the Nazi Abwehr and disclosed full details of all MI6 operations and personnel in Europe.[9] After the war, there was an ever increasing tendency for British intelligence to regard 'humint' as unreliable gossip (although some Western intelligence agencies, notably the Italian, continue to focus their activities on 'humint' rather than 'sigint').[10] Some British intelligence experts dismiss 'humint' because its targets – which they call 'the dark side of the moon' – are frequently too well concealed to be accessible to hostile agents (sometimes referred to as 'darksiders' for this reason). Certainly, however, as the Stasi files repeatedly demonstrate, 'humint' can provide useful additional detail to an emerging intelligence picture.

'Sigint' cannot, of course, pick up the private views of the political class, and Western intelligence takes great care to keep its activities secure from wireless interception. It is, however, very reliably reported that both Margaret Thatcher and now Tony Blair became strong believers in the importance of 'humint'.[11] In addition, it is true that many domestic British political observers, as well as members of the political class, set great store by what could equally well be dismissed as 'gossip'. Once a policy becomes public knowledge – say, for example, the 1979 NATO twin-track rearmament decision – it may seem that prior knowledge of it would have been of little use.

In fact, pre-emptive policy-making by NATO's opponents could not be developed without prior warning of such a policy. In the same way, predictive stories about the real views of political leaders, tales of high-level arguments or rumours of virulent hatred and quarrels hidden beneath a pacific veneer, whether in government or between governments, could and did reveal much of importance to Communist chiefs. There is no doubt at all that SED leaders, led by Honecker and Mielke, regarded such intelligence as both absorbing and of great value in developing policies and policy stances for the GDR. Indeed, intelligence digests (called *aktuelle Informationsberichte*) – of which a few copies remain – were obligatory reading for the leadership and testify to the sensitive nature of the material gathered by Stasi agents. Topics covered in some of the surviving digests include the future of Britain's nuclear deterrent, the Polaris missile, various economic summit meetings in London, disagreements on the Strategic Defence Initiative between Margaret Thatcher and Ronald Reagan, and even an inside British view of the talks between Helmut Schmidt, then Federal Chancellor, and James Callaghan, then British Prime Minister, on 14 February 1977, which said that, beneath the surface, relations between the two men and the two states were the opposite of cordial. The British were deeply dissatisfied that an agreement on the funding of the Rhine Army had been broken by the West Germans and also resented Schmidt's lectures on how to improve Britain's economy.[12]

Even if today we are suspicious of the value of such insights, it should not be a matter of indifference to us and our security service that the GDR believed, during the 1980s in particular, that such information was of value and that it was prepared to go to considerable lengths – and vast expense – to gain access to it.

Christopher Andrew and Oleg Gordievsky are well justified in describing this era as 'the most dangerous period of East–West tension since the Cuban missile crisis twenty years before. During the American presidential election campaign in 1980, Moscow had expected the anti-Soviet rhetoric of . . . Reagan to mellow . . . Not till Reagan entered the White House did the Kremlin fully grasp that his hostility towards the Soviet Union derived not from campaign tactics but from deep conviction.'[13] They show how the Soviets were firmly told that the new administration was not prepared to allow détente to be used as a smokescreen either for Soviet expansionism or for dangerous military growth. The US defence budget was accordingly increased by 10 per cent.

Andrew and Gordievsky also confirm that the Soviet leader, Leonid Brezhnev, was seriously rattled by this new hardline approach, even going so far as to try to convince the members of his Politburo that the US was 'actively preparing for nuclear war. There was now the possibility of a nuclear first strike by the United States. The Politburo had accordingly decided that the overriding priority of Soviet foreign intelligence operations must henceforth be to collect military-strategic intelligence on the nuclear threat from the US and NATO.'[14] Both the head of the KGB, Yuri Andropov (who was to succeed Brezhnev in November 1982), and his deputy, Kryuchov, shared the view that Armageddon lay just around the corner. Gordievsky himself was just about to come to London as an intelligence officer and in June 1982 was instructed in Moscow to ensure that he focused his intelligence gathering on NATO's plans for a missile attack by securing 'well-placed agents' there.

The detailed areas described by Gordievsky as being of concern to the Soviets, and therefore targets of one form or another for Soviet intelligence, mirror those identified and pursued by the Stasi as reflected in the Stasi files. Markus Wolf confirms that 'in the battle between supporters and opponents of the nuclear deterrent the public's view of Moscow's and Washington's intentions was all-important. We placed great emphasis on counteracting American propaganda about the Soviet threat.'[15] These intentions included the deployment of Cruise and Pershing missiles, scheduled for late 1983, hoping (against hope) that Labour might win the 1983 and 1987 General Elections to replace Margaret Thatcher and trying to assist this in any way they could. They knew that she was increasingly offering support to dissidents such as the Sacharovs, Aleksander Ginzburg and Lech Walesa, and was intent too on deploying new missiles. East Germans issued declarations of their own commitment to peace (which they believed would help Labour and Michael Foot, its leader, running on a unilateralist ticket into No. 10 Downing Street) and they tried to steer into the wilderness anyone in the British peace movement whom they believed might undermine the credibility of Communist 'peace councils' by suggesting that true disarmament could only be multilateral and that the Warsaw Pact should disarm along with the West.

Wolf wrote that his particular role in these matters 'was to concentrate on the effect of the disarmament campaign on the foreign policies of the NATO countries, and work out how the East could benefit from divisions within the Western Alliance'.[16] He added that it was vital to ensure that the Stasi were not seen to be manipulating leading figures in the CND, although the emphasis should probably be on 'seen' rather than 'not'. They watched with keen anxiety the emergence of the SDP to the right of the Labour Party (and, like the KGB, suspected the CIA lay behind it).[17] They looked for signs of a pre-emptive strike against the East, and for any indication that their own dissidents were gaining help and support from any Western agency.[18]

These affairs defined the Stasi's broad agenda in the 1980s; they were what the Politburo wished secret intelligence to illuminate and they became the Stasi's London tasks. In some ways, the needs of the East German leadership were not so different from those of the British government as set out by Sir Percy Cradock in his book *In Pursuit of British Interests*, in which he writes of the 'great prize' which all intelligence services seek: to 'read intentions' and to answer the question 'Will there be a disaster next week?' He adds, 'the art of predictive assessment lay in interpreting fragmentary usually ambiguous intelligence and constructing, on that basis, a picture of the other side's position'.[19]

The East Germans would have agreed with every word, although they were far more ruthlessly aware of the supreme political purpose behind their intelligence needs – to secure the position of Communism in Germany and beyond. In the best traditions of German bureaucracy, order after order makes this point in writing – and the Stasi files groan under their weight.

The Stasi chiefs wanted 'intelligence useable by recipient': intelligence capable of being understood by the ruling elite who might have the political skills necessary to exercise power in a Communist dictatorship, but might be easily misled by overelaborate interpretations or analyses. In addition, the processing by their highly trained analysts was designed to ensure that secret intelligence was exactly that. Inaccurate secrets, or apparent secrets which were not secret at all, were a major hazard to be excluded. Equally, the sources of genuine secrets had to be protected at all costs. Where such individuals might make themselves vulnerable if their information ever entered the public domain, a special note to this effect ('source protection vital') was made on the intelligence product itself. Like most governments, the East German one was inclined to believe that what came from a secret source was better, or more valuable, than what came from an open one.

## The Organisation of East German Secret Intelligence in London

The Stasi files show how espionage was conducted in a Western state other than the Federal Republic of Germany. Basically, the nefarious brilliance of the East German secret service relied most obviously on its remarkable and highly intricate structure which resembled a series of pyramids, each of which fitted perfectly into

another larger or, indeed, smaller one. To try to describe the way
they worked is less easy but the system that Mielke and Wolf developed was essentially fluid. In the case of the Stasi, the discrete
categories common to all intelligence services (officers, agents,
sources, targets and victims) merged almost effortlessly into each
other. Officers became agents, victims turned into sources – various
actors could be rotated around different axes, assuming different
roles, according to whatever arrangements were decided upon at the
time. Tactics which in other intelligence services would (as far as we
know) seem contradictory and counter-productive held, in the Stasi's
case, the key to much of its success. It was at once both extremely
centralised and strongly decentralised. Wolf himself, at the top of
the HVA pyramid, continued throughout his career to run about a
dozen agents.[20] There was the *Zentrale* (or *Zentrum*, the term often
used by military intelligence officers) in Normannenstrasse in
Berlin, which controlled everything from above. Some 15,000
people worked there. At the same time, groups of intelligence officers operated as small cells, recruiting agents as and when needed
for individual projects (always specified by the 'Centre'). Every
operation was treated as discrete. If those selected to take part in
it were not full-time officers in the 'Centre', they would always be
formally recruited into it and given a specific codename. That is one
reason why there is such a plethora of codenames. There were
undoubtedly large numbers of Stasi spies, but they did not all spy at
the same time. Frequently, spies would work on a specific subject
for a short period.

Some of the Stasi's British spies were formally signed up, while
others were encouraged not to regard themselves as spies at all.
Furthermore, all who spied for the Stasi, including those we would
call their agents, were themselves spied on by the Stasi. The category of 'victim' merged organically into the category of 'perpetrator'
on many occasions, both in the UK and beyond. In Britain, individuals were spied on by the Stasi while, at the same time, helping the
Stasi to do its work. While internally the East Germans referred to
the work involved in identifying, recruiting and then running such
people as 'agent work' (*agenturische Arbeit*), externally the word
'agent' was avoided.

The British Security Service usefully explains that

agents working within a target organisation, or reporting on individuals under investigation, represent [a] most significant source of secret intelligence. Agent operations are highly specialised and are often conducted over the long term. The work involves the identification, recruitment and subsequent careful direction of an individual within, for example, a terrorist group or a hostile intelligence service. Some agents, who can include members of the public as well as members of target organisations, regularly run considerable risks in their work. Substantial resources are devoted to providing support for the agent and the Security Service case officer, particularly to maintain the security of the operation. Close attention is paid to the welfare of the agents both during and after their agent career.[21]

With one or two obvious alterations, these words might just as easily have come from the pen of Markus Wolf although the terminology, of course, was different. Wolf writes, 'We never called ourselves spies but *Kundschafters*' ('seekers after knowledge').[22]

In Britain, the gathering of intelligence, where conducted from the East German Embassy, was chiefly undertaken by actual sources, sometimes called just that (*Quellen*), sometimes IMs, sometimes referred to as 'persons of trust' or shown in the Stasi files to be so, recruited and run by the East German officers in London, who – confusingly – were themselves called sources.[23] The real sources in Britain were largely British citizens, or British residents.[24] 'Illegals', British spies run directly from East Germany, were always co-opted workers, or IMs. At times, voices are heard suggesting that much of the Stasi's intelligence was derived from newspapers or open sources rather than from spies. In fact this assertion is totally contradicted by the evidence of the Stasi files. Where newspaper reports are used, they are in the form of clippings (of which there are a number in the files although they constitute perhaps less than 1 per cent of the material). Apart from the existence of 'illegals' there are other reasons for discounting the idea that this was not an active secret service on the prowl.[25] Most of the subject matter was material which never found its way into the media, personalities identified who never appeared in the newspapers and of whom even well-informed journalists will never have heard. In any case, the GDR had perfectly good reporters of its own in London – in the form both of journalists and those diplomats in the embassy who were not spies. In fact, we know that the MfS was convinced of the need to obtain secret intelligence that would go well beyond that which other sources would provide – indeed, the Stasi files prove that the 'Centre' always took its work very seriously indeed. No officer in the field could get away with palming off a *Times* editorial, for example, as a piece of secret intelligence. It is true that from time to time Stasi officers have claimed otherwise but the documentary evidence of the files shows that this is false and said simply to protect their sources in accordance with time-honoured traditions of spycraft. Where too few secret sources were being used, it spelled serious problems, including dismissal, for the officer involved.[26] This is also why the veracity of the 'Centre's' analyses was of such a high standard and has so far never been called into question by any expert.

There is a final reason for accepting that the secret material was precisely what it purported to be. As we shall see later, considerable sums of money changed hands. The Stasi was always very orderly about payments to its agents – they had to be registered, and the name of the officer handling the money was set down, usually in the form of his cover-name. The Stasi was well heeled, but this does not mean that it would have dreamed of paying for intelligence secrets that it could get itself without resorting to third parties, or that it would pay serious money for rubbish or pay intelligence officers to do what journalists or diplomats could do for less money (intelligence salaries were high in East Germany). As far as its sources and agents were concerned, the Stasi always liked to offer money as an inducement. But these payments were minuscule and were not to be confused with big sums offered for specific items. Viewed another way, Stasi cash can be seen to be significant for another reason too: it is sometimes said that individuals helping the Stasi did so without being aware that the people they were speaking to were intelligence officers or agents. Where money changed hands, however, it was plain to the recipient that what was going on was espionage.

*

At the top side of this structure in London, as in every other place where the Stasi operated, including East Germany, there existed a secondary level of officers for special duties (*Offiziere in beson-derem Einsatz*, or *OibEs*) as well as ordinary officers (*Offiziere der Residentur*). They are examined in detail later. At the bottom end of the structure we find talent spotters and go-betweens or middlemen (*Tipper* and *Ermittler*).[27] It is clear that in the UK these go-betweens played a critical part in transferring secret material from a source to an officer.

We still do not know who all the HVA people were, but, by piec-ing together various leads contained in the Stasi files we can identify *some* of them, including a number of the most dangerous officers and officers for special duties who were based in London. In the same way, we can now also know the identity of every single secret military intelligence officer in Britain. It goes without saying that secret intelligence work requires the greatest secrecy to be attached to the true identities of both 'officers' and 'agents' (in the English sense) – the 'sources' or 'persons of trust' (and the talent spotters and go-betweens) who worked together to collect the intelligence which was sought by East Berlin. Where the officers worked as diplomats, exposure would mean immediate expulsion; where they were not working from within the embassy, exposure would mean a long prison sentence. Expulsion would also mean an effective end to all further secret intelligence work anywhere in the West. These were things to be avoided.[28] Any identification by MI5 or others of the agents (in the English sense) would not only stop what they were doing but would undermine the confidence of fellow agents and deter them from assisting East German spy efforts (one reason why counter-intelligence successes should be publicised). The Stasi files show that agents were unnerved whenever spies were caught in the West, and required careful reassurance that this Western 'hysteria' would always quickly evaporate.[29] The reason for such deep levels of security is plain – to preserve secrecy and confidentiality to a truly fantastic degree. And security was, on the whole, effective. Had the Stasi files been destroyed by their original owners, as intended, the sanguine attitude taken by British intelligence towards the Stasi would have seemed justified since virtually none of the Stasi's UK intelligence gains left any discernible trace.

As far as the processes of East German intelligence gathering are concerned we can identify three distinct activities: intelligence gathering, collection, and evaluation. Evaluation was undertaken by the 'Centre' in East Berlin and consisted of two different processes: verification and distribution among core policy makers. These activities, directed by Werner Irmler, were adhered to with strict Prussian discipline although in outline the system was not dissimilar to the Joint Intelligence Committee in the UK.[30] Known as ZAIG (*Zentrale Auswertungs und Informationsgruppe* – the Central Evaluation and Information Group), it had a staff of over a thousand officials.[31]

These officials were charged with collection and analysis and central planning. They also fed information to those designated to receive it, including the various party bosses and government ministers. They were responsible for checking and evaluating the quality of material, for the central planning of all intelligence work, and for 'blue skies' thinking about its future.[32] ZAIG decided what the leadership should be told. This was done in a variety of ways. Items of particular interest were forwarded at once, but the weekly secret intelligence digests compiled by ZAIG. Ministers and high officials in the intelligence world were sent numbered reports which they had to read, initial and then return.

It is important to stress here that spying is in direct contravention of the 1961 Vienna Convention on diplomatic relations between all states who are members of the United Nations.[33]

Article 3.1 laid down precisely what diplomats were meant to do: 'protecting in the receiving State the interests of the sending State and of its nationals, within the limits permitted by international law; ascertaining by all lawful means conditions and developments in the receiving State, and reporting thereon to the Government of the sending State'. A number of articles set out in precise terms what was to be made available to the states signing this Convention. Article 22.1, for example, promised that the premises of the mission should be inviolable and immune from search. Finally, and by no means least importantly, Article 31.1 conveyed diplomatic immunity on any diplomat breaking the law of the receiving state ('a diplomatic agent shall enjoy immunity from the criminal jurisdiction of the receiving State').

Precisely because these freedoms were so far-ranging (they were, of course, mutual rights, enjoyed by the 'sending' as well as the 'receiving' state) there were penalties for failure to abide by the Convention. Two articles in particular (articles 41 and 9) made it entirely clear that states were neither to engage in espionage nor to interfere in the 'internal affairs' of the receiving state, and that any dealings between the embassy and the citizens of the 'receiving state' should be conducted through that state's foreign ministry. A failure to abide by these simple rules would result in the diplomat in question being declared 'non grata' and then expelled. As we shall see, there is no doubt at all that on every point East Germany broke the Vienna Convention deliberately and cynically.

What was the difference between embassy reporting and spying? In theory, the difference was obvious. According to the Vienna Convention, embassy staff were not permitted to undertake espionage. They were not allowed to recruit agents to collect secrets. The role of an embassy was to represent its country and its political leadership and, by overt means – examining the media, discussions with the diplomats and so on – to gain information which might help the formation of its own government's policy towards it.

In practice, it might be said that all embassies engaged in – and continue to engage in – secret operations. The US Embassy in London, for example, will have several officials working for the CIA and the FBI, the latter invariably legal attachés. However, the staff of embassies representing states which this country regards as its friend ought not to engage in espionage against us. The American intelligence community in London, for example, is expected to spy not on us but on mutual enemies and potential enemies who may operate from London. We, in turn, ought not to spy on our friends. There is considerable evidence to suggest that the UK does – and did – spy on its friends, including its partners in the European Union and upon the institutions and personnel of the European Union itself, although there is anecdotal evidence to indicate that we do not spy on the Americans, and have not done so in the past.

In the same way, there is evidence to suggest that some of our European friends spy on us.

Sir Michael Quinlan, a leading British former civil servant, puts it as follows:

> We have to acknowledge that effective espionage – at least and especially the 'humint' component of it – involves doing things which would normally be reprehensible – concealment, untruth, subterfuge, intrusion, illegality at least abroad, co-operating with or employing disreputable people, suborning individuals from their formal responsibilities. Secret intelligence cannot be conducted without all or anyway most of these actions, and I am not minded to condemn it accordingly . . . We were entitled to do certain of these things in order to penetrate and weaken murderous clandestine organisations in Northern Ireland. But in themselves such activities surely have to be assigned to the debit side of the ledger, just as does the fact that soldiers may have to kill . . . We cannot say – in the West, I know we do not say – that anything goes . . .[34]

Obviously, therefore, in those states with which we have a diplomatic arrangement, but which are likely to want to damage British interests, we will use our embassies to house a number of intelligence officers. We too are in contravention of the Vienna Convention. Equally, we too would expect the counter-intelligence authorities of those states to look out for our people and to employ their own intelligence staff in their embassy in London.

It is the task of our security service to uncover and expel, or prosecute, their officers and agents whenever they are found, just as it would fall to hostile or potentially hostile states to uncover, expel or prosecute our intelligence staff and agents in their country. Similarly, we might wish to conduct espionage independently of our embassy and must expect others to do the same here. Of course, 'illegal' espionage, which takes place without diplomatic cover, is a highly dangerous undertaking: those caught can expect very long sentences and, in times of armed conflict, even the death penalty.

If we do it, and did it, and the Stasi did it, we may wonder what the difference was between us? The answer is that liberal democracies are not the same as Communist dictatorships which regarded liberal states as their enemy. Western liberal democracies are states in which political power can pass peacefully from one group or party to another. This stems from a fundamental belief in the human and civil rights of all citizens to seek to influence the governance of a liberal democracy. Indeed, the need for open political debate to allow power to change hands makes democracies vulnerable. Fascist, Nazi or Communist regimes, on the other hand, rule by virtue of their control of the political institutions, including their police, intelligence and security services. Secret power is used to sustain their rule and, where necessary, to attack liberal democracies. The very existence of liberal states had always been seen by Communists and Fascists as a threat to their own illiberal regimes. With the possible exception of Gorbachev, all Communist leaders rightly and genuinely regarded the West as their enemy, even if only in a passive sense: their way of life and ours were contradicted by each other.

Communist systems never could, and never did, permit the free expression of human rights because to do so would eventually bring about the collapse of Communism itself. This is why every Communist intelligence and security service was charged with seeking to discover the secrets of Western policy, to undermine it wherever possible and to do everything it could to allow Communism to prosper at home. Right up to the end in 1989–90 Communist leaders continued to demand of their security and intelligence services that the fight against the West be maintained and even intensified. Nowhere is this point seen more clearly or more grimly than in the spying conducted by the Stasi.

Communist states are different in kind from Western ones, and their espionage is therefore different as well. The Stasi was far more similar to the Gestapo than either of them was to MI5. Our intelligence and security services are paid to defend our liberty. The Stasi, on the other hand, worked to preserve a frequently violent and always oppressive police state, to intimidate and, if necessary, liquidate all political opposition to the regime. It is therefore both inaccurate and unacceptable to equate the work conducted by Western intelligence services with the work done by Communist ones.

The Stasi files show, however, that there was one final, crucial, difference between any East German embassy and a Western one. Even if intelligence collection and agent tasking does go on in every embassy, whatever the state it represents, it is a fact that on 20 June 1980 Mielke ordered that in every East German embassy ultimate control of all political and technical operations conducted from within the embassy was thenceforth to lie with the HVA resident and *not* the ambassador.[35] It was not the person who appeared to be in charge, as far as the host country was concerned, namely the East German ambassador, who was in fact directing the embassy's most important tasks: it was the HVA resident.

As Christopher Andrew has pointed out in reference to the NKVD/KGB, it is true that what was of interest to a Communist intelligence service was not necessarily of interest to a Western one.[36] Such considerations apply equally to the Stasi. However (and it is a big 'however'), it does not follow that because an East German intelligence goal was of no immediate or apparent interest to Britain, British intelligence was entitled to assume that no harm would flow to us from failing to counter or contain the Stasi's pursuit of the goal in question. If the East Germans were concerned with a matter in Britain, it was because they believed it impacted on vital East German interests. British authorities could not assume that, because they might not be concerned with that matter, it must follow that an East German intelligence hit on it was of no importance.

Anything that contributed to maintaining the East Germans' position of power damaged Britain. It was therefore always in Britain's interests to prevent, if it could, the East Germans from making the gains they desired. Damage to Britain would always be associated with any profit made by the Stasi.

As we shall see, some of the core East German targets – Britain's NATO strategy, her defence policy and the UK's relationship with the USA and with the Federal Republic – were ones from which an alert British counter-intelligence service would immediately or automatically have wanted to exclude the East Germans. Others – such as the GDR's huge curiosity about the SDP or its concern with CND and END – might at first glance have seemed to need little or no intervention by MI5. The Stasi saw the SDP as a breakaway Social Democratic party and therefore something that might impact on the future of Socialism more widely. But today, with 'New Labour' and Tony Blair's second election landslide in 2001 behind us, can we believe that the Stasi's assessment of its impact was wrong? The Stasi was correct in thinking that the SDP might change the face of British politics and an evaluation of its policies in that light was of great use. It is interesting that the Stasi seems to have undertaken no targeted operations against the British Liberal Party before the end of 1988. Perhaps it did not believe in the much-vaunted 'Liberal breakthrough' in Britain.

Equally, CND had a double importance for the East Germans. On the one hand, its commitment to unilateral nuclear disarmament by Britain, its deep anti-Americanism and its willingness to deal with Communists greatly served the purposes of the Soviets. On the other, the proximity of the leadership of the Labour Party to CND would, if Labour had been returned to power in the 1980s, have dramatically improved the chances of Communism enduring in Eastern Europe and in Russia. This was because the arms race to which Ronald Reagan and Margaret Thatcher were so committed weakened the economies of the Eastern bloc and promoted internal unrest. To be shot of the Conservative government, and to gain a unilateralist Labour one would have reduced at a stroke the need for arms spending behind the Iron Curtain – and would have given the various Communist regimes more money to spend on the consumer culture it was believed would keep citizens loyal.

It might be asked why the British government and MI5 seemed to be relatively unaware of the extent to which the East German Embassy existed in order to facilitate Stasi espionage against the UK, especially since all states use their embassies for espionage. It is quite inconceivable that East Germany would have been allowed to carry on operating from 34 Belgrave Square, to the considerable extent that the Stasi files demonstrate it did in the fifteen years from 1974 to 1989, if MI5 had known then what we know today about Stasi activity in London. What MI5 – and Britain – got entirely wrong was the *extent* of that intelligence activity, in terms of both the numbers of sources that the Stasi could exploit and the numbers of areas to which it was able to gain access.

It is revealing that the aforementioned Sir Percy Cradock, a former chairman of the Joint Intelligence Committee from 1985 until 1992, when discussing the JIC's reaction to the recognition of East Germany does not mention the possibility that if the GDR were recognised it might use its embassy as a base for espionage against the UK.[37] We should recall that Stella Rimington has confirmed that the filling of Communist embassies in London with intelligence officers had gone on unchecked by MI5.[38] Interestingly, from 1976 to 1978 Sir Percy had himself been British ambassador in East Berlin.

It is bizarre that the person who evidently had the clearest idea of what the Stasi would do with its London embassy – indeed, the person who provided the most accurate picture of the awful reality of East German spying – was a writer of fiction, John le Carré. In *The Spy Who Came in from the Cold*, published in 1962 (thirteen years before the East Germans were allowed to come to London), le Carré set out a number of central motifs around their spying. These included not just the use of embassies as spy bases, but the way in which the Stasi worked, including their exploitation of British Communist Party members.

Examples are le Carré's description of Liz Gold's political world and the East Germans' close interest in the CPGB (and how the Stasi activated its friends there whenever it needed to – there is, as we see later, an exact replica of this story in the 1980s); the use made by the East Germans of those Communists who had spent the war in exile in the West; and the passage in the book where Fiedler, an HVA officer, says to Lemass: 'Your initial interrogation took place in the West, where [. . .] we used the Soviet Embassy at the Hague [. . .] *only an embassy could provide the kind of link we needed. The German Democratic Republic has no embassies in the West. Not yet . . .*' (my italics). What is interesting is not merely that Fiedler's prediction ('not yet') was perfectly correct (but made at a time when it seemed quite implausible), but that he should make such a strong connection between the desire for recognition on the one hand, and the secret service need for intelligence bases in GDR embassies on the other.

The Stasi files confirm, of course, how vital this link was to the East Germans – yet there seems to have been almost no awareness of this in the West and few, if any, worries about this aspect of recognition either in the UK or in West Germany.

Le Carré seems to have known such a great deal about the Stasi in the early 1960s, whereas most other people (in the West), even where they were professionally interested in East Germany, appear ignorant.[39]

It might therefore be thought that le Carré – who worked for a time in the British Embassy in Bonn, then the Federal capital – had inside information from British intelligence about what the East Germans might get up to in the event of their being recognised. This in turn would be intriguing because it would indicate that the British government did know much more about what the Stasi did than the record seems to indicate. (It would also raise rather interesting questions about why le Carré was allowed to publish, even as fiction, a work which drew on such accurate insights into the East German intelligence service.)

Le Carré himself provides the answer to this. When I asked him where his information on the Stasi had come from, and whether one could assume it was common knowledge on the part of the British authorities (on the basis that he was a government employee so that what he knew was, in effect, also known by the government) he replied:

> My answer does not match your curiosity. I can only tell you the truth: namely that I made the whole thing up, and if my guesswork turned out to be correct, that's basically a fluke. Of course, as a member of the British Embassy in Bonn at that time, and as an occasional traveller to Berlin, I was immersed in the German scene. But professionally I had no interest in East Germany and no insider's knowledge. If I had, my employing service would never have let me publish the book whereas, rather grudgingly, they passed it ahead of publication, confident that it bore little relation to reality. The awful Markus Wolf is on record as paying me the same compliment, but I must disown it.[40]

There was, then, a dangerous covert war being waged by the East German secret service against targets in the United Kingdom to help perpetuate its rule in East Germany and the rule of Communism more generally.[41] Its objective was to make an input into GDR foreign and domestic policy – defined by the SED leadership as an offensive policy, driven by the need to maintain a repressive regime at home.[42]

# 5

# 34 Belgrave Square

The East German Embassy at 34 Belgrave Square, which also incorporated the East German consulate, was the Stasi's major UK base, known in its secret role as Residentur (Residency) 201. In 1990 the building passed to the Federal Republic and today it houses the German Information Centre.

The British government, via the Foreign and Commonwealth Office, was responsible for locating the East Germans in an appropriate site. Doubtless in return for a prime location in East Berlin (on Unter den Linden), the East Germans were given the grace and favour of Belgrave Square. The East Germans had specifically asked to have their embassy in this building, which was just round the corner from the West German Embassy, and consequently made the obvious point that two German states were now represented in London. The resident West German ambassador at the time, Karl-Günther von Hase, recalled his considerable unhappiness at the proximity of the East Germans. In particular, he resented having to have the sign which read 'German Embassy' replaced with one which said 'Embassy of the Federal Republic of Germany'. It had been a basic tenet of the West German faith that the embassy represented all Germans, whether of West or East.[1]

Unfortunately, the East German officers in London were, like their comrades in East Germany, allowed to dissolve themselves, and destroyed all the records in the embassy before quitting it.

Today, however, thanks to the Stasi files, we know not only that 34 Belgrave Square housed several discrete groups of Stasi spies in the UK (HVA, HA and NVA intelligence operators were all present in London), but that – in order to preserve the total commitment to conspiracy – formally one group did not know who belonged to the other groups.

Rather less understandably, the Foreign and Commonwealth Office has destroyed virtually all of its files relating to the personnel in the GDR embassy because it lacks the space in which to store them.[2] It should be added that it was not the Foreign Office's job to keep files on the 'personalities' in the various East European and Soviet embassies (that is to say, records on which of them were believed to be 'spooks'). This means that the unit which kept an index of the personalities – not the Foreign Office – may still possess it.

We can, therefore, still not be entirely sure of the total number of spies who worked at 34 Belgrave Square although the London Staff Lists and the London Diplomatic Lists, which contained the names and posts of all diplomats accredited to the Court of St James, compiled annually, are extant – and not inaccurate. Since the Vienna Convention gives immunity to all diplomats, it is reasonable to assume that everyone working at the embassy was either an accredited diplomat or a staff member. We do, in addition, have some idea of the capacity of the premises: it had four floors and a basement and it is probable that at any one time in the region of thirty to forty people worked there.[3]

A reasonable description of the general direction of work at 34 Belgrave Square has been provided by Klaus Eichner, a former senior Stasi officer (working for Wolf in the 'Centre', not in London).[4] The importance of his statement is that it confirms what we know from the Stasi files, rather than providing any startling new insights (which, bearing in mind his status, is hardly surprising). In an interview, Eichner stated that Britain had possessed a 'certain priority both as a sovereign nation, and as a leading member of NATO', although the two chief Stasi targets were West Germany and the USA. He explained that the very first Stasi analysis of a NATO state's secret services was done on Britain – although he added quickly that the analysis of their goals, personnel and structure was done 'without a source, just relying on the cleverness of our own people'.

He explained that two departments took a particular interest in the UK: the NATO one and HVA III. Special focus, he said, was given to the British peace movement, parts of which (in particular END) were seen as likely to destabilise the Soviet bloc, and to certain individuals. Information about the UK also came via 'FERN', the West German secret intelligence code for the UK into which the Stasi had broken. Above all, he said, it had been vital to recruit agents in Britain: 'you could only win someone over if you knew their personality. Knowledge was not to be had from the streets. You needed sources to know what people were like.' The Stasi had to be opportunistic – 'we always exploited Comrade Chance', as Eichner put it – and the HVA in Britain, he said, understood only too well the possibilities of 'the British disease' – he meant homosexuality, as he laughingly explained – when it came to agent recruitment.

Markus Wolf, rather more grudgingly, recognises the existence of secret intelligence operations in the UK but indicates that intelligence had been 'gathered', at any one time, by a single 'resident' operating out of the embassy, by East German journalists recruited in the UK, or by a single spy, Dr Hagen Blau, who worked for the West German Foreign Office.[5]

But the idea that in the 1980s intelligence came from only one 'foreign intelligence resident' in London at any one time, as Wolf claims, is plainly absurd: as we shall see, the Stasi files prove that the GDR possessed at least twenty-one discrete sources of secret intelligence in the 1980s, not counting the half-dozen secret military intelligence officers also based in Residency 201, or the 'illegals', who were kept far from the embassy's confines. London was well stocked with Stasi spies.

## The Stasi's Work in the West

In order to uncover the extent of Stasi espionage in Britain, it is important to describe the various units, or Stasi departments, which operated in the West more generally.[6] First, there was the secret intelligence service, the HVA (*Hauptverwaltung Aufklärung*, or Main Directorate Intelligence), under first Markus Wolf and then Werner Grossmann, with 3,819 officers – the biggest single unit in the whole ministry. Various directives ordering the HVA to penetrate particular areas of civil society in the West have survived in the Stasi files.[7] Following East German recognition in 1973, a new Department III was established to deal with all embassy work, except in the USA; it was commanded by General Prosetzky. A new Department XII, led by Colonel Dr Klaus Rösler, with Colonel Karl Rehbaum as his deputy, did intelligence work on NATO and EU states as well. HVA Department XV of Leipzig, the HVA outstation there, was given special but by no means exclusive responsibility for Western operations in October 1982.[8]

Mielke took personal overall charge of all Stasi operations, including HVA ones, but increasingly in the 1980s first Wolf and then Grossmann became key links in the chain which connected the work of the HVA to the Stasi more generally and to secret military intelligence conducted by the intelligence section of the National People's Army (the NVA).[9] After the stationing of Cruise and Pershing missiles, the HVA became more interested in military intelligence, developing Department XII to set up a central information unit gathering intelligence on this topic.

In addition to the HVA, however, the Hauptabteilung I (HA I) with 2,319 officers, spied on Western forces and on NATO 'objects'; it was also concerned with the security of military intelligence units. HA II, led by General Günther Kratsch, with 1,432 officers, conducted counter-espionage in the West; it had a 'Working Group Co-ordination' which ran the central control of all the top IMs operating in the West, known as IMBs. HA II also had Division 9, whose 'focal point' was French and British intelligence. We know that in 1989 it planned to recruit about twenty non-Germans with 'links to France and the UK'. HA II plays a highly significant if complex part in this story. They not only advised Stasi officers whom to avoid because of perceived links to Western intelligence but also indicated who might be encouraged to draw close to Western intelligence on the Stasi's behalf.[10] HA VIII, under General Karli Coburger, spied on West Berlin and Western surveillance systems there. HA IX also undertook counter-intelligence assessments of UK sources.[11] HA XX, which sought to combat dissidents and the internal opposition in the GDR (including the Churches), also had extensive duties in the West, and particularly in the United Kingdom; HA XXII kept lists of terrorists, including members of the IRA. We know, too, that there were 477 agents or co-opted workers (IMs) operating against UK and US forces in the Federal Republic.[12] There were at least 150,000 co-opted workers working for the Stasi but we still do not know the precise number operating in the West at any one time.

The Federal Republic was the most deeply penetrated country. It has been variously estimated that, over forty years, the East Germans had some 17–23,000 operational spies working in the Federal Republic, but there were also significant numbers of spies in the USA, France and the UK. The names of 50,000 West German citizens have been listed as being IMs or co-opted workers but not all of them actually worked in the Federal Republic and a number may well have worked in the UK.[13] Equally, several 'West' German agents turned out to be East Germans, such as Günther Guillaume, the spy in Brandt's Chancellor's Office.

We know, too, from a few fragmentary files, that in *1989* the HVA had 700 IMs of its own in the West. The British case suggests the HVA had its own approach to recruitment and the gaining of intelligence, which was more opaque than that of the other parts of the Stasi or in West Germany. We also know how much information the HVA received from its sources or agents at particular points in time: in 1988, for example, Grossmann informed Mielke that the HVA had obtained 10,000 pieces of secret intelligence, of which some 25 per cent were rated 'valuable'. Two years earlier, Wolf had reported to Mielke that the HVA had received 6,708 pieces of intelligence and that this was 300 more than in the previous year.[14]

Under the slogan 'Fight Against War!', Mielke's predecessor, Ernst Wollweber, had begun the process of gaining Western Stasi agents, but his intention was simply to get intelligence about Western plans in order to forewarn GDR foreign policy makers. When Mielke took over the Stasi in October 1957, he refocused its work to underpin domestic repressive policy. This did not, however, mean that the Stasi's work in the West declined; in fact it was expanded greatly but its objective was now more firmly linked to the domestic health of the SED. Intelligence gathering was defined here as the 'defence' of Communism at home against all its enemies, of which the West was but one.[15]

By the 1980s, Stasi policy had been further refined to meet a number of directives issued by Mielke in respect of the organisation's work against the West in general, and the United Kingdom in particular (although, it is worth repeating, the core of this work was undertaken against the Federal Republic and Western organisations and institutions in West Germany).[16] Mielke had already sanctioned plans to enlist agents or co-opted workers (IMs) and sources (*Quellen*), aiming in particular at so-called 'Perspective IMs [PIMs]' – agents who were prepared to work for the Stasi out of ideological conviction, who were seen as preferable to those who could be blackmailed or bribed. (Robin Pearson, whose case is discussed below, became a PIM.[17]) Mielke was also prepared for his officers to play a very long game when it came to recruitment: he knew it was never likely to be an 'instant fix'. As early as 1976 Mielke had issued instructions that all Western visitors to the GDR were to be looked at with a view to whether or not they might be 'operationally interesting', which was defined as meaning suitable, in theory, for agent recruitment. Special attention was to be paid to university departments for this purpose.[18]

While warning of the danger of 'double agents' (IMs who were in fact working for MI5 or MI6), Mielke nevertheless instructed his officers to create 'a solid and highly active net of patriots working on the invisible front – a strong, successful, effective and conspiratorial intelligence force'.[19] In his Directive 2/79 he offered more precise orders: his officers were to 'gain intelligence on the aims, the agents, the means and methods utilised by the enemy which was both timely and reliable in order to preclude any surprise changes in the political, economic and scientific spheres'. They were to 'discover exact information about the enemy and his centres, and his potential, and to execute offensive measures against them and all hostile forces'. They were, in addition, required to 'secure the embassies and offices abroad' of the GDR, concentrating in particular on the United States, the Federal Republic, all NATO members and West Berlin.[20] Although it is not the subject of this book, it should be noted that electronic intelligence gathering was increasingly being developed in the 1980s.[21] The listening stations included a former Third Reich Atlantic one in Cadiz, offered by Franco.[22]

The Stasi also drew up lists of their targets in the West. The one that is shown in Appendix 1 has never previously been published. There were altogether about one thousand HVA targets of which the overwhelming majority were West German. Some eighty-two were in the USA, seventeen in the UK and fifteen in France. It is important to note that the Royal Institute of International Affairs (Chatham House) is not on this list, an important matter to which we will return.[23]

In working out who was doing what in Belgrave Square we need to set its work in the context of the Stasi's activities more broadly. By the time Grossmann took over, in 1986, the Stasi was manned by some 102,500 officers and in the region of 150,000 agents or co-opted workers.[24] Three years later, its annual budget was 3.6 billion Ostmarks – at Communist exchange rates, US $1 billion. One justification for this huge expense was the accepted fact that Stasi targets were of concern to the whole Eastern bloc.[25]

A highly revealing – and, as the Stasi files prove – wholly accurate account of how East Germany used its embassies for espionage purposes was provided by a former HVA resident who agreed to be interviewed in 1990. Identified only as Horst-Peter L., a specialist in Arab affairs and resident in Aden (1976–8), Baghdad (1978–80) and Beirut (1985–7), he spoke openly about his career.[26] Starting off as a straightforward diplomat with some counter-intelligence duties, he was recruited by the HVA. After additional study in the Stasi college in Potsdam in 1970, he was given work experience monitoring the Palestinian delegation for the World Games in East Berlin in 1973. After diplomatic recognition, he explained, the Stasi's work could expand, and he completed further special training in espionage. He then moved back into the GDR Ministry of Foreign Affairs. It was made clear to him that this was a conspiratorial move, requiring a complete change to his life. He had to acquire a new identity as a diplomat, collect personal records with his new name and signed accordingly. He had to get several previous years' worth of official stamps on his papers, to move to a new flat in a different part of Berlin, change all his registration files and remove all traces of his former work for the Stasi. His daughter had to move to a different school and at work he was asked formally to announce his resignation from the Stasi. A five-month intensive English course had to be taken and passed. Even his social life changed – his family's circle of friends was to be restricted to people they knew supported the Stasi's work. Effectively, the Stasi had made him re-invent himself.

Most of the information Horst-Peter L. sent back to the 'Centre' was encoded. For reasons of security, and because it liked to safeguard its own operations, the Stasi insisted that all key embassy posts were held by Stasi people. The resident, he explained, was also responsible for the security of the embassy and for communications with the 'Centre' in East Berlin. This included working with self-destructing containers sent in diplomatic bags.

Regular consultations would take place between the resident and the ambassador, and because, he said, the results of secret intelligence work were the basis for foreign policy decisions taken by the leadership of the GDR, the ambassador had a very strong interest in exploiting the secret intelligence emanating from his embassy. 'This form of co-operation,' he added, 'produced good results for political intelligence; I always found the ambassador a competent partner for discussion and evaluation.'

However, he continued, at all times he had to avoid arousing suspicion as to his real role: 'On the one hand, I was resident, on the other I had to fulfil my cover role as cultural attaché, press attaché, or scientific aide to the ambassador; the point was to ensure that neither other employees of the embassy nor the host country, and especially its secret service, would ever become suspicious of me.' He added, with considerable pride, that he had not been identified in any of the countries in which he had operated: 'not a single one'. Whether this claim is fully justified we cannot know: he had, however, never been expelled from any of them.

We can see that the Stasi had quite specific (if ambitious) goals: they wanted to know the intentions of the Western political leadership in respect of military and political initiatives against Communism, to uncover strategic and political plans directed at the Communist states and to steer them, wherever possible, towards the interests of the GDR. There was to be a focus on NATO activities in Britain, France, Belgium and the Federal Republic: they wanted to know about SDI, rocket technology, biological warfare, Eureka and the European Defence Initiative. They wanted to know who was who in the political class, how they could be used, and, if possible, subverted. They wanted agents, emphasising the role that students (especially those visiting the GDR) might play.

At first glance one might be forgiven for assuming that the Ministry's work against the West was conducted only by its secret intelligence service, the HVA. Not surprisingly, the HVA was highly active in the UK, especially its Department III. Yet, as the Stasi files show conclusively, several other arms of East German intelligence operated in London in considerable strength.

# 6

# The Stasi in Britain (I):
# The HVA Documents

The purpose of the Stasi's secret intelligence operations, conducted under the cover of the East German Embassy in London, was to reveal the true *aims and intentions* of various British policy makers and the prevailing views in the institutions that were responsible for the governance of Britain and its relations with the Warsaw Pact states. First and foremost, the Stasi wanted intelligence on the thinking of the British government in respect of its defence and European policies. Their next priority was to discover the plans and goals of the leaders of the British peace movement, especially CND, and, on a week-to-week or month-to-month basis, to find out which of the various Soviet proposals they would support or oppose. The Stasi was also deeply concerned to uncover the aims and ambitions of the leaders of the new breakaway Social Democratic Party, and what its impact might be on the Labour Party (and therefore on Labour's chances of winning a general election and possibly forming the British government).

The Stasi was always on the look-out for secret or classified documents, defence or otherwise. Documents were what British policy makers wrote and read; copies of them would allow the East Germans accurately to second-guess what the policy makers would do. From this material, the Stasi's intelligence analysts in the 'Centre' in East Berlin would make estimates and evaluations which would then be passed on to East German and Soviet policy makers.

They, in turn, would think of ways either of getting round or steering British policy to their own advantage.

There was very little interest in what might be called 'scientific systems analysis' intelligence. The Stasi did not 'do' broad-brush intelligence gathering, because the East German leaders wanted to know not how Britain 'functioned' but how its leading politicians would 'operate' under specific circumstances in specific policy areas. This was targeted and focused intelligence gathering.

Stasi intelligence was, like that of any intelligence agency, obviously prone to the shortcomings of its own particular political system. The East German leaders probably exaggerated their own ability to steer events in the long term, and (as is explored at the end of this book) they failed to predict that the killer blow to East Germany would come from their closest ally, the Soviet Union, and not from Western support for their internal enemies, as their leaders believed.[1] No intelligence service can choose its masters, and even if the Stasi was in possession of 'the big picture' in respect of Soviet thinking at the end of the 1980s (as 'off the record' they might have been), it is not clear that they could have done anything to avert the disaster that befell all of them.

It is, however, noteworthy that even if the Stasi could not save the state for which they were the 'sword and the shield', they were able to make careful provision for their afterlife: vast amounts of hard Western currency were stashed away before unification in 1990 made this impossible. By the beginning of 1990 some DM 50 billion had been safely deposited 'outside' (much of it in Austrian and Swiss bank accounts held in Zurich), using an Austrian company called Novum and the Austrian Communist Party.[2] Alexander Schalk-Golodkowski (known simply as 'Schalk') said in March 1990 that from 1972 to 1989 the East German government received DM 27 billion, channelled through the Stasi, as payment for the release of East German political prisoners.[3] A further DM 23 billion was received in the form of credits from West Germany and was likewise channelled through the Stasi. The Stasi chiefs established a special 'emergency fund' of DM 100 million. The decisions on where to place the cash were taken by Honecker and Krenz. German police have used a figure of DM 26 billion as a base line for the amount the

East German government actually had; to date they have recovered barely DM 2 billion. Virtually none of those Stasi officers involved in these matters has been brought to justice, and most of the documentary evidence could have been destroyed by the Stasi themselves in the first few months of 1990, making convictions complex.

It is interesting that the problems faced by many Stasi officers in aiming to be more alert and realistic than their political masters within both the Stasi and the Politburo were similar to some of the difficulties faced by the CIA during exactly the same period.[4] Internally, the CIA believed that, for political reasons, successive American presidents had overestimated the extent of the Soviet threat in order to gain increased spending on American arms. A more cautious use of CIA intelligence might have helped get the Soviets off the hook. It is by no means implausible to believe that, in bowing to pressure from the Politburo and the 'Centre', the Stasi overestimated the threat posed by NATO's rearmament and British (and American) support for the dissidents of Eastern Europe. On the other hand, it is certain that the dissident movement might have been far larger had there been less Stasi repression.

From 1986 to 1989 the CIA spent much time trying to find out the mindset and true intentions of Mikhail Gorbachev. Was his proposal for a 50 per cent arms reduction genuine or a ruse? In 1977 the CIA had estimated that Soviet growth was 1 per cent – the same as it had been in 1945. They deduced that the Soviet Union would have to get a new dynamic leader if the problem was to be solved, but what it got instead in the first half of the 1980s was a succession of very old and sick leaders. The circumstances of the Eastern-bloc states deteriorated seriously. Then Gorbachev emerged. But what the CIA did not know was whether he truly believed that low Soviet growth was the outcome of massive spending on arms, so that a lull in the arms race might allow the economy to recover and thus lead to renewed arms spending, or, as the CIA believed, he could see that the Soviet economy was in such deep decline that a conclusive halt to the arms race was the only way of trying to keep Communism alive. The CIA had conducted 'humint' operations in the 1980s to discover whether Gorbachev was indeed the genuine Communist he claimed to be (which they subsequently confirmed) rather than a

Boris Yeltsin (who could make the transformation from Communist to post-Communist). If the former, the CIA reasoned, Gorbachev would do everything short of war to ensure the survival of Communism; if the latter, he might actually lead the Soviet system into a new, liberal future.

When viewed from East Berlin, the issue of the arms race shows why the Stasi took such an interest in the British peace movement. Keeping up with the arms race while not allowing it to cripple the Warsaw Pact economies could only be a major East German preoccupation. CND, which supported unilateral nuclear disarmament by Britain and ultimately by all of NATO, was therefore regarded as a major boon to the East Germans. Similarly, those in the British peace movement who argued for multilateral arms reductions as well as human rights reforms in all the Iron Curtain states constituted a serious threat to the Communist position. All Warsaw Pact countries wanted enough arms to maintain the integrity of the Soviet empire; they certainly did not want human rights movements undermining their domestic control. They could not afford the level of arms spending to which they were already committed, and could afford any increase even less. To reduce the standard of living of their citizens to pay for more weapons was for the East Germans a nightmare scenario. Successful intelligence operations in respect of defence secrets and support for the dissidents were their only escape. And, since a lot of the talk about arms had to do with the type of weapons and the number of warheads each weapon had, military and economic intelligence was absolutely vital.

This is the context in which the few surviving fragments of Stasi secret intelligence should be viewed: it explains their significance and why so much effort and cash was devoted to their gathering.

This chapter presents examples of the secret intelligence collected by the HVA and other Stasi units in Britain; the following chapter examines the intelligence collected by the military intelligence unit in London. The Stasi files provide examples of two sorts of intelligence material. First, there are the descriptions of individual pieces of intelligence, known as the SIRA. (The indexes are included in Appendix 5.) Second, individual items of intelligence analysis have been found in the digests prepared for the top leaders of East Germany.

## The SIRA Material

East Germany's first post-Communist government permitted the HVA to destroy its own archives. Beginning work at the end of 1989, it had, by Easter 1990, largely accomplished this task. One set of encoded materials, however, was left intact for the simple reason that the HVA did not believe anyone would ever be able to decipher them. These were the indexes for the Information Research System – or archive – operated for research purposes by the Stasi. It is known by its acronym, SIRA, which stands for 'Information Research System of the HVA' (*System zur Informationsrecherche der HVA*). The Stasi chiefs were right to think – in 1989–90 – that this material, processed by Robotron computers (the technology was stolen from the West), was indecipherable.[5] But they were wrong to believe that advances in computer technology might not change the position, for what could not be decoded in 1989 could – albeit with huge difficulty – be deciphered almost ten years later.

It is vital to realise that this material is an archive of all secret intelligence material considered worth keeping for further research. It is, by definition, material that had been gained by covert and secret intelligence means, involving the full panoply of officers, agents and contacts. It was not material gained from diplomatic or open sources: although, like all intelligence services, the Stasi did use open sources, it laid by far the greatest weight on secret material, 'conspiratorially gained'. This reflected the leaders' conviction that if something was secret it was automatically important and likely to give a true picture of the aims and intentions of its enemies in the West, just as their own real goals were hidden from public gaze.

As we have noted, the central evaluation unit, ZAIG, based in East Berlin, screened all the material and anything not regarded as secret intelligence was not stored in this archive. The HVA's material was therefore the 'Crown Jewels' of the German Communist regime which it never believed would become public.

# The Secret Intelligence Digests Prepared for East Germany's Leaders

The SIRA indexes indicate the type of secret intelligence the East Germans wanted to collect, and they give us a benchmark of their success. However, the intelligence gained was not just archived but was also distributed in the form of digests to the leadership of the Stasi and the regime. Because each SIRA item contains the registration number of the 'source', and because some of the intelligence digests also include a registration number, we are able to link specific sources to specific items of intelligence.

This is the first time that these secret intelligence reports, some based on stolen British documents, have been published, or indeed seen by anyone other than the 'Centre' and the small group of government chiefs in East Berlin. It is also the first time that any government's secret intelligence reports relating to events as recently as 1989 have been placed in the public domain.

It must be stressed that at the time this material was collected, analysed centrally and then distributed, it was 'news' – the German word for intelligence was either *Aufklärung* (enlightenment), *Nachrichten* (news), or just plain *Berichte* (reports) or *Informationen* (information). It naturally had a sell-by date. Some news was more useful than other news. Even at the time it was being distributed in East Berlin, some of it would already have been out of date. Yet, where the intelligence dealt with the aims and ambitions of UK political leaders, it could still reveal the mindset of the individuals concerned. And mindsets were of the utmost importance to the East Germans in charting how far a particular approach could be taken, and when to dodge and dart around it. This means that for us to estimate accurately the true importance of the intelligence to the Communists – and, consequently, the damage that it did to British interests – we have to try to imagine the position the East Germans were in as the fruits of their espionage filtered through to them. In short, to reiterate that 'yesterday's news is today's fish and chip paper' does not automatically detract from the significance that was attached to the news at the time – nor the assistance that the Communist leadership of East Germany derived from its possession –

itself *prima facie* evidence that those who knowingly supplied to our self-confessed enemies were, if they were British, traitors pure and simple.

Every piece of material starts with the same sort of opening phrase, such as 'This is what the enemies of the GDR believe "internally"', or 'These are the inside views of those with power in the states which oppose us and do not contain the information our enemy wishes us to have (and passes to us by the normal diplomatic channels) but the facts it chooses to conceal from us.' Generally, the material which is reproduced below has to do with British high policy at various junctures. The SIRA pro forma in fact includes not just a grading system for truthfulness and reliability, but also one for 'actuality'. No one was more aware of the distinction between news and old paper than the Stasi.

As we shall see, this was only one form of secret intelligence in which the Stasi took an interest. They also had specific concerns with secret military intelligence, with the British peace movement and its links to East German dissidents – activities pursued under 'legal' cover from Residency 201 in Belgrave Square. But we should not forget that the HVA also undertook 'illegal' espionage against the UK and had an active policy on agent recruitment.

*Surviving items of intelligence material gained by the Stasi spies in London, listed chronologically*

1969 secret intelligence on nuclear weapons production
1970 on using the Irish model in German–German relations
1970 French negotiating ideas in respect of the UK's bid to enter the EEC
1970 on long-term developments in airborne armaments in NATO
1972 on the potential and structure of the energy industry of the UK
1972 on 'Eternal Triangle VII', the Rhine Army Divisional Exercise
1973 on security threats arising to the GDR from recognition
1973 on replacing Polaris
1977 on James Callaghan and Helmut Schmidt
1977 on the CPGB

1977 on the Western Economic Summit

1980 on HVA leadership in residencies

1982 on UK–GDR trade

1986 on British reactions to the SDI agreement between the UK and the USA

1986 on the current foreign policy of the Labour Party

1986 on UK–GDR relations

1986 on the visit of XXX from the British Labour Party to the GDR

1986 on British participation in SDI

1986 on the situation inside the British Conservative Party

1986 on British views on Ostpolitik and on the relationship with the GDR

1986 on disagreements within the leadership of the British Labour Party on defence

1986 on consultations between the Labour Party and leading British industrial circles

1986 on UK–GDR relations

1986 on British attitudes towards the arms-control process

1987 on British relations with the USA

1987 on British relations with the GDR

1987 on the British peace movement.

These secret intelligence reports were prepared for members of the Politburo in a very limited number of copies in digest form, varying from two to fifteen. At least three such digests were sent out each week. Virtually every one went to Honecker (or Ulbricht before 1971) as head of the Politburo (his name appears as 'Hon', ticked to show it had been received), Fischer ('Fi'), Axen ('Ax') and Winzer ('Wi'). Recipients were reminded that the material was not to be used in any published form whatsoever in order to protect the source. In effect, this meant that no public reference could be made to it. This indicates, yet again, that almost all of this secret intelligence came from agents. Using this material in any public way would, of course, have alerted British counter-intelligence to the existence of prime sources within the British government and in Britain more generally – not simply because the intelligence contained sensitive facts, but also because even to describe the context in which they were presented would be taken as evidence that secret thinking within the British government had been communicated to East Germany. This, in turn, would have been an immediate warning to British leaders that all was not well with its security. Indeed, this may well be one reason why official speeches in the GDR were anodyne and lacking any immediate newsworthiness (as any reader of *Neues Deutschland* would confirm): it was the safest way of ensuring that no cat was ever let out of the bag. Recipients were always instructed to return their copies of the intelligence reports, but fortunately (for posterity) not all of them did.

This intelligence did indeed contain a large number of 'cats', some of which are today probably still not out of the bag and in the public domain: the existence of KH-11, a US spy satellite on orbit over the west coast of Ireland to prevent arms shipments to the IRA; the use by MI5 of trickery in the form of free holidays to recruit agents in Ulster; the payment of £100,000 to IRA 'supergrasses'; and the eerie Arab contacts maintained by the IRA.

The documents that have survived demonstrate a wide range of East German concerns. Some involve very technical issues such as 'gas ultra centrifuge systems' and uranium enrichment; others outline carefully what was then the current negotiating position of various parties. They include the position of the French government on UK entry into the EEC at a critical phase (showing how the French sought to squeeze the best deal out of the UK to France's advantage) and the tactics Sir Geoffrey Howe, the British Foreign Secretary, proposed to pursue when dealing with East Germany in 1986 (motivated, the Stasi learned, by his wish that Britain should embark on its own course towards Eastern Europe, to resist what he regarded as unfortunate West German attempts to position themselves so closely to the various Communist leaders that the dissidents there would be seriously discouraged). This was a most useful piece of intelligence which alerted the East Germans to the potential dangers of Britain's new policy – and allowed them to quickly develop counter-measures. These are explored in later chapters.

The East Germans were interested in Britain's application for membership of the European Community (which they rightly saw as strengthening the overall position of the Community vis-à-vis the 'Socialist' states of the Communist bloc). They were also concerned to know about the aims and intentions of the Conservative government and the internal struggles within it. They were well informed about how the Westland Affair was rapidly spiralling out of control and about Michael Heseltine (who, as Defence Secretary, was of particular concern), and they clearly liked to hear about his chances of succeeding Margaret Thatcher (which their source correctly rated as slim). They wanted facts about the views of the leadership of the Labour Party, and they set store by knowing how Labour was handling the unilateral nuclear disarmament issue and how East German policy might be developed in order to make life as easy as possible for a prospective Labour government after 1987, one which was committed to enact the CND's proposals.

One very important piece of intelligence, set out in the next chapter, dealt with NATO's development of new tactical fighters, laser-guided rockets and innovations in radar and electronic equipment. Britain's special background in arms technology and manufacture was highlighted. Similarly, reassuring evidence that the Warsaw Pact would continue to retain numerical superiority over NATO in weaponry until 1985 was undermined by the intelligence that the firepower of the West would be increased while cutting back on the numbers of its aircraft. Western policy makers proposed that US forces in Europe and the rapid development of new weapons systems would also keep the Soviet bloc in check. Close attention was paid to the developing SDI argument. East German spies realised that, although there were those within British industry who did not believe that Britain's support for it would actually lead to big contracts for them, Margaret Thatcher was determined to stick to her line, even though she herself was doubtful about whether it would ever work.

Finally, the HVA's work on the IRA shows clearly that it was regarded as an ideological partner and potential military ally by the East Germans. At the same time, by 1985 the Stasi had plainly become fearful that the IRA's successful use of terror would endanger the GDR's global capacity to engage in terror attacks of its own, or to exploit, for its own purposes, any terror attacks that its 'partners' in the Middle East or Latin America might launch. As Wolf explains, 'the MfS and my own department were involved in a number of alliances with forces that used terror as a tactic'.[6] The Stasi took great pains always to introduce the IRA to the Politburo as a partner of the East German regime. On one occasion, for example, the Stasi pointed out that since the *twelfth* century the British had been engaged in a colonial class war against the Irish people. By the end of the twentieth century, the IRA, the Stasi insisted, was to be regarded as a working-class, national liberation movement with anti-imperialist and anti-capitalist ambitions. The IRA committed acts of 'terror' in Stasi eyes, it is true, but always directed only against a brutal and oppressive British regime, one which at times resorted to isolated acts of cold-blooded murder. When the Stasi spoke of the 'inhumane' conditions under which IRA prisoners were detained, which it insisted were an 'affront to human dignity', either it was displaying breath-taking hypocrisy or it was so ideologically constricted that it genuinely could not appreciate the irony of the fact that its own treatment of its political prisoners was considerably worse than that of the British government for most of the period of its reporting on the IRA.

The Stasi consistently emphasised that the IRA were in no way hostile towards the GDR, although it did note that IRA attacks on British bases and personnel in West Germany and West Berlin could conceivably damage what it referred to as East German 'equipment' in its vicinity. These would appear to have been unmanned electronic tracking devices installed near British bases.[7] Finally, and perhaps most chilling, the Stasi had clear information, both from their own sources and from the KGB, about the links between the IRA and other terrorist groups in Europe and the Middle East and specifically drew the attention of the East German leadership to an international terrorist conference held in Belfast in 1979, from which all further international links had been developed.

(In the following text it should be noted that some of the material was passed to me after March 2002, which means that the names of certain individuals implicated in terrorist activities, but not convicted of them, have been blacked out.)

Stasi File No. 69
HVA 05.08.70
760/70
10 copies

## The UK and EEC negotiations

It is proposed to have a relatively short transition period for all new
entrants including the UK. The reason is that France has a
particular interest in the rapid and unrestricted participation of the
UK in financing the common agricultural policy and the opportunity
for French agriculture of making a rapid impact on the British
market. The French are also unwilling to grant the UK concessions
on the industrial front where a long transition period might favour
Britain. As regards the Commonwealth, the French experts believe
that its goods should only enjoy entry into restricted areas of the
EEC.

As far as coal and steel union is concerned, the British will have
to give up existing practices which have protected both these
commodities. They will also have to supply a capital sum towards
the European coal and steel industries, the size of which is to be
determined during the negotiations themselves.

This report is based on an original document which is seventy-
three pages long. It can be requested if required.

This information may not be used in any published form to
protect the security of the source.

———

Stasi File No. 11/77
14.03.77

## On the CPGB

Within the CPGB some want a resolution in favour of Amnesty
International (AI) which would make specific mention of the so-
called political prisoners in the Socialist States. The member of
the Executive Committee, Hodges, recently took part in an AI
conference. Opposition to any contact to AI came, above all,
from Bert Ramelson. Because of its revisionist ideas, the party

leadership is responsible, according to several named Communist rank-and-file members, for the decline in the membership of the party, its lack of activity and the decline in sales of the *Morning Star*.

———

**Stasi File No. 20/77**
**1.Hon [ticked]**

## On the summit of leading capitalist industrial states on 07–08.05.77

According to material we have obtained, the British government is satisfied with the course and the results of the summit although its premise here is that neither a comprehensive solution of the politico-economic problems nor any single agreed set of ideas on how to make progress is possible under existing conditions. The British government was able to protect its political and economic interests. The British line of working very closely with the USA has proved itself successful, even if this has caused dissatisfaction with the Federal Republic and France. In opposition to the position taken by the latter two states, the United Kingdom totally supported President Carter's position on energy policy. The UK has done the same thing in exploiting the West's position of strength in respect of food supplies to the Socialist States. British political circles emphasise that at the conference the British government supported the continuation of the East–West dialogue, which was then in general accepted by the US delegation. It has to be noted, however, that the British government believed that in the human rights question, President Carter had intervened in order to avoid any significant disturbances in the East–West relationship, not least in respect of the follow-up to the Helsinki cooperation and security process.

———

**Stasi File No. 9/82**
**MfS HVA ZI 13.09.82**

## On UK–GDR trade

If British economic circles are saying that in connection with the
1982 Leipzig fair economic relations between Britain and the GDR
are at a very low point and unlike other Socialist States, the GDR is
actually becoming less interesting to the British. The reason for
this is the negative picture of the GDR painted by the British
government and the media, which focuses on its indebtedness.
This gives the GDR a poor credit position. If the GDR wishes to
improve this it must follow other Socialist States and supply
accurate statistics.

———

**Stasi File No. 57**
**MfS HVA**
**Nr 4/86**
**27.01.86**
**15 copies**

## Information on the current foreign policy of the Labour Party

Internally, leading members of the Labour Party are saying they
want an extension in relations with the SED, especially when it
comes to consultations over security and disarmament questions.
They are interested in the current relationship between the SED
and SPD which is due to be intensified in this area. The Labour
Party is keen to have detailed information about Soviet plans. The
Labour leadership do not regard the Soviet three-stage plan as one
which can be realised in the immediate future, given Reagan's
persistence over SDI and what they regard as the unwillingness of
the American administration to consider disarmament properly. On
the other hand, they believe this will strengthen West European
opposition to SDI. There is a lack of clarity within the Labour Party
as to whether the surprising non-inclusion of British and French
nuclear potential in the estimate of European nuclear weapons
signifies a change of attitude on the Soviet part. It is clear,

however, that tactical missiles systems based in the GDR and Czechoslovakia are part of the plan. The Labour Party faces difficulties unless British nuclear weapons are included in the first stage of any disarmament programme because the official position of the Labour Party is that, on gaining power, they would immediately disarm all nuclear strike capacity.

———

**Stasi File No. 57**
**MfS HVA**
**Nr 7/86**
**17.02.1986**
**15 copies**

## Information on the visit of XXX from the British

## Labour Party to the GDR

Leaders of the Labour Party regard XXX's visit to the GDR as extremely satisfactory and valued highly the open atmosphere in which talks were conducted. They note, however, that the solution of certain humanitarian problems would make things easier. The Labour Party has a special interest in relations with the SED, the Soviet and Polish parties. There was no objection to the sending of a Labour Party study delegation to the GDR to discuss security and disarmament issues.

———

**Stasi File No. 57**
**MfS HVA**
**Nr 12/86**
**24.03.1986**
**15 copies**

## Information on the situation inside the

## British Conservative Party

In the view of leading members of British industry, there are now serious conflicts within the Conservative Party. They stem from the complex economic and domestic political situation at present, as well as from the current economic policy of the Thatcher government which militates against the interests of British industry. The conflicts are to be seen in the context of the forthcoming elections and the possible decision to defer the elections planned for 1987 to the first six months of 1988 simply in order to overcome the differences in opinion, and to be able to establish a united and uniform party line in order to once again win a majority in Parliament. The party conference originally planned for 1987 may now take place at the end of 1986. However, further polarisation in the positions of power seems likely to occur. At the moment there is an increase in the influence of the previous Defence Minister, Michael Heseltine. But his chances of succeeding M. Thatcher are seen as slight.

———

**Stasi File No. 57**
**MfS HVA**
**Nr 15/86**
**14.04.86**
**15 copies**

## Information on British views on Ostpolitik and

## on the relationship with the GDR

Important circles in the British Foreign Ministry point to the foreign policy speech made by the Foreign Secretary, Howe, on 17.03.86 to the Foreign Press Association, in which he emphasised the ongoing strong interest of the UK government in intensifying relations with the Socialist States. His words, however, were motivated by Britain's fears that it might find itself playing a subordinate role to the other West European states in their relations with the Socialist States. The British government clearly intended to normalise its relations with the GDR. This was seen as an important precondition for British trade and the presence of British firms in the GDR as well as for successful competition with French and West German companies in the GDR and the other Socialist States. For this reason, the British Foreign Office wished

to have political talks with the GDR Foreign Ministry and hoped that
the visit of Foreign Minister Fischer would be realised in 1986.

———

**Stasi File No. 57**

**MfS HVA**

**Nr 24/86**

**23.06.86**

**16 copies**

## Information on consultations between the Labour

## Party and leading British industrial circles

British monopoly capitalist circles have been engaging in the very
first discussions with leading politicians in the Labour Party, in view
of the possibility that Labour might win the elections which now
seem likely to take place in 1988. In these internal discussions,
the Labour leadership has stressed a concession to industry in
the form of a major modification to its present economic policy.
Their aim is to win industry's support at the time of the next
election.

Consequently, Labour has agreed to a constructive and active
policy to strengthen the UK's position in the European Community
and to engage in intensive cooperation with France and the
Federal Republic. At the same time it will abandon any plans to
regulate industry in ways which could constrict its capacity for
foreign trade. Any attempt by the state to interfere in economic
policy so to increase the international competitiveness of British
industry will also be strictly limited. However, in view of the
contradictions within the British Labour Party, its leaders could
make no concrete foreign policy statements. It seems likely,
however, that their goal of strengthened economic and political
relations with the European Community will lead to a weakening
of ties with the USA.

———

**Stasi File No. 518**
**MfS HA XX**
**Foreign Policy Information**
**02.02.1987**

## A British evaluation of the 13th meeting of

## the joint/mixed government commission GDR–UK

Internally, the head of the British delegation evaluated the course of the 13th meeting as a success. He expressed himself satisfied that the GDR was taking account of British wishes. This flexible attitude had allowed the power of those wanting economic cooperation with the GDR to be strengthened. There were high hopes of the readiness of the GDR to involve the UK in major projects and work with British firms. This will remain the core objective for the British government in its relations with the GDR and will play an important part in the visit of Trade and Industry Minister Clarke to Leipzig early in 1987.

## The British evaluation of Western economic

## summit in Venice 08.06.87

British economic circles speak in an internal evaluation about the far greater real threat of a world economic crisis than appears in the final communiqué. In the area of arms control, the discussion was hallmarked by confusion about the Soviet policy, and the main issue was how the West could be pulled out of its defensive position.

# Examples of the material on the IRA

**Stasi File No. 17219**
**MfS HA XXII**
**Department XXII/8**
**20.10.1986**

## Evaluation of the extremist organisation 'IRA'

### 1. History

The development of Catholic Ireland has been stamped by the colonial policies pursued by Britain since 1167. The conflict caused by Britain has taken ever more revolutionary forms, all subscribing to national self-determination and against the colonial policy of the ruling class of Britain. The working class in Ireland grew at the beginning of the twentieth century and engaged in multiple strikes. The revolutionary movement in Russia influenced that of Ireland and in 1910 Sinn Fein ('We Alone') was established.

By 1970 the movement had split into two wings: the official wing, which turned its back on armed struggle and wished to use democratic means to establish a democratic Socialist republic, and a 'provisional' wing, called 'provos', who fight for Christian Socialism without Socialists and Communists. They use arms and terrorist methods. They are led by a 'General Headquarters Staff' with six members. In 1981 Sinn Fein was refounded with Gerry Adams, born in 1948, as president.

Further evaluation of the IRA relies on the results of analyses of our informal collaborators' materials and includes evidence gained from the Western media about the repressive measures used by British security organs and the British government.

In 1976 the IRA became a secret army to operate against the 120 members of the Special Air Service, or SAS, sent to Northern Ireland. They were able to penetrate the IRA and caused considerable damage. This caused the IRA to regroup, disbanding its companies, brigades and battalions and establishing conspiratorial cells of three to five members. They successfully countered the British plans and goals of destroying the IRA.

Terror attacks are targeted at leading British politicians, British

and foreign diplomats, senior officers, and buildings belonging to
the British Army and the RUC, senior civil servants, especially
those involved in legal measures against the IRA, members of
Protestant paramilitary organisations, in particular the UDR and
the UDA, British economic interests, forces in their own ranks to
create ghetto security in Catholic areas who undertake 'knee-
capping'. Anyone cooperating with British forces is shot. Since
1974 the IRA has transferred its operations to mainland Britain
but the anti-terrorist unit of Scotland Yard was able to destroy it in
the capital prior to the creation of cells. Since 1978 it has met
with success: on 20 July 1982 eleven members of the Queen's
Life Guard were killed and the Harrods bomb on 17 December
1982 killed five and wounded eighty. The first of these attacks was
to oppose Thatcher's Falklands campaign which contravened
Article 51 of the UN Charter. Their most spectacular attack to
date was on 12 October 1984 against Thatcher and her Cabinet.

There have been hunger strikes against the inhumane prison
conditions, which are an affront to human dignity, used in the
political struggle against the ruling British classes, reaching their
high point in 1980–81.

The Thatcher government rejected the claims for political
status, exclusion from work, housing in special wings, and did not
react to the deaths of the hunger strikers. There are no signs of
any common West European sympathy hunger strikes as there
were in 1985 in the case of the 'RAF'.

The UK government uses 325 'supergrasses' recruited from
IRA members to betray their own organisation. They get freedom
from prosecution for all offences, except murder; financial
assistance up to £100,000, free passage to any English-speaking
part of the Commonwealth but chiefly to Australia, South Africa or
Canada. Secret Service specialists construct new identities for
them and have authorised plastic surgery in some cases.

The IRA attempted to counter the 'supergrass' strategy by
taking family members as hostages, pretending to become
informers and then withdrawing all allegations, staging a mass
outbreak from the Maze prison on 26 September 1983.

There is no evidence that UK forces operate 'death squads', as do the Spanish. But individuals do hunt down and kill IRA members. Immense sums of money are expended by the reactionary forces in Northern Ireland and the ruling classes in Britain.

The IRA's international links include the Basque terrorist organisation ETA and a contact to the Red Army Faction through Jean Carl Raspe, who came to the UK in 1971. There was a meeting in Belfast in 1979 which included representatives of terrorist organisations from West Germany, Italy, various Arab states, Japan, France and the Netherlands. The linkage between the IRA and West German terrorist groups generated the recent attacks on the UK Rhine Army.

There is confirmed information that in 1980–82 the IRA worked together with the 'Carlos Group' in France and had contact with the 'Revolutionary Cells' in West Germany as a result. An attempted attack in Gibraltar was foiled by the SAS in March 1988. Three suspects were shot in cold blood by them. Our understanding is that they had worked with the Basque ETA organisation.

Unofficial information states that two further Red Army Faction members are developing links to the IRA but that firm contacts have yet to be established. Our operational knowledge of the Red Cells shows no contact between them and the IRA in West Germany.

The British Secret Services undertake subterfuge to recruit sources from Northern Ireland by pretending that they have won so-called 'lucky-dip holidays', their names having been allegedly selected by computer. They are then taken to locations in southern Europe where they are approached and asked to work for MI5.

The IRA has no hostile intentions against the GDR. It will not join in the 'anti-imperialist Fighting Front'.

The individual who planted the bomb intended to kill Margaret Thatcher has been observed making contact with XXX who on two occasions was trained in Libyan camps. On 29 September 1984 a type KH-11 US satellite spotted the *Marita Ann* carrying weapons to Ireland delivered by a Canadian ship.

We will continue to monitor the IRA constantly. We will test all new operationally gained information for its impact on the GDR and, if necessary, introduce the necessary operational intelligence and control measures.

Agent XV 5414/85 will continue to be activated and operational tendencies and activities will be documented in the operational files.

——

**Stasi File No. 19156**
**MfS HA XXII**

Index notes on Berkeley, Liam Thomas Brendan. Operational information: Cherry Park, Belfast, no. 11. Is undertaking a lecture tour to West Germany and has possible links to Hughes and Rooney.

**HA XXII, Dept 8**
**25.09.89**

## Operation 'Feldwebel'

Since 1988 there has been a considerable increase in IRA activities in the Federal Republic. Thus far two people have been killed and twenty wounded, in some cases severely. There has been much damage to property. The methods used were bombing and direct attacks on targets with automatic weapons. The IRA is of the view that one dead British soldier in West Europe generates greater publicity in the world than one dead Protestant policeman in Ulster. Given that on the one hand we are dealing here with the political and military interests of the ruling class in Ulster and on the other with the demands of the IRA for the withdrawal of British troops, and the creation of a reunified Ireland, the two sides cannot be reconciled. Further IRA activities are therefore to be expected.

This requires us to undertake further work in this field with the following focal points:
- locations of British troops in West Germany and West Berlin
- condition of military bases and living quarters
- the proximity of UK bases to operational quarters or equipment of the GDR or other Socialist States
- in what way are our quarters or equipment endangered?
- the location of Irish students and workers in base areas

- all connections and contacts of the IRA and its political wing
  Sinn Fein in West Germany and West Berlin
- IRA recruitment there
- which persons are used for logistical purposes by the IRA in
  West Germany and West Berlin?

As we see, what the East Germans were after in Britain, not least as
the proxies of the Soviets, had real value – and, of course, what
remains is simply a fragment of what once existed. This was first
division intelligence work, with focus and depth. Its authenticity as
secret intelligence stems not just from its location in secret intelligence files, nor from the comment that the material was not 'what
our enemy wishes us to have and passes to us by normal diplomatic
channels, but chooses to conceal from us', but also from the fact that
it mirrored what Western intelligence wanted to know about the
Soviets in the 1980s.

In this context, it is revealing to recall some comments made by
Margaret Thatcher about the uses leaders make of different kinds of
intelligence. She wrote about her own wishes as a user in respect of
intelligence about the Soviet Union:

> On the one hand, there were those who played down the differences
> between the Western and the Soviet systems and who were generally
> drawn from political analysis and systems analysis . . . I remember
> a remark of Robert Conquest's that the trouble with systems analy-
> sis is that if you analyse the systems of a horse and a tiger, you find
> them pretty much the same: but it would be a great mistake to treat
> a tiger like a horse. On the other hand, there were those – mainly the
> historians – who grasped that totalitarian systems are different in
> kind, not just degree, from liberal democracies and that approaches
> to the one are irrelevant to approaches to the other . . . My own view
> was much closer to the second than the first . . .[8]

# 7

# The Stasi in Britain (II):
# The Military Intelligence Documents

Within the East German Embassy at 34 Belgrave Square, working
under deep cover, there was a discrete military intelligence unit
whose existence has never before been publicly revealed. This unit
(whose story is told in Chapters 8 and 9) collected facts and documents not just about military hardware but also about political
matters which might impact on military planning issues. East
German military intelligence officers in London were as concerned
with the British peace movement as with the latest weapons technology. Some of the material they collected was also filed in the
SIRA archive, usually mediated through an HVA 'source' (the HVA
had overall authority over the military intelligence unit), and,
because of this, military intelligence also found its way into the
digests prepared for the leaders of the East German regime. Some of
this material, as these shards show, plainly predates the establishment of a military intelligence unit in the embassy. We know,
however, as has already been noted, that at least one military intelligence officer was operating in London before the opening of the
embassy, in the GDR's trade mission.

# Military Intelligence Material in the Intelligence Digests

**Stasi File No. 154**
**MfS HVA**
**Nr 1114/69**
**Intelligence Digests**
**10.12.69**
**7 copies**

## Information concerning West German–British–Dutch co-operation on the 'gas ultra centrifuge project'

A reliable source states that in mid-July 1969 the British government's future plans in respect of this project are to solve two problems: the first is how the gas ultra centrifuge technology can be used for military purposes and the second is the site for the organisation which is to run it. These problems are to be solved separately; the British will not consider the second problem until the Dutch make concessions on the first.

The British government has made it entirely clear that it will not yield on the issue of military use and seeks to win the German government over to its point of view. Information was required by XXX about West German plans for uranium enrichment.

Other reliable sources state that there have been lively discussions in American government circles about the creation of enrichment plants by the three. There is a suggestion that the technique, based on gas diffusion, which is currently secret, should be made available to other groups. The aim would be to prevent gas ultra centrifuge units from being constructed. Because of the low investment costs, American circles are concerned about nuclear proliferation.

A further American measure would be to offer the guarantee of enrichment services at special prices for a longer period. This, too, is seen as a sign of American discomfort.

This information can not be published in any form in order to protect the security of the sources.

Stasi File No. 793/70
14.08.70
2 copies only

## Information on the long-term developments in air

## armaments of leading NATO states excluding West Germany

[. . .] It is evaluated that most changes will come from the USA. In West Europe apart from France and the UK, Sweden (in the form of its all-purpose fighter, the SAAB 37 – one of the most modern constructions in its class) will have a certain influence on the development of tactical aircraft. This applies also to Japan which seeks complete independence in armaments and will almost certainly achieve its goal by 1980.

In the period 1975–80 there will be a trend towards simplification and uniformity in air armaments, excluding the USA, whose military-strategic position demands weapons systems which are either too costly for European NATO members or are unsuitable. The armed forces of the Warsaw Pact will not, over time, be able to avoid a similar trend.

If the West European NATO states do not soon fundamentally alter their armaments strategy, NATO European Command will, when the tactical fighter the F-104 becomes redundant, not be able to utilise a uniform airborne NATO weapons system [. . .] NATO states with their own armaments industry will, except where there are bilateral developments, no longer possess a common weapons system. The smaller NATO states are already thinking of ways of prolonging the life of weapons systems already in use.

One expected result will be that the influence of neutral states as well as France (which does not belong to the military organisation of NATO) will increasingly be felt on the arms market and play a part in the arming of individual NATO states. An example of this is the cooperation in armaments (the purchase of weapons, bilateral developments) between Denmark and Sweden, Belgium and France, Norway and France and Italy and Spain (a joint helicopter construction). Internally thus far we have known only about the bilateral arms work conducted by the UK and Spain to develop a marine variant of the helicopter WG/13.

The following aspects of air armaments are seen as core ones:

- the introduction of new types of aircraft (fighters and trainers such as MRCA-75, Super Harrier, Mirage F-1, G-4 and G-8)
- the development of new air to air and ground to air rockets
- the improvement of radar and electronic apparatus including the use of electronic data analysis
- the development of the NATO integrated early warning system (NADGE).

Current plans show [. . .] that the West European NATO states are not planning major strategic or tactical changes for the air strike command. In general, the goal is a fewer number of aircraft with the same fighting strength. The numerical and technical superiority of the Warsaw Pact states over the West European NATO states will not alter in the coming years. The numerical superiority will last until 1985. For this reason, stress is laid on the military significance of the presence of US air strike forces in Europe.

The UK (note that possible changes in armament policy connected with the change of government in the UK are not included in this digest): as the only militarily integrated West European NATO state with a large arms industry, Britain is certain to have the improved or new weapons systems. Alongside the Polaris A3 nuclear powered submarines carrying intercontinental ballistic rockets, there are the fighter planes the Harrier, Jaguar and MRCA–75 as well as various helicopters. Long-term budgetary considerations rule out both the development of intercontinental ballistic rockets or the building of an anti-rocket defence system. However, the following developments in British arms are to be expected by the beginning of the 1980s:

- the further development of Harrier fighters into the Super Harrier
- a laser-steered ground to air rocket
- an automatic transfer system for air intelligence
- an airborne early warning system against low-flying aircraft
- a medium range ground to air rocket
- a plane to support ground fighting.

There will be only minor reductions in RAF personnel.

———

Stasi File No. 386

MfS HVA

718/72

31.07.72

6 copies

## Information on 'Eternal Triangle VII':

## the Rhine Army Divisional Exercise

It is reliably informed that from 22 September to 15 October 1972 a divisional exercise of the first division (staff site Verden) of the British Rhine Army in Lower Saxony will take place. As part of the autumn manoeuvres it will involve combat exercise, code-named 'Eternal Triangle VII'. It will consist of 11,900 troops and include 590 Danish soldiers with 2,400 track vehicles including 100 MLC-24 or a higher class, 560 armoured vehicles and 240 tanks (220 with rubber tracks, 20 with steel chains). Thirty-one helicopters will be used.

———

Stasi File No. 386

MfS HVA

782/72

23.08.72

9 copies

## Information on the potential and structure

## of the energy industry of the UK

The UK's entry into the EEC will increase its energy potential and strengthen its position vis-à-vis the Socialist States. The nuclear potential and its relatively small coal industry will increase the role of the UK. The integration of the energy industry, especially in nuclear affairs, will not be easy. However, the reserves and the potential will continue to fail to meet requirements, especially in oil and natural gas. To address this, a policy of 'economic cooperation' will be offered to third-world states in which stability will be given in return for natural resources.

The UK has coal reserves of 15.5 billion tons of which 12.3 are regarded as secure. It is the most efficient producer in the EEC, and will deliver 46 per cent of the entire EEC coal production. Prior to 1971, its production of oil and natural gas was small. Since the discovery of relatively large reserves (some 137 million tons of oil and 1,000 billion cubic metres of gas) great steps are being taken to increase production. From mid-1972 to 1975 consortia are engaged on the enterprise. By 1975 the so-called Forties Field should produce 35,000 tons of oil per day and the Auk Field 14,000 tons. Natural gas should reach 113 million cubic metres per day by 1975. The nuclear potential of the UK will be greatly increased by entry into the EEC. It is a leader in the use of nuclear energy and will introduce significant industrial, technological and financial potential into the EEC as well as research capacity. The UK has considerable experience with fast-breeder reactors.

———

**Stasi File No. 386**
**HVA**
**06.10.73**

Information on the possibilities of a choice of rocket systems for the strategic offensive arms potential of the UK

The ISS has investigated the choice of future rocket systems for the strategic offensive potential of Great Britain and has put its conclusions in the form of a memo.

Experts regard this memo as a first comprehensive verdict on the situation for a possible replacement for the Polaris rocket system used in UK nuclear submarines. West German experts are of the view that the ideas set out in the memo are in wide measure a reflection of those held by the Royal Navy and the British government. The latter has, however, not yet come to a decision on the matter.

The memo is subdivided into three sections. It adduces conclusions which flow from keeping the Polaris system, alternatives to it and currently thinkable solutions to the problems raised.

In the memo ideas are set down on the future effectiveness of the Polaris offensive system as affected by their ability to penetrate the Soviet anti-deterrent systems and the usefulness of U-boats. In addition, other factors influencing the life of Polaris are considered, as well as the political consequences of a diminishing cooperation between the UK and the United States and subsequent cooperation with France.

The results of this investigation can, according to West German military experts, be seen as follows:

1. The Polaris system remains an effective instrument of deterrence for the UK only for as long as the USA and the USSR place limits on anti-ballistic missile systems. If it were necessary, the UK could increase the offensive potential by deploying multi-headed war heads (MIRV – multiple independently targetable vehicles).
2. The USA will give up Polaris by 1980 at the latest. This would put a question mark on the exclusively American support for its offensive weapon. This problem would – if Polaris were to be maintained – have to be very carefully considered.
3. The political consequences of keeping Polaris are many. The American readiness to support the UK's offensive weapons in the future could be reduced as a result of foreign policy developments. In terms of cooperation with France, the maintenance of the offensive potential could allow the present contradictory positions of France and the United States to be bridged. Currently, the still existing technical difficulties here are increased by the completely differing political goals of the two states. Time, at any rate, is needed to get rid of these differences.

In the second part of the memo alternatives to Polaris are seen as being the American Poseidon weapon system, the future US system, or cooperation between the USA and France, which would lead to problems for the United Kingdom.

If the UK chose Poseidon, it would have a rocket system with a greater potential to penetrate than with a MIRV-adapted Polaris

system. It would have the additional advantage of ongoing US
support. But there are technical and political obstacles to this. Even
if the UK chooses Poseidon there is no guarantee that the US will
continue to support Polaris for the whole of its life. There may be
SALT II difficulties standing in the way of the purchase of Poseidon.
It could also undermine attempts at greater European integration if
there were no Franco-American agreement on nuclear cooperation.

Experts believe therefore that the UK could wait until after 1978
when the submarine long range weapon system ULMS-I (undersea
long range missile system) and the Trident submarine are ready
because until this date the US will still be using Polaris.

There are therefore three choices for the UK: two with Polaris
and one with Poseidon. No decision will be taken before 1977–8.
This date is very important because it will be the first test of the
ABM Treaty with the Soviet Union. The ULMS-I system and Trident
can, of course, be purchased from the US before 1977–8. But the
politics are the determining factor. To choose Poseidon would imply
a special relationship with the US and damage the relationship
between the US and the European Community.

The Expenditure Committee of Parliament, as we are reliably
informed, has therefore asked François Buchene, director of the
ISS, an additional question and his answer is that a decision by the
UK may be necessary before the question becomes technically
relevant. Buchene has advised the Committee that the cheapest
measure was to keep Polaris and the most expensive was to
acquire Trident. In between at the cheaper end was keeping Polaris
but acquiring MIRV, next to acquire Poseidon, next to acquire
ULMS-I. His advice to the Committee was to retain Polaris.

———

**Stasi File No. 7/77**
**14.02.77**

On the discussions between Prime Minister Callaghan
and Federal Chancellor Schmidt on 23/24.01.77

British government circles evaluate the outcome of the talks on the
current relationship between Britain and the Federal Republic as

unsatisfactory. This could be seen especially in the collapse of
discussions on a new agreement on foreign exchange in respect of
the payments for the Rhine Army and also in the West German
view on how Britain ought to solve its economic problems.
Callaghan believes the Federal Republic is not paying enough.
Schmidt insists that he will not move from the position of his
government that the West German support of credits for the UK
from the International Monetary Fund represents a very
considerable contribution to Britain. The British government
believes it is heavily burdened by the CAP contributions. During the
course of the discussions Schmidt actually increased the pressure
on Britain to make greater contributions to the CAP. It can by no
means be excluded that the British government will feel itself
forced to surrender to the German position on this matter, at least
in part. Schmidt also made it clear that he expected the British to
reverse their recent cuts in defence expenditure once they had
overcome their economic problems.

——

**Stasi File No. 57**
**MfS HVA**
**Nr 2/86**
**13.01.86**
**15 copies**

Information on British reactions to the SDI
agreement between the UK and the USA

British government circles regard the political support given to SDI
by the Thatcher government to be merely an attempt to secure
British interests. The doubts about the actual efficacy of SDI and
the nuclear deterrent aspects of it are simply being ignored. The
economic expectations placed on SDI have not been met by the
Americans. The agreement contains no guarantees or obligations
on the part of the USA towards British firms to permit them to
gain preferential treatment in the awarding of any contracts, or to
offer any technological help in dealing with competition.

All the Americans said was that if the agreement were signed speedily, British companies could look forward to lucrative contracts. The US also made it clear that priority would be given to technology which would secure the success of the entire venture. Signing represents a weakening of West European economies in competition with America. At the same time, this has led to a devaluation in European programmes such as Eureka or Esprit because, in expectation of greater profits, European companies are now going to concentrate the leading-edge technology on SDI projects instead.

———

**Stasi File No. 57**
**MfS HVA**
**Nr 8/86**
**24.02.86**
**15 copies**

## Information on Great Britain's participation in SDI

Right up to the last minute, Britain's signature of the memorandum of understanding on British participation, on 6 December 1985, was in doubt. The Department of Trade and Industry had reservations about the regulation of patent and property rights which did not pay sufficient attention to British interests. It is still not known what compromises enabled a signature to be given since the memorandum was considered so secret it was withheld from Parliament . . . [other] sources indicate that the concessions were all procedural and not material. They establish a roof under which the American administration can deal with British firms, universities and research institutes, relying on the good services of the Ministry of Defence.

———

Stasi File No. 57
MfS HVA
Nr 18/86
12.05.86
16 copies

## Information on disagreements within the

## leadership of the British Labour Party on defence

Internally, leaders of the Labour Party believe that the use of the US Air Force in the bombing of Libya has heightened the deep contradictions in Labour's defence policy. In particular, there are differences concerning the demand of the left-wing forces in the party that all US military bases in the UK should be closed. Those who support the idea of complete unilateral nuclear disarmament, including WW and XX, on the assumption of power are now pressing more strongly for this. They insist that in the event of a Labour victory in 1988, the party must declare that the Polaris fleet is to be disbanded immediately they take over. YY, on the other hand, insists that such a goal would be used by Margaret Thatcher to strengthen her position in the election campaign, since a majority of the electorate is clearly opposed to unilateral nuclear disarmament. According to AA, the Polaris question should be resolved only as part of a general disarmament negotiation with the Soviet Union.

———

Stasi File No. 57
MfS HVA
Nr 32/86
18.08.86
16 copies

## Information on British attitudes towards the

## arms-control process

According to British Foreign Office circles, Great Britain is in principle interested in maintaining the arms-control dialogue of the

USSR with the USA. It would, they believe, correspond to the interests of Western Europe if new arms-control structures were developed. The SALT regulations were symbolic and lacked military-strategic or negotiating significance. Recently, the demands made upon the West have become greater because the Soviet Union has, thanks to its leadership, increasingly succeeded in representing its policy as dynamic and flexible. The Reagan administration, on the other hand, has been able to introduce only very scant forms of innovation or new proposals into the arms-control negotiations. The British Foreign Office believes, however, that the Soviet focus on Western Europe is chiefly tactical in nature, so as to enable Western Europe to exert a stronger influence in the more important Soviet–American relationship.

The UK expects the Americans to make practical suggestions for the development of a system of mutual restraint, or some other form of compromise, in order to maintain arms controls as an instrument of security policy. The UK is afraid that the internal debates and the lack of clarity in the Reagan administration about the next steps in arms control and about its reaction to the expected new set of Soviet proposals will prove disadvantageous to the overall American position.

—

**Stasi File No. 518**
**MfS HA XX**
**Foreign Policy Information**
**19.01.87**

## The British evaluation of British relations with the USA

Leading British government circles are disturbed that Great Britain is finally losing its status as a privileged ally of the USA. These fears are the result of an insufficient readiness on the part of the USA to take note of British views on arms control which makes it difficult to work out a Western alternative to the peace initiatives of the USSR. Within the British government the ignoring of the British interest in the modernisation of the nuclear potential of Great Britain by the United States has produced dissatisfaction. From the

British viewpoint the Americans ought to develop a better
relationship with their NATO partners in respect of gaining
agreement to decisions and information and taking one-sided
steps, and consider the effectiveness of consultations with the EU
on economic matters as an indicator.

British government circles are also deeply disappointed by the
American failure to honour the unconditional support given by the
UK for the SDI project. The British Prime Minister herself was
displeased about Reagan's refusal to take account of her ideas in
respect of an increased effort to come to an agreement in the
Middle East or showing greater flexibility in respect of Central
America. Despite this, Margaret Thatcher aims to de-escalate the
disagreements with the USA and to construct the relationship with
the USA as tightly as is possible.

This, then, is the nature of the secret intelligence that the Stasi
acquired, some of which appears to be high-grade. What links the
whole is its impact on the security of the GDR. The demand that this
be protected at all costs is the common thread that runs through all
the reports.

# PART III

# THE INVISIBLE FRONT

# 8

# The Military Intelligence Unit in London, 1972–84

The situation in the London residency is optimal. It produces a continuous flow of successfully executed tasks. Excellent work is being done here. And the way in which the roles of resident and legalist are played alongside each other is exemplary, and highly motivating (*'Die Situation in der RoD ist optimal und gewährleistet eine kontinuierliche Aufgabenerfüllung. Das Zusammenspiel zwischen Resident und Legalist ist beispielgebend und wirkt motivierend'*).[1]

This glowing verdict on East German intelligence-gathering in London, made at the end of 1988 by a somewhat grudging 'Centre' in East Berlin, is hard proof of the Stasi's considerable satisfaction that it was getting the goods it wanted. A few months after the above comments were made, on 27 January 1989, the 'Centre' reiterated that 'excellent work' had been done and that it was more than pleased with the '209 pieces of information obtained in 1988'. Its judgement, however, was in this instance not on the HVA or other Ministry spies, but on a small, discrete group of specialist East German espionage officers and their agents who were self-evidently bringing home the bacon, a fact conceded by Stella Rimington, who writes that the 'massive assault on the West' waged by Communist intelligence 'had its successes, not surprisingly. It has been estimated, for example, that about 150 weapons systems depended on technology

stolen from the West.'[2] For behind the smart white stucco façade of
34 Belgrave Square there lay concealed not only an elaborate Stasi
and HVA apparatus but also the London section of the East German
military intelligence unit.

Although there are still gaps in our knowledge of the London
operations of the HVA, the nature of military intelligence work there
is depicted in considerable detail in the Stasi files. Modelled on
the GRU – Soviet military intelligence – the East German officers
managed with great success to obtain secret information, and covertly
penetrate their key British institutional targets, while *appearing*, with
almost flawless skill, to respect the strict etiquette of diplomatic life.
None of those Britons who had professional dealings with the military
spies had any idea that that is what they were. This was the tradecraft
the Stasi knew to value: the opportunistic and relentless recruitment
of agents to collect intelligence about the issues which concerned the
political leadership in East Berlin.

Through careful piecing together of single files and fragments of
files, we can in fact do more than document the work of the unit in
the 1980s. As a serious espionage unit, the military intelligence officers were obliged to deliver a precise record of their security
situation to the HVA at regular intervals, using, as one would expect,
their codenames. There, however, the real names of the officers
were appended on further sheets before being forwarded to the
archives of Army intelligence (presumably because the Stasi, rather
than the People's Army, kept the records). These sheets survive
along with the examples of their work listed above. They provide us
with a rare opportunity to align cover-names with the real identities
of the officers. Thanks to the HVA shredders, however, most of
the names of the unit's British agents (whose real names the Army
did not need to know) and full details of their intelligence were
successfully obliterated.

Two unique files, which (from the Stasi's viewpoint) ought to have
been prioritised for rapid destruction in early 1990, tell us that the
first military intelligence officer in London, Jürgen Wahner (code-
named 'Hampel'), was stationed here from 1970 to 1973 – that is,
*before* East Germany had been recognised and before there was an
East German embassy.[3] He was employed as a trade adviser. From

1973 to 1976, under the codename 'Kretschmar', he worked as a secret intelligence officer in Beirut, returning to London in 1977, where he spent two years building up the unit before going back to East Germany in 1979.

Following recognition, Gerd Kreissig ('Haupt') arrived and spent three years in London. In 1976 he was joined by Bernd Knott ('Hoppe') – legally an 'economic attaché' and formally on the 'staff list' of the embassy rather than the 'diplomatic' one – and a year later by Peter Escher ('Hohlfeld'). In 1981 Escher was replaced by Hartmut Linser ('Harald') and in 1983 Dr Oswald Schneidratus ('Helios') joined him. In 1985 two new officers arrived, Stefan Wetzel ('Hecht') and Friedbert Krebs ('Hammer') and finally, at the end of October 1987, Jörg Döring ('Harke'). Compared to its Soviet analogue, the GRU in London, which contained fourteen GRU officers, the East German unit was small – but, according to Oleg Gordievsky, it was very good.[4]

The files also show that the British agents recruited by the unit had the following cover-names: 'Adler', 'Astor', 'Barber' (a British spy within CND), 'Bill', 'Baldur', 'Basalt', 'Isak' and 'Ivo' – and at least four more ('Aktion', 'Akzent', 'Palme' and 'Rave'). 'Adler' was a specialist on the IRA and had access to a British institution which knew about it.[5] There is, for example, a record of intelligence he gained on the IRA hunger striker Bobby Sands, dated 3 July 1981. The East Germans clearly used a list of codenames for their agents which was devised according to some internal formula. We cannot be certain that all of their British agents were aware that they possessed these codenames, but it seems likely that at least some of them would have been. Not all had special training as agents, but where they received cash payments from people they understood were East Germans, they would have understood that they were spies, betraying their country. The files say that 'Bill' had been recruited by Kreissig (that is to say in the period 1974–9).

Some of them may have thought they were spying for a fellow NATO country (called 'recruitment under a false flag'), though they would have had to have been fairly dim to believe that states supposed to be our NATO allies wanted secret intelligence about the UK, for which they were prepared to pay. In any case, collecting *any* secret information about Britain's defence forces was treachery, no matter whom it was for. We know, too, that some of them lived in the London area.[6]

The argument that is sometimes trotted out by MI5 and the FBI as to why none of these was ever apprehended is that a good security service does not seek to expel individuals unnecessarily – once they are known about, they can be prevented from doing harm. Nor does it want them to be named when they have been uncovered because, as long as their identities remain secret, this, combined with their treachery, may allow them to be used operationally by themselves or the Americans. In the case of military intelligence or HVA officers and agents, this seems totally implausible. For one thing, the evidence we have suggests that none of these spies believed their operations had been unmasked and, if MI5 did spot some of them (as seems likely), they were clearly never caught red-handed, for none was expelled. The option did exist. One hundred and five Soviet 'diplomats' were thrown out of Britain in 1971. Expulsion was, in fact, a very effective measure and it certainly scuppered KGB operations in the UK.[7]

The Stasi was, of course, always alert to the possibility that MI5 might cause trouble for it. Oddly enough, on one occasion in 1981 MI5's hand had been clearly detectable, but the Stasi had failed to make the connection. On 16 July 1981 it had picked up a letter sent to the Council of Ministers of the GDR by one R. G. Killope, giving his address as 3 Kingsland Park, Knock, Belfast BT5 7E, Northern Ireland. Claiming to be a football fanatic, Mr 'Killope' had written in excellent German (itself perhaps a touch suspicious) to say that he was collecting facts on all football league clubs in Europe. He needed precise information on every East German club, a list of players ('by club'), their dates of birth, their heights, their weights, their usual position and their membership of previous clubs (if any). He also wanted to know how often they played, what their results had been and whether they kept files showing how the various teams had fared in every European competition. He ended his letter by emphasising that this material was to be published in a book on European national football teams.

The Stasi had a good laugh about this, as is clear from officers'

notes in the margin. They correctly identified this as an attempt to
waste their time in a big way. They saw that Mr 'Killope' had not
only realised that the East German government might want the
GDR's teams to appear in a book on European national football
teams, but that, if it did, the onerous and time-consuming job of
compiling the facts would be passed to the Stasi. The letter was
classed – correctly – as sabotage, but was wrongly believed to come
from an Ulster sympathiser of the East German dissident movement (and for this reason it was dealt with by HA XX, which
operated against dissidents and their supporters in the West).

Had the Stasi been slightly quicker off the mark, it would have
realised that it was unlikely that many Northern Irish football fans
would have been able to write such fluent German, that there was in
fact no such address to be found in Ulster, and that there was no
record of anyone called 'Killope' in the whole of Belfast. In fact, the
letter was almost certainly no more than a classic British intelligence wheeze, dreamed up by some bright MI5 officer.

To conduct military espionage against Britain, the Stasi used
a system similar to that employed by the HVA. An officer grouping
in the 'Centre' in East Berlin, in this case directed by someone
known as 'Hans-Georg', ran agents or co-opted workers akin to actual
officers. The agents (in East German terms) ran agents (in the English
sense) called 'persons of trust', or 'contacts', who were the real sources
of the intelligence, but working with them was called 'agent work'
(*agenturische Arbeit*). We know from the files that similar methods
were used by the Stasi in Paris.

The Stasi files show that all the cover-names of the officers in the
London unit began with the letter 'H'. The files also indicate that, on
coming to London (and adopting the 'H'-led codename), the officers
gave up their earlier codenames. This shows that, in military intelligence, codenames were attached to a particular posting. Most of
the British agents' codenames began with the letters 'A' or 'B',
although there are two that begin with an 'I' and one each with a 'P'
and an 'R'. There are several major contacts listed here, in
particular 'Barber', in the British peace movement (CND and END).
In addition, these files contain the real names of individuals whom
the military intelligence unit hoped to recruit as agents or contacts.

When linked to each other, the files, and the fragments of files, give an excellent picture of the areas assigned to secret military intelligence. On 15 April 1989, an East German secret intelligence officer set them down as follows: 'our tasking area is focused on defence, security and intelligence matters as well as issues in international relations'.[8] He will have been instructed that, translated into precise targets, this meant collecting intelligence on MI5, MI6, GCHQ, the Ministry of Defence, the Foreign and Commonwealth Office and the institutions connected with them, including the Institute for Strategic Studies and the Royal United Services Institute.

Everything which had a connection with military and strategic issues, including policy issues, was deemed to be the remit of the unit. Military intelligence also fed into political intelligence – for obvious reasons: as Wolf said, 'Satellites can tell you where missiles are today but only a source in military intelligence can tell you where they will be tomorrow.'[9] At various points, the targets designated and described in the files of the secret military intelligence unit provide direct links to the subject matter of the SIRA and intelligence digest reports.

The military spies were also required to engage in counter-espionage work against MI5, MI6 and the CIA. The files show that they were remarkably effective, and not just in 'agent work', exploiting their secret sources as a *Kewa* against the Foreign Office, the Ministry of Defence, the Institute for Strategic Studies, and possibly even MI5 itself. The unit also worked against both CND and END (frequently stealing confidential documents from both). This enabled the HVA (which had the responsibility for this more sensitive part of the secret work) actively to seek to steer both CND and END, if it could, towards a position which suited East Germany. Two further vital functions, that of the *Tipper* – a British talent spotter – and the *Ermittler* – the go-between, who could guide the East German officers towards what we would call their agents and contacts, and serve to put space between the East Germans and their source – are also well highlighted in this material.[10]

The 'Centre' believed that this was a job for skilled young officers with excellent English. The reason for this focus on youth was the

belief that young men had the best opportunities for 'winning contacts', particularly among female secretaries (or gay men) and
younger employees in the arms industry (who might be easily foxed
by them). If necessary, they could also pose as doctoral students,
and so on. Young officers had another advantage: as freshmen in
secret military intelligence, they had no past. Most came straight to
London from training in East Germany (about which MI5 could
have known nothing). For obvious reasons, older officers stood a
much greater chance of being on the files of British, American,
German or French counter-espionage.

These files illustrate one other, vitally important, thing. They
decisively give the lie to the claim that the East Germans did not
take intelligence collection seriously and that the central analysis
department in East Berlin was incapable of distinguishing between
newspaper stories, material gained as a result of the diplomatic
cover the officers enjoyed, and the genuine fruits of high-class espionage. It is crystal clear from these documents that the 'Centre'
rejected substandard intelligence, and that those who tried to get
away with supplying it suffered severe penalties. What the Stasi
wanted had to be very good, or, at least, good. This was not just
about seizing opportunities and showing initiative. It wanted its
spies to be ruthless, to know and recognise the 'enemy' and display
single-minded 'fighting instinct'. As the following case proves,
where this did not happen the Stasi spies were sacked.

In the detached view of the 'Centre', military intelligence gathering in London was sometimes less than a resounding success. It was
not until the mid-1980s that the East German officers began to generate the sort of material that pleased the 'Centre' – and even then
not all was plain sailing.

The story behind this issue begins in earnest on 3 November
1980 with an activity report written by the senior military intelligence
officer in London at the time, Peter Escher (known as 'Hohlfeld').[11]
It is worth reading with great care – but not for the reasons that
Escher hoped, for what makes his report so revealing is the fact that
the 'Centre' was deeply unimpressed with his progress. Escher
had got into trouble: he had allowed himself and a colleague to
be photographed in conversation with a Soviet military attaché,

indicating a professional link between them which ought not to have been exposed. Knowing that the 'Centre' was going to be furious, he decided (as others, understandably, if not professionally) to conceal this error in an elaborate maze of unconvincing explanations.

Oberleutnant Escher/'Hohlfeld' had headed the unit in London since 18 March 1977. Trained as a teacher, he had moved to administration, spending eight years as an officer and senior officer in the 'Centre', with five years spent on foreign policy work in embassies abroad. He spoke good English. He had been a member of the SED since 1965. What made his failings worse was that he had been deemed by the 'Centre' to possess all the necessary qualifications for brilliant work in London. He had been promoted from second to first secretary and awarded the title 'Richard Sorge intelligence officer' (*'Richard Sorge Aufklärer'* – Sorge being the legendary spy who had warned Stalin about Japan's Second World War plans, and been executed by the Japanese) and also the silver service medal of the National People's Army.

For 1981–2 the 'Centre' had instructed the unit to accomplish a variety of tasks. These included the recruitment of one new 'person of trust' ('agent' in the English sense), to undertake two exercises, to define one additional military target, to work on two discrete projects requiring secret information and to undertake basic espionage against three different objects.

But Escher had not delivered and had offered various reasons for his failure, including pressure from MI5. 'Whereas in the past,' he said, 'MI5 had operated chiefly against the Soviet Union, the Czechoslovak People's Republic and Bulgaria, there were now ever more signs that it was beginning to work against the officers of the GDR.' He added that the British government 'had inspired the making of television programmes which suggested that Special Branch was no longer able to protect foreign diplomats'. This was a 'direct invitation to terrorists' to attack them, he insisted. Indeed, the East German Embassy in Belgrave Square no longer had a policeman guarding the entrance, leaving just its bullet-proof glass to keep prospective terrorists at bay. Who these 'terrorists' were, or what their motives might be, was not explained. The relations between the Stasi and the major terrorist groupings in the Middle

East, Ireland and Latin America were good, and they were therefore unlikely to cause the East Germans problems.[12]

The 'attacks by MI5', Escher went on, had culminated in what he believed was an MI5 plot to 'intimidate' 'Hoppe', his junior colleague Bernd Knott, who had been photographed with him in conversation with the Soviet attaché. This had led the first secretary of the US Embassy (whose name is given in the file) to seek to make contact with him. He had even been invited to his flat, to the embassy, and out for lunch. The American had asked him about the embassy, and Escher had subsequently been informed by his Soviet colleague that the man was a CIA officer. Even worse, the person, he believed, had tipped off the second secretary at the South African Embassy, a man named van Schoor, who also approached him and asked him questions about East German links with the ANC and SWAPO. Escher said he now believed van Schoor was an officer working for BOSS, the (then) South African secret intelligence service.

The 'Centre' was disgusted by what was regarded as unconvincing special pleading. Escher's superiors were trained secret military intelligence officers and they were not willing to let anyone, least of all one of their own officers, pull the wool over their eyes. Escher's report precipitated his dismissal from his London post. It was not just that Escher had allowed himself to become 'noticed' as a possible military intelligence officer, but that he was using what he claimed were the objective difficulties of his work in London to pass on poor intelligence. Nevertheless, the 'Centre' concluded that, despite these errors, there was no evidence that the resident himself (Escher) was 'in danger' from MI5: they did not, in the 'Centre's' view, add up to deconspiracisation.

However, a further in-depth assessment of Escher's performance was carried out (to be attached to the Official Diary of the Military Intelligence department in Berlin as a 'top secret' record to be kept 'under lock and key'). It proves, once more, that the Stasi took their spying seriously.

Dated 4 June 1982, its subject was the period from December 1981 to May 1982 and the 'themes raised' were set down as 'morale, political conditions, leadership and security issues'.[13] It recorded an analysis of the work of the London unit examining Escher's 'poor execution' of his tasks, in particular the failure of his fieldcraft in respect of making contacts and talent spotting. Instead of directing espionage and spying himself, he had spent far too much time 'acquiring' information from non-secret sources and, in particular, sending on reports rather than materials. Despite some good results (sixteen pieces of the unit's reporting were deemed 'valuable' and thirty-six 'usable'), overall Escher's performance was said to be totally unsatisfactory. He seemed not to comprehend that his work was to recruit contacts and links. As a result, 'the intelligence gained was chiefly the product of the clever use of information acquired by virtue of his cover function'. It yielded 'no deeper secret military intelligence that would go beyond the generalities of military policy making'. He possessed 'too hazy a picture of the enemy', his character was 'defective in this regard' and he 'lacked fighting instinct and firm will'. Basically, the 'Centre' judged, he was too pleased with himself to be an effective intelligence officer. The 'Centre' confirmed that Escher should be relieved of his London tasks as soon as was practicable (the end of 1981). Its parting shot was a decision to issue a 'formal disciplinary warning of the imposition of a penalty' to lie on Escher's file – where it can be seen today.

This scathing report was signed by two colonels, Schuricht and Koch. A footnote, delivered more in sorrow than in anger, recorded that Escher, 'like no other cadre', had been given all the assistance necessary to become a good intelligence officer.

In Peter Escher's final weeks in London, a further potential problem for the unit arose. One of his prime contacts in Britain was a woman called Helene Koblizek, an Austrian citizen. Her contact with him had lasted a comparatively long time, from 1978 until 1982. During discussions with her about an Israeli in whom he was taking an interest, Escher noticed a photographer taking pictures of the two of them speaking in a London street.[14] Once again, however, the 'Centre' deemed this not to be catastrophic. It is possible that the photographer was an HVA agent, testing Escher.

The 'Centre' hoped that things would look up with the arrival in London of Harmut Linser, Hoppe's replacement, code-named 'Harald', who had arrived on 1 January 1981. Linser had been trained as a lawyer and had joined the SED in 1976. Thus far he had not been operational.[15] Born on 2 March 1954 in Meiningen he was recruited for the HVA in 1978 when he was just twenty-four. It was his career in the National People's Army which indicated to the Stasi that he was a good recruit to secret intelligence work. His personal file said that he had demonstrated a 'strong technical interest in weaponry'. He was, however, said to be a heavy smoker and so fond of beer that he had developed a sagging waistline which, his recruiters told him, required attention if he was to be attractive enough to fulfil his duties. This advice was given not in respect of his personal life (he was already married) but as an order to square him up for his operational duties. In London, his legal cover was that of the East German consul. He was formally initiated into his secret tasks by the 'Centre' at the usual conspiratorial meeting (not, as was common for the HVA, in one of two Berlin safe houses, quaintly code-named 'Albert' and 'Connie', but in an office in Prenzlauerberg) prior to his departure. They were set down as follows: first, and foremost, he was to work on recruitment with a view to winning agents (*operativer Personenhinweise in Richtung Agenturischer Mitarbeit*). Second, he was to select, develop and lead another category of agent, the 'persons of trust', to the East German cause. Third, he was to engage in secret military intelligence work himself, and to monitor the British order of battle. Fourth, he was to participate in other operations in London, as required, including safeguarding 'the security interests of the Centre'. Finally, he was to take every opportunity of increasing his understanding of the methods of work and the techniques employed by the British counter-espionage agencies. His annual salary was to be 1,177 Ostmarks, paid by the Stasi, plus 926.50 from 'the cover organisation' – that is, the East German Foreign Office – and a monthly allowance of 250.50 from the National People's Army. He would get an additional allowance of 75 Ostmarks per month for personal expenses, and an operational bonus of 75 Ostmarks per month over ten months each year.

We note that his Stasi salary was significantly higher than his Foreign Office one. This underlines, yet again, the priority given by East Germany to espionage. An order dated 27 January 1982 placed him on 'active service' in London. His tour of duty was to end in March 1986.[16]

The first 'quality evaluation' of Linser's duties took place on 3
March 1982. He was told by Colonel Koch that, as a new member of
the diplomatic community, he should expect MI5 to show most
interest in him at the start of his posting. A checklist was later
appended to this report which showed the 'Centre' was satisfied
that he was displaying the duties of a 'foreign officer', and had met
the requirements of practical work laid upon him, including those of
his cover function as East German consul.

His first tasks had been to analyse a British 'Foreign Office document' which had been 'acquired', to spy on journalists working for
the East German *Neues Deutschland* newspaper, and to learn how to
do the work of a consul. He was reminded of the basic needs of 'contact work': security, alertness and conspiracy. Finally, he was
indoctrinated into some special duties concerned with observation
techniques, and told how to construct a 'legend' for himself – the
Stasi term for an alibi – in case he was caught while on operational
duties.

The seriousness the Stasi attached to the security of their agents
can be demonstrated by the almost obsessional care with which
each possible MI5 observation was recorded and analysed by the
'Centre' (all were, in the event, discounted as 'contacts with British
counter-espionage').

From the moment he arrived in London, Linser kept a record of
what he feared might be MI5's surveillance of him. At the end of
December 1981 he believed a twenty-minute observation of the
East German Consulate had been conducted by men in a vehicle
parked in Belgrave Square. On 23 January two Jehovah's Witnesses
had tried to discuss religion with embassy officials (might they be
MI5 officers? he wondered). At a reception on 27 January at the
Bulgarian Embassy, Linser had been introduced to two men who
claimed to be police officers from Scotland Yard. The 'Centre' was
certain, however, that none of these incidents had anything to do
with MI5.

The 'Centre' took a slightly different view about three further
incidents in the period from June to October 1982. The first arose
when Linser reported that the East German Embassy had been
'observed' on two further occasions by men in a car, and that his West

German opposite number, the consul von Rohr, had invited him to a garden party. This was a very awkward invitation because von Rohr was a proper diplomat – as were, presumably, most of the other guests – but Linser was not. Might this be an attempt to 'out' him? The 'Centre' declared that it had to be assumed that MI5 was testing him to see if he was what he pretended to be. Their feeling was, they said, confirmed by further possible 'contacts' with MI5 the following year: in February, Linser and his wife were photographed outside their London home and 'British officials' had spoken to him during a visit to the docks at Hull and Flixborough.

Linser also said that he had been disturbed by an approach from an Austrian citizen who had offered material about Israel. He wondered if this might be a 'provocative act' – a pretend 'walk-in', set up by MI5 and designed to reveal his true professional duties. What the files reveal, but he did not, and could not, know was that this citizen, a woman, was none other than Helene Koblizek, Escher's prime contact. The 'Centre' merely told him to be careful; it did not reveal Koblizek's real status. It told him that it was possible MI5 was testing his cover as part of a general drive against the 'Socialist' embassies in London.

At the same time, the 'Centre' reflected on whether, if MI5 was being particularly active, Escher should not warn 'Ivo', another of his prime sources, about this. It was in connection with this sense of unease that the 'Centre' decided that, for the time being, the relationship with another British Stasi agent, code-named 'Barber', should be broken off. The reason was that the HVA had informed the 'Centre' that a third (unidentified) Stasi agent had warned them that 'Barber' had made certain 'verbal attacks' on the East German government. However, on 8 November 1982, the resident in London ruled that if this were so, there were no (which was underlined) security implications for the work of the military intelligence unit. 'Barber's' critical utterances were designed simply to conceal his closeness to the GDR from his colleagues in END, enhancing his own cover. There was, therefore, absolutely no evidence to suggest that 'Barber' was working to expose Linser.

The 'Centre' decided that this was the right time to indoctrinate Linser into the existence of two English agents, the 'person of trust' code-named 'Baldur', and the operation being conducted together with 'Isak'. The identities of these four agents of the East German military intelligence unit in London – 'Barber', 'Ivo', 'Baldur' and 'Isak' – remain secret, even though it is clear from the SIRA and secret intelligence digests that these four provided excellent material. By piecing together two different files, we know that 'Bill', mentioned elsewhere, and 'Baldur' were both journalists.[17] They were both to be used to gain secret intelligence because of the cover provided by their profession. One of them, most probably 'Barber', may also have been one of the HVA's sources. Thanks to German rules of grammar, we know that he was male, and that he and 'Freundin' (the peace movement spy whose case is discussed below) were not the same person.[18] About 'Isak' we know only that he had no systematic training as an agent but had been taught 'on the job', and that he seems to have spent some time working for an East German firm in East Germany.

Linser continued to make a note in the files of anything which might conceivably indicate that his cover and his true activities in London were being broached by MI5 or the CIA.[19] These notes reveal that he had yet another complicated issue to resolve. On 19 January 1984 the secret military intelligence unit was approached by a man calling himself Roger Gagnon, who turned up at the embassy and claimed that he worked for the United States Army in Britain. He seemed genuine and to have important technical material to offer the Stasi. But was he an authentic 'walk-in' – or an MI5/CIA stooge? It has not been possible to trace Gagnon to put these allegations to him.

In 1983 'Hoppe' (Bernd Knott) had been replaced by 'Helios' – whose real name was Oswald Schneidratus. Linser instructed Schneidratus to take up contact with Gagnon. Gagnon was taken to the consulate, within the embassy building, where he told Schneidratus that he was prepared to sell the East Germans five top secret documents on computers, including instructions on the building of a flight simulator, an electronic warfare subsystem and an operational flight trainer. He wanted £250 for these but, intriguingly, said that for more money (he did not specify a sum) more material would become available.

Schneidratus noted that Gagnon seemed very nervous. He told the East Germans that he had been stationed in West Germany until recently but was now living in Woodbridge, Suffolk. He added that on no account would he agree to a further meeting in Belgrave Square, and as a venue suggested Ipswich or Felixstowe instead – preferably the latter, proposing the King's Head pub there on the next day, 20 January, at eleven o'clock. As proof of 'good will', he said he was prepared to leave the material overnight for them to examine, without immediate payment: he knew that what he was offering was of value, and he was certain the Stasi would take up his invitation to buy more of it.

Ever conscious of the need for security, and trained to be obsessively suspicious, Linser weighed up the case carefully. As a general rule, neither the military spies nor HVA liked dealing with 'walk-ins' (the Stasi called them *Selbststeller*, or SS). A report by 'Operational Security' in East Berlin dated 25 May 1984, attached to an analysis supplied by a Colonel Marowski, dated 23 January 1984, had drawn the embassy's attention to the fact that, in the last quarter of 1983, all East German embassies in Western Europe and North America had been approached by supposed 'walk-ins'.[20] The HVA had discovered that almost all (but not every one) were members of the US Army. For this reason, the existence of the London volunteers had been put to Colonel Schramm of the HVA. The 'Centre' had decided that any volunteer should be deemed to represent a political risk and that, as a general rule, it should be assumed that such volunteers were working for either the CIA or MI5.

Linser was, probably like intelligence officers everywhere, thrown into a quandary. The fact that the American officer was very nervous, and did not wish to return to Belgrave Square, indicated that he might genuinely be a potential agent. But the fact that the material he offered was of special interest could indicate that behind Gagnon lay the hand of MI5 or the CIA (because they would know that, for the Stasi to get interested, something genuinely significant had to be put on the table). However, it might indicate simply that here was a disaffected officer, ready to betray his country, or NATO, who could end up providing valuable intelligence.

Linser decided to be cautious. He was running other contacts (as outlined below) and did not wish to be knocked off course by a possible MI5 or CIA counter-attack. He was also worried about Schneidratus's handling of the incident: several errors had, in his opinion, already been made. One of these was to lead Gagnon to his office, in an area designated as the consulate (which automatically linked the consul – Linser himself – to espionage); another was to try to persuade the officer to return to the embassy to collect his cash the next day, giving him a codeword to use at the time. Linser advised the 'Centre' to agree to ignore Gagnon (though not before carefully photocopying all the documents and sending them on to East Berlin). He believed it would be dangerous to go to the King's Head, and advised that, if the American returned, the HVA in London should be warned so that they could photograph him.

Meanwhile, two further 'walk-ins' offered themselves to the East German Embassy. On 31 January 1984 a letter was received at Belgrave Square from a 'J. Kohler', offering to spy for the East Germans. Then, on 17 February 1984, a man who said he was called 'Beutel' turned up at the embassy, offering intelligence. Neither Linser nor Schneidratus could form an opinion as to the reliability of either. Both appeared genuine – but were they?

The 'Centre' decided that the two, apparently discrete, approaches by Kohler and Beutel were probably too much of a good thing. Linser was instructed that it would not further the current duties of either men to accept any new agents for the time being. The 'Centre' ordered that the two were to be dealt with in the following way: they were asked to state their motives, to say whether they had visited any other Eastern bloc embassies, and to explain why they had visited that of the GDR. The slightest doubt about the veracity of any of their answers should, Linser's instructions continued, evoke three 'provocative' questions. The first was 'Who is your task master?', the second 'Why do you wish to compromise the Embassy of the German Democratic Republic?', and the third 'How will you feel when we pass this material to the British Foreign Secretary?' This, it was assumed, would be sufficient to make Kohler and Beutel realise they were wasting their time (and simultaneously be given a nasty fright should they be undercover reporters for the *Daily Mail*). It is worth stressing, however, that there was no reason to believe that either of them was not prepared to be a traitor.

Meanwhile, Roger Gagnon was getting even more nervous. On 8 March he returned to Belgrave Square. On being asked why he was approaching the East German Embassy, he replied that the other Eastern bloc embassies were 'too obvious' and therefore too dangerous. He complained bitterly that he had gone twice to the King's Head in Felixstowe but that no East German had turned up, and he insisted that, had he not been willing to do an honest deal with them, he would hardly have returned at such personal risk. Linser noted that Gagnon seemed genuinely deflated by this failure to meet him, and concluded 'our impression that this man is honest has been confirmed by his second visit to us'. But, as always, the 'Centre' was to make the final decision. It, too, was forming a favourable impression about Gagnon's 'honesty'. But it could not be certain. If it was decided to proceed with Gagnon, he was to be told that 'the firm for whom he wished to work was interested in his application'. However, the next meeting with him would take place in Austria and if he agreed to this, a second formal meeting (the word 'Treff' was used, from the German word *treffen*, to meet) should be arranged in a 'Socialist' state. Gagnon was also to be given £100 in cash as a token of thanks.

The 'Centre' instructed Linser to send 'Baldur', another English agent, to check out the Woodbridge address and see if he could enter Gagnon's home secretly. Once again, it gave precise instructions as to how this was to be done.[21]

'Baldur' was not, the 'Centre' ordered, to be told Gagnon's name or his precise address at this stage. He was to observe who went in and out of numbers five to seven Tennyson Close in Woodbridge. He was to find out whether it was close to any military 'objects' or to an airport, what the police in Woodbridge were like, how active they were, if there were any signs that particular houses were under observation. He was also to check out the amusement arcades in Felixstowe, to see if there were any flight simulation computers in any of them (the 'Centre' wanted to check that Gagnon's material was genuine) and generally to take photographs of the area. Linser was to run this operation, which was to be completed by 31 March and telegraphed to East Berlin by 1 April, and to devise a 'legend', or alibi, should 'Baldur' be stopped by anyone.

Regrettably, the file stops at this point. On balance, it seems likely that Gagnon went on to become an agent for a while. Had he been positively identified as a stooge or been discarded, this would probably have been minuted.

The May 1984 security report which the 'Centre' compiled also gave interesting details about the work of the military intelligence unit to date. It is clear that the 'Centre' was not displeased with Linser's work. So far, the report stated, in addition to the work on the British peace movement, 'relatively good results had been achieved in the collection of data' on military matters, and materials had been gained 'without exposing the comrades [in the unit] to an irresponsibly high degree of risk'. So far agents had not been used for this area of activity, it was noted.

The military intelligence espionage was currently being conducted on three 'objects', or targets, the report said. The first of these was the 'NATO-supreme command Channel'.[22]

The East German spies, we learn, visited Northwood, home to the UK NATO command, 'once a week, but twice daily during all exercises and manoeuvres'. Both Linser and Schneidratus were involved in this work. We may safely assume that this espionage consisted of straightforward observation – spying at its most simple: the East Germans would have either rented a room near the headquarters (a likely step), or simply parked their car somewhere and sat on a bench with a tape recorder and a camera (which might have been a touch chilly). Their task would have been to identify every visitor, especially those not in British uniform, and possibly, if their room or car were close enough, to try to pick up a wireless signal. What was so vital in such work was the detail: it was the detailed analysis of hardware and personnel that could do much to enhance intelligence obtained by other means or actually discover facts that other sorts of intelligence had failed to uncover. As Wolf had rightly pointed out, if you wanted military intelligence, you needed military officers to supply it. Only they could tell what it was that they were seeing.[23]

The 'Centre's' 1984 report outlined other apparent problems with the security of the military intelligence unit in London. Gagnon's first approach to Belgrave Square could, in the view of the HVA (which, it will be recalled, had overall control of all military intelligence affairs in London) have been spotted by MI5. The HVA had formally concluded, the report stated, that 'there was a high possibility of hostile observation' from cars parked in Belgrave Square, from what the HVA believed (with some authority) was an MI5 outstation in the Norwegian Embassy, from the observation point disguised as a flower stall (it was perfectly true that there was – and still is – a flower stall standing somewhat incongruously at the corner of Belgrave Square which looked on to the East German Embassy) and from a damaged vehicle which was attracting the attention of what appeared to be Metropolitan Police special protection officers. Finally, the HVA believed they had detected signs of special police interest in their Hendon apartment complex, and, during the night of 24–25 January 1984, there had been a suspicious break-in at the embassy. Property had been stolen (none of it secret) and some fine furniture destroyed, but there was a possibility that this implied something untoward in respect of security (although MI5's hand was not seen in this break-in, not least because the Stasi always believed that, were it involved in any break-in, MI5 would not leave behind evidence of entry).

There was also a personnel problem, the 'Centre' noted, concerned with Schneidratus: he had been implicated in the Gagnon business, thanks to a potential error made by Linser, who had asked him to meet Gagnon, establishing a secret link between the consul, Linser, and an embassy official. Were Gagnon to prove to be a Western agent, this would be a major blow. What made this worse was that Schneidratus's previous post, working for the UN in Cyprus, might have aroused British counter-intelligence interest in him and there was a fear that his Cypriot secretary might have been in the pay of British intelligence.

In order to ensure security as far as possible, the 'Centre' advised that extreme care should be taken with the location of the special radio equipment that was used to transmit information from London to East Berlin. This equipment consisted of what looked like ordinary radios (we learn that one looked like a 'Braun', one a

'Teleton', one a 'Satellit') but all included a device, known as a 'burst transmission unit', which allowed encrypted messages to be transmitted at high speed using short waves. Encoding devices, and the 'containers' in which they were hidden, were also issued to the two officers. All were kept in the officers' homes. Were they to be noticed, of course, the radios would arouse suspicion straight away because, the 'Centre' suggested, the British authorities would wonder why East German rather than British radios were being used. Close examination would reveal their secret and this would then disclose the true activities of their owners.

However, it should be noted that all this merely displayed the extreme level of caution (which some might regard – quite wrongly – as verging on the pathological) that was the Stasi's hallmark. In fact, these fears were certainly obsessive but they were not pathological. The obsession with security was a core Stasi strength. If the Stasi wanted its intelligence to be very good, its officers had to take the greatest care. There is no reason to believe that any other intelligence agency would not have proceeded along precisely the same lines. In the event, all the problems were listed by the 'Centre' as potential, rather than actual blows, and – as far as we can tell – this is what they remained, since none of them led to the discovery of any of the East Germans.

All was not gloom, however, because, as the report described, in May 1984 the unit had gained a new talent spotter and go-between who had been successfully 'taken into our network'. In addition, the report stated, there was one courier who would be active by August 1984 and one contact to an unnamed and unidentified source used by the embassy. In May 1984 the two officers had ten operations on the go, five to be developed, and three 'to be taken into the net'. Yet this success suggested to the ever anxious 'Centre' a possible over-stretching of the officers' time. Running too many cases (eighteen was seen as too many) might cause them to drop their guard in some way, or to fail to gain the maximum return from the Stasi's investment in them.

The 1984 security report came to the firm conclusion that 'no acute danger exists for our comrades in London'. As a consequence, there was 'no need to hem in their work in any way', but they did 'need to be ever more watchful, especially in the preparation and execution of agent tasking', particularly where potential agents were being 'observed and recruited'. Intriguingly, the report suggested that the two officers should look for wholly plausible legitimate reasons for working with their agents – perhaps by staging formal events together with them. To do so would provide a good 'cover' and conceal the other sort of secret activity – which the 'Centre' wanted, at all costs, to keep from MI5.

# 9

# The Military Intelligence Unit
# in London, 1984–90

By the early autumn of 1984 the Stasi's military intelligence operations in London seemed to be coming along very nicely. The focus
on particular areas of British political and strategic affairs was
paying dividends: Linser was doing well and the 'Centre' was happy.
Then, in the early hours of 4 October 1984, an urgent message was
flashed from London to East Berlin. It looked likely to knock everything pear-shaped. At half past midnight on that date, Linser's car –
a Mazda, travelling at high speed – had mounted the pavement
on the North Circular Road and then bounced at full force into a
lamp-post. Linser, by then thirty years old, was killed immediately.
The Metropolitan Police informed the embassy about the fatal
accident at half past one in the morning.[1]

This was bad enough – especially of course for Linser's family –
but far worse was to follow, as the 'Centre' was quickly to discover.
By daybreak, the London unit was already working flat out trying to
avoid a potential catastrophe. Totally by chance, the Met might
have got their hands on an East German spy. The first question
from the 'Centre' that morning was whether Linser had been on
operational duties at the time of his death and whether he was trans-
porting anything that might indicate that he was rather more than
the East German consul the Foreign Office believed him to be, and
which might allow his agents or his secret work to be spotted by an
alert counter-intelligence service. There was another question, but

it was not asked, demonstrating that the 'Centre' knew it could rely on its professionals: despite his known fondness for beer, Linser had not been under the influence of alcohol when the crash occurred.

The police brought some of his effects round to Belgrave Square on 5 October and the news now relayed to East Berlin was not at all good. The Met had found Linser's diary and had been in possession of it for one and a half hours. But, as the HVA resident in London now telegraphed to the 'Centre', it was still not clear whether those hours had been used to good purpose. The accident had occurred in the middle of the night, and the police had no reason to believe that Linser was anything other than the East German consul and so they might not have examined the diary in any detail. Much depended on how alert one could expect the traffic police to have been.

Later that same day, the 'Centre' was informed that London could now unfortunately confirm that Linser's diary had contained a number of highly significant 'operational' notes, all of which would be prime leads if MI5 or Special Branch were minded to investigate them. They included the following: a codename, 'Günther'; a Berlin telephone number (541 0891), as well as a private phone number set down by Linser as belonging to the 'FO person who was about to become operational in the UK in October', although this had been listed under 'Lon' (for London) rather than under the name of the person herself (the use of the feminine form of the German definite article shows that this person was indeed a woman). Even the proverbial 'Inspector Knacker', *Private Eye*'s fictional police hero, would have had little difficulty unravelling the identity of this individual since all he had to do was ring the number and find out who answered. However, it would not necessarily imply to MI5 what the HVA knew, namely that this was an East German *agent*. But it was a definite clue and there was no getting round that.

What made it worse was that 'FO' – written in this way – would be taken by MI5 to mean either Foreign Office or hostile target (*Feindobjekt*). It was perfectly true that 'FO' was also Stasi shorthand for *Führungsoffizier* (supervising officer), and only the context in which it was used would make it clear what had been intended, although an officer would never be referred to as a 'supervising officer person'. This means that it was just about conceivable that MI5, were it to get hold of this, would quickly come to the conclusion that Linser's scribble referred to an agent in the Foreign Office, or possibly (but less grammatically), one in the 'hostile target'. In fact, as the Stasi would have worked out, both letters, however they might have appeared, made the same point: whether in the Foreign Office or in a 'hostile object' (which could denote the Foreign Office or any British government institution) the East Germans were proposing to run a spy, to become operational at precisely this moment. 'Günther', they thought, was not a problem: this could be the first name of someone called 'Schmidt' (and thus presumably a German) although his phone number was 'clearly incorrect' (the HVA had obviously dialled it).

The diary also contained the real name of an individual (alas not identified in this report), whom the HVA knew was the Stasi's agent 'Palme', although there was nothing to indicate this. Then, tucked away among other scribblings, the HVA found the real name of an East German 'co-opted worker' with whom Linser could not credibly have had contact in his legal capacity as consul, but whom he could perfectly plausibly have known as a personal friend from the friend's 'East German stay' and who was now back in London. The diary also contained dates of meetings with individuals, some of which relied on Linser being the consul, but some also upon his being the military intelligence resident.

Scotland Yard or MI5, it was thought, would soon work this out if they thought to do so. The diary contained the home phone number and central London address of 'Isak' (but not his name or codename). There were diary entries for meetings with 'Baldur', 'Aktion' and 'Akzent' using their real names (again not set down here), and with someone called McMillan (sic). The HVA resident said that each of the individuals could (the word was stressed in the original) have a legitimate cover for dealing with Linser in his capacity as East German consul, and it might therefore be assumed that their real names were all known to British counter-intelligence as those of individuals in touch with the East German consul for professional reasons. (We know, however, that their importance to the Stasi was as *agents* because the HVA resident spoke of their plausible 'cover function', implying that this was in fact a cover, and not the real nature of their relationship with Linser.)

Finally, there was a note against the previous day – 4 October 1984 – the day of the accident. It said simply, 'Derek, 1800, Residency'. The appearance of the word 'Residency' was, the HVA believed, catastrophic, even though no one could have any knowledge of 'Derek', whether this was a real name or a codename, or what the 'Treff' was about. The British authorities, it was assumed, would see that the use of the word 'Residency' would betray Linser's true role, although it was also true that in English 'residency' could simply mean the ambassador's residence.

The good news, the 'Centre' was told (optimistically), was that, on hearing of the accident, Schneidratus had immediately gone to Belgrave Square, collected all Linser's 'operational documents, and materials, including his encoding and decoding equipment', and locked them away in the residency safe.

The 'Centre' wired back its initial instructions. This was to be regarded as an emergency and help was to be brought in; for the time being, however, it was not to be regarded as a real danger to the unit. Media coverage of the incident indicated that a fatal accident had occurred but there was no interpretation of Linser's duties. This was a positive sign. Even so, East Berlin suggested a number of next steps. The HVA resident should not make any contact whatsoever with any of Linser's contacts in the 'operational area'; he ought, however, to call 'Rave', who was to be informed of Linser's death and the possible consequences for him. All operational contacts with 'Palme', the 'Centre' went on, were to be dropped at once, even though in the past these contacts had had a perfectly acceptable cover (or 'legend') as being 'official contacts of the embassy' with him in his professional role. We do not know who 'Palme' and 'Rave' were, nor why 'Palme's' professional duties enabled him to have legitimate cover for having contact with the East German Embassy: his name does not show up in any other file nor in any of the SIRA material or any other list. Since military spies' intelligence does not seem to have been sourced under their cover-names, it is quite possible that material supplied by 'Palme', and indeed 'Rave', may be listed under one of the cover-names to be examined later.

The HVA's London resident, who had, as we have seen, the formal duty of protecting the security of the military intelligence unit, immediately took steps to discover who 'Derek' might be, to warn him if necessary, and to find out the consequences for the embassy should MI5 decide to pursue him. A minute in Linser's files in Belgrave Square reveals that 'Derek' was in fact one Derek Furze, a forty-year-old journalist, and that from 1972 to 1975 he had studied politics at Southampton University and from 1975 to 1978 at Durham. He was a bachelor who liked to travel and was happy to undertake commissions for research on political subjects. The HVA resident had said that Linser had claimed 'Furze would do anything for money, and is of a left-wing persuasion'. Linser had believed he could be recruited for the Stasi, hence this 'Treff', which would have been the *second* one.

On the other hand, the HVA noted, Furze's meeting with Linser could very plausibly have been in connection with his cover as consul (even though the Stasi files make it clear that Linser wanted Furze for '*our* purposes as well as for the cover ones'). Linser's widow had, in the meantime, confirmed that her husband had promised to be home by eight on the 4th, because he had a meeting in a pub that evening. The HVA had discovered a further name in Linser's diary, the resident added, that of another 'Treff' partner who, if worked on, and if the person behaved incorrectly, could be identified as a member of the US Army. Finally, the resident said, the Foreign Office had sent its regrets and the police had confirmed what no East German had even considered – that there was no alcohol in Linser's blood (despite the 'Treff' in the pub).

The 'Centre' ordered all contact with 'Isak' and his wife to be halted for the time being. As for Furze, the 'Centre' instructed the HVA to execute another 'Treff'; this was one the HVA did not want to get away.

Who any of these individuals were, or are, is not known. Efforts to trace Derek Furze (who possibly had absolutely no idea of the nature of the interest in him displayed by the East German secret military intelligence unit) have so far drawn a blank. Who McMillan might be is also impossible to say. There was someone called Hamilton McMillan (spelled this way) who had an intelligence interest, although the 'Centre' believed that there was probably a legitimate explanation for any of the names that MI5 might have found, and contact between Linser and McMillan would have come into that category.[2] There is no reason to suspect that McMillan – whoever he was – had acted in any way against the national interest. However, even though the follow-up files have been destroyed, it is clear that MI5 does not seem to have put two and two together. Indeed, there is no evidence that MI5 ever got hold of Linser's diary. Sources close to the Security Service seemed genuinely unaware of this entire incident.[3]

This can be seen from a further surviving document which outlines the activities of the military intelligence unit in 1986 and 1987.[4] This report began with a note on MI5 which said that a tactic it appeared to enjoy was 'provocation'. This was directed at all the Socialist embassies, not just the GDR's, but it had led to pressure being applied to 34 Belgrave Square. Staff believed their telephones were being tapped and their post opened, and there was also evidence of increasing cooperation between all Western security services. The various terrorist attacks in London had been exploited by MI5, which was now clearly engaged in what the East Germans rather quaintly (and singularly lacking in self-awareness) liked to term 'criminal and illegal acts' against them, which included stealing their passports and breaking into their cars. (We cannot know if MI5, whose sources tittered at the suggestion, or simply London street crime was really to blame for this.) There were also more stories in the newspapers about spying by Communist agents, and more and more they were finding that their 'contact partners' were subject to questioning. Letters sent by courier increasingly had a habit of disappearing, diplomatic immunity was being ignored and parking 'transgressions' were being treated more aggressively than usual.

The military intelligence unit in London deduced that all this was as a result of a new security policy of trying to make spying more difficult. Its political context, they assumed, was the rhetoric of 'opposition to détente', in which they believed both Thatcher and Reagan were indulging too heavily. However, the London officers insisted, 'wide sections of the British public, forces in CND and the

Labour Party' did support the Soviet peace proposals. This was making it politically harder for MI5 to target just the Soviet Embassy, and perhaps MI5 would start looking more closely at 34 Belgrave Square. They concluded that there were now more concrete factors militating against their work. As a result, greater emphasis than ever would have to be placed on the individual members of the residency 'in developing new cover functions' and continuing to build a 'differentiated circle of contacts'.

The London officers believed that 'the importance of penetrating the military-political and political centres of decision making in the enemy's institutions' was gaining in significance all the time (a belief examined from another perspective in Chapter 13, dealing with the 'round table' plan). They were pleased to report that they had executed the comparative studies required by the 'Centre' (we do not know what these were) and had fulfilled all tasks set to uncover the 'structures of the HO' – this time spelled without a full stop after the 'H', and so meaning *Hauptobjekt*, or main object. This almost certainly designated the Ministry of Defence, though it could have meant MI5 and possibly the Home Office. They were proud that there now existed 'an agent in the HO' (possibly the woman alluded to above), albeit one who could supply only a 'PHW', 'due to the limited possibilities that presented themselves'. It is not clear what a 'PHW' might be, but it is fair to assume it was not what, ideally, they may have wanted, since they added that 'conspiratorial infiltration' of the HO was something 'still too complicated to achieve'. It seems likely that 'PHW' stands for *Personenhinweis*, that is to say a who's who of the institution in question. Thus the unit would appear to be saying that it had a personal contact, or a source within the Ministry of Defence who possessed an internal telephone directory – very useful, but hardly earth-shattering.

However, the officers continued, their work against the Greenham Common and Molesworth observation points (Cruise missile sites) was wholly successful, thanks to the help of 'volunteer observers' recruited on site – that is to say English volunteers. Equally, the unit had created the preconditions for the successful 'conspiratorial infiltration' of the NATO 'Okdo' channel command at Northwood, which, however, were awaiting an unspecified event before proceeding.

Finally, the unit stated that its suggestions for new operations against 'new targets of military and military-political significance' would be forwarded separately. Sadly, the file which contains them has so far not been located.

In January 1986 the London office reported that the 'operational position' had become more complicated. Margaret Thatcher's government, they said, had slipped into crisis as a result of the Westland Affair (analysed in some detail), causing her, they claimed, to order a tightening of national security. The East Germans, however, believed that MI5 was still not on to them, despite a number of possible attempts to break their cover. They were discomforted, however, by an increase in the number of parking tickets issued, which were then, allegedly, used to threaten fellow Socialist 'legalists': the Hungarians, for example, had been told that unless they paid their fines four of them would be expelled. No similar threat, they reported, had been made to the East Germans.

In the Stasi files we find two new problems which the HVA thought might endanger the security of the military spies.[5] The first (something to which they returned in due course) had to do with a serious, if understandable, error committed by 'Helios', Dr Oswald Schneidratus. In his legal capacity as an arms-control expert, he had been invited by his American counterpart to a meeting on 28 January 1986 to discuss arms issues. Absentmindedly, he had left his briefcase at the meeting. Was this Linser's diary all over again? the embassy wondered. The 'Centre' was informed about this on 17 February 1986. It telegraphed back at once to ask whether there were incriminating documents in the briefcase (Schneidratus said there were none), and whether it was an 'ordinary' briefcase or had a secret container (it had none). However, Schneidratus had then made a second mistake: he had asked his wife to slip over to the embassy to retrieve the briefcase. The 'Centre' reasoned that the Americans would ask themselves why he had not asked an embassy official to collect it, and might deduce that Schneidratus had not wanted to tell the embassy about the incident. This, in turn, might cause them to feel that there was indeed something odd about the East German diplomat, and might prompt them to get to know him a little better or even to try blackmail if a dereliction of duties existed.

Suspicious as ever, the 'Centre' decided that Schneidratus needed prodding. He was asked why he had detailed his wife to fetch the case, and if there was really nothing in it which might be embarrassing. Schneidratus insisted that, as the briefcase was his personal property, and did not belong to the office, it made sense to ask his wife to retrieve it. He told East Berlin that he had now had a chance to look through all the papers in it and there was nothing that could have alerted the Americans to his true role, since what they would have found could just as easily have related to his 'legal' duties.

The 'Centre', smelling blood, demanded a detailed account of the contents of these 'papers'. There was, it was told, a cutting from the *Sunday Times* dated 23 June 1985. There was no problem about this. But it was not at all pleased when Schneidratus admitted that the Americans must have found an old slip of paper with a note of a lecture he had given to the Doncaster CND group on 26 March 1985, almost a year earlier, and a name, address and telephone number of a contact. Although Schneidratus could read his own writing (the name was 'B. Marshall') he doubted whether the Americans would have been able to do so.

Although none of this indicated activities incompatible with his proper duties, it might cause more questions to be asked. Perhaps the worst clue to what he was really doing in the UK came from another note. It had been written, but not sent, to a 'contact' of his called Bill Bowring, a London borough of Lambeth councillor at the time (not to be confused with the 'Bill' listed as an agent in the previous chapter). The 'Centre' concluded that no direct danger existed, but that indirectly clues had been provided which could reveal the identity of an agent (in the English sense) called 'Basalt', since 'Basalt' had fixed the invitation to Doncaster's CND group. This link might be confirmed if the Americans were able to decipher B. Marshall's name, since he was one of the CND organisers. We do not know the identity of 'Basalt', but it is possible that this was the codename that the military espionage unit assigned to Professor Vic Allen of Leeds University, one of the Stasi's CND sources. (Both military intelligence and the HVA spied on the UK peace movement.) The 'Centre' determined to take a longer and harder look at Schneidratus and his future in military intelligence.

On 8 August 1986 the security in the embassy was tightened following the receipt of what were regarded as 'threatening letters'.[6] One was headed 'Twenty-Five Years of the Wall', and the other contained a report of planned 'hostile acts against the residency'. In the meantime, East Berlin was obliged to address a second problem. Another walk-in had turned up. On 22 September 1986 a courier arrived in Belgrave Square with an urgent letter. Krebs/'Hammer' was out, and his wife accepted it on his behalf. It read as follows:

*Sehr geehrte Herrn!* [sic], I wish to offer my services to the people of the DDR [sic]. This after deep and careful thought. Being British, white, divorced, and having access to many interesting institutions, I think I could be of great benefit to your good selves. Knowing of no other way of contacting you (other than flying to Tempelhof and taking the S-Bahn to Ost Berlin [sic]), I had this delivered to you by minicab. I watched it being delivered. If you are interested in my offer, please follow these instructions:

A. On Sunday 28 September at precisely 1300 a man from your office is to be at the bar of the Grosvenor Hotel, Victoria, and order a Pernod with water.

B. At precisely 1315 he is to leave the bar and walk to the hotel's toilets. Here there is a telephone on the wall. On the right of the board a small lip of a card will be just visible. On it will be the time and place of the rendezvous. I am taking these initial precautions as I have no desire to be detained by the Queen, please.

Signed: Onyx.

The Stasi was getting increasingly bored with walk-ins. It recorded 'Onyx's' letter but did not consider for a moment going anywhere near the Grosvenor Hotel to liaise with him.

The dossier on Dr Oswald Schneidratus into which the HVA now fed his errors makes grim, if interesting, reading.[7] It illustrates yet again the relentlessness with which the HVA monitored its agents in order to exact the very best results from them, and also the career path of a highly ambitious and skilled operative. Schneidratus/'Helios' had been born in February 1941 and lived in Ohm Krüger Strasse in Berlin. He had joined the SED in 1969 at the age of twenty-eight, and had originally been recruited into HA I – the Stasi division which spied on Western forces and on NATO targets. He ended his career (in 1990) in HA II, that is to say as a counter-intelligence officer in the division which had special duties working with (and protecting) top Stasi Western spies and seeking to counter British intelligence efforts to uncover Stasi spy networks.

Despite his being an excellent spy, the 'Centre' formed the opinion (partly because of the mistakes he had made) that Schneidratus would never make a prime intelligence officer. Although the 'Centre' minuted in his personal file that he 'always passed on all relevant political operational materials', it believed that ultimately he wanted to end up as a proper ambassador rather than a spy. This, his report insisted, had meant that 'in his activities as an intelligence officer [*Aufklärungsoffizier*] there had sometimes been a discrepancy between the objective opportunities open to him and the intelligence he had extracted'. He had a tendency, it said, to put himself 'in the centre of things', and that sometimes meant a penalty had to be paid when it came to gleaning information. According to his successor, 'Harke' – or Jörg Döring – he had also made his military interests too obvious. Although his 'cover function' allowed him to demonstrate a reasonable knowledge of NATO, he had once referred to himself as a 'military expert'. Döring/'Harke' believed that this had been unwise, although his security had not been breached.

On 24 October 1985, a minute on Schneidratus's file recorded that his name may have been on the list of contacts of Oleg Gordievksy, 'of the First Main Directorate'. Gordievsky had been in the UK since June 1982, 'becoming a traitor in August 1985', the minute continued, and his 'operational cadre plan' had included contact with East German military intelligence. Accordingly, the HVA produced a 'Gordievsky action plan, involving cadres' dated 23 September 1985 (unfortunately, its actual contents have been destroyed).

It was possibly in connection with Gordievsky's defection, the file continued, that Schneidratus's car had been broken into in London, and the Met had taken fingerprints from it, including Schneidratus's. The Stasi thought that MI5 itself might have been responsible for the break-in so as to get a set of Schneidratus's prints. In 1987 his parents had come to visit him in London. This sort of thing was not normally permitted, and the fact that it did happen might, the Stasi believed, have alerted MI5 to the idea that Schneidratus was in some way 'special' (there is, however, absolutely no evidence that this was considered). Overall, however, Schneidratus had done excellent work, and there was no reason to believe that anyone suspected he was anything other than a bona fide East German diplomat. As far as we can tell, he left London in 1987 with his cover fully intact. As we shall see from the chapter which explores the Stasi's assets (see Chapter 14), no one who came across him in the public world which he was paid to penetrate and subvert said that they had had any idea of his real purpose in London.

A few weeks before Schneidratus left, in February 1987, the embassy received its very first bomb threat, from an organisation calling itself the 'Homosexual Liberation Front'. There was considerable puzzlement as to why the East Germans should be a target as it was not an issue on which they had any line. The police were informed, but no bombing ensued.

Schneidratus's luck ultimately ran out – but only after he had left the UK, and not because of any possible contact with Gordievsky. On 3 August 1988 Colonel Augustin of the HVA added a supplementary note to his file saying that there was now a suspicion that MI5 had recognised that Schneidratus might be a member of a hostile intelligence agency and had been placed on the 'NATO list' as such. Another note, dated 14 September, from an IM, stated that he now possessed only a limited personal attachment to military intelligence and recommended that he be transferred to the Foreign Ministry proper. This was agreed, and in February 1989, at the behest of HA I Schneidratus joined the GDR delegation to the Vienna disarmament talks on conventional weapons.

Schneidratus/'Helios' was replaced by one of the Stasi's most impressive high-flyers, Jörg Döring ('Harke'). In 1985 Friedbert Krebs, code-named 'Hammer', had taken over from Stefan Wetzel ('Hecht') as the junior in the unit, and 'Harke' and 'Hammer' formed a formidable duo. Under Döring and Krebs, military espionage in London reached new heights of success. Both men were canny operators. In particular, they understood that the British government had become increasingly obsessed with its secret institutions, but in a bizarre way which allowed spies ever greater freedom to operate. The Spycatcher Affair had encouraged the British Cabinet to regard its own intelligence community as constituting as much, if not more, of a potential threat to Britain's security than the activities of hostile spying agencies.

The element of farce in this – which the military spies understood, and none better than Döring, who played every ball he was thrown for all it was worth – meant that the heat was no longer on them, and it became more easy than ever for them to use their cover functions to gain the secrets that they wanted. They worked out that significant numbers of the British political class would begin to regard intelligence and security activities as something of a joke. If Britain could not trust its own spies, the argument went, the point of MI5 and MI6 might be queried to the Stasi's gain.

Döring's file shows that before coming to London his code-name was 'Louis' and before that 'Jochen Ducke'. Interestingly, he had completed a course in political science, gaining a 'diploma in foreign affairs', before being inducted into military intelligence. Like all the other military intelligence officers, however, he was subordinate in every way to the HVA – in his case, HVA I's security group. From 1982 until 1986 he had served in Paris as head of the military intelligence residency. In June 1986, after he had completed his tour of duty, the French security service, the DST, appeared to show a special interest in him and tried to recruit him. Because of this, there was a possibility – as noted on his file – that another Western intelligence service might try to track him in London.[8] He was recruited for the London job on 11 March 1987 in the Stasi safe house in Berlin known as 'Albert'. The plan for this, outlined here, said he should first be told of the cases of 'Kröte' and 'Baron', colleagues who had been recently targeted by an (unnamed) 'imperialist secret service' and warned 'how disastrous it would be for the GDR if the enemy' were to discover that 'certain officials in the embassy were in fact intelligence officers' – the reason being that 'light-headed espionage' would undermine the credibility of 'the GDR's efforts to promote détente'.

By May 1988 he was considered to have successfully completed his training in the following fields:

1. Recognising intelligence attacks and using counter-intelligence methods against them
2. Recognising weak points in the Stasi structure which might invite an attack by the enemy
3. Analysis of indications of operationally significant behaviour
4. Recognition of propitious conditions for possible espionage activity
5. Analysis of information on the activities of hostile intelligence and counter-intelligence services
6. How to behave if confronted by hostile intelligence services.[9]

Two other documents offer yet another slant on the importance of the London residency through their details of two further OibEs arriving in London.[10] OibEs, it will be recalled, were officers on special duties with special sorts of training. The first of the new arrivals was 'Clarus', or Dieter Rost, registration number XV 7214/81, and the second was 'Waldner', or Ulrich Köster. Rost's file, dated 8 May 1989, states that he was an 'OibE', in Britain as part of an exchange programme within the Stasi. His duties were to replace Chief Lieutenant Riesner as head of the London radio station (*Leitung der Funkstelle London*). A 'Wolfgang Riesner' is recorded in the London Diplomatic Lists, not as a diplomat, but simply as an 'administrative assistant'; he was in London before July 1987.

Rost's work, we learn, was to consist of maintaining communications between the embassy in London and the Centre of Department N-X/1 'under all circumstances'. He was also to assume responsibility for the 'telephone technology' installed in the embassy and the Trade Division. The regulations governing his work stemmed, we are told, from an agreement made between the Ministry for State Security and the (East German) Foreign Office. As such, Rost was to execute duties for Department VIII of the HVA, making him an OibE for HVA III.

Köster/'Waldner', on the other hand, was a top Stasi telephone security officer. He had previously worked in 'K' in Oslo, and 'S' in Milan (we do not know what these letters stand for) but had also been on active service in New York. He had been responsible for setting up the 'distance observation technology' (*Fernbeobachtungstechnik*) in the Washington residency. He was sent to London from March to July 1989, testing the 'distance observation technology' installed at 34 Belgrave Square.

## The Final Period

The final period in the life of the military intelligence unit in London was hallmarked by an operation already underway by 1988 (it is examined in the following chapter) and a bizarre story of what was wrongly viewed by the military spies as a turf war between themselves and the HVA.

As luck would have it, the military spies were getting better and better as East Germany was running out of steam, and Döring was undoubtedly their most skilled operator. On 10 November 1988 the 'Centre' informed Döring that a new opportunity for recruitment in London had arisen. A new agent, or informal collaborator, called 'Distel' had been successfully transferred to the UK.[11] She was an East German citizen who had married a British citizen working in the GDR, and had three children. The 'Centre' had instructed her to work as a talent spotter and to act as a link between the intelligence unit and possible contacts. Cross-referencing shows that 'Distel's' real name was Barbara Walters.[12] She was highly rated: for this reason she was to be allowed to 'rest' until 1990. She was then to be approached via an agent rather than by any London officer and told to send the 'Centre' a letter addressed to the Ministry for Higher Education and Training in Berlin. It was, however, to be forwarded via the East German consul (who would, though she did not know this, be her supervising officer). In this way, the contact between the embassy and Barbara Walters/'Distel' would be established without an officer from Belgrave Square having to seek her out.

On precisely the same day Krebs/'Hammer' had an interview with his supervising officer in East Berlin. He said that Döring/'Harke' wished to report the latest in a series of security alarms. He had noticed that his office had been searched for a second time; on the first occasion, he had come across a ballpoint pen which had obviously been left behind by the intruder. Three weeks earlier he had noticed that he was being observed by someone outside his flat, and that the individual had taken notes. Other East Germans were housed in the same apartment block, however, and he could not be sure that he was the target. He did not believe this had anything to do with MI5, rather with an HVA operation being conducted from outside the embassy by the new HVA resident, Siegfried Reichel, who had arrived in the autumn of 1988, replacing explosives expert Erich Schwager. Reichel believed that Döring and Krebs were working too closely together and thwarting the HVA's attempts to investigate this. Döring and Krebs, however, did not know that Reichel was not acting off his own bat but was following the HVA's instructions.

The 'Centre' was not best pleased to hear from its London officers that they believed a turf war (common in all secret services) had broken out between the HVA proper and the military intelligence staff. It had already been decided that the post of consul would be removed from military intelligence in 1990. The 'Centre' suggested a new agreement between HVA III and itself to avoid unpleasantness in the future and to ensure that the 'high demands on himself' made by Döring were properly supported by the HVA resident, Reichel. Reichel, the 'Centre' noted, had twice placed Döring/'Harke' at risk and 'took every opportunity to pick on him'. Krebs/'Hammer' had tried to calm things down but believed that Döring was right and Reichel wrong.

Tension had increased in the residency thanks to what Döring believed were MI5 attempts to break his cover involving his young daughter. Krebs informed the 'Centre' that, during the absence of her parents, their daughter (aged five) was telephoned three times and asked, in German, if she was alone, where her parents were, and the work they would be doing. Three policemen subsequently called at the flat and informed the embassy that a child was alone in it. The 'Centre' did not know who had called the police, nor why three policemen should then have gone round. Döring's daughter had been perfectly happy by herself, Krebs had stated. When her parents reappeared, she asked them what all the fuss had been about, and why people had been phoning her and shouting at her through the letterbox. In addition, Döring's car had been vandalised yet again. Krebs believed that 'in the present political circumstances, sympathy for perestroika in the USSR, GDR as a state is not going fully in this direction', a focused attack by MI5 on the embassy might have been viewed by the Home Office as appropriate. Both he and Döring were working to ensure that any MI5 operations would fail to notice them and their agents.

The 'Centre' was not certain that MI5's hand could be detected in any of these incidents, but it ordered a high level of alertness in its officers' surveillance of objects. Krebs told the 'Centre' that the London officers did not always share the evaluations made of their work in East Berlin. He was told that this was understood, but intelligence work was always concerned with the evaluation of the facts obtained, and not the methods used to extract them. Notwithstanding any of this, the supervising officer in East Berlin congratulated both men once again on the excellence of their achievements in London in 1988–9, which were said to be entirely first-rate. At this 'Treff', Krebs agreed to continue to serve in London until June 1990. After this, he was told, he would be sent to Paris. In view of the loss of the consul's post, the residency would have to be reorganised in any case, but the 'Centre' promised that the new ambassador, Joachim Mitdank, would be much more amenable to military espionage than his predecessor, Lindner.

A meeting took place in East Berlin on 8 December 1988 to review the various security issues that had arisen as a result of the turf war. Those present included Wesser, Mewis (the head of Section IX), Zillmann, and Section III, represented by Gäbler and Thalheim. As to reports of an increase in car break-ins, the HVA concluded that there had indeed been an increase, but, contrary to Döring's views, there were no clear indications that the British secret services lay behind them. Döring's fears, they said, were 'purely speculative'. The 'Centre' discounted his belief that over the past few years MI5 had been monitoring them. Section IX confirmed that there was no reason to believe MI5 had become aware of 'Harke's' work and they also shared the view that UK 'military counter-intelligence' were equally ignorant of the activities of the *Kewa* – the Stasi cell – in the UK. Firmly, the 'Centre' said that even if MI5 had been monitoring, neither Döring nor Krebs would have got to know about it, given the fact that they were known to be the masters of technological surveillance. In short, the Berlin meeting of 8 December 1988 concluded that 'the overall conditions' in the London residency were 'good' – and the intelligence generated first-rate. Section IX of the Stasi, who also had counter-espionage duties, it was minuted, added that they too believed there was no evidence that MI5 had become aware of Döring's operations, and it was said that they shared the view that no other UK military counter-espionage personnel were aware of the activities of the two military spies in Britain. This verdict was formally confirmed on 27 January by General Gäbler. Noting that Section IX had been required to look into 'Harke's' 1987 fears that MI5 might have been on to him, he recorded that this had been rejected out of hand, a verdict he shared. He wrote that 'Harke's work is of a very high quality and contains no security risks'.[13]

In a paper headed 'The Development of the Situation in Respect of Our Agents', dated 15 April 1989, Döring attested that there had been 'no major change in the situation of our agents. As before, the whole situation facing our agents, both for their operational work, and for the residency and also for its impact on the work of our illegal forces [that is, the officers – in the English sense] is complicated and requires continuous evaluation.'

On 5 August 1988 Döring sent the 'Centre' a further draft of the new Official Secrets Act. He argued, once again, that the Act could make life easier for the Stasi in London by taking the heat off it and transferring it to former MI5 officers. This was because its main emphasis seemed to Döring to be to suppress 'all exposés by former members of the British security and intelligence services'.

Döring summed up what he called 'the consequences for our agents' (*die Agenturische Lage*). There was, he said, likely to be a 'new intensity in the legal framework protecting state and service secrets'. The truth was that the whole set of targets worked on by the London residency was now covered by the new law: 'defence, security and intelligence questions as well as international relations'. The new regulations, he added, would also affect the FCO and the MoD:

'We must prepare ourselves for the eventuality that the amount of information we can acquire from official sources of finite intelligence data will decline.' They would have to be even more on their guard for the 'enemy', and their civilian contacts in the 'state apparatus' would become increasingly wary of them.

Döring warned that 'our contacts to people working in the state apparatus of the UK will become more complex, and their active involvement in counter-espionage will increase. That is particularly so for our work against the FCO and the MoD. At the same time, it can be determined that the GDR Embassy will as before not be at the centre of hostile attacks against Socialist countries which will be focused on the USSR, the CSSR, and Cuba.' Döring revealed in this document that East German military intelligence officers had 'contacts' and 'persons of trust' within the FCO and the MoD.

The very last report from the London military intelligence unit was dated 10 November 1989 and looked back over the past twelve months. Döring told the 'Centre' that HVA III – the unit that dealt with 'legalists' in the East German embassies – was still not paying sufficient attention or respect to their own work. As far as security events were concerned, he said that he had 'participated' in the CND annual conference from 18 to 20 November 1988, but that on the 18th his official Mazda had been broken into and searched. The windows had been smashed and a record of his official journeys, kept in the car, had been removed. An attempt had been made to steal the radio but his clothes were left untouched. Police in Salford had been informed. He had remained at the conference. The next day, he said, the same thing had happened to 'our Czech colleague who also informed the police'.

A minute on the file noted that 'Hans-Georg' believed that MI5 might have been behind this, as part of a general drive to make the East Germans feel insecure. On 17 November 1988, it was added, the London fire brigade had appeared at 34 Belgrave Square to 'investigate smoke seen coming from the roof of the embassy'. Special Branch were spotted observing an unnamed East German ship in London (Krebs/'Hammer' was on board at the time), but the 'Centre' concluded that the residency would continue to operate with its 'legend secure' and that none of the incidents added up to the view that MI5, 'the enemy', had either 'direct evidence or proof' against any of the East German officers.

The events of 7–11 October 1989 in East Germany (Gorbachev was visiting and 'Gorbymania' had broken out in a big way) had, Döring stated, been fully noted in the British media, and William Waldegrave, the Conservative Foreign Office minister, had commented on them on 9 October. He was obliged to report – fatefully – that, 'as far as the contact work of the embassy and our operational contacts are concerned there has been a noticeable growth in the reserve towards us'. The East German intelligence community was now obviously aware that the future of the East German state was increasingly being questioned and, naturally and correspondingly, the willingness of its British 'contacts' to work for East Germany was beginning to falter. Döring foresaw 'the clear possibility of direct hostile action' against the embassy. Actually, their time was almost up.

Indeed, it was at this point that the last file was closed. In his flat, in the company of Barbara Einhorn, a British academic (see Chapter 13), Döring watched on television as the Berlin Wall was opened up. We may imagine what he felt as he saw his future being dismantled before his eyes. He stayed in London long enough to welcome East Germany's last ambassador to the Court of St James, Ulrike Birkner-Kettenacker (who had been recommended to the interim East German government by Canon Paul Oestreicher) – and to destroy all his London files in the back yard of 34 Belgrave Square.[14]

# 10

# The HVA's London Team

So far in this book we have re-created both the purpose of and the background to the Stasi's UK operations, and we have also presented some of the surviving fragments of the secret intelligence that the Stasi collected. Now, however, we must begin to see if we can identify more of those who supplied it to the HVA. Trying to exploit the Stasi files to do this is rather like trying to solve a jigsaw puzzle from which most of the pieces have been stolen. The files of the HVA are even scantier than those of the military intelligence unit. We were never intended to uncover the real identities of the HVA's UK officers and their British sources – and the shredders did their job all too well. However, the Stasi files do contain important clues. Stitching together pieces of different files, fitting SIRA material to specific sources and then cross-matching them with other documentary evidence allows us to get substantially closer to – and at times actually to reach – an acceptable account of what precisely was going on and who was involved in the UK espionage.

Certainly, it cannot be right that, to date, every single one of the Stasi's London officers and agents is still at large – hidden, unchallenged and free. The Stasi was an organisation dedicated, in its own country, to the brutal repression of all dissidents, and abroad to secret intelligence operations, recruiting agents and collecting materials. In addition, the Stasi also underwrote subversion by supporting and training various foreign groups (chiefly Arab, Latin

American and West German) who were prepared to use terror against Western interests. So when we talk about East German intelligence officers, co-opted or otherwise, we are not simply talking about highly skilled and ruthless operatives, masters of secrecy and adept at avoiding detection. We are also talking about some very dangerous people.

The first thing we need to do in order to uncover the identity of the Stasi spies is to group the pieces of HVA SIRA intelligence around the cover-names of those who collected it. We know that the Stasi used officers, 'co-opted workers', agents, go-betweens and sources. We also know that the officers, 'co-opted workers', agents and sources all had cover-names. But we cannot automatically deduce from SIRA whether any single cover-name applied to an officer of some description (who would have been an East German) or to a real source (who would have been British). By grouping the intelligence passed on to East Berlin around the individual cover-names we will not only be able to see the areas they covered, but also make reasonable assumptions as to whether the cover-name belongs to an officer or a source. This is because sources, where located in British institutions, would only ever have had access to specific sorts of intelligence, whereas an officer, as a recruiter and collector, would plainly be able to boast a more catholic selection.

As we embark on this task, we must not forget that the entire system, from beginning to end, was designed to prevent members of the Stasi from being identified. The conspiratorial approach to recruitment and to all operations had but one purpose: to ensure that in the event of a defection only a very small number of identities could be disclosed. In operational terms, it was a blind cell system, frighteningly effective.

As Wolf himself explains:

Quite early in my career I had worked out a complex cross-referencing system which meant that anyone trying to identify an agent from our files would need to obtain access to three to five (depending on the security rating) pieces of separate information and security clearance to read three sets of interconnected documents.

The central registry contained both agents (organised by first name, last name, date of birth and place of birth) and hundreds and thousands of other persons who were registered for completely varied reasons. Card registers were kept separately in each Department, each one handling at most 60–100 agents. For each agent there was a card with a codename, address and territory . . . The cards never carried the agents' real names and the small card pack in each Department was usually kept in the custody of a trusted senior officer . . . any unauthorised person would have had to trawl physically through a massive quantity of paper in search of a match . . . I and my senior officers kept the names of our most important agents in our heads . . . I have never trusted computers.[1]

Wolf elaborates further:

Mielke was desperate to have me provide a central index of agents. I refused point blank . . . I was proud to say that under my tenure nowhere did there exist a single record of all our spies. I was determined no card index or computer disk should ever hold all our operational details. Instead I developed a process through which the identity of a source could be determined only if three to five key details were already available. Before a search could continue, each detail had to be checked blind against the other. We did have information cards on perhaps hundreds of thousands of individuals including many names in the West . . . Each card carried a codename, address, territory and file number. The number referred to a dossier containing real information on the individual spy. The small stack of cards in each Department was usually kept in the custody of a trusted senior officer and if this dossier did cover a spy, the handler had a cover story ready. In war or times of high tension, the officer's job would have been to remove a spy's file from the ministry to our temporary HQ.

Any unauthorised person going through the cards and files would have had to physically trawl through a massive quantity of paper in search of a match. Such a conspicuous operation to match the codename of an agent with his real one would inevitably attract attention, quite the opposite of what would have happened if ever these separate files had been kept on computer disks. The ungainliness of the system troubled me little because I and my senior officers kept the names of the most important agents in our heads . . . In its own way this decentralisation increased our security . . .[2]

A former senior British intelligence officer confirms that there is every reason to believe that Wolf's account is wholly credible: 'Purely on general principles the idea of a complex (overcomplex) system of safeguards for agent identities has the ring of truth about it, as does the possibility of agents being double-counted – but I haven't sat down to evaluate the system as described (which probably is simplified anyway).'[3]

## SIRA Material Presented from Residency 201, Grouped around Specific Sources

By far the largest amount of mid-1980s secret intelligence material – comprising reports on facts and on British views, together with freestanding British documents (the most highly prized catches of all) – was offered to the East German spymasters in the HVA by 'Eckhart' and 'Kraft'. Careful analysis allows us to offer a firm identification of 'Kraft' and 'Eckhart', and a very plausible one of 'Freundin'. Cross-matching fragments of evidence shows that 'Kraft' and 'Eckhart' were German, but that 'Freundin' was British.[4] Yet it is important to recall that, where German officers hide behind these cover-names, that is by no means the end of the story. Behind the officers – probably behind all of them but certainly behind most – there lurk British agents and sources. The officers collected the material but their recruited agents supplied it. This is what intelligence officers do. We should not forget, however, that, in addition to the three sources mentioned here, there are at least twenty-one other 'sources' named in the SIRA material who provided material on similar targets, of similar quality. We should also recall that the officers were very professional and very good, and the intelligence they gained was often high grade, as the examples given earlier indicate. Every item described here was included in the

SIRA archive – which, by definition, held only material deemed to be of ongoing secret value.

As our lists show, during the 1980s they describe: 'Eckhart' (who presented a vast and broad array of material, ranging from the views of Dr David Owen, Michael Foot and Neil Kinnock, to details about the British chambers of commerce, other commercial matters, the British Communist Party and UK policy towards China); 'Dreher' (with knowledge of British economic life, trade issues and industry); 'Brücke' (who gained inside knowledge on the CPGB); 'Jäger' (with Foreign Office viewpoints); 'Granit' (who worked on the Labour Party); 'Rat' (who did likewise); 'Holz' (who, like 'Dreher', spied on the British economy as well as on the relationship between Margaret Thatcher, Francis Pym and other leading Tories at the time of the Falklands crisis in 1982); 'Helfried' (who knew about British attitudes towards the GDR and the viewpoint of Frank Allaun MP); 'Direktor' (who worked on the senior Foreign Office official Michael Jenkins); 'Erich' (who knew about British planning in the event of a nuclear war and about CND); 'Gregor' (who worked on the foreign policy of the Conservative Party); 'Doktor' (who worked on the SDP); 'Lutz' and 'Kunze' (who had spied on CND, the Conservative Party, Edward Leigh and Julian Lewis, both MPs and dissenters in Mrs Thatcher's government, on E. P. Thompson and other British academics, as well as on NATO); 'Häussler' (who obtained documentary material on the Royal Navy); 'Gerald' (who supplied top secret information shared between the Defence Secretary, Michael Heseltine, and the West German ambassador in London and was discovered to be Gaby Gast, a West German intelligence officer); 'Freundin' (whose special area of operations was the British anti-nuclear movement, and who had tracked Hella Pick, the well-known *Guardian* journalist); 'Wien' (who worked on UK nuclear systems); 'Kraft' (who got hold of numerous documents, including one on 'Eureka', a top view on Soviet disarmament plans, various views from the Labour Party's Shadow Cabinet and the plans being made for the British General Election in 1987); 'Johann' (who offered the view of a leading British personality on the development of the GDR and the probable Western reaction to Soviet disarmament plans in 1987); and 'Merten' (who had unique insights into British–German relations).

# Narrowing the Field – the *Quellen* 'Eckhart', 'Kraft' and 'Freundin'

'Eckhart' – also written as 'Eckhardt', but with the same registration number (XV/175/75) and therefore the same person – deserves our special attention. He collected from February 1981 to June 1986. 'Kraft', who collected from July 1985 until April 1987, comes a close second, and 'Freundin', from June 1984 until the beginning of 1986, may be ranked third. Documentary detective work, exploiting a variety of evidence in each case, allows us to be almost certain about the identity of all of them.

This is a list of some of 'Eckhart's' most important material:

'Eckhart' (XV/175/75)

The UK Foreign Office and Poland, Chatham House study on NATO financial policy on Poland, Document on British ideas on the creation of NATO contingents for operations outside Europe, Documentary Report: a Chatham House study, Commercial relations between East and West Europe, a UK Foreign Office minister on Nigeria, a Chatham House document on the arms industry, a Chatham House study, a Chatham House study on arms control, Document on the international position of Chatham House, a Chatham House assessment of the development of the international situation, a symposium of an Arab research centre in London, a SSES report on East German identity, the Foreign Policy of the SDP, Labour attitudes to the Falklands Conflict, a document on a British evaluation of the Falklands War, on the Corn weapon, a Conservative view of the Falklands War, on the European contribution to NATO, on power and violence in East Germany, on UK defence policy after the Falklands War, on the SDP evaluation of the internal and external effects of the Falklands War, on UK–China technical co-operation, on the SDP leadership's views on the UK political situation, on the view of the Foreign Policy Committee of the Labour Party on a new West German government, on the view of the UK government on the new German government, UK policy on China, Dr David Owen as foreign policy

spokesman of the SDP, the 3rd Gulf Cooperation Council's conclusions, David Owen: an internal evaluation of the current political situation by the leadership of the SDP, the SDP leadership's
views on the current political situation, on the Trident Programme,
the Report of the UK Committee for Peace and Security in
Europe, Burden Sharing in NATO, on Foot, Shore, Kinnock
and Healey, on Trotskyists in the UK, on the SDP leadership's
evaluation of the forthcoming elections, the UK position on the
Williamsburg Summit, Current Questions in the British Peace
Movement, on Nuclear Weapons in France and Britain, on the
current situation of the CPGB, on British Foreign and Military
policy, on South Africa, on planned manoeuvres of the British
navy, a UK view on the FRG–GDR relationship, on the CPGB, on
a Mozambique contract, the visit of the South African President to
the UK, on the Position of Leading British Military Figures on
waging Nuclear War, on the German Foreign Office's influence
on Geoffrey Howe, Document on British Defence White Book,
the Sacharov hearing, a conference of the UK Chambers of Commerce, a Document on SDI, Reactions to the Reagan–Gorbachev
summit UK and US views in London, the UK view on the SED
Congress, the UK Participants to the GDR Roundtable, a UK view
of the Paris END convention, the UK Labour Party's study group
to the SED congress.

'Kraft' (XV/6900/82)

Report on speech of Mozambique Foreign Minister at Wilton Park,
Document 'On Eureka', Report on UK–Albanian relations, on the
UK Peace Movement and GDR, UK–Albanian relations, Document
on UK views on SDI Research, Document UK Defence White Book
1986, Document Research work on SDI Project, Document UK
Assessment of SDI Programme, Report on a UK Assessment of
World Peace Congress, on the election plans of the Conservative and
Labour Parties, Report on Development of END, Document on US
military structure and staff, Document on 6th END Convention,
Coventry, Report on Berlin's 750th anniversary, Document on END
Convention, Coventry, Document on UK views on SDI Research,

Report on UK position on US position on ABM Treaty, Document on Structure of UK Armed Forces, Document on Development of nuclear weapons, Document on Defence White Book, Document Developments within the CPGB, Report on Amnesty International.

'Freundin' (XV/4555/83) produced documents in English on END, a report on Einhorn, Childs, Williams, documents on END, a report on Hella Pick, a document in English on END, on END and travel, on the perspectives of GDR Peace Activists, and on the GDR group in END.

All in all, these materials, taken with the rest of the SIRA evidence, show that the East Germans managed to acquire intelligence on certain preselected aspects of the high policy of the British state, especially its defence and foreign policy, and those subjects in which the East German leadership took a special interest.[5]

It is immediately obvious that what both 'Eckhart' and 'Kraft' collected came from a variety of sources. While both of them shared similar areas of broad concern (and while 'Kraft' continued to collect after 'Eckhart's' name disappears from British SIRA), 'Eckhart's' work had a particular focus on the SDP, on leading Labour and Conservative figures, on British military strategy and defence thinking, and on international affairs. 'Kraft's' forte, on the other hand, was getting hold of documents, something at which he truly excelled, achieving startling success. 'Freundin's' *œuvre* was rather more modest and essentially focused on one specific area of the British peace movement. This suggests 'Eckhart' and 'Kraft' were intelligence officers but 'Freundin' was a British source.

Since agent 'Eckhart' (XV/175/75) was therefore an HVA officer, he was also obliged to be an East German diplomat. While it is true that the same officer could have more than one cover-name, his registration number would never have been changed (except in the rarest of cases). Since we know that 'XV/175/75' ceased to operate after 1986, and that 'XV/175/75' was 'Eckhart', we can bag him because, as a 'diplomat', his name must have been recorded on the Diplomatic or Staff Lists. SIRA tells us that 'Eckhart' was listed as a UK source from February 1981 to at least June 1986 (which would be an exceptionally long period of duty for a 'diplomat'). In the event, there was only one East German diplomat or member of the support staff in London for this length of time – Edgar Uher (a third secretary). Of those who had been there in 1981, Uher was the only East German still at 34 Belgrave Square in 1986. He was gone by the end of that year. The dates fit and, not unimportantly, the cover-name 'Eckhart' is similar to his real name, 'Edgar'. Sometimes, the Stasi chose cover-names which sounded like their officers' real names. Though this might seem insecure (which in a sense it was), it allowed security to be maintained if, by some error, an officer used his cover-name in the wrong circumstances. For example, had Uher called himself 'Eckhart' Uher by mistake, anyone discovering that he was called 'Edgar' would think that 'Edgar' was the name they had heard.[6]

This, however, still leaves open the more perplexing question of who sourced 'Eckhart'. For if Edgar Uher were this diplomat he was, at the time, a very young man (in his mid-twenties) and therefore unlikely to have had personal access to any significant official British secrets. Rather, his task would have been simply to channel cash, or some other benefit, to those of his British agents who did have the secrets, and which he would collect from them, either directly or more probably through a go-between. We know that the Stasi had cash galore, but we should not forget that they could exploit fully a panoply of other inducements, ranging from professional help to sexual favours.[7] 'Romeo' operations, as Wolf (and many others have reminded us) were often an excellent means of obtaining secrets and confidences from lonely women (Bonn's secretaries were always at risk) and, of course, gay sex could be used where targets were homo-sexuals. Markus Wolf has wryly observed that 'if I go down in espionage history it may well be for perfecting the use of sex in spying'.[8] His colleague at the 'Centre', Klaus Eichner, has reminded us that the Stasi were well aware of the 'English disease'.[9]

As we shall see, the East German intelligence officers paid out considerable sums of pounds sterling for items of intelligence. Behind this German 'Eckhart' there was at least one British 'Eckhart', as it were, one British citizen acting as a source for the HVA, able to reach those areas denied to the East Germans.[10]

Though plainly skilled (since MI5 never caught him), Uher was by no means the most sinister of the Stasi's London spymasters and spies. It is a matter of record that some of the Stasi officers received special training in electronics, chemicals, explosives and biological weapons. They were the 'officers on special duties', the OibEs. According to Joachim Gauck, 2,448 OibEs had been identified by September 1990 and a further 582 were then still under investigation.[11] OibEs were instructed to enter key positions in the GDR and its institutions, including its embassies abroad. They were absolutely forbidden to reveal their link to the Ministry for State Security. In the event of any crisis, they were authorised to take supreme power in whatever institution they happened to be located.

Several OibEs were stationed in London. After 1983 there were at least three of them, of whom one can today be shown to have been an expert in explosives and in chemical, biological and nuclear weapons. Another had special training in radio transmission. From their personal files and their past records we know that all would have been committed Communists and 'Chekists' who accepted that human rights – indeed human life itself – counted for nothing in the struggle to maintain Communist rule in East Germany. Not only are we entitled to accept that these people were inherently highly dangerous, even murderous perhaps, but also to ask who they were – and what they were doing in London.

Netting Uher was comparatively easy thanks to the length of time he was in London. The others are much more of a problem. However, in addition to the Stasi files and the SIRA material, we have three other sources of help which, unlike the CIA's 'Rosewood' files, we are able to consult. The first is a list, allegedly found in a Berlin garage, and passed to a leading British journalist.[12] It affixes 'sources' and their registration numbers to what appear to be particularly interesting pieces of intelligence. It seems reasonable to suppose that a renegade HVA officer compiled this list (while shredding the documents to which it referred) in the hope of selling it one day. Second, there is another list which a former Stasi officer (who may well be the same person responsible for the list mentioned above) did sell to a German journalist. This is a sort of accounts ledger, derived either from a Stasi accounts department, detailing some items of expenditure, or from a post-1990 German police report, seeking to link cash accounts with lists of Stasi sources. (The latter interpretation is regarded by Stasi archivists as most probable.) This list not only gives the real names of some of the HVA intelligence officers and the payments that they made on the HVA's behalf, but it also gives the registration numbers of some of the officers and their agents. Finally, the Stasi Archive in Berlin has compiled a register (*Who Was Who in the GDR*) containing the names of some officers. It is, however, incomplete and the names of officers known from other files do not often show up on it. With one significant exception, none of the names in the Berlin garage list matches the *Who Was Who in the GDR* list, and only two names on the accounts ledger produce hits. However, when these various sources are read in conjunction with each other, they do reveal the names of some officers and a few British recruits, and the cover-names of agents engaged in military intelligence. This is because the Stasi – unlike MI5 and MI6, or the CIA and the FBI – combined domestic and foreign intelligence work under one roof, encouraging cross-fertilisation between branches and generating thereby a documentary record of it. They can also be set alongside the London Lists of Diplomats and Staff accredited to the Court of St James.

## The Cash Connection

The Stasi files themselves contain some evidence of cash transactions. The HVA's finance division at Potsdam kept chits in a card index box entitled '*Operativgeld*', or 'Operational Payments', on which individual payments were listed as HVA expenses. This card index is vast, but even a cursory glance at it shows how 'sources' listed by codenames and/or registration numbers paid out sums in sterling to other codenames and registration numbers.

For example, 'Rolf Peters' handed over £1,300 between 20 September and 16 October 1988; XV/2145/86 gave someone £1,000 on 11 December 1989; XV/400/86 £500; 'Piet Atten' handed over £2,500 on 20 November 1989; XV/2567/80 paid out £500 on 4

July 1989 and the same amount again on 29 June 1989. XV/4883/88
paid someone £500 on 26 June 1989.

We cannot assume that just because the payments were made in
sterling they were necessarily payments made in the UK. But it is
reasonable to believe that they were made to Britons or people wishing to have sterling (because the Stasi had every currency it
required), and the round numbers suggest that they were payment
for specific pieces of information – every part of the Stasi was always
very careful about expenses; every pfennig had to be accounted for,
with signatures and counter-signatures, in true German bureaucratic fashion.

The Stasi accounts ledger is vital not just because it shows that
during the 1980s Stasi officers paid out large sums of pounds
sterling to their agents (identified here only by their codenames
and, sometimes, by their registration numbers). It also gives the
real names and the registration numbers of the officers who were
handing over the money. Using these numbers, we can refer back
to the SIRA material to link a source with a particular individual
and cross-check it with the 'garage list' of key secrets and the
registration numbers and cover-names of agents involved in their
collection.

The very fact that the Stasi paid out these considerable sums of
money in cash is in itself significant. It proves (were anyone to
doubt this) that the Stasi was running agents in London. Officers
with registration numbers (and therefore officers in the English
sense) would not pay themselves sums in sterling for gaining information, for that was what they were employed to do. Equally, if the
information obtained in London had been material to which the
Stasi would have been given access in their disguise as diplomats,
there would also have been no need to pay for it.

Since we know that there was always one registration number for
each spy in any single operational area, where the same registration
number shows on different cover-names in Britain, we can be sure
we are dealing with only one person. 'Eckhart', for example, has exactly
the same number as 'Doktor' – and is therefore one and the same
person. Similarly 'Erich' and 'Mark' are one person, as are 'Helm'
and 'Rathmann'.

Similarly, where the registration numbers are different, it is clear that we are dealing with two different people. Where one registration number with one cover-name pays another registration number with another cover-name, this is evidence of a cash transaction between an officer and an agent. Where someone appears as a source in the East German sense (*Quelle*) but can be seen also to be a paymaster, we may be certain that the East German *Quelle* is not the actual source of the intelligence that has been paid for. 'Erich' and 'Mark' were both listed as receiving cash, but since we know (from the registration number) that they were the same officer, elsewhere listed as paying out cash, they also clearly paid others for the information they gained (for no one paid themselves). Here we have proof that a source possessed a source (a 'co-opted worker' running an actual source). This was conspiratorial intelligence gathering writ large, designed to ensure that the actual spy was at three or four removes from the case officer in East Berlin – or the record of the cash that was handed over.

Above and beyond the records of the HVA's card index, there is the fuller accounts ledger. This list is highly fragmentary, and not in any discernible order. It exists for only two years, from 1985 to 1987. It shows that in Residency 201 in London there were at least three HVA intelligence officers who paid out sums in sterling during these years. Their names are Erich Schwager, Klaus Pfenning and Dieter Rost. All three, the British Foreign Office was told, were 'diplomats', and all show up on the Diplomatic List. Four others (Ingo Schröter, Holger Krüger, Ulrich Köster and Hartmut Schulz) also made large payments in sterling, but are not on the Foreign Office register of diplomats in London. Schröter may be identical to the 'super Romeo' Schröter mentioned by Wolf, in which case the payments to him will have funded sex visits to Britain.[13] If so, it would be interesting to know whom he was seeing here. Unfortunately, neither 'Eckhart's' cover-name nor his registration number show up on this fragment.

At various times over just two years, Stasi officers paid out £206,895; most of these payments were round numbers, most of them over £1,000, and on one occasion – in 1986 – a single payment of £11,500 was registered under the expenses of Erich

Schwager, apparently to a single agent called 'Schumann' for 'operational purposes'. From July 1986 to June 1987, Ingo Schröter paid out twenty-three times, to a total of £46,230.

Single payments were almost always for £1,000 or more (single payments included £1,500, £2,000, £1,200, £2,500, £2,000, £4,100, £10,000, £1,650, £9,000 and so on), always in round numbers. These were amounts worth having – the larger sums would have provided a down-payment on a nice flat in London, for example.

The 'Kramers' ('Sonja' and 'Werner') received a total of £33,000 from September 1985 until June 1987, always in round numbers. It is important to realise that this 'Sonja' is plainly not the same woman as 'Sonja Schulze', because by 1986 Sonja Schulze and her husband Reinhardt were both securely in a British prison and would therefore not have needed paying in June 1987.

The following are listed under their codenames as having received sterling payments: 'Erich Kraft', 'Erich Jahn', 'Klaus Mark', 'Robert', 'Sonja Kramer', 'Werner Kramer', 'Gerd Lange', 'Frenz', 'Blümel' (listed as an IM), 'Helm'/'Rathmann' (share the same registration number), 'Notar', 'Franz' (listed as an IM), 'Bodo', 'Günther Münster', 'Frank Beyer', 'Jörg Wolle', 'Franziska Vogt', 'Thomas Gerlach', 'Alfons Paulsen', 'Assistent', 'Harry', 'Park', 'Johannes Faber' (equals twenty-four codenames, where 'Helm' and 'Rathmann' have the same registration number, XV/00265/82, and are therefore the same person).

It is interesting to compare these codenames with those on SIRA material, recorded as having come from Residency 201, and those on the garage list. Most names do not match up. The following SIRA codenames were used: 'Birke', 'Brücke', Dieter', 'Doktor'/'Eckhart', 'Dreher', 'Erich', 'Freundin', 'Fröbel', 'Genf', 'Granit', 'Gregor', 'Häussler', 'Helfried', 'Holz', 'Jäger', 'Johann', 'Kraft', 'Kunze', 'Lehrer', 'Mark', 'Pepp', 'Stern', 'Wald', 'Wien' (equals twenty-five codenames, where 'Eckhart' and 'Doktor' have the same registration number, XV/175/75, and are therefore the same person). The ledger also shows that 'Kraft' and 'Erich' have the same registration number and are therefore the same person.

All in all, therefore, it seems obvious that some of the codenames belong to East German officers and some belong to their British sources. According to the *Sunday Times* journalists John Goetz and Stephen Grey:

> half the hundred sources are thought to have been British and the other half German. One contact was Alf Lomas, a former Labour leader in the European Parliament who provided political support. Other Labour sources gave Berlin internal party documents. Two former Left wing activists, David Mourton and Stanley Hodgson, have also been identified as former contacts. Both men have denied that they did anything to help the East German regime. Lomas flatly denied that he had ever received any special information or used any material sent to him by the East Germans. 'I am sure they [the East Germans, not the Stasi] regarded me as a supporter, which I was. But anyone who suggests I was working for them in any way is barmy, or making it up.' It is understood that Lomas, Mourton and Hodgson are not on the MI5 list of suspects being considered for prosecution.[14]

The *Sunday Times* continues:

> the material suggests that there were at least two agents inside the Labour Party. The first code-named 'Rank' provided more than 100 reports on Labour including 47 internal party documents between 1973 and 1976 and nine documents from Labour's national executive committee marked 'internal' or 'secret' between 1973 and 1976. The second agent 'Wien' supplied 13 reports on foreign policy from Party HQ and wrote reports on Denis Healey and Neil Kinnock. One document dispatched by 'Wien' was a copy of a report by Mike Gapes . . . now MP for Ilford South. Gapes said yesterday that in common with other Labour officials, he had often met diplomats from the East German Embassy to explain his Party's position, and to criticise their country's record on human rights. He named two diplomats who liaised with Labour and attended Party conferences. Both are known by the *Sunday Times* to have been full-time Stasi officers. There is no suggestion that Gapes passed any documents to the Stasi.

During the *Sunday Times* investigation, Colonel Günther Bohnsack, a former East German intelligence officer, identified Alf Lomas as a political contact known as 'Alf' to the service's propaganda department. The *Sunday Times* adds that Dave Mourton was 'listed in the Stasi files as "Dave"'. He was formerly married to an East German and was once a member of the CPGB. In the Stasi files 'Dave' is alleged to have supplied nineteen different documents in 1986 and 1987: all were academic texts on defence issues. At the time, he was studying at the London School of Economics. He said, 'it is possible that I came across some of the documents listed in the Stasi files at this time but I have no recollection of ever handing them over to any kind of Stasi agent'.

Mourton recalled, the *Sunday Times* said, contacts with a diplomat from the East German Embassy who is known to the *Sunday Times* as a former Stasi employee. It is not suggested that Mourton was aware of this. 'It's all a mystery to me,' he said. 'To my knowledge, I never had any direct contact with the Stasi'. Hodgson, another British contact, now works in South Africa but has made no comment.

A leading East German journalist, Rainer Oschmann, named by Goetz and Grey as the real name of agent 'Helfried', has denied the claim that he was a Stasi spy in London. Oschmann, currently press spokesman for the Party of Democratic Socialism, is reported as having said that he had been a foreign correspondent in London from 1981 until 1986 and foreign editor of *Neues Deutschland*. He had, he said, written 'situation reports' – but said that he did not know whether he was an 'IM' or not. He stated that he had been asked by the HVA to write articles which might appear in West German newspapers, and that for this purpose he had been given the name 'Helfried', which was his middle name. In London he said he had been approached by a member of the East German Embassy. He realised this person was an HVA man and he agreed to give situation reports on the government and the Opposition. On 2 April 1983, during a visit to Lloyds, he claimed he was approached by a member of Britain's domestic security agency, MI6 [sic], and was asked to become an agent. He refused, and told the embassy about this. The Stasi broke off all contact to him at this point, he says, and he left London in *1985*, implying that for their own story Goetz and Grey needed to have him in London for a further year. Oschmann claims that he told this to the *Sunday Times* but they did not report him properly. He strongly denied that his reporting post was just a cover for HVA work. As for 'Eckhart', the *Sunday Times* claims to know his identity but refuses to reveal it (for reasons that are hard to explain).

As we have discovered, the SIRA material and the accounts ledger found in the Berlin garage show that 'Eckhart' and 'Doktor' have the same registration number (XV/175/75), and are therefore the same person. Their periods of espionage do not conflict. Why, then, do they have two codenames? It is a fact that some agents were given different codenames for operating in different areas – Gaby Gast, the West German secret intelligence spy, was sometimes 'Gisela', sometimes 'Gerald' and sometimes 'Reinhard', depending on what she was collecting – and this may have applied in this case: the location of the sources serving XV/175/75 may well have necessitated two different codenames. Of the sources, one was, as we shall see, at Chatham House. Another may have been 'Barber', the END and military intelligence spy, who was clearly British. One telling (and perhaps chilling) aspect of Uher's operations is that no one interviewed for this book had ever even come across the name; there was no record of him in the Security Service or the Foreign Office, nor could any individual interviewed for this book recall having ever met someone of his name or description. It is possible that as 'third secretary' (he was never promoted) he rarely, if ever, stuck his head out in public, since his 'legal' persona was so slight as to have no standing in the wider diplomatic community. If he had attended Chatham House as an associate member in 1981 and 1982 – which was technically possible, as we examine in the next chapter – he left no trace of himself there. No one there remembers him. He could not have been a member of Chatham House after 1982 (also explained in the next chapter), yet the HVA's interest in Chatham House topics and the dovetailing of their intelligence with those topics continued unabated, as a glance at the SIRA material confirms.

What can all this mean? Having seen the evidence, and reflected on its significance, and having compared this case with others, it must be concluded that 'Eckhart's' sources were British. Because of his nationality, but also because of his youthfulness and lack of standing in London, it is probable that 'Eckhart's' espionage operations were predicated on his putting considerable distance between him and his British sources. Had Uher been an urbane and established figure on the British scene it is possible that he could have connected with his sources directly. But everything we know about him suggests he was simply a conduit for cash and intelligence. His name does not even feature in the Stasi Archives who's who or in any other available study. It is tempting to suggest that this meant Uher was so important that special care had been taken to remove all traces of his existence, but this is unlikely: the bigger the reputation, the more numerous the marks left behind. The few traces left by Uher confirm the verdict already reached – that he was an insignificant messenger of highly significant messages.

This being so, the greater the weight that has to be attached to his sources. What made 'Eckhart' so successful in Britain (which is why he stayed here so long) was that he was very good and teamed up with at least one outstanding source. It is perfectly possible that this source did not even know of 'Eckhart's' interest in him (given the nature of British public life at this time, the source is much more likely to have been male than female). If we recall that at times an HVA relationship could function at three removes ('co-opted worker', go-between and source), the source may not even have realised that he was the object of HVA interest, or that the things he was passing on were winging their way to East Berlin and the Politburo. If the link between 'Eckhart' and the source was direct, and knowing, the source was plainly an East German spy. But if the link was maintained using a go-between, the status of the source becomes more fluid, just as the HVA would have intended.

At this juncture it is absolutely vital to emphasise two points (to which we shall return): that the vicious and invasive way in which the Stasi searched for sources meant not only that they understood well how to exploit fully this fluid territory, but that their preying on people who might well have been vulnerable for one reason or another frequently resulted in British Stasi sources also being, in a very real sense, Stasi victims.[15] This might not excuse what they did, but it helps to explain why they did it. As Wolf himself states,

'there were many people we were content to run in the grey middle
ground as sources without pushing them too hard, lest they be
reminded of their loyalty to their own country and turn away from
us'.[16] Time and time again, the Stasi files confirm the prevalence of
this sophisticated but corrosive strategy.

Clues to the identity of 'Eckhart's' source here can be gleaned
from some of the pieces of intelligence. There is a clear pattern to
these but it is a rather original one – and not everything that
'Eckhart' collected fitted into it, because several sources served
him. 'Eckhart's' source is well informed about the SDP, what its
leaders think, and its foreign policy, about the Labour Party, about
leading Conservatives, strategic and security issues, and about
round table meetings between prominent Britons and East Germans.
He is also, plainly, close to Chatham House. It has to be stressed,
however, that this source may not have known of 'Eckhart's' interest
in him – in which case, it was the go-between who erred. Given
'Eckhart's' five-year relationship with the source, however, it
stretches the imagination somewhat to believe that the source could
have remained entirely unaware that behind the go-between there
lurked an intelligence officer. At the same time, we know that the
Stasi often used 'false flag' recruiting techniques (pretending to be
members of Western intelligence services), which may have further
muddied the waters of espionage.

Uher was German, but, as we see later on, we can also be confident about the identity of 'Freundin', who was British. If 'Eckhart'
was not just a source but also a recruiter, and 'Eckhart' and
'Freundin' figure on several lists, it is possible that 'Freundin' was
also a recruiter in some form or another.

Turning to the codenames 'Kraft' and 'Erich', we have already
noted that they were the same person, because they have the same
registration number (XV/6900/82). The accounts ledger tells us
that this is the registration number of Erich Schwager. Schwager
was therefore both 'Kraft' and 'Erich'. And if Schwager was one
source (in the East German sense) who paid out money to agents,
the other named officers on the same ledger – Klaus Pfenning
(XV/00502/87), Ingo Schröter (XV/4393/83), Holger Krüger
(XV/3389/76), Ulrich Köster (XV/1687/76), Hartmut Schulz (whose

registration number is missing) and Dieter Rost (XV/7214/81) – were plainly doing the same sort of thing: recruiting and paying British agents. As we know from other files, Rost was a military intelligence officer, code-named 'Clarus'. Not all of them show up on the Diplomatic Lists: presumably they operated directly out of East Berlin and came to London as and when required.

Yet this information about Schwager is also interesting for an entirely different reason. If we look at the Diplomatic List we can see who he replaces and by whom he is replaced. We know that Heinz Knobbe was an HVA person because he was betrayed as such by an embassy worker (see Chapter 4). He was replaced by Schwager by June 1984, and when Schwager went he was replaced by Siegfried Reichel (who we know from the files of the military intelligence unit was the HVA resident in 1989). This makes Knobbe, Schwager and Reichel the three most obvious candidates for the title of successive London HVA residents in the 1980s.

Schwager is perhaps of most interest since he was plainly one of the most dangerous East Germans in London. The who's who compiled by the Stasi Archive clearly identifies him as a senior HVA OiBe who had special skills in 'operational-technical matters concerned with arms, munitions and chemical weapons'; he was, in short, an explosives and weapons expert. His last post, in 1989, was head of the ultra-secret Department BCD, which dealt with armaments and chemical 'services'.[17] He was also qualified to direct nuclear radiation protection measures, was responsible for the radiological fallout protection of senior Stasi officers, for chemical weapons protection measures, and also for the training of Stasi officers in explosives, new weapons technology and chemical warfare. By 1989, he had 176 officials working under him.[18] We may ask what someone with his specific expertise was doing in the UK in the 1980s. It is important to recall that in a key interview in *Die Welt* in April 1990, a leading member of the East German regime, Alexander Schalk-Golodkowski, admitted that the GDR had channelled arms to the Middle East to the tune of DM 650 million by 1989.[19] The chief recipient of these weapons had been groups in Iraq, Jordan and Egypt (Schalk-Golodkowski denied that arms had been given to Chile or South Africa). He added that the

Stasi had used a 'technical engineering company' to conceal the GDR's lethal trade in arms. Schwager's particular penchant for blowing things up, and his knowledge of chemical weaponry, strongly suggest he was at the time deeply involved in the secret arms trade, selling East German weapons to Arab and Latin American terrorist groups from his London base and possibly to the IRA as well.

Where are these individuals now? As Ian Cobain of *The Times* discovered, Erich Schwager is today a successful businessman, running a company called Moha, and a very frequent visitor to the UK.[20] Cobain did not know, however, what Moha did. In fact, Schwager runs two companies – the other one is called MZB, which claims to be a firm devoted to the 'worldwide direct sales of motorcycle spares for MZ, JAWA and Bajaj'.

Schwager's fellow managing director in MZB is none other than Edgar Uher. MZB's website lists an Edgar Uher as 'the general manager and the contact for people who speak no German, but English, French or Russian': Uher's photo may be viewed on the internet.[21] He must have been an attractive and fetching young man in London, which may help to explain his considerable success. No photograph of Schwager exists. Moha says that it is part of a company which undertakes 'industrial engineering', established in 1986 by a Mr M. K. Hadeed, with a head office whose address is listed as PO Box 921 678, in Amman, Jordan. Schwager was, as we have seen, not a military intelligence officer but an HVA officer. It follows that his duties were not to spy on Western weaponry with a view to alerting the East Germans about developments which might affect East Germany's security, but to gain intelligence on the supply of arms to groups whose goals the East Germans sought to further. There is no reason to believe that his current connection with Moha Engineering, a company based in the Middle East, has anything whatsoever to do with his previous interests in chemical and nuclear weapons, explosives and new weapons technology. Given his expertise, however, some will be alarmed by any link between a former Stasi arms specialist and any Arab company, even one whose business is entirely honest, given the tensions flowing from the aftermath of a Western world cast under a deep shadow by the events of 9/11. It is breathtaking that, at the time of writing, Schwager had not been called to account for his activities in the 1980s.

While it would be facile to allege a direct link between the Stasi and current Islamic terrorism, there is very plainly a historical connection between the Stasi's work with certain Arab radical and terrorist groups in the 1980s, and current events involving highly organised and well-trained fundamentalist groups. We know that the Stasi helped build up intelligence organisations for certain Arab states, and that they trained groups of Middle Eastern radicals in explosives and chemical weaponry. Using their embassies in certain Arab countries, they also trained those states in secret police work and how to secure political power. The Stasi may not necessarily be the 'father' of organised Islamic terrorism, but it may be its 'grandfather'; those who it trained twelve years ago may now themselves be the trainers.[22]

The Stasi's involvement with terrorism, in particular Middle Eastern and Islamic terrorism, was not known about before February 1990. [23] Initially, it was said that in the mid-1970s Erich Honecker, as head of the national defence council, had instructed two ministers, Hoffmann and Kessler, to prepare the Springsee complex in Beeskow as a training centre for West German terrorists. By June 1990 the arrest of Susanne Albrecht, who had murdered the banker Jürgen Ponto, showed an even more chilling aspect of the Stasi's links with international terrorism: in 1977 the Stasi had arranged for her to find refuge in South Yemen.

The link between the Stasi and the government of South Yemen was subsequently shown to be a very strong one. The South Yemen secret police had been set up and trained by the Stasi. It was there that the Stasi supplied Albrecht with false identity papers to enable her to enter Czechoslovakia in 1980. On 21 June through his lawyer, Friedrich Wolf, Honecker denied having given safe haven to terrorists. He added that he and the rest of the SED leadership had always opposed terrorism and indeed were part of the international fight against it. He said the accusation was part of a campaign to destroy 'the good reputation of the GDR as the home of peace throughout the world and to criminalise the East German leadership'. A former MfS officer contradicted this statement, however, when he admitted that the terrorists had been required to commit themselves to further attacks on West Germany. Two HVA XXII officers had informed him about this. Their job was to work against terrorists and in this capacity they had made contact with the Red Army Faction.

In June 1990, an interview with an unnamed senior Stasi officer revealed more facts about the connection between Stasi officers and Arab terrorism.[24] He stated that the Stasi did not refer to 'terrorism' in connection with Middle East politics; if they spoke of 'state terrorism', they meant Israel or the USA. The Stasi, he testified, had actively sought to gain influence in the Arab world, and Yasser Arafat, it believed, was the linchpin because Arafat had made the first move towards East Germany. Honecker, he said, had told Arafat that the GDR was opposed to 'terror' but the Stasi officer insisted that this was a straight lie (*Augenwischerei*); in fact, Arafat was assured that the GDR would help him in his 'anti-imperialist struggles'.

The officer explained that the first move was the delivery of weapons to the PLO. The second step was to offer them training in security and intelligence issues in the GDR. The Stasi established a designated 'chair for international relations' at its college in Potsdam, secretly located near the complex but not actually in it. He said that, since 1969–70, the Stasi had offered intelligence courses there to Arab groups. He claimed too that within the SED there was an international department which regulated all political support for so-called illegal parties. It was here that the decision was made to support the pro-Communist Chilean exiles, and from here that the Stasi was ordered to cooperate with the PLO. He added that every year since 1995 Department II of the HVA had run summer courses for the 'exile cadres', designed to teach them basic self-defence, conspiratorial work and explosives training.

The officer stated that 'the PLO seemed to know more about explosives than we did', but they were very ready takers for intelligence and security work. He went on, 'Mielke had said "We are everywhere in the world", and this was our motto. We undertook the training of African and Arab services from states with a "socialist orientation". It was a programme shared with the KGB, with the GDR handling Yemen – we had about fifty people there until recently.' Both Arafat and Daniel Ortega of Nicaragua had been guests of honour at the fortieth anniversary of the GDR. George Habash, the militant Palestinian leader, kept a flat in Dresden. 'If you went into the main building of the Yemeni state security,' the officer continued, 'you would have thought you were at home with us. We even supplied the notebooks.' The same could be said about Mozambique. The officer further claimed that they had not only helped Mengisthu to power in Ethiopia but had stabilised him – 'at one stage when he looked shaky we had two hundred people there'. The Stasi had given the Ethiopians a railway security unit, 'just like the one we had', even though there were apparently only twenty-five kilometres of track.

He stated that East Germany had been quick off the mark in establishing Stasi residencies in numerous other Arab and African countries. Under Nasser, Egypt, he alleged, had been its first host, followed by Ghana and Guinea. It had cost the MfS a vast amount of money (*Schweinegeld*) and, the officer insisted, 'all a complete loss'. At the end, he said, no one but Mielke knew how big the entire operation was. Not surprisingly, perhaps, within three days Wolf had denied this officer's suggestion that there were links between the Stasi and West German terrorists – 'not at all in my memory'.[25]

According to this testimony, Schwager's Stasi colleagues also earned the GDR hard Western currency derived from Western purchases of Middle Eastern oil. Weapons were stored at a base in Kavelstorf, the only such base that existed. Further evidence of the Stasi's interest in promoting Arab terrorism, especially in Iraq and the Lebanon, emerged from a further 1990 interview.[26] The Stasi had trained all sorts of people as its agents, he claimed, 'all different – traders, representatives of firms, advisers in ministries, university lecturers, doctors, diplomats and so on. What they shared was their proven experience in intelligence work whether in the GDR or outside.' Above all, he said, they all had 'the connections which were important preconditions for secret intelligence work'. He concluded by repeating that the most vital work the HVA had done in the Middle East was with the Palestinians: 'our chief work'.

For all these reasons the story of the Stasi's British operations is clearly an important one. We must now turn to their British sources.

# 11

# The HVA's London Sources

In Britain, as we have seen, the Stasi organised the gathering of secret intelligence using an elaborate and fluid structure which was designed to generate effective intelligence while maximising the security of all those involved – from officer and 'co-opted worker' to actual source. 'Co-opted workers', though often described in the Stasi files as 'sources' (*Quellen*), were often not the true sources of the material, since they themselves ran further agents, also called 'sources', or 'persons of trust'. The distance between the provider of intelligence and those who collected it and passed it on was a sort of safety net which protected officers and sources from the Official Secrets Act – and from being caught. The Stasi was also able to minimise the risk of detection by expanding the gap between officer and real source by employing talent spotters and go-betweens.

As we have seen, 'Eckhart' and 'Kraft' were German and 'Freundin' was English. However, the overwhelming majority of those whom the Stasi recruited or exploited – the actual providers of the intelligence that it passed on – can only have been British because East German 'co-opted workers', as Germans, could simply not have had access to the secrets that the 'Centre' and the Politburo in East Berlin desired so ardently. Behind each East German officer there lay at least one Briton, often several. For this reason, it is not unfair to assume that the figure of one hundred individuals as the number of Stasi agents, sources and so on, given to Parliament by the Home Secretary on 21 October 1999, was reasonable and derived from estimates similar to those made here.[1] The Home Secretary did not say how many of these were German and how many British (though sources close to MI5 suggest that roughly half of them were British). It is important to be clear that what hangs on this issue is not just the question of the identity of those Britons who betrayed this country and its liberal values in favour of a Communist secret police, but also a matter which offers key insights into how the Stasi organised its secret intelligence operations.

Although the identification of most of the East German spies requires the careful cross-referencing of various fragments of evidence, some spies' names can be derived from the Stasi files without much trouble. We know, for example, that 'Hans Reichert', a long-serving and senior Stasi IM, was in fact Gerhard Lindner, the ambassador in London from 1984 until 1989.[2] The record of his registration number has been destroyed but his interests, as the only surviving part of his Stasi file reveals, touched on UK affairs in respect of the British peace movement. Lindner, who has never been asked to account for thirty years of spying, including his espionage in the UK, disappeared after 1990. He may be living under an assumed identity anywhere in Germany or, like other high-ranking officials of the GDR, he may have moved to the Middle East. He was an accomplished and highly skilled secret operative and a maker and executor of high policy over many years. In Britain he devoted his energies to gaining intelligence about CND and END, and ran some of the Stasi spies within both organisations. Yet, despite his exalted position in the diplomatic world, he was not the *leading* Stasi agent in the UK: this was always the HVA resident. The Stasi files indicate, too, that he was termed a *Quelle* but was one who himself ran other *Quellen*. He was an IM and therefore not an officer, in German parlance, but was far more than 'an agent' in the English sense. Equally disturbing, he successfully avoided discovery by MI5. By even the most conservative measure, thanks to his training and his extensive list of contacts, including British ones, he still represents a danger to Western interests and British security.

Another important Stasi source of information in London, whose codename does show up in the SIRA documentation, is Dr Hagen Blau, or 'Merten'.[3] He was an IM who received a substantial regular monthly income from the Stasi. Most of his personal records were successfully destroyed. He was identified as a spy, however, in 1990, subsequently tried, and later named by Markus Wolf.

Apart from Blau, Wolf speaks of only one 'resident' in Britain (at any one time, presumably). Wolf clearly wishes us to believe the London spies in the 1980s were all 'diplomats' from the embassy, and were far fewer in number than Jack Straw's and MI5's one hundred individuals. He therefore does not mention the twenty-one SIRA sources and does not tell us how many of them were 'diplomats', how many ran agents, or who was English and who was German. Nor does he disclose the existence of the military intelligence spies (about whose presence in London he plainly knew).

Certainly Hagen Blau did huge damage to Britain's national security, but he was in London for only three years, from February 1971 until 1974. Working as private secretary to Karl-Günther von Hase, one of West Germany's most highly respected and influential ambassadors to the Court of St James, Blau, it is confirmed by his superior, saw and heard all that passed through von Hase's office, as was normal for any private secretary to an ambassador.[4] 'I have often asked myself,' von Hase elaborates, 'what Blau did *not* know. At the time of his espionage in London, Britain was anxious to enter the European Community and the official policy of the Federal Republic was to expedite this in every single way possible.' The Federal Republic, von Hase explains, and especially he himself, enjoyed 'the fullest confidence of various British Prime Ministers, Edward Heath especially, but also Harold Wilson and James Callaghan'. Heath had even invited von Hase and his family to Chequers to spend Christmas with him. Blau would not normally accompany him to Downing Street and was not at Chequers, but he would be told everything after every single meeting. 'Telegrams, letters – he saw the lot,' says von Hase today.

Von Hase adds that an important embassy, like the London one, dealt with a large number of highly sensitive military matters, and received reports of all top secret NATO military discussions (though not necessarily reports of all technical matters relating to weaponry). Blau saw each and every one. He also saw all Western European Union material, as well as secret economic. There is no doubt in von Hase's mind as to the consequences of this: 'all of it will have been of very considerable assistance to the East German regime'. Von Hase believed that the West German government's drive for better relations with the GDR prompted the very security disaster which the Blau case illuminates so clearly.

Von Hase had never heard of Blau before being asked by the head of the West German foreign ministry to have him in London in 1971. He was even asked to employ him for an additional year, which at the time von Hase found 'surprising, if not necessarily suspicious'. Today von Hase recalls that Blau drank too much and was obviously overeager, 'almost too dutiful towards me'. But he did not think for a single minute that he might be a Stasi spy. The security of the embassy as a whole was a matter for the British government, although all vetting of embassy staff was carried out in Bonn. 'We all had the greatest respect for MI5,' von Hase insists, 'we were certain they were bugging our phones – it made us feel secure. We felt safe that they were there and, if they did not express any concerns, we did not have any either.'

Even after Hagen Blau was uncovered (and tried and sentenced to a short period in jail in Germany for spying against the Federal Republic), rather to von Hase's surprise no MI5 officer ever bothered to visit him, either to explore the full extent of Blau's spying or to offer an apology for this most significant of security lapses in the early 1970s. Blau did as much harm to Britain and NATO as he did to the Federal Republic, but he was never required to face a British court. Today Blau, now in his late sixties, is a leading member of a local Communist Party organisation in the Ruhr.

How did the Stasi's London officers physically obtain their secrets? In particular, how did 'Eckhart', the youthful honeypot officer Edgar Uher, face up to the tasks the 'Centre' had placed on his not very experienced shoulders?[5] Whom did he recruit – and how?

As a young blond HVA officer, 'Eckhart' may not have had much experience of high diplomacy, or how to tap the best minds of Britain's political class, but there were some important prizes which could be won with good looks and sheer attentiveness. Time and time again the Stasi files show how attention to the personal life of a target was used to access the secrets that flowed from its public life.[6]

Nevertheless, because of the fluid way in which the Stasi operated, we should never assume, without clear proof, that its British targets had any understanding that this is what they were. To be recognised as a likely target by the Stasi did not automatically imply that the Stasi was recognised *by* the target. Go-betweens played a crucial role here, as did 'false flag recruitment' (pretending to work for Western intelligence agencies).

The HVA (as has been frequently emphasised) was allowed to destroy documentary evidence of its activities. Naturally, it began with the most sensitive files – those giving the identities of its Western agents, its positions, and how the Stasi worked on them and with them.

On this specific matter, Wolf actually does provide a clue but, as always, it is shaped to meet information already in the public domain. His clue does little to illuminate the question:

I valued information from foreign correspondents and columnists highly because they often seemed to me better informed than Western diplomats. Over the decades, we tried to recruit a number of US and British journalists as sources, but we failed. Our only journalistic sources were German and mainly on minor newspapers. Among our own journalists we did not consider it proper to recruit directly although bureau chiefs of the East German news agency and our newspapers who were stationed abroad were expected to confer with members of the foreign intelligence residency in our embassies; we were aware of the reputation of the American and British FBI and MI5 and proceeded very carefully before launching operations in those countries.[7]

One explanation for the provenance of the SIRA material (or at any rate a large part of it, mostly provided by 'Eckhart') – an explanation which MI5 offered in 2000 (but seems to have been persuaded to abandon in 2002) – is that it was collected, overtly and quite legally, from the Royal Institute of International Affairs, otherwise known as Chatham House, at 10 St James's Square in London. On the face of it, a large number of SIRA items do appear to be connected with events staged at Chatham House. Although Chatham House liked to present itself as a 'holy of holies', in which the most important and often sensitive issues in foreign policy were explored for its audiences, it was not, in fact, a secret institution; nor, strictly speaking, did it claim to be one. For this reason, so MI5 argued, the Stasi's Chatham House 'espionage' was not a threat to British national security and so it did (and does) not constitute 'a problem' in the eyes of the Security Service.[8] Chatham House, like the British Council, was never used for secret purposes by British intelligence (nor were any of its employees ever recruited as agents of British intelligence).[9] We should recall that the HVA was highly professional and that the documentary evidence of the intelligence it collected was not the sort of material which would be generated by any public, or semi-public event, despite what Uher (or any of the other 'Eckharts') may have subsequently claimed about their being able to palm off reports of Chatham House meetings in this way. It is true, however, that in 'Eckhart's' case we have only the descriptions of the contents, not the contents themselves. It is also clear that some of his intelligence was similar to subjects raised at Chatham House.

To any outsider with interests in Britain and its foreign policy, Chatham House might well have been seen as an Aladdin's Cave of national and international secrets. It was certainly a very smart institute, in the smartest part of London. It was meant to come over as the heart of the British Establishment – and it did so, in the 1980s, with rare panache. In 1980 HM The Queen visited Chatham House and made an important speech (published in the annual report) in which she said, among other things:

> For sixty years leading figures from the world stage – statesmen and scholars, businessmen and journalists – have come here to talk about their problems [. . .] Now that Britain is much more at the mercy of fast-moving events abroad it is that much more vital to try

to see the way events are going as clearly and as early as possible.
The day of the specialist is here and you have, I am glad to hear, met
his [sic] demands by providing expert and detailed studies . . .

Her Majesty was absolutely right to make the point that *leading* figures were frequently to be found addressing Chatham House
audiences. A glance at the most celebrated of Chatham House's
speakers from 1981 to 1990 reads like a who's who of international
affairs at the very highest level. All these people spoke either at
'open' members' meetings (which outsiders could attend) or at
'closed' ones (for invited members only). It is safe to assume that all
these speakers would, at one time or another, have shared in their
nation's most sensitive secrets. However, every single one of them
would have understood the need to keep quiet about matters which
they might have knowledge but which could not be properly disclosed in public lectures. Their speeches and talks did not, and
could not, in themselves, constitute secret intelligence.

Even so, perhaps partly for marketing purposes, Chatham House
liked to portray itself as a quasi-secretive body. This could be seen
most obviously in the emphasis it laid on its world famous 'Rule',
which read as follows: 'In order that speakers may feel free to
express their opinion, all meetings of the Institute shall, unless otherwise stated, be strictly private. Those present shall be free to use
information received at meetings of the Institute but it shall be the
condition of such use that the speaker's name shall not be quoted,
nor the fact mentioned that the information was obtained at a meeting of the Institute.'

The Rule implied that important confidential truths, if not actual
secrets, would be disseminated at Chatham House events. It was, of
course, hardly a deterrent to any serious hostile intelligence service
who were not going to give two hoots about this Rule, but it made
Chatham House sound mighty important.

In addition, its original regulations on its own membership
implied that Chatham House was a site where important national
and international confidences might be exchanged since full or
nominated membership was confined to British or Commonwealth
subjects. This was later revised to offer full membership to United

States citizens and then to citizens of the European Community. The regulations were changed again towards the end of the 1970s to include Soviet bloc diplomats as 'associate corporate members'. However, Communist bloc citizens were still denied membership. This procedure allowed a small number of diplomats nominated by the East German Embassy to take advantage of some of Chatham House's facilities (its occasional fee-paying conferences were open to anyone prepared to pay for them). They could attend all public meetings but they could not vote at AGMs, were deemed outsiders rather than insiders, and were not invited to study groups or 'closed' meetings.[10]

Clearly, Chatham House's original idea had been that its meetings should be confined to those who were stakeholders in the British system and, it was assumed, would not want to betray it (indicating that such a possibility existed); membership was then extended to all Westerners, following the same logic. When East European and other Communist diplomats were given access towards the end of the 1970s, this was done in the knowledge that no real secrets would ever be disclosed at Chatham House events and that the wish to be inclusive might win friends behind the Iron Curtain and dissolve fears about Western intentions. Naturally this meant an East German intelligence officer pretending to be a diplomat could easily become a 'nominated member' by virtue of the embassy's corporate associate subscribing membership. However, he would gain nothing of actual intelligence value from doing so.

Today Chatham House says that it did realise that some of those who were put forward for associate membership by the embassies of Communist states might be intelligence officers. Yet it was given no guidance as to its policy on this by MI5.

The changes made to its membership rules showed that, in the eyes of those who ran it, Chatham House needed to move away from any pretence of being a major repository of Western and British secrets and of wishing to trade on this basis any longer. At the same time, like all good clubs it did not want to abandon exclusivity altogether. Even though its security was hardly leading-edge, Chatham House did accept that in some cases its meetings might touch on sensitive material, or that its speakers might make unguarded comments, and that not everyone should have access to them. This was the reason for its having 'open' and 'closed' meetings ('private discussion meetings' and 'study groups' respectively). Associate corporate subscribing members were only eligible for admission to the former so long as they agreed to abide by the Chatham House Rule. The East Germans fell into this category. Admission to study groups, however, at which some of the most sensitive issues were discussed, were by invitation only and not open to associate members. They were, however, allowed to consult the library and the press cuttings.

There seems, then, to be some plausibility in the idea that SIRA material could have been lifted by 'Eckhart' from Chatham House's public or semi-public meetings. As we have seen, Uher himself has made this claim and several journalists have been inclined to follow this line. The *Sunday Times*, for example, wrote on 26 November 2000 that:

Agent Eckhart was a prolific London operative, [wrongly] reported earlier this year to have been employed by Chatham House, the influential think-tank. When the *Sunday Times* traced him through a former controller, he ridiculed this report. He was in fact a diplomat at the East German Embassy and is now a businessman. He agreed to be interviewed on condition that he was not named. 'I laughed my head off when I read that I was supposed to be an employee of Chatham House.' In fact, he said, he was a fully paid-up member of Chatham House, not an employee, and met many public figures there when politicians and senior officials came to speak 'off the record'. He said that he had roamed freely among the great and the good and had found no shortage of willing sources of information . . . 'I was the most productive of all the agents in London,' Eckhart said. 'But if you looked at my reports, you would notice that many were nothing but accounts of events at Chatham House. All that information was available to people who paid the membership fee.

Is it true, then, that 'Eckhart's' intelligence gathering in this particular sphere (he did other things as well) was simply lifted from reports of Chatham House's public or semi-public events? If the answer is 'yes', the story about the provenance of this part of Uher's espionage ends here. If, however, the answer is 'no', there has to be an entirely different explanation for the intriguing connection which binds 'Eckhart' to Chatham House – and which Uher's subsequent statements are designed to conceal. The answer is 'no'. 'Eckhart' has obviously lost none of his black arts. What is more, this conclusion makes it plain that most of what 'Eckhart' collected truly would have been secret intelligence. The facts suggest that Chatham House was indeed of concern to the Stasi, but, during almost all of 'Eckhart's' spying, only at one remove. As we shall see, over time 'Eckhart's' interest in Chatham House turned into an interest in a particular individual with immediate and better access to it than he could gain himself.

By the late 1980s, when 'Eckhart' was no longer listed in SIRA as a source, Chatham House began to solicit more active East European involvement in its affairs by explicitly inviting individuals from Soviet bloc states, including East Germany, to come and 'work' there. In the annual report for 1989, for example, Sir James Eberle, the Director, noted that 'a succession of visiting scholars from East European countries' had visited 10 St James's Square in 1988–9, and that 'intensive discussions about a future European architecture was taking place between the RIIA and participants from Hungary, Poland, the Soviet Union and East Germany'. He was blissfully unaware that the East German 'scholars' included at least one experienced Stasi spy, H. H. Kasper, and the research institute from which they came – Institut für Wirtschaft und Politik, the IPW (Institute for Policy and Economics) – was a Stasi front.[11] By 1989 it was actually listed as a partner. Having such people on the inside of Chatham House after 1989 was a very different matter and clearly a very dangerous one. In the event, however, by this time the HVA *already had a source inside the building*, so not much changed. Fortunately, the GDR was shortly to collapse in any case, so the damage would have been minimal.

For all that has been rightly said about the formal absence of secrets at Chatham House, some research was undertaken behind the scenes into confidential and, at times, secret matters. In addition, major political figures, who knew how to keep their mouths shut in public, were bound to be less cautious in private. If the Stasi's interest in Chatham House can be shown to have revolved around these private deliberations and discreet conversations, rather than its public or semi-public events, information about them could become genuine espionage and would constitute a serious breach of security both for Chatham House and the UK. It was at this level that secret intelligence could certainly be generated, and collected. A brief glance at some of the brilliant and highly influential people who worked behind the scenes at Chatham House in the 1980s shows them to be individuals whose private views were occasionally worth soliciting for intelligence purposes. They included David Watt, Director until 1984, when he was replaced by Sir James Eberle, a senior British admiral; William Wallace, a key adviser to the then leader of the Liberal Party, David Steele; Keith Kyle, a highly regarded British journalist; Pauline Neville-Jones, said to be the cleverest woman in the Foreign Office; John Roper; Nick Butler, a key adviser to British Petroleum, close to major reformers in the Labour Party; and Laurence Freedman, an expert on security policy. They, and other leading figures, all came to think and debate with their peers at 10 St James's Square in the 1980s.

Of course, no ordinary member, and certainly no associate, would ever have been allowed anywhere near high-level chatter or activities such as the important defence research undertaken by Ian Smart and Laurence Freedman on nuclear weapons, or the work done in 1984–5 by John Roper, enticingly entitled 'The Future of British Defence Policy'. The fruits of this research would generally be published, but whatever was published would obviously be carefully vetted: none of Chatham House's able researchers would have wished to publish sensitive material which might harm Britain. Roper himself was (and still is) a leading defence expert, at the time exceptionally well informed about official thinking in the British government and NATO, and some of his work was highly sensitive.[12] Outsiders were kept well away from these matters. Yet, as the SIRA entries for 1983–4 prove, the Stasi did get close to the hidden treasures of Chatham House – far too close – and almost certainly by chance, through what was probably an unforeseen and unexpected encounter with someone who had easy access to what was going on there. It was not Chatham House, the institution, that attracted the Stasi, but some of the people who stopped off there for a time, carrying out research.[13]

One reason for believing the Stasi was interested in some of the transitory personnel there, rather than the institution itself, comes from the fact, already noted, that in the mid-1980s they drew up a list of the HVA's institutional targets in the UK at this time. This list did *not* include Chatham House, which means that the Stasi believed that, as an institution, it had no formal secret role and was therefore not worth targeting as one. Interestingly, the HVA and MI6 came to exactly the same conclusions. Yet we know that some of what 'Eckhart' got his hands on had a Chatham House link, *and* that it was rated as secret intelligence by ZAIG (the central evaluation unit), which as we have seen, was organisationally distinct from the Stasi's collectors precisely so that it could maintain high professional objectivity – and to avoid being duped. Had ZAIG not been satisfied that what 'Eckhart' was providing was secret intelligence, it would not have been included in the SIRA archive. Of course, it might have been possible for 'Eckhart' to dupe them, had he so wanted, but it is unthinkable that he could have done so successfully for five years, between 1981 and 1986. If 'Eckhart' had acquired so much of value from slipping into public meetings at 10 St James's Square, or even into meetings which he was not permitted to attend, and had he thereby been able to get his hands on secret intelligence, accepted as such by ZAIG, Chatham House would undoubtedly have been a formal HVA target.

Since it was not a formal target, and since the intelligence was genuine, the connection between 'Eckhart' and Chatham House and the actual origin of the intelligence cannot have been an institutional one. It can only have been a personal one, tying 'Eckhart' to a member of Chatham House, either directly or using a go-between. To put it another way, 'Eckhart' was running a spy in Chatham House, either directly or indirectly; there was some third party involved in the arrangement. The importance of Chatham House to the Stasi was its source there, rather than Chatham House itself.

This conclusion is supported by strong evidence from other quarters. If we compare SIRA material with actual Chatham House events, the first thing that becomes obvious is the *lack* of use the Stasi made of the star speakers. Very few of the celebrities speaking at St James's ever show up as named personalities in Stasi materials. One or two of them (to whom we shall return) were of interest to the 'Centre' in East Berlin, but a considerable number of renowned individuals were completely ignored by 'Eckhart' and his Stasi colleagues in London. The Stasi could not have cared less about the high calibre of its public speakers. Indeed, it is as revealing to note, rather, how the HVA did *not* use Chatham House than record how they did. Theirs was not a broad-brush approach to British thinking. Rather, the SIRA documents and the intelligence briefings show that the collection was focused on certain specific subjects and individuals. The HVA did not share the British penchant for listening to the views of political has-beens, however illustrious the posts they might once have occupied. SIRA is evidence of the clear, strategically driven and cool assessment by the HVA of the true requirements of East German secret intelligence.

A careful analysis of all Chatham House events and the SIRA entries under 'Eckhart's' name shows clearly they were almost never straightforward records of Chatham House events. Of 149 pieces of relevant SIRA intelligence which superficially appear to be connected with Chatham House, no more than 6 can even be indirectly related to the *precise* topics of the talks and speeches given there. The number of pieces of intelligence which may have been triggered by such talks and speeches is greater – but 110 pieces of SIRA intelligence bear no relation whatsoever to anything officially presented at Chatham House in the 1980s.

Where superficially there appears to be a connection between the topics analysed at Chatham House events and those addressed by 'Eckhart' in his intelligence work, closer examination shows they were, in fact, quite different from each other.

On 28 July 1982 'Eckhart' despatched material on 'the SDP's evaluation of the internal and external effects of the Falklands War'. Dr David Owen, we find, had spoken at an open meeting of Chatham House on 10 June. 'Eckhart' may have been in the audience. But Dr

Owen's topic of discussion was an entirely different one, which had nothing to do with the Falklands War. (It was entitled 'Common Security: The Views of the Palme Commission on Disarmament'.) Here is an example of a topic – disarmament – which it might be expected would have been of interest to the HVA. Had 'Eckhart' reported on it, his bosses might have been well satisfied. Yet this was *not* the subject of 'Eckhart's' report. Instead, he disclosed information on another object of the HVA's concern, the Falklands, which had proved that under Margaret Thatcher Britain was prepared to use military force in pursuit of a political objective.

It is as if Dr Owen's presence at Chatham House had a public dimension (the Palme Commission) which sparked a subsequent private HVA investigation (on the Falklands) and that it was this private one which 'Eckhart' submitted as secret intelligence, rather than Owen's actual speech. A few weeks earlier, on 20 and 27 April 1982, there had been two open meetings on the Falklands at Chatham House, with SDP speakers present. The day after the second meeting, 'Eckhart' filed his secret intelligence, a document (entitled 'A British Evaluation of the Falklands War') rather than a report. Plainly, there was some connection between this document and the two meetings, but it was neither straightforward nor obvious. In some way, 'Eckhart' seems to have got hold of a document, possibly one which informed, at a private level, the two public meetings.

Another example can be found on 1 February 1984, when 'Eckhart' submitted another document following a speech at Chatham House on 4 November 1983 by the then British Foreign Secretary, Sir Geoffrey Howe, entitled 'The Future of the European Community'. Yet 'Eckhart's' document addressed a 'UK View on FRG–GDR Relations'. The document may have been linked in some way to Sir Geoffrey's speech – but the two subjects are most definitely not one and the same. Was the document (nonetheless of the greatest interest to the East Germans) generated in some way by Sir Geoffrey's visit to Chatham House, even if his talk was on something entirely different?

Other examples lead inexorably in the same direction. A series of intelligence pieces sent by 'Eckhart' and his comrade 'Kunze' in 1984 (for example, the document 'On English Defence', dated 24

March 1984, the report on the British arms industry, dated 10 May 1984, the report sent on 26 November 1984 on 'The Position of Leading British Military Figures on Waging Nuclear War') clearly relate to sensitive British defence issues and do not chime with any specific Chatham House event apart from an open meeting addressed by Sir James Eberle on 15 November 1984. What they do chime with, however, is the research and study group on the future of British defence policy, underway behind the scenes, to which 'Eckhart' could not possibly have had personal access. It is as if the HVA was able to consult its source on individual topics, and that this view, rather than a discussion of the topic itself, formed the basis of the secret intelligence.

On 28 January 1982 'Eckhart' sent papers to East Berlin on 'The Foreign Policy of the SDP'. On 11 December 1981, Roy Jenkins – still President of the European Commission – spoke at Chatham House on the 'case for UK membership of the European Community'. The SDP had been formed on 26 March 1981, so although Jenkins himself did not win a seat in Parliament for the SDP until March 1982, 'Eckhart' was right to spot the key part of his platform was that, unlike the Labour Party, at the time committed to withdrawal from Europe, the SDP would be a European party. Yet the precise topic of 'Eckhart's' interest and the topic of Jenkins's speech were different from each other. It is as if Jenkins's public words – as President of the Commission – had, in some way, led to a more private and internal discussion about Jenkins's personal plans – as prospective parliamentary leader of the SDP.

Usually, then, a piece of 'Eckhart's' SIRA intelligence would focus on a specific aspect of a wider topic considered at Chatham House. It would seem that what interested the HVA about this were the background discussions within Chatham House that paralleled public discussion of the topic. Areas which might have been of prime interest would have concerned the reasons for the choice of topic, the private thoughts of the experts and politicians in developing the topic and so forth – but not the actual delivery of the public speech itself. It can be readily seen that whatever 'Eckhart' said in the *Sunday Times*, his intelligence work did not consist of simply writing about what had been said at public or closed meetings at Chatham House. It would have been nice to prick the bubble of Markus Wolf's proud boast that the Stasi was the finest secret intelligence organisation in the Communist world; if anything, the Chatham House spying confirms that it was.

It is not merely that 'Eckhart's' topics and those of Chatham House differ in their exact substance, but, where the topics do dovetail, comparing their respective dates reveals a most peculiar feature about the items sent to East Berlin. It will be recalled from the SIRA material that in East Berlin the 'Centre' recorded the precise date on which SIRA material was sent to it from London and when it arrived. The Chatham House annual reports, on the other hand, set down the dates on which its meetings were held. By comparing the two sets of dates, we can see that many pieces of intelligence were delivered to East Berlin *before* the Chatham House meeting to which they refer took place. Repeatedly, it can be seen that these Stasi reports which relate closely to Chatham House topics anticipate and predate the actual Chatham House discussion of them.

On 14 May 1982, for example, 'Eckhart' sent a document on 'the European Contribution to NATO' to Berlin. This was a typical Chatham House subject – indeed, Chatham House did run a series on NATO. But the series did not start until *June* 1982 – thus the document of 14 May preceded the talks to which it was supposed to be related. On 13 October 1982 'Eckhart' wrote on 'The View of the Foreign Policy Committee of the Labour Party on the Creation of a CDU/CSU/FDP Government in the Federal Republic of Germany'. German affairs were certainly a subject with which Chatham House concerned itself, but its series on West Germany did not start until *November* 1982. Once more, the report preceded the actual meeting.

Similarly, in June 1982 there were some meetings on the European contribution to NATO but 'Eckhart's' report was compiled in May. There are many other instances of this. In December 1982 and March 1983 there were reports on 'Burden Sharing in NATO'. This was a topic for a study group to which the East Germans would not have had access. The Chatham House report on this matter was published, but not until after April 1983. Yet it is possible that the papers for this study group, which would plainly have been of interest to the East Germans, may have lain around inside Chatham House since December 1982 and been picked up by 'Eckhart'. Certainly, associate members were not supposed to be privy to the discussions which generated this 'policy paper'.

According to Chatham House the position on these papers was as follows: 'The Falklands papers were prepared in a great hurry; copies would *not* have been sent to members or associates automatically; a few might have been sent out for comment or review before in advance of publication.' Chatham House itself concludes: 'It might be that "the agent" had access to the papers when they were in preparation.'[14]

On 1 April and 7 April 1983 'Eckhart' sent one document and one report on British preparations for the Williamsburg Summit. This may sound like a Chatham House event, but it was not. What is more, both the report and the document preceded the summit, which took place on 28 May 1983.

From 1981 to 1983 it is just possible that Chatham House may have sent papers in advance of forthcoming events to the East Germans in Belgrave Square. If this did happen it would have stopped in 1983 for a simple reason explained below. What this suggests, yet again, is that where this happened after 1983, the Stasi had someone in Chatham House who was not only supplying the material but was also, in some way, giving what the Stasi thought was an authoritative British view upon it. It can be seen that, on some occasions, a Chatham House topic appears to have been lifted straight into an East German report. But frequently it is mediated by a 'British view' on the topic.

Some pieces of intelligence are, however, undoubtedly linked directly to Chatham House events: a good (if rare) example is a report sent to the 'Centre' in East Berlin on 8 October 1982 entitled 'UK Policy on China'. This seems to have come from a *closed* meeting (to which no East German could have been invited) on the 'Chinese Communist Party', convened by an expert on the subject, Dr Jonathan Mirsky. Another is an *open* meeting addressed by Denis Healey on 7 December 1982 on 'Labour's Foreign Policy': on 2 March 1983 'Eckhart' sent a report to East Germany entitled 'On Foot, Shore, Kinnock and Healey'. Another report sent on 15 September 1983 by him, entitled 'Nuclear Weapons in the UK and

France', could well relate to an *open* talk given by Colonel Jonathan Alford, the strategy specialist, on 28 July; this was entitled 'The Place of British and French Nuclear Weapons in Arms Controls'. The links here *seem* plain but we cannot be sure because the materials themselves have been destroyed.

As to the confident assertion that 'Eckhart's' espionage flowed from the East German membership of Chatham House, when scrutinised this can be seen to be quite unconvincing. The insistence that his intelligence stemmed from his own membership of Chatham House was a lie, designed to protect his sources as any intelligence officer is taught to do.

Although the East Germans were indeed registered associate corporate members from 1979 until April 1983 and then again from April 1987 until 1990, they were *not* recorded as associate members of Chatham House for almost four of the six years when 'Eckhart' allegedly obtained his material from going along to its meetings (lists of members were published in each annual report and corporate membership, at this time, ran from March to April, a financial year). Even if Chatham House had been sending the East Germans material including papers they were not entitled to receive prior to April 1983, no such material would have been sent after April of that year. And if 'Eckhart' were anywhere in St James's at this time, he was ogling elegant hats at Bates's, or buying smart City shirts at Lewin's, but not attending Chatham House meetings. The general practice in respect of study groups (which the East Germans were not entitled to attend) was to send out papers to members in advance of the meetings, although this would be done for members only and the papers marked 'confidential'. It is possible that papers may have been left lying around in Chatham House where a resourceful spy might conceivably have laid his or her hands on them. But if they were subsequently deposited in the library, there was no open access to them. Speeches were taped but not, as a rule, transcribed, although sometimes some speeches would be published after delivery in *International Affairs*. In short, there was no legal 'general access' to what was discussed at study groups, and digests for talks were not filed for 'general access' to the library in advance of their being given.

Since he was, in fact, not a 'fully paid up member' after April 1983 (as the *Sunday Times* wrongly suggested), he would not have been able to attend any of its meetings, whether general, open or closed. They were, as we have seen, by invitation only. Although Chatham House sources suggest that non-members were sometimes invited to these confidential meetings if they had specialist skills, when it came to NATO, or British defence policy, the East Germans had none (or not the ones Chatham House had in mind). And Chatham House confirms that, where membership dues remained unpaid, it would not have invited non-members to attend over a continuous period of four years. This means that, from April 1983 until the end of his time in London, 'Eckhart's' SIRA material did not emanate directly from his corporate East German membership of Chatham House and probably not before then either, when he was technically a member. At the same time, it has to be stressed, there plainly was a link between 'Eckhart' and Chatham House which continued until he departed. There is no reason to suppose that this link was a direct one, or that 'Eckhart' ever entered 10 St James's at any point.

What possible explanation can there be for the lapse in East Germany's membership of Chatham House in 1983, given 'Eckhart's' ties with it and the potential such a connection offered for espionage? How are we to explain the resumption of its membership by March 1987? The East Germans had moved towards it in 1979, away from it in 1983, and then back again towards it in 1987. Each of these dates is significant in its own way. Furthermore, knowing from its files how the Stasi operated, and its massive attention to detail, it is highly likely that, if the reasons for its apparently contradictory behaviour were different each time, they were always consistent with the highest attention afforded to the logic of conspiracy. We must remember that we are dealing here with 'Chekists' – well-trained but fanatical subversives.

If 'Eckhart' had used Chatham House as MI5 have suggested, it is unthinkable that the East Germans would have let their membership lapse for four years. The response that staff at Chatham House may have been incompetent, and may never have checked the membership of people attending its meetings, lacks credibility, as does the idea that the Stasi might have been trying to save money. Not only could the Stasi not bank on official incompetence over a four-year period, the risk involved in turning up for meetings as lapsed members would have been immense. We may recall that the Stasi was almost pathologically cautious about being discovered. From the Stasi point of view, any of its officers masquerading as a diplomat being challenged as to why he was attending meetings when he was not entitled to do so would have compromised the entire security of its Chatham House operation. For all the Stasi knew, Chatham House, becoming instantly suspicious of the East Germans, might have run straight to MI5. As for money, the Stasi had more than enough. Is it conceivable that they would have tried to save money, given the risk it would entail? The answer is obvious; they would never have done so.

Much more probable is that the East Germans joined Chatham House initially for entirely diplomatic reasons; and, because the West Germans were also members, it made further sense to be seen to be there as well. Chatham House itself was not, in the mid-1980s, an HVA target. During these years, however, it seems likely that 'Comrade Chance' introduced the HVA to a member in whom they proceeded to take increasing interest, either directly or indirectly through a go-between. It was this member (who could also have been an employee) who was the HVA target. Then, in 1983, something happened to this member which obliged the HVA to instruct the East German Embassy to withdraw its membership of Chatham House.

What this 'something' was may no longer be a mystery. Extensive research reveals exactly how this apparently bizarre behaviour should be interpreted, for we know from many other examples – in military intelligence files and elsewhere – that it was classic Stasi spycraft to distance any obvious East German presence from 'operational objects' on which they were working, but with whom they lacked a legitimate relationship that could account for the contact.[15] What was signified by this particular move was that the Stasi's target had found himself or herself more closely involved with Chatham House than he or she had previously been. To minimise the danger of any overt link being made between events inside Chatham House and the Stasi, the embassy needed to step back. To the outside world the distance that the Stasi put between itself and Chatham House after 1982 suggested indifference towards 10 St James's Square. In reality, it meant exactly the opposite.

In 1987 things changed again. This could indicate that their source had moved away from Chatham House, that a way had been found for constructing a legitimate connection between him or her and the East German Embassy, or that the East Germans had become aware of a new opportunity, the value of which would outweigh earlier caution and make rejoining plausible, if not entirely risk-free. There is indeed a clear indication of one highly attractive incentive, which would also have prevented any legal relationship with their source from raising any questions. As noted, in 1988 Chatham House had been host to two researchers from West Germany – and also from East Germany – working under John Roper, at that time Director of Studies at Chatham House. Clearly, such a plan would have had to have been developed before 1988. The Chatham House plans were of great benefit to East Germany both as a public statement that it was now accepted in the UK as the 'other' German state, and, of course, it automatically presented the HVA with even more ways of using a legitimate cover to gain intelligence. What better way for the GDR to demonstrate its commitment to the high ideals of Chatham House than to rejoin?

This explanation for the Stasi's behaviour may seem Byzantine and far-fetched, but it is far from so. Close analysis of the Stasi files shows time and time again how committed the Stasi was to working out every detail, to analysing each option (or 'variant') and to moving carefully, but always single-mindedly, forward.

From the Stasi's point of view, there was one Briton whose exceptional career in British public life must have attracted its interest. Discreetly and distinctively it spanned the Labour Party and the SDP, British defence and security policy, and NATO issues. It provided numerous points of contact with those very fields in which we know, from SIRA and the intelligence digests, that the HVA took such a strong interest. Convincing circumstantial evidence allows us to suggest who that person might have been. This is a subject to be explored later.

There are two final points worth bearing in mind, both of which strongly support the suggestion that 'Eckhart' had an agent inside Chatham House after 1983. The first, explored in Chapter 13, is concerned with the fact that the Stasi got hold of two of Admiral Sir James Eberle's passports and photocopied them for their files. Sir James was not appointed to Chatham House (where he kept his passports) until 1984. The HVA may have had someone working for them at the Passport Office in Petty France, but it is probably more likely that his passports were taken (on two separate occasions) from Chatham House. Second, it is an astonishing fact that all Chatham House's own written records of its relations with the East Germans are today inexplicably missing. If the Stasi had collected most of their British material from Chatham House, this would suggest not just that it mistook covert for overt intelligence but that it was one of the few sources actually available to it. This in turn would show MI5 in a favourable light, because it would indicate that it had closed all other openings. Since, however, the *real* link between Chatham House and the Stasi was indeed a secret one, and quite different from that first claimed by MI5, the charge still stands that the East German operations represented a serious threat to British national security, on a par with the sort of covert intelligence operations which led to lengthy jail sentences for individuals involved with it.[16]

In his 1989–90 Chatham House report Sir James Eberle wrote: 'We have continued to provide briefings on both immediate and long-term issues for policy makers. Our staff have briefed the Labour Party's new European Committee . . . We have welcomed our regular and increasing flow of visiting fellows from partner institutions in Europe', and he listed the East German Institute for Policy and Economics among them. Had he had sight of the Stasi files at the time (which he can hardly have done) he might have added, 'We have also briefed the East German secret intelligence and secret military intelligence services and have welcomed visiting fellows from the HVA in East Germany.'

In short, the reassuring view, originally supported by MI5, that Stasi intelligence gathering stemmed from its officers' listening to erudite meetings at Chatham House is simply unsustainable. In fact, the collection of foreign policy materials by the Stasi in London followed the same principles that governed the procurement of its secret intelligence in other fields, notably the British peace movement, to whom we now turn.

## PART IV

# PENETRATION AND RECRUITMENT

# 12

# Penetrating the British Peace Movement

So far, the Stasi files have shown that the chief intelligence collectors in London were the officers of the Stasi (HVA and military intelligence officers and 'co-opted workers', or IMs). Those who supplied them with the intelligence – the Stasi agents, further 'co-opted workers', contacts and persons of trust, in short the Stasi's real sources – were all embedded in one way or another in what the Stasi called its 'British objects' (that is, the British institutions, policies and personalities in which they took an interest). We have noted that when the Stasi thought they would derive an advantage from doing so, they were happy to exploit the fluid structure of their intelligence and security system to conceal the skill with which they targeted recruits and sought to influence the flow of the events that concerned them.

On one level, the Stasi trusted no one, not even its own 'co-opted workers' and officers in the field, not its sources, persons of trust or contacts. Nor did the Stasi, as a general rule, like volunteers. The Stasi chose you, not the other way round. But – logically – in order to be chosen, you first had to be a Stasi target. Yet those on whom the Stasi spied, but did not want to select as spies, were also targets. Targets were therefore always victims. Some, however, became recruits and sources. Some remained victims. Joachim Gauck, the 'father' of research into the Stasi, wrote in 1991 that it was often very difficult to distinguish between 'perpetrators' and 'victims' when it came to the East German secret police – what he called '*die schwierige Grenzziehung zwischen Tätern und Opfern*' (the difficulty of drawing a dividing line between perpetrators and victims).[1]

This book is an account based on the Stasi's own files (which it did not for one moment think would ever enter the public domain). It is a Stasi eye view of East German concerns in the UK, of British individuals it wished to target, of its agents and sources in the UK. It is also a Stasi eye view of those it regarded as its intelligence assets but at all times about what the Stasi *believed*, in its inner secret core, to be true. The claims that are made are always clearly shown to be claims made by the Stasi; but just because it believed something to be true, it does not automatically follow that it was the truth, or that because it believed it was making a gain in any particular area, Britain or the West were actually being harmed.

The files show that the list of people who had contact with the Stasi is large. Most of these were neither 'sources' (in the East German sense) nor agents (in the English one), but just people in whom the Stasi had a serious interest and about whom it wished to know more. Most of them did not seek the Stasi's attentions and many rejected them out of hand. Where they did so, they were, as we shall see below, always left alone. Merely to be targeted by the Stasi as a source of intelligence, or even paid by them without realising who was making the payment, does not prove such people either did or intended to do harm.

The main names of those caught up in the web of espionage that is reflected in the Stasi files range from Sir Rudy Sternberg (Lord Plurenden), Harold Wilson's confidante in the 1950s (whose files tell us much about the 'Wilson Plot'), to Lord Roper, currently Lib-Dem Chief Whip in the Lords who had contact with the Stasi from at least the mid-1980s to 1990. Many well-known names were the objects of Stasi interest. Most of them, however, were simply the targets and never assisted the East Germans in any way at all.

However, some of them did provide assistance to East Germany, a state which regarded Britain as 'the enemy'. They were the Stasi's persons of trust. How do we know? Not just because the files prove the Stasi trusted them (though not more than it trusted anyone, including itself) and acted on what they said, but also that they obviously trusted the Stasi, or those East German 'diplomats' they believed reported to the Stasi. This is why none of them has ever disclosed their relationship with the East German secret police until now. Some of these persons of trust were also the 'victims' of Stasi spying, themselves spied upon. Paradoxical perhaps, but the hallmark of Stasi spycraft was that, on a deeper level, no one who worked for it could go unmonitored and no one would ever be let go. As Wolf put it: 'It amazes me that otherwise intelligent Westerners believed they remained masters of their own destiny. No cooperation with an intelligence service is ever forgotten. It can be unearthed and used against you until your dying day.'[2] He was spot-on.

It must be stressed that without the help of the CIA we remain uncertain about the precise relationship between some of those investigated below, and the Stasi *Quellen* as set out in the SIRA material (see Appendix 5) ('Birke', 'Brücke', 'Dieter', 'Dreher', 'Eckhart', 'Fröbel', 'Genf', 'Granit', 'Gregor', 'Kraft', 'Mark', 'Pepp', 'Stern', 'Wald', 'Wien') and in the files of the military intelligence unit ('Adler', 'Akzent', 'Astor', 'Baldur', 'Barber', 'Basalt', 'Bill', 'Isak', 'Ivo', 'Palme' and 'Rave'). Some of these *Quellen* were officers, some British agents. Yet, where the Stasi used real names in their files, we do know the identities of the people who helped them. Where those named made statements or gave reports to the Stasi, there is no problem about concluding that these were some of the people who gave the Stasi the items of intelligence in question, which it then retained on file.

We should not forget that – in the words of a very senior British secret intelligence officer – the Stasi were 'very, very good': they had lots of money, they were given a free hand by the KGB, and they were the heirs to the German tradition of ruthless efficiency. We must recall that at various times in a two-year period the Stasi paid out £206,895 for operational purposes – that is, for intelligence. This was not peanuts and it was not used to buy any. We cannot know how much of the intelligence listed below was paid for; nor can we know, as yet, who received Stasi cash for handing over material. But it is as plain as a pikestaff that some did.

In all, the Stasi spying generated at least eight thousand pieces of intelligence about British politics, including documents, attributed

to almost one hundred sources from the late 1970s to 1989. Some of
these sources may be identical with other HVA and Stasi sources,
and if so will include individuals whose names we do have. It also
produced an estimated two thousand pieces of secret military intelligence and an unknown quantity of industrial espionage. It is true
that some of the sources (in the English sense) may not even have
realised their contact was an East German intelligence officer –
the East Germans were brilliant linguists and could also, *in
extremis*, always pass as West Germans.

Let us turn now to the files concerned with the British peace
movement and with British support for the East German human
and civil rights movement (from the Stasi's viewpoint, at times these
two fields merged into one).[3] Before chasing the leads some general
observations must be made. The first thing to bear in mind is the
*context* in which these secret intelligence files must be seen.

To those who knew little about the GDR, the obvious central concern of the East German leadership with the British peace
movement, and with peace issues more generally, might seem curious. Similarly it might not be immediately apparent as to why these
materials were seen as secret *intelligence*, or necessarily *secret*,
even though the fact of their location in the Stasi Archive means that
it must be accepted that the East Germans regarded the information
as secret intelligence. But secret intelligence it was, and on reflection it is obvious why this should be so.

We know its status for the simple reason that it was placed in
secret intelligence files (and not in the diplomatic files of the East
German Foreign Office, for example). The Stasi also made it perfectly plain when named sources (in the English sense) gave it
information of their own free will. This, naturally, put them at huge
risk. Finally, where they were used to steer the peace movement in
Britain, they were executing one important aspect of the work of any
secret intelligence service.

There are two main reasons why this field was considered to be
absolutely crucial by East German policy makers and quite fundamental to the survival of the Communist system. They wanted
Britain to disarm unilaterally and to neutralise those in the British
peace movement helping East German dissidents who were fighting

for disarmament but also for civil rights. The East Germans, like the Soviets and the rest of the Soviet bloc, were seriously rattled and weakened by the harsh policies pursued by NATO since the 1979 twin-track decision to deploy Cruise and Pershing missiles in Europe to counter a new perceived Soviet ICBM threat. Most observers today believe that the Communists knew they could not afford the massive rearmament into which NATO policies obliged them to enter. They therefore had every reason to seek ways of minimising the impact of NATO's rearmament.

Several strategies were pursued by the East Germans (and the Eastern bloc as a whole). One consisted of trying to stress in Britain and other Western countries that the 'Socialist States' were peace-loving and had not initiated the arms race, which was, therefore, unnecessary. We may recall Soviet Foreign Minister Gromyko's famous words to Nancy Reagan – 'whisper peace in your husband's ear every night'.[4] Another was to seek to promote the fortunes of those political forces within Britain which shared the East Germans' opposition to NATO's rearmament, in particular CND, which was committed to Britain's unilateral, or one-sided, nuclear disarmament, irrespective of any corresponding disarmament within the Soviet bloc. The East Germans liked CND's unilateralism, and wanted it to succeed, although they were not stupid enough to make this obvious in public. They were particularly pleased that so many leading members of the British Labour Party – not least its two leaders during the 1980s – were members of CND and declared that they would put unilateralist policies into practice were they to be elected. The Labour election manifestos of 1983 and 1987 both committed a Labour government to unilateralism.

The Labour Party leader from 1980 to 1983, Michael Foot had been involved with the anti-nuclear movement since the 1950s, and Neil Kinnock, who succeeded him, and his wife Glenys had joined CND as students at Cardiff University in 1961.[5] Kinnock was also a member of the CND 'Committee of 100', an even 'more radical offshoot' of CND. He left CND in 1991 when his party abandoned unilateralism, giving up, in the words of his biographer, 'a political and ethical attachment which had lasted twenty-five years'. Even a young Tony Blair had fought his first election, in

1983, on a unilateral stance and his election manifesto at the time claimed that he, too, was a CND member. For these reasons, spying on and penetration of both CND and END, a peace group within CND, whose members were also CND members, were vital goals of the Stasi's British operations. On the whole, the Stasi met with frightening success. Above all, the East Germans wanted the CND to carry on pursuing left-wing policies which they figured out ran parallel to their own interests. They did not want to see CND move towards multilateral disarmament. Indeed, on an official visit to Moscow as leader of the Labour Party, Kinnock and his wife evidently got into trouble with the Soviets by indicating that they were as happy to be multilateral as unilateral disarmers and objecting to the Russian claim that this made CND the 'agent of capitalism'.[6]

Similarly, where CND members were unilateralist and ignored East European civil rights campaigns, as several key figures such as Bruce Kent did, the East Germans were perfectly content. But when END members – and in particular END's remarkable leaders, E. P. Thompson, the celebrated academic and social historian, Mary Kaldor, a distinguished strategic studies scholar and broadcaster, and Ken Coates MP (known to his friends as 'Ken Coatesky') – marshalled END support for multilateralism or linked the peace movement's goals to the fight for human rights in East Germany (and other Eastern bloc states), both they and END became a major threat.[7]

It has to be said straight away that just because the East Germans liked CND it does not follow automatically that CND members were 'controlled' by the East Germans, even if some important CND leaders were fond of East Germany and believed in its 'peace policy'. On the other hand, it has to be accepted that the East Germans had a considerable interest both in penetrating CND to discover precisely how its aims were being developed and in steering END to the advantage of the GDR, should this prove in any way possible. As Stella Rimington reminds us, 'Soviet and East European intelligence officers were also trying to subvert Western democracies by funding and directing national Communist parties to try to gain influence in legitimate protest groups . . . like CND.'[8] The information that the Stasi received was to be used by the East Germans to 'exert influence' on Western policy-making or to subvert a hostile movement from within – as Mielke himself had put it: 'let us hit the enemy in such a way that he becomes entangled with himself and puts us to one side'.[9]

There were several ways in which this could be done: END, as a group, could be played off against the much more powerful CND. END could be 'subverted' from within (the German word was *Zersetzung*; the MI6 term, as used by Daphne Park, a former MI6 officer, was 'disruptive action') by instructing the Stasi's people in it to behave in a particular way for a particular result.[10] This was not a major problem for them: END members were all 'self-appointed'.[11] Anybody who said they were interested in peace and civil rights issues could join. This provided opportunities for Stasi incursions. Alternatively, the East Germans could arrange for certain individuals in the peace movement to be better briefed about 'Socialist' peace policy than others. Some might be seen to possess international standing and to be able to project themselves as major statesmen (and women) where in fact they were lightweight, posturing on a 'world stage' constructed by the East German propaganda machine. After all, access to every major political figure and organisation in East Germany (and other Eastern bloc states) was carefully controlled by the governments of those states. Without that access important routes of international dialogue were closed to CND or END and their *raison d'être* slipped away. The East Germans could use the patronage that they possessed both in respect of East Germany and the Soviet Union to raise the profile of those Britons they wished to see prosper.

The Stasi files reveal, horrifyingly, that all of these things took place. Indeed, what is worse is that, right or wrong, the East Germans believed that, by 1986, they had won the argument for the hearts and minds of the British peace movement and convinced them that there was no alternative to British unilateral nuclear disarmament. They were also confident that they had scuppered E. P. Thompson's plans for linking peace to civil rights as far as the GDR was concerned and neutralised the individuals in END who were both multilateralists and minded to support the East German dissidents.[12] As one leading member of END has attested: 'by 1986 the END East German group had fallen apart', adding 'the END women's group (who were deeply concerned with the East German dissidents) dissolved itself as well'. In this sense, too, the Stasi did succeed.[13]

Opportunities were arranged to allow the Stasi to penetrate CND with their own agents (certainly more than one because the files show that 'Barber', a peace movement spy, was checked up on by another Stasi source within CND – making at least two agents) and, consistent with this, enable the Stasi to attempt to steer CND.[14] More than one Stasi military intelligence officer travelled round Britain speaking in support of unilateral nuclear disarmament.[15] The Stasi exploited its ability to grant access to East German and Eastern bloc leaders for END and CND leaders. It helped the CND leader Bruce Kent, for example, to establish an international profile for himself. It did its best to ensure that its contacts did well within the various organisations. It goes without saying that all such strategies *had* to be secret ones.

Its British assets were recruited to ensure that the Stasi might be able to achieve those goals. As Wolf himself wrote:

> One of the greatest pressures on governments East and West throughout the 1970s and 1980s came from the burgeoning peace movement . . . We were in the awkward position of trying to support the peace movement in Western Europe as a propaganda weapon against Washington while our secret police in the East spared no effort to repress 'ideological diversion' among burgeoning peace groups at home . . . we were aware that the peace movement had taken root in our societies and that it represented a potential challenge to Soviet influence in East Germany.[16]

He added that the Stasi feared these groups would join to form one big anti-Communist protest movement in Eastern Europe.

END's line, and why it threatened the East Germans, is well illustrated by the 'Prague Appeal' of 11 March 1985, written by Jiri Dienstbier, the leading Czech dissident, and others for 'Charter 77' (but according to the Stasi files generated from London and not Prague) which showed how far Eastern European dissidents had taken heart from the link between Western and Eastern peace and human rights movements.[17] It shows precisely how END's ideas were not merely revisionist in the context of European politics as a whole, but would spell the end for East Germany.

'Europe,' Dienstbier said, had been 'one of the main points of friction between the two power blocs. Were a war to break out here, it would be fatal for the entire planet. Europe is divided. Our common hope lies in overcoming this division.' He added that 'citizens should not only exercise public scrutiny of governments but find ways of loosening ossified positions . . .' He concluded with a rallying cry to all dissidents, especially those in East Germany, tempting them with the dream of unity (and echoing E. P. Thompson's END line):

> A democratic and sovereign Europe is inconceivable as long as individual citizens are denied the right to take part in decisions affecting not only their everyday lives but their very survival. If our aim is European unification, then no one can be denied the right to self-determination and this applies equally to the Germans. Let us acknowledge openly the right of Germans freely to decide how they wish to unite their two states.

This verbal dynamite (which may have seemed romantic and idealistic but was – as the events of 1989 showed – anticipatory and predictive) did more than worry the Stasi hugely. The East Germans noted that no one in Britain had endorsed the Prague Appeal with more enthusiasm than E. P. Thompson.

The Stasi and the East German leadership reasoned that they had to do two things in response. First, they had to do all they could to win the battle for the hearts and minds of the British peace movement; second, they had to stymie and subvert those members of the peace movement who wished to join peace policies with the demand for human rights. At all times, the Stasi had to ensure that the official state-run East German Peace Council, Moscow's stool-pigeon, was regarded as an authoritative exponent of a real 'peace policy' which would prove how deeply committed East Germany was to 'peace' – on its own terms. It was vital to ensure that CND and the British peace movement continued to hold the Peace

Council in high regard and that it stamped firmly on E. P. Thompson's scepticism about it – and thus subverted his aim of dealing with the unofficial peace groups of Eastern Europe. As we shall see, on the whole the Stasi was successful in doing this in the GDR. It also managed to get Western opinion formers to continue to put their trust in the totally cynical Soviet bloc peace councils. By droning on about them, the East Germans made useful propaganda to the effect that they were busily supporting peace themselves through what they termed their 'peace' initiatives.

*The GDR Review*, that nicely produced East German propaganda paper, devoted issue after issue to the East German Peace Council, and its various offers of 'peace'. What is more, it was able to report on how gladly these offers were taken up, by CND in Britain, and by what the *Review* called leading British opinion formers like 'John Klotz and Jack Berlin' (whom few, if any, had ever heard of), in Europe as well as in Australia and other English speaking countries (where some held strong sympathies for the GDR).[18]

To 'interfere' in CND and END for its own ends the Stasi needed reliable intelligence – both detailed knowledge of the ins and outs of CND policy-making and how East German aims and ambitions could be realised within it – as well as detailed knowledge of who the dangerous peace activists were, and how they could be neutralised or even subverted. So important was this strategy to the East Germans that, as we have seen, both the HVA and the secret military intelligence officers were deployed to work on it. But this was not just an operation in Britain. It needed parallel work in East Germany. This was because the dissidents had slowly come to see how they could use the internal logic of the regime's stated support for peace and civil rights against itself, not least by gaining external publicity for their demands.[19] It is not possible here to give a comprehensive account of dissident activities in this period.[20] Ulrike Poppe, one of East Germany's finest and most courageous dissidents, has provided a general account of the Poppe–Bohley circle.[21] In the early 1980s, organised dissent based on a demand for peace and civil rights more generally became a real threat to GDR internal security.[22] As Poppe later explained: 'By being incriminated and persecuted, we were pushed into a formal opposition to the regime. This is how we discovered the issue of human rights'.[23]

This opposition, notwithstanding the truth that it was based on support for values that the state *itself* claimed to stand for, was nevertheless opposition to SED control over peace issues.[24] Since it was self-evident that the control of peace activities, like every other political activity in the GDR, was itself a core Communist strategy, this automatically made the dissidents anti-Communist in fact, even if strictly speaking not in theory. It is generally accepted that the awareness among many dissidents that they were becoming anti-Communists – if the definition of Communism was what the SED stood for – dawned on them only very gradually. At the start of their journey into opposition, they regarded themselves as committed 'Socialists' (as in the *Socialist* Unity Party) because they genuinely believed in respect of peace what the SED state said about itself. Indeed, every primary school textbook in the GDR made its devotion to peace quite explicit.[25]

There was, however, influential support for dissidents in Britain: END was committed to the idea that peace and human rights would go hand in hand.[26] Thompson's book, *Protest and Survive*, edited with Dan Smith, reveals much more about his aims in the section entitled 'Appeal for European Disarmament' than in his more widely read opening chapter from which the book takes its title.[27] In 1980 END had published the 'Berlin Appeal', made by a noted East German dissident, and gained an impressive set of signatures supporting it (two signatories, Robin Cook MP and Michael Meacher MP, were to become leading ministers in the 1997 Labour government).[28]

On 23 November 1981, E. P. Thompson had himself come to 'Westberlin' (as the East Germans called it, to differentiate between it and their capital 'Berlin') to give a speech in which he declared that: 'the Eastern and Western peace movements should work together . . . there is an immediate link between real disarmament and the development of democratic movements in the Socialist states. *Furthermore, the creation of democratic movements in them is a precondition for forcing the Socialist states to disarm'*.[29] Thompson was not simply urging Eastern and Western peace movements to cooperate, but stating that together they could pressure the Soviet bloc. To add insult to injury, Thompson had insisted that 'pressure on the Soviet Union must be increased' alongside pressure on the USA: Thompson's line, intriguingly, came increasingly to demand that the Soviets disarm before NATO. Not merely multilateral, rather than unilateral (which was CND's position), it in fact reflected the 'Zero Option' which Reagan and Margaret Thatcher came to support.[30]

The East German dissidents took great heart from Thompson's audacious but intellectually irresistible formulation. They responded to the Stasi's intimidation of them by coolly adding demands for civil liberty to those for peace, adopting the line that both aims were formal state aims of the GDR anyway, and ought therefore to be sanctioned by the SED, and that the Stasi's attempted suppression of the women dissidents showed that, without civil rights, the call for peace could not be properly made.[31] Since the East German constitution guaranteed the right of association and free speech, the dissidents' request seemed hard to formally contradict.[32] Poppe recalls: 'Peace to me did not mean simply non-war and rocket-reduction. Peace was indissolubly linked to the human rights issue'.[33] Initially they believed that dialogue with the SED would deliver it.

The Stasi files show that in the view of the SED, dialogue with Poppe and the others was not on the menu. The Stasi had other ideas. Although it was fairly certain that Poppe and her circle were not an invention of END, which it had been monitoring via its agents, to the Stasi's inventive minds the END link offered an immediate means of dealing with the dissidents, who were also all under constant surveillance (Poppe's flat, for example, was permanently bugged).[34]

The Stasi believed that if the opposition leaders could be successfully intimidated, the organisation they led would quickly crumble. It soon began to see that its very work in the UK could provide the necessary means of achieving this. The Stasi knew that END as a group, and the GDR–END group within it, was offering Poppe support. If it could prove that Poppe was accepting it, and conspiring with END against the Soviet Union and the GDR, she and her colleagues could be charged with high treason and with working for foreign intelligence. This would discredit them all as traitors, puppets of the West and enemies of 'Socialism'.

London therefore provided the Stasi with the ideal opportunity of neutralising Poppe and the threat she presented, the single most serious opposition to the GDR as a whole. In London, in addition to the work against the peace movement more generally, the Stasi's people were now charged with destroying E. P. Thompson's plans, fortifying the unilateralists even more strongly and developing a plan to use the dissidents' London links against them. Exploiting the British feminist academic Barbara Einhorn, who was not unsympathetic to the GDR, an elaborate trap was set which Poppe and Bohley had no chance of avoiding. This proved to be a textbook example of the 'disruptive action' examined in some detail later on.[35]

Serious Stasi reporting on END (said to have been founded in April 1980 and located at that time at 227 Seven Sisters Road, London N4) began at the end of 1981 when E. P. Thompson's presence in Berlin was picked up by the Stasi, and evaluated. From then on, there was a continuous flow of material about END and its leaders and members. On 14 November 1983, for example, a detailed report was prepared for Markus Wolf on END's contacts to the East German dissidents which he personally forwarded to General Paul Kienberg in HA XX.[36]

It was based, the report stated, on espionage from Britain ('unofficially, reliably learned from the Operational Area'). It explored the activities of the women members of END who had, it was said, close ties to 'Westberlin' and 'regular contacts to active representatives' of the East German 'independent peace movement'. It sought to 'publicise the hostile activities of these people in the Western media' and its leaders were said to be Barbara Einhorn and Jane Dibblin, aided and abetted by David Blow, the BBC's Berlin correspondent. The report alleged that they had close contact with Bohley and Poppe. They were attempting to construct a more secure means of conveying information from 'Westberlin' to East Berlin: 'the previous BBC correspondent in Westberlin was regularly active as a courier, but his successor is only occasionally ready to transport material'.

On 3 February 1982 the HVA's CND spies told Wolf that 'John McWilliam and John Evans, both CND members and MPs, have been elected on to the Parliamentary Select Committee for defence. They thus have access to documents coded "COSMIC"'. On 6 December 1983 one of Wolf's CND spies passed him a list of 'operationally relevant contacts and links of hostile-negative people' (that is 'hostile to East Germany'). An example of the distortions inherent in 'humint', it contained some fairly wild assertions. On the list we find David Blow, Sheila Taylor (said to be a link with MI5), John Sandford (also believed to have a link with the British secret service), E. P. Thompson (who, the END spy said, had 'close connections to the US Embassy in London'), Judith Eversly, Karin McPherson, Anne Marie Bathmaker, David Childs (said to have contact with the British Army and author of books hostile to the GDR), Peter Lawrence of Loughborough University, F. Carter of London University, Graham Coe (of the British Embassy in East Berlin) and Ian Wallace.

Six weeks later, on 23 January 1984, HVA III (the main unit operating from the London embassy) passed to East Berlin a revealing (and highly confidential) account of an extremely heated END meeting held on 8 January 1984. Paul Oestreicher, who had been general secretary of the British section of Amnesty International, was a leading Church of England diplomat working for the Archbishop of Canterbury, a canon of Coventry Cathedral and a fluent broadcaster on the BBC, could be found ferociously attacking Einhorn for 'talking too much' to the Stasi (who had detained her at the time while she was caught up in the Stasi's 'disruptive action' against the East German dissidents) thereby endangering them; she had, the report said, 'made the organs of the GDR aware for the first time' of possible problems in the relationship between END and the dissidents, and had led to the arrest of Bohley and Poppe, a sinister and telling incident which reveals just how the Stasi worked. The HVA's source also mentioned that several END members had said to each other that they believed that Bruce Kent had been 'bought by the GDR' and that his personal contact to 'the GDR representatives exceeded the normal measure'.

A further internal note on the Einhorn case followed on 30 March 1984. END leaders were said to have concluded that her arrest had meant the GDR now knew everything about END, and that Einhorn had acted 'irresponsibly, endangering the work of women in the GDR'. END members were currently debating whether she lacked 'common sense or experience'. The analysis ended with a list of future measures END was proposing, including a stepping up of its campaign against East Germany.

It is important to note that the 'source' (*Quelle*) for this report was given at the foot of this document. It was XV/45555/83. It is very rare for a source's code number to be attached to a specific piece of information at this level. It was, in fact, a serious mistake to do so. Even though the Stasi never imagined that its files would come under scholarly scrutiny, one of Markus Wolf's rules regarding conspiracy had been broken. A link had been made between a source, and an account of an intelligence operation. As we shall see in Chapter 14, this code number links the source to the SIRA material, to END and CND as well.

Further intelligence was received from 'progressive forces in CND' on 30 March 1984, noting END's increasing influence in it.[37] On 29 May the Stasi was given an internal and confidential verbatim report of a meeting held between END and a leading East German functionary, Werner Rümpel, deputy chair of the East German Peace Council. On 29 June 1984, the East Germans were told of secret Labour Party plans to invite a prominent East German to the annual conference which were being discussed at a private END caucus meeting. Oestreicher, their spy told them, had advised against inviting anyone who was too obviously 'a party horse'.

Another major report on END was sent to Wolf on 9 July 1984. END aimed to wage 'a common struggle in East and West against the manipulations of peoples by their rulers, and the defence of human rights', and was attempting to gain control over CND. Its work in Eastern Europe was 'especially lively'. Under the leadership of the Eastern Europe Group, the report warned, specific committees had been formed to 'work on' the USSR, the CSSR, Hungary, Poland – and the GDR. The report also said Thompson had now been seen repeatedly entering the US Embassy in London, and was thought to have links to MI6. The Stasi could see here an opportunity to discredit him, but a CIA source has stated that the idea that

Thompson might have been briefing the CIA in London was extremely far-fetched).[38] Perhaps his visits were to try to secure a visa.

In April 1985 the Stasi was told by its spy that in February of that year Patrick Burke had met between fifteen and twenty East Berliners on behalf of END. On 20 May 1985 Wolf received a report from the KGB on a meeting of the 'campaign for worldwide disarmament' held in Oxford. It was obviously a private meeting and this time the source was a KGB contact rather than a Stasi one. The report claimed this group had 'secret plans to oppose the World Peace Council'. A few days later a Stasi minute on the Labour MP Tony Benn declared that 'he plays an ambiguous role in the peace movement, according to informants in left-wing Labour circles'. Benn, the HVA had learned, 'is on the one hand engaged in the UK anti-rocket campaign while at the same time strengthening his links to [the Polish] Solidarity movement and making, quite openly, anti-Soviet and anti-Communist remarks'.

Further Stasi files contain a long report, with stolen confidential documents attached, plainly compiled at the end of 1985 on END, based, it says, on 'information from a source which has immediate access to the leaders of END, and has personally looked at the instructions and files of END'.[39] The identity of the source is, of course, not set down. Although we know that 'Hans Reichert' – the East German ambassador, Gerhard Lindner – liked to speak to various members of END, it is scarcely conceivable that he would have been allowed to rifle through its 'instructions and files', or that he would have had 'immediate access' to Thompson and Kaldor. The HVA received a confidential END report on two meetings with East German dissidents and on discussions with East German 'peace women', dated January 1985, as well as a draft letter from the women on the subject of 'beyond the borders', which was an initiative being undertaken by women in five Western and Eastern European states.

The final bundle of material handed over to the Stasi by its END contact consisted of private END correspondence, a report on a meeting held in Athens by Mary Kaldor with other Western peace movements on 17 December 1984, a 'position paper' written by the chairman of the END 'GDR group', Jan Williams, and material on a number of meetings and seminars attended by British experts on Germany and the GDR.

This spying against END by someone who was obviously a member and had, as the Stasi files state, direct access to the END leadership, was not likely to put Britain's security at risk. But it was material which could be exploited to do serious damage to END and, conversely, help the Stasi in its campaign against its own East German dissidents. Documentary material of this kind was, of course, always especially sought after because it allowed the 'Centre' to evaluate with some accuracy exactly what an organisation was up to. This material was examined by General Wolfgang Schwanitz, the deputy head of the HVA, on 20 January 1986 and sent to General Kienberg.

As for spying against CND, Wolf was told that CND would accept an invitation to visit the East German Peace Council in February 1986 and informed as to who would be in the delegation (including Stephen Brown, said to possess 'active contacts' with dissidents from his time at the Theological Faculty of Humboldt University in Berlin in 1983 and 1984).[40]

Another highly sensitive report, dated 3 February 1988, prepared by HVA III/A/I, contained internal material on END and its East German links as well as internal and confidential material on the current plans of CND (said to include a campaign against the US's 'Star Wars' plans and its stance on NATO). Bruce Kent had addressed the question of 'how Great Britain could be taken out of NATO' and concluded that, for the time being, it was best not to 'put this on our agenda'.

The Stasi was particularly interested in END's leaders. They had learned as early as 26 October 1980 that: 'Thompson goes so far as to make the removal of SS-20s his first demand'.[41] A further note on him, dated 19 February 1982, claimed that he had said END would never join the World Peace Council because 'it would be deceitful to tie END to an organisation which only opposed NATO' and not Soviet rearmament.[42] He had added, 'the pressure on the USSR must be increased . . . Eastern and Western peace movements could work together. Western rearmament has had the negative effect of strengthening the bureaucratic elites of Eastern Europe'. There were, he had insisted, 'no good democratic bombs and bad Communist ones, no good proletarian ones and bad imperialist ones'. The Soviet leaders, he insisted, 'would have to realise that millions in the West whom they dismiss as anti-Soviet are people who support civil rights and oppose certain aspects of Soviet conditions. That is why END refuses to deal with National Peace Councils.' Many more reports carried the same message.

Mary Kaldor was said in a report on her in the Stasi files dated 9 June 1984 to be a 'member of the disarmament committee of the Labour Party and has contacts to 'hostile-negative groups' in the GDR; she was one of 'the most active fighters in END'. On 21 October 1984 it was said that she was 'a representative of the right-wing anti-Socialist position and one of the leading ideologists of END'; on 12 December 1984 she was reported as having stated that 'what was clearly unacceptable to the Soviet Peace Council was our support for independent peace groups, something on which we cannot compromise . . . as long as we continue to support these groups, they will interfere in our peace movement, i.e. encourage the Stalinists'. Of Ken Coates the Stasi said repeatedly that he was 'known to HA XII [which operated against terrorist organisations!] as an active disseminator of Trotskyite views . . . according to unconfirmed reports, he has contact to the enemy's secret services'.

Even though we may believe that these sorts of reports and comments seem, from a British viewpoint, to be relatively harmless, from an East German perspective they contained material which did not merely cause alarm but could have led to very serious consequences for those being 'denounced'. Thompson, Kaldor and Coates were portrayed as dangerous enemies of the GDR – more dangerous in some ways than the dissidents because they were well-known British citizens who could not simply be rounded up and neutralised through terror. All three of them had a proven ability to lead others. The Stasi, as far as we know, did not operate in the same way as the Bulgarian secret service, one of whose London targets, Georg Markov, was assassinated in a London street in 1978 with a small poisonous Ricin dart fired from an umbrella (developed by the KGB).[43] But both Thompson and Kaldor were frequently out and about and those spying on them clearly put them in harm's way.

The Stasi files gives numerous other examples where individuals were endangered. On 6 December 1983 information from a British spy was sent to the 'Centre' that 'Sheila Taylor, Secretary of the GDR–UK Friendship Society, is a Communist, regarded as reliable and not ambitious' but that she had links to the British Security Service, as did John Sandford, a Reading academic who worked on the GDR. It goes without saying that neither of these people knew that this was being said about them (and, as we see, Sandford himself has formally declared that he had absolutely no links with MI5 or MI6), a fact the Stasi had confirmed. In January 1986 a tip from a Stasi officer, 'Jutta May', was passed to the HVA on 'John Theobold from Leicester' pointing out that he was 'very interested in contacts with the GDR'. A minute was made in East Berlin on 6 October 1986 that 'Jackie', identified as 'Jackie Hanouf/Hope', who was thirty years old, was an Oxford student writing a thesis on 'GDR Literature, the Environment and Peace Policy'. IM 'Manfred' had been asked to watch her.[44]

Now who, we may now ask, supplied the Stasi with the information that it sought? The Stasi files do allow us to identify some of its assets. The END spy, for example, was clearly an insider. It is, however, worth recalling that those who were targets were also, sometimes, sources.

The group who, from their own perspective, were sometimes targets and sometimes assets are obviously the most complex. They illuminate the truth that in espionage, as in life more generally, things are indeed rarely 'black' or 'white' but frequently various shades of 'grey'. Like any intelligence service that exploited 'humint', or human intelligence resources – people – the Stasi could not afford to be choosy. It would extract whatever it could from whomever it could. Someone who at one stage was prepared to give the East Germans something might at another refuse to do so; a friend of East German Communism could turn into its enemy.

What would the perfectly decent members of CND or END have thought of the Stasi's interference in their internal affairs? What would they have thought of those whom they regarded as their colleagues having *secret* meetings with East German 'diplomats' who worked for a secret police who abused the very dissidents they believed they were supporting? What would they have made of the 'guidance' and 'steering' to their organisations that the East Germans provided?

The idea, put about by some GDR fellow travellers, was that since not all the dissidents were behind bars all the time, they were, in effect, permitted to function more or less freely as dissidents. This showed, they opined, that the Politburo was less vicious than one might assume. The Stasi files show the falseness of this view. Where individuals were left free, it was indicative of the increasingly sophisticated methods used by the Stasi to control them, usually *from within*. The East German IM 'Karin Lenz', one of a vast army of apparent dissidents who actually worked against them, has said: 'When I have found out where I can hit someone to maximum effect, how I can finish them off – and that is usually with psychological methods – and if that person is my enemy, then that is what I do'.[45] A Stasi directive 'for developing and working upon operational objects' states that it aimed at 'promoting discord amongst hostile-negative forces' by the 'systematic organisation of professional and social failure, the undermining of self-confidence of individuals, and the creation of mistrust and mutual suspicion'.[46] The means to be employed included 'the use of anonymous letters, phone calls and denunciations to the police and the propagation of specific rumours and acts of indiscretion' but no mass arrests. Far from existing happily in 'niches' as germs of an alternative political culture, the dissidents were successfully undermined by the spying, steering and control exercised by the Stasi which placed total faith in the ultimate victory of Communist *Gleichschaltung*.[47] As Wolf Biermann famously noted, 'we were all like rats in a laboratory'.[48]

To repeat: some of the Stasi's British informants were also its victims. Today they may insist they were guilty only of naivety or that they believed they could, by speaking to East German intelligence, support the East German dissidents more effectively by proving to the Stasi that the dissidents had friends in Britain. They may claim that if END seemed weakened by the mid-1980s, this was not the outcome of their information-giving but of contradictions within END itself. Finally, they may say that since the story ended with the collapse of the Stasi and the victory of the East German dissidents, this shows that they were doing the right thing. However, had the Wall not come down the Stasi's London sources would not only have been seen by the Stasi as supporters but no one in the West would ever have known otherwise.

Everyone who gave the East Germans information realised, one way or another, that this was exactly what they were doing – at best they were squalid collaborators, at worst Stasi spies. And a considerable number of those identified in the files, whom it has been possible to interview, have formally attested to the fact that they always suspected the East Germans with whom they were dealing were either themselves intelligence officers, or would pass on what they said to those who were.

Other Stasi informants do not appear in the files to be victims of any kind. There are numerous examples of known Communists, or those sympathetic to what they wrongly claimed were the 'ideals' of the GDR, giving aid to the Stasi. The Stasi files show, obviously enough, that they were considered assets. Two good examples of such 'assets' are Peter Jarman and Vic Allen.

Peter Jarman was a leading British Quaker. There are two entirely straightforward instances of Jarman supplying 'Hans Reichert' with highly confidential information about END's plans and its goals. Even if he did not know, as seems likely, that in passing these facts to Lindner they were actually being passed to his Stasi alter ego, 'Hans Reichert', the facts themselves could only prove highly damaging to END. In short, it was irrelevant to Jarman whether he was, or was not, communicating with an East German spy.

From the files we discover the following:

18/19.11.85 'a responsible functionary of the British Quakers, Jarman, tells us Oestreicher had tried to include Einhorn in a visit to the GDR planned for 1988. His idea was accepted 36:4 because Rümpel had said there would be no ban on her'.[49]

In a report dated 25.11.85 it is said that 'the East–West Secretary of the Quakers, Peter Jarman, member of the Liaison Committee of CND, stated in a personal conversation with our source that one was currently thinking about how one could change the hard line adopted towards the Eastern bloc. He said it was not just a question of tactics, but contents. There were better ideas around of how to come into contact with officials in the Socialist States.'[50]

Nevertheless, Jarman went on, 'co-operation with "the independent" peace movement [i.e. the dissidents] would also be conducted'.

A subsequent minute on the file made it plain that, in the Stasi's eyes, the views expressed by Jarman had come from confidential internal discussions not intended for general dissemination. Today Jarman says he was concerned 'to keep channels of communication open in a bitterly divided Europe'.[51]

The second individual, Professor Vic Allen, formerly chair of sociology at Leeds University and a leading CND member, helped the East Germans in precisely the same way. He clearly went to a lot of trouble on behalf of the East Germans and should have known that the information he was offering them was highly sensitive – and that it would end up in the Stasi's files, irrespective of whether or not he realised that Lindner was 'Hans Reichert'.

In a file dated 1 February 1985, the Stasi receive a report based on 'words expressed by Vic Allen' (the German is *Auesserungen*). Allen once again tells the East Germans that 'the political situation in the leading caucuses of the CND has changed to the advantage of anti-Soviet forces'. The report continues: 'according to his evaluation the pressure from hostile forces in END and NATO has increased. These forces have as their goal to use as a pretext the defensive measures adopted by the USSR in response to the twin-track decision in order to further anti-Soviet tendencies and forces in the international peace movement.'[52] 'These forces,' he said, 'are planning an anti-Soviet demonstration in March 1985, when Foreign Minister Gromyko is to visit London.' Allen says he believes that 'the political forces who are opposed to constructive co-operation with the forces for peace in the Socialist States are already in a majority amongst CND's leadership. At the last CND national conference only one-quarter of the delegates came from progressive forces who were ready to come to agreements with the Socialist States.' He believed, however, that the 'anti-Soviet forces' were doing less well at grass-roots level.

We also have a written report of an oral communication from Vic Allen to Lindner in which the latter says that the former recommends 'that the Peace Councils of the Socialist States should make contact with the regional divisions of CND and invite the corresponding delegations . . .' (the German phrase is *er empfiehlt deshalb*).[53] The very fact that Professor Allen makes recommendations to the East Germans shows not merely that he is giving them his considered advice, but that he realises that the person to whom he is speaking is someone with the authority to process his recommendation (because otherwise there would be no point in recommending anything of this nature). In a report dated 1 February 1985, Allen warns the East Germans that 'END uses the CND logo and that its fundraising had begun five years earlier, in April 1980'.

In a letter of 14 March 1985, sent from 'Bank House', his home, Allen provides more information to Lindner. Later, in another report, he is said to have 'told us', 'reported to us', 'analysed for us' and 'suggested that' ('[Allen] *teilte mit*' . . . '*berichtet*' . . . '*schäzt ein*' . . .'*schlug vor*'). Allen had thoughtfully provided his private address so that anyone wishing to pursue his suggestions further could contact him discreetly. He warned 'Hans Reichert' that CND was 'currently under great pressure from END and in particular from a member called Jane Mayes who did not openly tell CND leaders she was also an END member. He said that Sheila Oaks was 'very dangerous' and that so far 'her real political background is unknown to me'. He advised Lindner that on behalf of the Shipley CND group, he would invite Dr Liebig from the German Embassy in London to its fortieth anniversary Dresden event.

Vic Allen was, however, not the only source in CND. On 16 November 1981 the Stasi was reliably informed from someone other than him that Bruce Kent had just declared that Josef Luns's claim 'that CND was funded by the Soviet Union' was a lie.[54] The number of Communists in CND was, in fact, small: Lord Jenkins had been replaced by Joan Ruddock rather than John Cox, a CPGB member and veteran CND member.

Another important asset for the East Germans was Ion Bader of the British Peace Assembly. He told the Stasi's intelligence officer on 23 July 1982 that it had become 'increasingly hard to work with CND' which was moving in an anti-Soviet direction because the Trade Unions were not represented, making the organisation ever more 'middle class'. Bader added that even Frank Allaun had signed the END's Berlin Appeal, although 'James Lamond MP was one of the few who understood what was going on, and had refused to sign'.[55] Lamond confirms the truth of this report and adds that he did not believe CND should diversify by supporting campaigns for political dissidents.[56]

The files indicate that the Stasi subverted CND and END in two major ways: first of all, by sowing discord and suspicion between its British members and the East German dissidents and, second, by instigating vitriolic rumours about individuals and futile ideological arguments – such as E. P. Thompson's alleged links to Western intelligence – and setting one member against another by suggesting breaches of good faith, and dishonesty. In the atmosphere of the 1980s, when many lost their faith in British and American security services, any apparently well-founded suggestion that a particular individual might be working for those services would immediately cause major ructions and might prompt the exclusion of the person involved. No CND or END member was going to work with a 'spook'.

The Stasi reports were reports of intelligence gained, yet also of an intelligence service in action, crushing those it regarded as its enemies. They indicate clearly the presence of British spies within these organisations and the sorts of policies that the Stasi's London intelligence officers were minded to promote. This follows not only from the provision of inside reports and the stealing of documents but from the record of conversations the Stasi had with certain named Britons. They reveal the incredibly tortuous and malign way in which the East German intelligence officers manipulated the GDR's friends and foes alike. The reports illuminate the identities of those on whom the Stasi relied as its most sensitive sources.

Even so, it must be emphasised that these reports were the Stasi's view of END and its activities. Where they came from its spies inside END or CND, the reports represented the analysis of the spy in question, not of the 'Centre'. Frequently, different spies would spy on the same organisation or individuals. This is why within the Stasi files there seem to be so many reports on the same subjects, but each with one or two significant and often contradictory verdicts on individuals. In this way, Wolf's people at the 'Centre' believed they could arrive at a true reading of an intelligence item. Good examples of this form of reporting can be seen in the case of several individuals; for example, both Sheila Taylor and John Sandford are said by one spy in December 1983 to be agents of the British secret service, but numerous other documents and reports attest to the fact that they were trusted by the East Germans who continued to deal with them, proving the lack of a link with British intelligence. Yet the same spy also said that David Blow was operationally interesting and supported the dissidents. This was not only true, but it was matched with a November 1983 report on Blow, also true, which said that he, quite properly, was not very keen to act as a courier (it conflicted with his duties as a journalist).[57]

The Stasi's spies made judgements on the basis of what they always believed was an objective evaluation of individuals or plans. What their spies could never know was who else might be a Stasi source or what they might be spying on. They simply carried out orders according to the rules of conspiracy established in Lenin's day. The Stasi spied on its spies. An individual could, for example, be reported as behaving in a way hostile to the GDR's interests, or saying something specific against the GDR, without the reporter knowing that the person had been told to act in this way for the Stasi's own purposes. There are several examples of such behaviour in the files.

Lists of individuals said by the Stasi's British sources to be hostile to the GDR might therefore include the names of those who were actually Stasi spies. The reports would never indicate this, although the leaders of the HVA and HA XX would always know who was their particular person and who was not. For this reason, the files must always be read with particular care and attention to detail.

One thing, however, must be carefully noted. It was perfectly possible to say 'no' to the Stasi, even if one were inside East Germany at the time. There were a number of straight British and American academics and journalists whose work took them to the GDR who simply told the Stasi to get lost. Good examples are: Mark Brayne, the distinguished BBC journalist who had studied at Leipzig in the late 1960s; Anne McElvoy, the journalist; Professor Ian Wallace, a noted GDR expert; and Professor Jim McAdams, an American scholar.[58] Brayne, for instance, says that although no one had specifically warned him about the dangers of recruitment, he knew that this was a possibility. He had enjoyed his time in the GDR but seen at once that it was a 'crap system'; he stayed away both then and subsequently from any likely recruiter.

A Stasi file shows how Anne McElvoy and four Americans, all visiting Humboldt University, were targeted.[59] McElvoy was spied on by the Stasi continuously from September 1986 until June 1987; they noted an ethereal quality about her and that she had failed to make an impression on anyone, which they found suspicious. They discovered that she had 'given three talks on the BBC about her time in the GDR which had been libellous and slanderous' and included the charge that East Germany was secretive and that the Free German Youth were not 'merely' boy scouts, but had, in the past, been Stasi agents. A second file on her is not open for research; this indicates that the Stasi put strong personal pressure on her to work for them and that she resisted it with courage.[60]

The Americans were also closely observed. One was alleged by them to be an active homosexual which, they said, made 'operational control of his East German contacts difficult'. Another, a female professor, was said to be having a sexual relationship with a colleague who, it was claimed, was a noted academic from Bate College. The Stasi saw a possible lever here, but dropped him when told by 'our brother organ' (that is, the KGB) that he was known to have unspecified links to the CIA.

Anne McElvoy has herself described how a 'sweaty' East German asked her to write reports for him. She said no. Today she says:

The classic defence of informants is that they did not do anyone harm. That will not do. They were not in a position to know whether they were doing harm or not. Anyone who denounced a fellow Briton in East Germany condemned that person to the attentions of the Staatssicherheit and thus invaded their privacy. Far worse, they also steered the attention of the Stasi towards a target's friends and acquaintances in the East with potential consequences that were far worse.[61]

She is certainly right. Ian Wallace, in Leipzig in 1977, was approached by several individuals and walked firmly away from each one. Jim McAdams, researching in East Germany in the 1980s, was repeatedly propositioned. He was, on several occasions, offered 'expenses' (which he refused) and quickly formed the view that the Stasi was actually very good and that he needed to be very cautious. Today he says, 'The Stasi needed to be hard-working – the GDR knew that through excellence in intelligence-gathering it could box above its weight.'

It is for this reason that the all-embracing, highly refined yet ruthless work of the Stasi must be deemed the defining dynamic of the political development of the GDR. Timothy Garton Ash is right to argue that by the early 1980s the GDR was not just totalitarian but a real-life example of Orwell's fictional nightmare state.[62]

# 13

# The *Kewa* and John Roper

In their relentless search for new contacts and sources, the Stasi in London showed initiative, resourcefulness – and extreme caution. The Stasi's drive for British informants was focused on the areas designated by Mielke himself in his 1968 directive: 'The enemy's centres of politics, and the centres of their military, economic, scientific and intelligence communities.'[1]

The Stasi's considerable skill at identifying likely prospects in these locations emerges clearly from various fragments of its files. As we have seen, the Stasi was highly suspicious of 'walk-ins', volunteer spies in London, always fearing that they might be working for British or American intelligence. On the other hand, it needed contacts, particularly in the UK. Selecting them and, where possible, recruiting them, was, after all, the main purpose of its presence in London. Although at the end of the day it was the Stasi who decided whether someone was to work for it or not, it was ever ready to exploit those Britons who wanted to be its friends, provided, of course, they had no direct connection to British counter-intelligence. This vital question, the *sine qua non* of successful espionage, was rigorously checked out by HA II, a special unit established for the purpose. Wherever HA II signalled there was a risk that the object of Stasi interest might be inclined to spill the beans to MI5, the Stasi walked away fast.

The Stasi was specially welcoming to anyone well-disposed

towards it who had an insider's knowledge of British public affairs. Such people could, if risk-free and properly handled, become prime sources of information, and one or two of them might, like the Soviet moles of the 1930s and 1940s, provide more insights than a whole army of poorly placed agents. Given the small size of the British political class, and the fact that its members tended to know each other (often from university), in 1983 Wolf had determined that HVA efforts in Britain should be concentrated on winning a small number of key contacts – those that were embedded in the British political class (or capable of being so in the future) – rather than approaching large numbers of potential recruits, some of whom might reveal the fact of this approach to MI5. In his 1983 order, Wolf had spelled out clearly that it was not 'a question of gaining vast numbers of IMs, but rather to get those we have into areas where, if questions of war and peace exist, they will be able to provide the decisive information we need . . . At the same time officers must collect comprehensive information about likely personalities in these communities in order to compile dossiers on them, with the aim of recruiting them, or simply being well informed about them.'[2] In Britain, the Stasi correctly perceived that quality was more useful than quantity.[3] Plainly, this view was right, for we know that none of those wooed in this way ever disclosed the Stasi's interest in them to MI5.

The Stasi used what it called 'conspiratorial methods' to get close to a designated target. In this mode, it referred to itself as a conspiratorial cell, a *Kewa*, or *konspirative EinwirkungsApparat*.[4] Recruiting individuals, whether as spies, sources or agents of influence, could prove to be a difficult, incremental process and, if it were necessary, the Stasi was prepared to spend years waiting, convinced its patience would bear fruit. It was one reason why Wolf was so depressingly justified in claiming that the Stasi truly was 'the best intelligence service' in the entire Soviet bloc. Stasi approaches usually followed the same pattern: a British expression of benevolent interest in East Germany, made by a sufficiently important person, might trigger an invitation to a cocktail party in Belgrave Square, then further private meetings and projects could follow and, where appropriate, an investigation by HA II. Then, and only then, the Stasi might ask for something in return, or suggest an area of collaboration which itself would deliver what it wanted. In this way, the trap would be set and the intended victim would fall in, usually head first.

The Stasi files show how Mielke's and Wolf's orders were carefully carried out to the letter in the United Kingdom. Whenever a prominent Briton asked it for any sort of favour, the Stasi was ready to grant it if the favour could be turned to its advantage. Because all such connections were so secret, most of the evidence of them was destroyed in 1990. Some dossiers, however, did escape the shredders.

On 13 February 1989, for example, our old friend the East German ambassador, Gerhard Lindner (shortly to be replaced by Joachim Mitdank), sent a teleprinted message to the 'Centre' in East Berlin to say that, on 10 February, he had been visited by a very senior British Liberal MP, Sir Russell Johnston, then MP for Inverness. The Stasi knew perfectly well that from 1983 to 1985 he had been his party's defence spokesman.

In strictest confidence, Sir Russell had made a tawdry plea: he wanted the East Germans to buy him an air ticket from Budapest (where he had official business) to East Berlin so that he could visit the leaders of the East German Liberal Party, the LDPD. Lindner urged immediate agreement because he reckoned the request could prove extremely useful to the East Germans for two quite different reasons. The first was that the LDPD was simply a Communist front, an organisation run by the Stasi through several of their people, one of whom was Lindner himself. It existed because the East Germans wished to retain the semblance of democratic life by pretending that theirs was a multiparty state. A visit to the East German Liberals by someone as prestigious as Johnston would do much to sustain this fiction ('prominent British Liberal leader visits the LDPD', *Neues Deutschland* could then report). But the second reason for agreeing to Sir Russell's request for a free air ticket was that to pass him something by way of a useful gift, and to have him in East Berlin, would present the Stasi with the operational potential to do something with him. In this way, the *Kewa* could begin its work and Sir Russell, they hoped, be turned into a 'source' (in the English sense) or even something more.

Lindner, who was keen to see Sir Russell ensnared, was of course well versed in Stasi tradecraft. He had joined the East German Liberal Party in October 1946, when only seventeen.[5] Trained as a lawyer, he had first been recruited by the Stasi in September 1956 as their co-opted worker inside the party, and then again, in August 1959, to spy on the international peace movement. His file recorded that in Britain he would be warned that MI5 was on to him in the following way: two men would approach him and say, 'we come from the Lindner company. Where should we put the wardrobe', to which Lindner would then respond, 'I ordered neither a wardrobe nor a bookcase.' Cumbersome but, sadly (from a British viewpoint), never put to use. In 1976 Lindner received a medal for his services to the Stasi, his citation reading: 'politically, he is absolutely reliable and has made a major contribution to the development of the LDPD, the Peace Council of the GDR, the British–GDR Association and the Olympic Committee'.

The Stasi files do not relate what happened to Sir Russell in East Berlin. Sir Russell (now Lord Russell-Johnston) confirms the incident. He got the ticket and visited East Berlin, where he was given what he calls the 'red carpet' treatment. It was his understanding that the East Germans had taken the initiative in wanting him to have an 'open invitation' to visit the GDR![6] His case shows how very, very careful such British personalities had to be. To have accepted a free trip to East Germany and been entertained there could so easily have put him in harm's way. At the very least, as the surveillance on Ron Hayward had shown, his every word would have been recorded by the Stasi, to be used at a later date as and when necessary.

The Stasi did not always wait to be approached. Sometimes it formed a view that a particular figure might be worth further investigation, perhaps because one of its sources had recommended such a course, or because it mistook the transparent ease with which members of the British establishment chatted in private to each other – chatter which might include criticism of those in power – for a potential willingness to provide the East Germans with intelligence.

One of those in whom the Stasi decided to show an interest was

Admiral Sir James Eberle, one of Britain's most distinguished naval chiefs, who on retirement became Director of Chatham House in 1984.[7] From 1979 to 1981 Sir James had been Commander-in-Chief of Britain's Polaris submarine fleet and NATO supreme commander. Before 1983 he was also known privately (and publicly thereafter) to be critical of what he regarded as NATO's 'overkill' capability in the nuclear field. NATO, he had said, had enough nuclear weapons to destroy the world 'ten times over', when 'once would be enough'. He had also, he said, had two very sensitive, major disagreements with Margaret Thatcher. One concerned her belief that she ought always to be consulted about any NATO plans involving nuclear weapons of any kind, including depth charges to be tested in North Atlantic waters, the other much more serious – about Trident and Cruise missiles, and the necessary retargeting programme if British submarines were to be armed with them. She had wanted the British Polaris fleet to destroy all the 'central organs of Soviet state power', including Moscow, even though they were all also US targets. Sir James believed there was little point in both Britain and the USA setting out to destroy every Soviet city twice, advising instead that British missiles be aimed at five cities only. Mrs Thatcher was not impressed.

During Sir James's first two years at Chatham House, he also became the blameless victim of a tip-off to the Stasi, one almost certainly emanating from the Chatham House source. Plainly, someone of his standing, with a reputation for disagreeing with the Prime Minister on nuclear strategy, might prove a valuable Stasi asset. Whoever passed his name to the Stasi may well have thought, quite wrongly, that Eberle's views might indicate a readiness on his part to speak to the East Germans. Because of his considerable importance, HA II was wheeled in to check him out; given his security policy background, it was fair to assume that he might still have links with British counter-intelligence. They quickly discovered the truth. Not only was he entirely loyal to the Crown, but, on becoming Director of Chatham House he had, off his own bat, acquired the habit of holding regular but entirely unofficial meetings with an MI5 official working in the MoD. Although Sir James believes he told no one about these informal encounters, it seems possible that

HA II got wind of them, as a result of which the Stasi dropped him like a hot brick.

Until today, Sir James had no idea that he had been targeted at all. HA II's report on him, of which only a few telling fragments remain, was compiled during October 1985. It noted his long interest in missile technology, stating, for example, that from 1953 to 1957 he had attended an advanced training course on guided missiles in the USA. His dossier shows that HA II also obtained photocopies of two of his passports, one issued in 1975 which expired in 1985, and the other he acquired thereafter. They clearly wanted to check out his international contacts.

These passports are themselves testimony to the Stasi's remarkable and frightening ability to get hold of any material it wanted. The 1985 passport, issued in London, may have been obtained in 1988, when Sir James visited East Berlin for a conference (his visa was signed by a man to whom we shall return later – Jörg Döring, the East German 'consul'). His 1975 passport, however, issued in Newport, *cannot* have been copied in the same way. We may be certain about this because Sir James was absolutely forbidden to visit any Iron Curtain or Communist states on account of his high rank and position. Nor did he do so, and his 1975–85 passport accordingly contains no visas or stamps for any Communist state anywhere in the world.

How did the Stasi get them? It is conceivable that either the Stasi had agents inside the Newport and London passport offices, who would copy passports at HA II's behest, or, more plausibly, a single agent inside the London office (which issued the second one). The Stasi agent there could have copied both the old and the new one at the same time during the renewal procedure in 1985. Alternatively, but far more credibly, it is possible that Sir James's passport may on two successive occasions have been stolen from his desk at Chatham House, copied and immediately returned without his knowledge. This would have had to have happened twice, because the HA II copy of the 1975 passport is of a valid one, without the triangle cut from the top right-hand corner that indicates it has expired. While Sir James would have had both passports in his possession after his new one was issued in 1985, the 1975 one would by now have been clipped.

If HA II was able to gain access to the London Passport Office in Petty France (located round the corner from the Home Office in Queen Anne's Gate, from where political control of MI5 was exercised) what chance of other subversive and conspiratorial groups operating in Britain, from the IRA and the KGB to Arab terrorists, having access to the same facility? If, on the other hand, someone within Chatham House was able on two occasions to steal Sir James's passports, it was clearly home to a Stasi spy at this time. What seems, on the face of it, to be a small matter of an admiral's passport falling into the wrong hands is in fact evidence of a real and serious breach in British security at a very fundamental level.

Since there is no further reference to Sir James in any other extant part of the Stasi files, we may safely deduce that the Stasi immediately lost interest in him, deeming him entirely unsafe from its point of view. Sir James has no recollection of contact with any East German prior to his 1988 visit to Berlin. Whoever passed his name on to the Stasi had clearly made a grave mistake, confusing his robust honesty towards a Prime Minister with a readiness to betray his country to the East Germans.

## The *Kewa* and Lord Roper

By far the most unsettling and damaging targeting by the *Kewa* in London was against Lord Roper. In the 1980s he was properly regarded as one of our most prominent defence experts, with legitimate access to Britain's defence secrets. He went to work at Chatham House, in whose affairs he had always taken an interest, in the autumn of 1983. Roper's contact with the Stasi can today be documented in surviving fragments of files. It lasted until the fall of the Wall in 1989 brought it to an abrupt end. It illustrates the way in which an alert and highly efficient hostile intelligence service exploited each and every opportunity for recruitment that presented itself, even in respect of those who, like Roper, understood something of the Stasi. Ultimately, and certainly by 1989, Lord Roper became what today we would call an 'agent of influence'.

The earliest extant evidence of a direct HVA interest in Roper can be found in a SIRA document, dated 23 April 1986. However, as is explored below, there is every reason to believe that by this time the Stasi had already established a link to him, but that all the files relating to it, which would have included giving him a code-name, were almost certainly destroyed in 1990. It is important to re-emphasise that individuals in whom the HVA took an interest were invariably given codenames; equally there is no reason to deduce that those who received a codename would have known this or that such an attribution implied some written contract between the target and the Stasi. The Stasi did not always offer a written contract.[8]

From the Stasi's viewpoint, Lord Roper was a richly fascinating prospect. Their mutual interest in each other stemmed from Roper's impressive pedigree as a left-of-centre politician, with great under-standing of security policy and East–West relations. He was at the very pinnacle of the second division of British politics, hardly (at the time) a household name but nonetheless extremely well connected. He had a CND background (since abandoned but one the Stasi had uncovered), and retained an expertise in defence and security matters that was second to none. There was the Labour Party and SDP link, and, while at Chatham House, he was deemed to be one of their best brains. He was also very close to several leading West Germans (and therefore well versed in the West German policy of seeking ever closer contacts to East Germany). He had a personal and long-standing interest in Eastern Europe and a clear view of what he regarded as the undoubted benefits of détente. We may deduce that, to borrow the Stasi's phrase, he was a 'bear' well suited for 'washing'.

The backdrop to Roper's 1986 contact with the Stasi was a fasci-nating change in British policy towards Eastern Europe, completed in 1985. The Foreign Secretary, Sir Geoffrey Howe, had decided to undertake a major new initiative which was designed to promote dissidents' fortunes in the satellite states and weaken Soviet influ-ence there by quietly driving a wedge between these states and Moscow. Its context was the view that the growth of the dissident movement in the Communist bloc, and the emergence of Gorbachev as Soviet leader, presented Britain with a new opportunity to stress its commitment to liberty and human rights in Europe and to speak to those keen to break away from the Kremlin.[9] Needless to say, the

East Germans had been warned. One of their spies, 'Komet', had sent a note to East Berlin with details of proposed changes to Britain's foreign policy as early as 10 August 1984, and on 1 March 1985 'Eckhart' had sent a report 'on the influence of the German Foreign Office on Howe' (whose relevance becomes clear from the passage below).[10] Ironically, in the case of the GDR, the policy's only outcome was to give the Stasi additional opportunities to get closer to British security and defence communities, a classic example of a policy having, in one area, an effect which was the exact opposite of the one intended.

One of Britain's most eminent diplomats was asked to draw up a memorandum, or despatch (the highest level of Foreign Office communication), to provide the guidelines for effecting the changes.[11] Never made public before, it can be seen to provide a novel and imaginative means of transforming the 1975 Helsinki commitments on human and civil rights into reality. Britain, it affirmed, wanted a better relationship with the Soviet Union and its allies, but not at the cost of jeopardising 'our own aims of increased security'. Britain could not actively promote 'evolutionary change' in Eastern Europe unless it drew closer to regimes it regarded as 'unpleasant or nasty', but this was potentially dangerous. The despatch suggested a way of doing this without risk (aware, however, that the US might find aspects of it hard to understand because it favoured a more 'adversarial' approach to the matter).

The argument set out went like this. Gorbachev's accession to power in the Soviet Union had given East European leaders more 'room for manoeuvre' in an attempt to safeguard the continued viability of Communism. Kadar of Hungary and (far less plausibly) Honecker of East Germany were cited as examples of leaders who might be so affected.[12] This 'room for manoeuvre' could allow Britain to increase 'Western influence in all areas and at all levels' in Eastern Europe so as to encourage dissidents there to become a 'quiet, long-term challenge to the dominance of the Communist policy'. In short, a chance now existed, the despatch stated, of exploiting chinks in the curtain to reach out to those East Europeans who might be open to Western ideas, and to Britain's emphasis on human and civil rights – and would not damage its security.

The policy further stated that there would be an undoubted advantage in giving the Eastern Europeans an 'accurate exposition of Western policies on defence and arms control'. However, the policy emphasised (a point vital to our story) that the Warsaw Pact was still the 'major adversary of the West and that Eastern Europe was a vital part of it'. Correspondingly, the document emphasised the point about the primacy of security once more that *we cannot afford to lower our guard'* (my emphasis). In establishing new links to Eastern Europe, nothing should be done which might sustain Communism, or in any way compromise Britain's safety.

In implementing the new policy, Sir Geoffrey Howe became the first Foreign Secretary to visit Poland, East Germany, Bulgaria, Romania and Hungary for many years, in the course of his visits meeting members of the various Communist governments, but trying, too, to speak to dissident leaders. In this way, Howe hoped to contrast British policy with that of the West Germans. It was thought that both Helmut Kohl and Hans-Dietrich Genscher were cosying up to Communist leaders – in effect bolstering them – and forgetting the dissidents (which was probably true). The British and American endgame, however, was the disintegration of the Soviet bloc, even if the former was adopting more of a 'softly, softly' approach.

Three centres were established by the Foreign Office in London, one dealing with Russia, one with China and a third with Eastern Europe. All were charged with setting up a series of round table meetings, to consist of influential Britons selected by the centres, and various East European groups, chosen by partner institutions behind the Iron Curtain. It was considered important that the centres should be the channel between Britain and Eastern Europe rather than the various Communist-controlled Friendship Societies which would seek to interfere with the choice of British members and might be used by the respective East European regimes to prevent the round tables doing what they were intended to do: further the fortunes of those who wished to break away from Soviet-led Communism. The noted diplomat, Sir John Birch, then head of the Foreign Office's Eastern European Department, asked Alan Brooke-Turner to take overall charge of the operation.

Each side would field its own team. Sometimes, Sir John says today, this worked; sometimes it did not.[13] The Polish round table, run by the Polish Parliament, was rated a success, whereas those with Bulgaria and Romania were examples of what Sir John calls 'dead losses'. His explanation is significant: the delegations from the latter two states were always accompanied by 'secret police minders'.

In 1986 it was decided to include East Germany in the process but, as Sir John says in the full knowledge that the East German regime was 'the main proponent of Communism', and the payoff might be slight. Interestingly, he recalls that the East Germans were highly delighted to be included, and there was a 'lot of sucking up' by Gerhard Lindner to get the GDR in on the act. We know today that he had received early warning from the Stasi spies of a discussion in the Foreign Office as to whether it would in future regard the GDR as 'West' or 'East', and Lindner's efforts to convince the British that it was an 'eastern' state, to be put alongside all the others being invited to the round tables, was wholly consistent with East German aims.

There was, however, a fatal contradiction in including East Germany, one which will have explained Lindner's enthusiasm for the idea. This was that in the GDR's case the British team could have no chance at all of going over the heads of the Politburo and addressing the East German dissidents directly. Indeed, this was the last thing the GDR would allow. Conversely, by talking only to East German *apparatchiks*, Britain was clearly not going to be able to do anything to help the dissidents. In fact, there was even more to this than just a contradiction. An alert Foreign Office would have realised that any East German team would not merely exclude the East German opposition but inevitably include members of the Stasi or those under its sway. Regrettably, no one in the Foreign Office or MI5 was aware that Lindner himself was a leading Stasi spy and warned Alan Brooke-Turner accordingly.

The organisation designated by the East Germans as the partner for the British team was the IPW, the Institute for Policy and Economics (*Institut für Politik und Wirtschaft*) in East Berlin. As members of the team, Sir John went for leading politicians, diplomats and the odd academic. Roper was invited by Brooke-Turner to organise the East German round table.[14] The British fielded, at various times, Pauline Neville-Jones, also in the Foreign Office;

Richard Davy, a distinguished writer and journalist; Edwina Moreton and Tessa Blackstone, then at Birkbeck College and subsequently a government minister.[15] However, Sir John makes one point absolutely clear. It was *not*, he says, either their purpose or their intention to have any dealings at all with any individuals whom they believed, or suspected, might be official members of the intelligence communities of Eastern Europe. Not only was there no point in inviting foreign spies to attend round tables, but formally, it would, from the East European angle, have made them intelligence operations. This was absolutely not what was desired, as Sir John repeatedly emphasised. For the same reason, no members of MI6 were ever invited to attend any round table meetings. These meetings, then, were plainly not intended to be intelligence briefings (nor to produce any).[16] To ensure that members of foreign intelligence were excluded, Sir John says he looked to the British Embassy in East Berlin, who handled the detailed arrangements on the East German side, to screen any known Stasi contacts.

But, as the Stasi files reveal, intelligence briefings are precisely what the East German round table became – briefings conducted by British experts for the benefit of East German intelligence! This came about partly because it was how the GDR worked, and partly by choosing the 'Institute for Policy and Economics' as the East German partner to select the East German team. The designated partner in East Berlin was in reality simply a front for the HVA, as Wolf has since confirmed:

> We despatched two men, armed with the pretext that they were rep-
> resentatives of *the Institute for Policy and Economy, a name we
> occasionally used as a handy cover* [my emphasis]. The useful thing
> about this story was that a Westerner, if he had any knowledge of
> East Germany or even much common sense, could gather that he
> was talking to the foreign intelligence service without the need for
> the embarrassment or fright . . . from a formal introduction. We used
> both shadow and light to conceal ourselves, unlike the Americans
> who always struck me as ready to admit openly that they came from
> the CIA.[17]

Lord Roper, leading the British team at the GDR round table, says today that he was delighted at this particular link with an institute which he regarded as 'a sort of Chatham House think-tank close to the Politburo'. 'The interesting thing,' he remarks, 'is that it was the IPW, and *not* the one in Babelsberg which is generally thought to have had the most intelligence links.' He concedes that the IPW was 'a party institution' but its job was 'primarily to work for the Central Committee of the SED' – that is, for the government of East Germany, and not the Stasi. The IPW was directed by 'Professor' Max Schmidt, who had a young aide by the name of Gerd Basler.

In the event, the East Germans who – as a direct result of the establishment of the GDR round tables – were able to infiltrate themselves into Britain or, if based here, gain valuable access to prime British sources included over the three years some six IPW agents, at least two London Stasi spies – in the persons of Lindner ('Hans Reichert'), and H. H. Kasper (who went on, with Roper's full approval, to become a research fellow at Chatham House).[18] By 1987 two military intelligence officers (Dr Oswald Schneidratus, or 'Helios', and Jörg Döring, or 'Harke') had been given opportunities through the round tables to expand their activities in the UK although the personal file of the former shows that it was only the latter who was ordered to exploit them.[19] No one on the British side seems to have realised that all these particularly unsavoury individuals were, formally, spies who (if they were present in the UK) should never have been allowed to enter this country and (when encountered in East Germany) should have been avoided like the plague. Even if Roper did not know for certain that by 1989, in addition to the IPW input, there were two Stasi spies and two military intelligence officers exploiting the round tables, he himself has declared that he did know that the IPW might include Stasi sources and even intelligence officers.

He accepts today that, at the time, he knew that within the IPW, at any rate, 'there were people producing stuff for the Stasi, at least we always assumed they were'. But, of course, the people 'producing stuff' for the Stasi were themselves the Stasi, as Wolf himself confirmed. Chatham House, after all, insists it did not write reports for

MI5 and MI6, and MI5 and MI6 insist they did use Chatham House staff as agents. So why should the IPW work 'for' the Stasi unless it *was* the Stasi? Indeed, this Stasi work should have been no surprise to anyone who had thought about it for more than five minutes. Lord Roper, whom the Stasi files show to have been at special risk from this Stasi presence at the round tables, insists that he was not caught off guard in any way since he understood, at the time, that any dialogue with East Germans would include people close to the Stasi, if not the Stasi themselves: 'this would,' he says, 'not have been a surprise'. He was, he claims, always well informed about the East German intelligence service and it would, as he puts it, have been a 'very naive person' who thought that 'you only had to worry about the KGB'. But he goes even further: in his view, the presence of Stasi spies at round tables had been a positive boon. When asked whether this did not mean that the Foreign Office might seem to be actually helping the Stasi to spy on Britain, he replied: 'if the Stasi understood us better, so that East German decision-making about the UK would improve, this would lead to more rational policies – and that was in Britain's interest'. He added: 'the East Germans agreed to join our round table because it gave them the opportunity to get sources – to meet a number of people in British life'. Richard Davy recalled being strongly encouraged to develop relations with East Germans outside of the round tables.[20]

'This operation was intended by the Foreign Office,' Roper says today, 'to make the point [that] although these people were our enemies, it was probably rather better that they knew what we were about than that they didn't. I suspected at the time that the East Germans were convinced that this was a British intelligence operation rather than anything else. As far as I know, none of the British team was directly involved in intelligence, but no doubt there were Foreign Office people there taking full notes.' He was certain, too, that the British Embassy in East Berlin would know which of the East Germans were 'involved in intelligence' and 'who were relatively clean' (a wholly unwarranted and over-optimistic conclusion, as it transpired).

Lord Roper, who, as he affirms, had no personal connection with British intelligence or counter-intelligence, says that since the

British Foreign Office had authorised such meetings, it would have ensured that British intelligence was fully informed about them. He had frequently been warned, as had other round table members, of the possible dangers of interacting with the East Germans, and 'people who were in Chatham House and attending meetings of this sort were often told by the Foreign Office to be careful'. He had, he said, once had personal experience of being set up in Romania, while still an academic (he had been given 'a very nice dinner and the Romanians got absolutely nothing out of me'). He had been confident that he could easily handle any hostile approach.

As supporting evidence of their caution he recalls how, at a second round table held at Wilton Park in Sussex, mention had been made of Germans who had spent time there immediately after the Second World War. For some reason, there was a suggestion that documents relating to this should be shown to the East Germans, but then one of the British participants had said that it might not be such a good idea to give them the names of Germans with this sort of connection with Britain (of whom some might have been British agents). This was, he said, 'an example of the attentiveness that we had at all times in our operations and dealings with the East Germans'. Although there are evidently confusions in Lord Roper's testimony (that on the one hand the British Embassy in East Berlin could be relied upon to ensure East German round table participants were 'relatively clean', but on the other it was not a surprise to know today that East German spies had attended the round tables and that they gave nothing away), it seems entirely clear that he conducted these meetings on the basis that spies might be attending them. This can be seen not only from the fact that, as he says, he was very careful not to reveal the names of post-war German contacts of Wilton Park to the East Germans, because that might cause problems for them if they now lived in East Germany, but also from his view that having intelligence agents present was advantageous. Ultimately, however, Lord Roper remains absolutely convinced that it was a situation he could handle well. Lord Roper appears not to have known that MI5 operated an 'exclusions policy' designed to withhold visas from spies.[21] But if he did know, he rightly assumed it was ineffective because it was meant to exclude the Stasi from the UK, yet here they were. His assumption that they could and did come here shows too how important these opportunities were from the Stasi's point of view.

There would appear to be one small, if niggling, discrepancy at this point, probably attributable to the vagaries of remembering details of events over thirteen years ago. Both Birch and Brooke-Turner insist that at the round tables no contact was consciously to be made with Stasi officers, and that, had this been done, it would have contradicted and compromised the entire purpose of the round tables. Lord Roper says the exact reverse was true. Such contacts, he says, were made, and were entirely consistent with British goals for this exercise. Sir John, however, was not told at the time what Roper's views on this were. When asked about these matters today, having been told of the evidence of the Stasi's presence at the East German round table (something he had not known until now), Sir John says that he *now* believes there could have been some good in speaking to East Germans, who might have been Stasi members, or close to the Stasi, because in some Eastern European states the intelligence services themselves contained dissidents.

It is perfectly correct to say that in some former Soviet satellites, post-Communist elites had indeed partly evolved from existing intelligence services. But this never happened in the GDR; even in early 1990 the Stasi used its remaining power to destroy incriminating evidence and stash away its millions in hard currency. Before 1989, the Stasi not only did nothing to support a transition to democracy, but it countered it at every juncture. Nor, thankfully, did the Stasi become part of the post-Communist democratic elite. Good British intelligence would have pointed out that it was a very far-fetched notion that it ever could be so. Since the Stasi's *raison d'être* was to fight for Communism (in whose survival its officers had the strongest of vested interests) it would take rather more than an agreeable round table meeting to make them wobble, let alone recant. We may wonder if Sir John, a diplomat to the core, is not attempting to square this extraordinary circle in a less than satisfactory way. For either the Foreign Office meant to engage with Stasi officers (which seems incredible) or it did not (in which case Lord Roper's recollection is wrong and disturbingly so). Sir John adds, in an attempt to be reassuring, that the Foreign Office was always careful to defer to MI5's concerns in dealings with East Europeans and, if anything, MI5's hand lay 'rather too heavily' on Foreign Office 'initiatives'. In fact, the evidence from the Stasi files shows that, if there was a problem about MI5's 'hand', it was that it was not nearly heavy enough.

Sir John says, on learning now that Stasi officers did attend his round tables, he can entertain some sympathy with Roper's viewpoint. It might possibly, he concedes, have been 'important that the East European leadership should hear from us even if through their intelligence officers', adding that for them to know the UK 'was serious about arms control' directly from the UK rather than via the Russians, made sense too. It was useful to 'explain to the East Europeans why we were deploying Cruise missiles – because of Soviet SS-20s'. Even so, he adds, he had been right to insist that the important issues that were discussed at these East German round tables were discussed *only* at the round tables. There was to be no 'cosying up' outside the meetings. It was important that the British delegates 'did not drop their guard' and engage in any hidden negotiations. For this reason, Sir John points out, all round table members were reminded at a private team dinner about the importance of security, and warned about the hazards of meetings outside round table events. Indeed, all members of the Foreign Office and the Ministry of Defence had to record every single contact with any Eastern European for this precise reason (although Sir John himself was exempted because his duty was to have as many contacts as possible). Sir John is absolutely adamant about this central point: 'the last thing we would have wanted would have been for the round tables to be used for intelligence services passing messages to each other'. Yet while it is perfectly true that messages were not passed to 'each *other*', it is also true that the British views were directly communicated to East German intelligence.

Initially, these round table meetings had been set up to raise broad and not too delicate questions (nothing 'earth shattering', Sir John says). But the growing significance of dissident activity meant that more serious subjects had to be raised which would hopefully filter through to the dissidents and potential dissidents of various

Soviet bloc states, including the GDR. If discussion at the round tables had been confined to flowery cultural issues, the presence of the Stasi might not have mattered at all. But the discussions went well beyond the anodyne. And where the subject under discussion was British defence, the potential for serious damage to British interests was much greater. It was one thing to be honest about British defence, in talks with people who could be regarded as Britain's future friends in a post-Communist Europe, quite another when these people were not just the representatives of a hardline regime but members of its intelligence and security service.

For some East German round table members, the completely official status of the East German team (and the absence of any dissidents) was a very negative aspect of the enterprise. Two members of the British side, Pauline Neville-Jones and Richard Davy, have said it made the round tables of very limited usefulness. Dame Pauline has written: 'East Berlin was regarded in the FCO as something of a lost cause and contacts were more vigorous and significantly more productive with other central Europeans.'[22] Richard Davy has said that 'the East German round table was the least productive and, unlike other ones, it did not include dissidents'.[23] However, he believes that this 'was not time nor money wasted', explaining that he believed the British view was that 'by dealing with these people they could perhaps penetrate, and effectively subvert, a closed system'. He also insists that, like John Roper, he knew that 'virtually all the East Germans were either intelligence officers or afraid of them', and that this was a 'common assumption' – though not, it would seem, a belief shared by Foreign Office officials and Sir John Birch in overall command.

Yet even if East German intelligence were members of the round table, Davy insists, nothing of intelligence interest would have been passed to them: 'People like myself,' he says, 'had no secrets.' Essentially, he says, we 'trotted out our line and they their line'. He does concede today, however, that some of those who were invited to the UK may have been East German intelligence officers who would otherwise not have been allowed in to the UK.

Yet this view – that nothing of any real consequence took place at these round tables – contradicts the careful argument advanced by

Roper that the whole purpose of these meetings was to make serious points. Indeed, as we have seen, Roper believed that the seriousness of the enterprise was illustrated precisely by the fact that their East German opposite numbers were conduits to the HVA and the Politburo. These were certainly not trivial affairs. Roper has said quite specifically that the British actually 'gained more from the round table policy than the East Germans. We were ambitious, knew a lot of them were Stasi and did not give anything away. We were not unwitting sources.'[24]

At this point we should pause and reflect on precisely what the Stasi files have revealed about the round tables. Here was John Roper, one of Britain's leading experts on strategy, defence policy and the highways and byways of the centre-left and left in British politics, dealing directly across a table with the Stasi who regarded Britain as its enemy, and against whom it was waging an intelligence war. The Stasi was given unique access to some of Britain's best strategic and foreign policy thinkers. What is more, the Stasi members who were present were not simply Stasi spies but included at least one military intelligence officer. We cannot know precisely what the HVA extracted from the round tables because its files on them have been destroyed. But it was obviously of value because the contacts continued.

It is, perhaps, worthwhile pointing out that when, during the late 1930s and 1940s, similar sorts of exchanges took place with the Abwehr, Hitler's generals or members of the Third Reich's secret intelligence service, the British team always consisted of counter-intelligence officers and the meetings were conducted as counter-intelligence operations.[25] Even this did not prevent the British from being duped. The 'Venlo Incident', as mentioned in Chapter 4, is a telling example.[26]

It was both foolish and unwise to exclude British counter-intelligence officers from the round tables, denying them the chance to monitor the East Germans. Had they been included, round tables with the East Germans would have then been made secure. To include them would have required the approval of Sir Gerry Warner, the MI6 counter-intelligence chief at the time, who would have run the meetings just as they should have been run – as counter-intelligence operations. In the event, MI6 did not even know they were underway. Roper says today he believed that someone in the Foreign Office was keeping an eye on the round tables, which made them safe. He could not have been more wrong. Sources close to British counter-intelligence say, unequivocally, that if any knowing contact with East German intelligence was being made through these meetings, that would indeed be a matter of very serious concern to British national security.[27] Such contact was made. And Lord Roper remains convinced that his contacts with the Stasi were entirely consistent with British aims. He says: 'the FCO clearly wanted this to be done. To that extent I was executing a bit of British policy.'

In fact, however he may put it today, both Sir John Birch and, perhaps even more crucially, the Foreign Office despatch which produced the round tables, stipulated properly that Britain's bottom line was always to do nothing with them which might endanger Britain's security. There are, of course, those who will argue that as they were being conducted under Roper's leadership they would appear to be yet another serious potential source of harm to our national security. It was almost as if the round tables were doing the Stasi's work for it, not only allowing real information to flow from West to East but introducing individuals from East Germany to significant British figures who might then seek ways of following up those contacts to their own ends. Yet we should not forget Lord Roper's insistence that this was not a situation out of control: far from it, he indicates; we got much more out of it than did the Stasi.

To those inclined to be critical of the plan to use the East German round tables in this particular way, the error will seem compounded by the fact that neither Lord Roper, nor anyone else at that round table, had any official role within British counter-intelligence, nor any professional knowledge of how counter-intelligence operations should be undertaken. Often, where individuals have overstepped the mark and knowingly brushed up against the officers or agents of a hostile intelligence agency, they have pleaded that they were doing so on behalf of British intelligence, or in pursuit of British policy. Where the evidence contradicts any such authorisation, it is inevitable, at the very least, that eyebrows will be raised.

When asked whether he was surprised that the revelation of these meetings had made a very senior British counter-intelligence officer turn apoplectic, Lord Roper replied – with characteristic bluntness – that he was 'not surprised at all!' Sir Rodric Braithwaite, a former senior diplomat and adviser at 10 Downing Street (speaking generally, and not in connection with these precise issues) has written that anyone claiming that he had been authorised to deal with people whom he knew to be East German intelligence officers was in effect claiming they were a British 'agent'.[28]

So what can have been at the back of Lord Roper's mind? What was the point – from a British angle – of talking to the Stasi about British defence thinking? Would a truthful account of our peaceful intentions towards the East Germans diminish their confidence in themselves? Was it not more likely to increase it, and therefore go against British aims? The East Germans were interested in British views but only in order to gain from them, not to be changed by them. Where intelligence officers were involved, such a gain would inevitably be intelligence. That is what intelligence officers do – and what they did then. At the same time, the net effect of holding round tables which could – and, as we have seen, did – include East German intelligence officers was not simply inadvertently to assist East German intelligence gathering. It also allowed the East Germans to filter their own, carefully contrived positions, which would have been underscored by Stasi disinformation, to senior British figures. Unless the British participants disregarded virtually everything the East Germans were saying, the Stasi's goals would have been achieved.

Today Lord Roper accepts that it is perfectly legitimate to consider whether or not this policy was wise. It was, he says, a bit like deciding whether during the Cold War years a 'fat Russian was less dangerous than a thin one'. There were always going to be risks. However, he says, he and his colleagues were 'grown-ups' and always 'had things under control'. The *policy*, he says, may be criticised as risky and counter-productive in that it shored up the very people Britain hoped would vanish. But he believes it would be quite wrong to blame the *people* charged with executing it – that is, people such as himself. If he is arguing that it was the intention of the Foreign Office knowingly to bring highly influential people like himself and Pauline Neville-Jones together with East German intelligence officers, that would be an indictment of Foreign Office policy (and contradicts Sir John Birch's claim). If, on the other hand, he is suggesting that links at this high level were inherently risky, we may concur – although even here we may very seriously doubt the risks were justified by any concrete result, let alone by an advantage to Britain. Lord Roper himself makes the point that it was just as well the Berlin Wall fell, and the West won the Cold War. Had this not happened the FCO policy might, he wryly notes, be seen as having supported those we wished to see disappear.

As we shall see, however, Lord Roper was not content with the formal policy, or what appears to be his bending of it to encompass the Stasi. He developed further plans, independently of Sir John Birch's outfit, and of his own initiative, in order to take his relationship with the East Germans to new, and even more dizzy, heights.[29] It was one thing to involve HVA professionals in Sir John's round tables. It was quite another to seize the initiative to offer them tailor-made entrées into Britain's secret world of security and defence policy.

Before moving on to the next instalment of this dark story, there is one further point worth considering. As we have repeatedly seen, it was strict Stasi policy and practice to move well away from areas where its own intelligence activities might come to light. In theory, the round tables chaired by Lord Roper could well have been viewed by the Stasi as attempts by British counter-intelligence to uncover its agents (as Roper himself has suggested). Yet quite obviously the East Germans did *not* think there was any risk to themselves in working together with Lord Roper or other British round table participants, because they continued to want to participate in them right up to the fall of the Wall in 1989. How, we might ask, could they have known that British intelligence and counter-intelligence had no part in, or watched over, these meetings? Even if Sir John Birch or any other senior diplomat had told the East Germans that intelligence services were not welcome at the meetings, the Stasi would not have taken his word for this. What is more, the HVA was absolutely right to be sure MI6 knew nothing about the round tables, which makes the incident even worse from the British point of view. How *did* they know?

One answer is that one of their own London officers – 'Eckhart' in fact – had confirmed that, from the British end, these were not intelligence operations because none of the participants was working for British intelligence. How did 'Eckhart' know? Lord Roper says he believed that British intelligence was watching over the round tables, via the FCO. That there was no evidence of this secret guard might not be at all surprising. Yet in the event, no watch was kept. And for at least one of his subsequent major projects involving East Germans and Britain in 1989, there cannot have been any question of a watchful British eye in the background, since Roper promoted them of his own initiative. 'Eckhart' was perfectly right. As the SIRA files show, in April 1986 he sent a report on the proposed British team. We do not know precisely what was in his report, but we can be sure that it raised no intelligence objections because the meetings went ahead. To state, to the 'Centre's' evident satisfaction, that Pauline Neville-Jones, Edward Pearce, Edwina Moreton and John Roper himself owed no formal duty to British intelligence indicates deep knowledge on 'Eckhart's' part. How on earth could he have got it, except from his acquaintance with the members, or a member, of the British team? This, too, is no trifling matter for it is a further trace of the Stasi's focus on John Roper and his expertise, and we must revisit it later on.

Sources close to MI5 have confirmed that they are now seriously worried about these matters.[30] Before being presented with the evidence concerning the round tables with East Germany, they had known none of the details outlined here (they were not party to these events). At first, however, they were not sufficiently motivated to speak to Lord Roper about them and believed the 'Roper' in question was the eminent historian Hugh Trevor-Roper. Lord Roper has confirmed that, up to June 2001 at any rate, no one in MI5 had interviewed him. As a senior political figure, he supports their line, believing that a debriefing twelve years after the event would serve little purpose.

It is interesting to compare these details concerning the round tables with a commentary provided by Colonel Roy Giles, a former senior British military intelligence officer with extensive experience of secret intelligence operations inside East Germany. When asked if, while serving, he would have had informal contacts (unregulated by British counter-intelligence) with Stasi officers, or even with those whom he knew to be connected to the Stasi, he replied that any such meeting with a member of the East German intelligence community, or with anyone believed to be reporting to it, would have been treated as 'highly suspicious' and would have been studiously avoided. If such a meeting had by chance presented itself, Colonel Giles said unequivocally that 'clearance would have been sought *at once* – some decisions a British officer can make on the spot but this would not have been one of them'. As to the view that in 1989 the Stasi ought not to have been regarded as Britain's enemy, but be seen as a useful conduit to those who wanted to reform Communism, he could only deliver the pithy expletive 'bollocks'. He could recall one US military intelligence officer who had privately bought some Meissen china from an East German. He had been sacked immediately. Another British officer developed an interest in art and was invited to visit the flat of an East German. Colonel Giles recalls that 'everyone was absolutely horrified'. Such behaviour, he believed, was 'completely unacceptable and this view was widely shared'.[31]

By 1986–7, then, John Roper was ensnared in the Stasi's net of contacts and was regarded as a person in whom the Stasi could place its trust. He was known not to be a member of the British intelligence community and he was plainly keen to build bridges to East Germany's Politburo. He was indeed something of a catch.

At this point his story took a dramatic turn. A new boy turned up on the block. This was Jörg Döring/'Harke', a military intelligence officer, freshly arrived in London. One of his first duties was to connect to Roper.[32] We must remember that so far the Roper operation had been an HVA project. Schneidratus ('Helios') had been involved in setting up the round tables with Roper,[33] but there is no evidence of any military intelligence interest in Roper before November 1987. We do know that the military intelligence officers believed the HVA treated them as junior partners and did not share resources with them which, understandably, led to more than a little friction. But as the round tables moved into discussions of defence and security issues, it is not surprising that East German military intelligence should want a look-in as well. Döring arranged to be present at a round table planning meeting over food at 34 Belgrave Square on 23 November 1987. Demonstrating the almost pathological suspicion that was the hallmark of the Stasi, Döring came to believe that Roper had been covertly taping the conversation. This, Döring concluded, implied that Roper was not what the Germans had taken him to be, namely a reliable friend of the GDR, a bit of detective work he duly reported to the 'Centre' without delay.

A Stasi document dated 24 November 1987 describes how, on the previous day, acting on instructions, Döring made contact with Roper and a Chatham House researcher, Adrian Hyde-Price (now a professor at Leicester University), working then as Roper's junior administrative assistant. The two men agreed to come unaccompanied to Belgrave Square to discuss further contacts through the round tables. During the talks, however, Döring thought he saw Roper fiddling with a small tape recorder. It was in fact a Psion Organizer, only recently on the British market and therefore not familiar to the East German.[34] He immediately feared the possibility that this was an MI5 sting – with Roper doing the stinging – and he asked his military intelligence chiefs in East Berlin to check him out.

The Stasi files provide a fascinating account of Döring's version of the meeting and the subsequent conclusions to which the 'Centre' in East Berlin came on Roper.

24.11.87 Minute:
In line with 'Harke's' duties, there was a meal on 23.11.87 given by Bock with representatives of Chatham House, Roper and Hyde-Price. 'Harke' noticed that Roper was taping the whole of the conversation conspiratorially on a tape recorder. 'Hans-Georg' was immediately informed. The evaluation is that it was a targeted measure. Roper, clearly, belongs to the circle of employees at Chatham House who work for MI5. This observation must be noted in the operational work. However, in security terms there was no incrimination of 'Harke' and it does not endanger the *Kewa*. Suggest a detailed evaluation of the whole matter at the Treff in the Centre in December.

What is revealing about the response, which came from Section IX of the Stasi, the investigation unit, was its verdict:

> . . . on 23 November 1987 the legalist 'Harke' informed us about the monitoring of a discussion with the member of Chatham House, Roper. There is a reference to this in the country file. Section IX knows of no such fact. After analysis of the contents of 'Harke's' report, Section IX evaluates that it cannot be concluded that there was a targeted action against the legalist. The British are leaders in the operational use of technology. Were we to suppose that there had been a Secret Service targeting by Roper, it would have to be premised with the question as to why he was doing it in such a way as the legalist was able to note it. What we would need to examine is whether the legalist 'Harke' is perhaps asking more questions than his cover allows. This could conceivably be a possible explanation for why Roper was recording the conversation. But here, too, the question exists as to the purpose of the recording.

In fact, back in East Berlin, the suggestion that Roper might be working for MI5 was quickly rebuffed (for one thing, it contradicted 'Eckhart's' information from April 1986 and the decision to go ahead with the first round table meeting in October 1986), although it is not clear whether the military intelligence chiefs knew this, since, for reasons of conspiracy, there had been no earlier need for them to know. As this document shows, Döring's query was passed to Section IX which dealt with internal investigations.[35] They then asked the specialist unit, HA II, to become involved. We know this because we have a remaining fragment of the dossier they provided on Roper at this time (it contains material up to and including 1987 but not later).[36] It is plain, as we see below, that HA II produced nothing which suggested any link to MI5, but the choice of HA II to investigate him is, in itself, interesting – and chilling.

HA II was, as we saw in Eberle's case, the department which investigated important Stasi sources or potential sources, in particular those individuals who had a connection, formal or informal, known or unknown, to the Stasi.[37] The fact that HA II investigated Roper shows how seriously the Stasi took him as a source. However,

HA II was also the unit charged with undertaking counter-intelligence checks for a special category of Stasi co-opted workers. These were IMs who had the unique advantage, from the Stasi's viewpoint, of possessing a link to Western intelligence services (the Stasi expression was '*IMs mit Feindberührung*', 'co-opted workers who could touch the enemy').[38] Such people were, obviously enough, very special Stasi assets because as long as they were deemed reliable friends of the GDR, they provided a way of penetrating Western security. On the other hand, where they had not declared to the Stasi their potential links to Western intelligence, they were deemed to be hazards who might be double agents, and therefore enemies. HA II knew, or guessed correctly, that Eberle had active links to British intelligence so he was deemed by the Stasi to be unreliable and was dropped. Roper was treated entirely differently. There were no such links – and they therefore trusted him.

The meaning of HA II's involvement in this incident is ambiguous. It could suggest that these fragments concerning Roper were part of Döring's file, that he was the co-opted worker (he was indeed one) and that Roper was the suspected agent of Western intelligence. But if these fragments are all that remains of *Roper's* HVA file, which the Stasi Archive can neither confirm nor deny but is a strong possibility, this carries with it an unhappy implication to which we shall come in due course.[39] These papers include a photocopy of his passport easily copied during one of his numerous visits behind the Iron Curtain. They also refer to the fact that, as a student, Roper was an active member of CND. This was a useful snippet of information which the Stasi will have relished, given their interest in subverting CND. Lord Roper has said this was common knowledge – not least because it appeared in his entry in *Who's Who*. In fact, the *Who's Who* entry for the 1980s says: 'Roper . . . read PPE at Oxford; president of UN Students' Association 1957; organised University referendum on nuclear disarmament' – not quite the same as stating, as HA II does, that 'as a student he was active in the anti-nuclear weapon movement'.[40]

In the event, HA II plainly confirmed Section IX's view that, whatever his connections to British intelligence might be, Roper was not in any way working *for* MI5 or MI6 (which was, as we have

seen, patently the truth both then and now, since at the end of 2001
MI5 was still confusing him with Hugh Trevor-Roper).

Section IX duly told Döring his suspicion was unfounded and that
he had not been targeted as he suspected. There was no evidence that
Roper, whom they clearly felt they all knew well enough to describe in
familiar terms ('the *member* of Chatham House, Roper' – Döring, it will
be recalled, had ignorantly termed him a 'representative'), was any sort
of security threat to them at all. Indeed, they suggested that if MI5 had
been involved, it would have been done so skilfully that Döring would
never have known – his noticing should, in fact, have told Döring that
Roper was no MI5 spy. The 'Centre' plainly agreed because they
insisted that contact with Roper be maintained. This still leaves the
question open as to why, if Döring thought Roper were an MI5 agent,
he could conclude that his unit had not been endangered. The answer
seems to be that Döring had not used the meeting with Roper and
Hyde-Price to try to ensnare Roper. They had no idea that Döring, for
the military intelligence spies, might be interested in working alongside him. Since Döring had given nothing away, there was nothing for
Roper to uncover about him. At this point, the 'Centre's' conviction
that Roper was not an MI5 plant kicked in. As Döring's reaction
shows, he was not aware of the 'Centre's' view of Roper. This is not surprising not only because Döring was new but because the competition
and conflict between the HVA and the military intelligence officers
was a matter repeatedly noted in the Stasi files.

Döring had been certain that Roper, even if he had been an MI5
agent, could not have deduced that he, Döring, was a military intelligence officer, and not a diplomat, and, for this reason, the incident
had not endangered the *Kewa*. What he did think, however, was
that all further contact with Roper – as we have seen in full accord
with Stasi spycraft – should be suspended or broken off. But the
'Centre' had disagreed. They knew Roper had no MI5 role. What is so
sinister, of course, is that the contact was indeed maintained, not that
Döring, newly on the scene, should have believed Roper was, from the
*Kewa's* viewpoint, a likely MI5 agent. There was, therefore, no reason
why the 'Centre' should instruct its officers to cease all further work
on Roper's plan to introduce IPW members into Chatham House,
which we have seen the Stasi found enticing. Had the 'Centre' had the

slightest doubts about him, the *Apparat* would indeed have been in trouble. As it turned out, they played ball with Roper into 1989, to encompass two further projects initiated by him.

There were two further peculiar aspects to the Belgrave Square meeting between Roper, Hyde-Price and Döring. The first was that Roper could not remember ever having met Döring, but even fifteen years later Hyde-Price recalled him immediately and clearly ('a youngish, overweight embassy official'). Second, not only did it not occur to Hyde-Price that Döring might have been an intelligence officer (Hyde-Price points out that at the time he was 'very new to the game' of international contacts and had no intelligence links himself) but also he attests that he believed the East German round table was solely a Chatham House affair. This means that he had not been told of Sir John Birch's role in them, or that a Britain–East Europe centre existed. Indeed, today Sir John Birch's name still meant nothing to him at all. It is obvious, therefore, that Roper wanted the East Germans to accept that he was the leading British figure in the relationship with the East Germans and would use his position at Chatham House to their advantage.

Lest there be any doubt about the Stasi's belief that Roper was, from its point of view, entirely clean, we can adduce one final bit of evidence on this from the files. On 27 January 1989, in discussing Döring's strong record in London, the 'Centre' mentioned that MI5 lacked any knowledge of Döring's real identity as a military spy. Had the Stasi believed that Roper were an MI5 agent, or even reporting to it at any point after 1987 and before January 1989, it would have assumed that Döring had been 'deconspiracised' – that MI5 knew what his real job was. Yet at the 'Centre' General Gäbler had specifically stated not only that Döring's work in London was 'of a very high quality' but that it contained 'no security risks'. This is corroborated by the evidence that the Stasi regarded Roper as fertile territory in 1989.

While Döring was being informed about Lord Roper, Roper himself was devising yet more ways of constructing working links with the East Germans, using Chatham House as a base. He was now seeking to establish further contacts with his East German opposite numbers from the Institute for Policy and Economics so as to bring them to 10 St James's Square as 'research fellows'. He did so entirely on his own initiative as Director of Studies, as Sir James Eberle has confirmed: 'I have no recollection that any of our Chatham House visiting fellows came from East Germany. If there were, I am sure that John Roper would know, for it would only have been in connection with the Chatham House International Security Programme which he ran. I can be reasonably certain that no such initiative – if indeed there was one – originated from me.'[41] But fellows did come, and it seems certain that the idea was entirely Roper's. He had thought they might write a book on détente. He decided, however, not to edit the project himself, but to get his fellow round table member, Richard Davy, to do so. Leaving aside the issue as to what, precisely, it was thought 'research' by the East Germans in the UK might contribute to British understanding of détente, having East Germans in Chatham House would dangerously extend the range of possibilities open to the Stasi in London.

The book (entitled *European Détente*) finally appeared in 1992 and contained only one chapter on East Germany, written by H. H. Kasper. Although Roper was not aware of this, or had forgotten it, Kasper had in fact been an 'attaché' at 34 Belgrave Square from 1984 until 1987, when he returned to East Berlin to take up the post at the IPW. Davy has spoken of the enormous difficulties he had in getting Kasper to deliver his chapter. When it finally arrived it was very dull. The reason was not hard to decipher: Kasper was more of an HVA spy than a scholar.

Yet further dramatic evidence in the Stasi files shows that this was by no means the end of the Roper affair with the Stasi. It was at this very critical stage in his relationship with the Stasi that Roper crossed the Rubicon and became their agent of influence. We have plain evidence from June 1989 showing Roper furthering the aims and ambitions of the Stasi, in the knowledge that doing so would find favour with the East Germans. Roper began to use his considerable influence to help establish a favourable view of East Germany in British public life, help which would enable doors to be opened for the East German intelligence community which would otherwise have been firmly kept shut. His depressing readiness to act as the agent of the East Germans came to fruition from their point of view in the early summer of 1989, as the Stasi files reveal. On 16 June 1989, Lindner's replacement as ambassador, Joachim Mitdank, sent a secret wire to Horst Sieber of the Central Committee of the SED, to General Krabatsch of the Stasi, to a Professor Schmidt of the IPW and to his predecessor, Lindner.[42] His message read as follows:

1. On 15.06 I invited members of the 3rd round table GDR/GB, leader of delegation John Roper, into the Embassy. A very positive evaluation: course of meeting, atmosphere and organisation of round table. The discussion of the problems in the sense of a constructive conflict of opinions was especially thanks to Professor Schmidt. The members of the British Delegation asked for their best wishes to be conveyed to him. There was great interest in a continuation of the discussion in the same way in the future. Of exceptional usefulness was the strengthening of trust as well as the construction of greater willingness for contacts. Chatham House and the EEC [Centre for Eastern Europe] are particularly interested in continuation of contacts especially with the IPW and IIB. A stay in Dresden and especially talks with local politicians would be useful and very informative. The British side is concerned to prepare for and execute the 4th round table in a similar way.

2. In the period before the 4th round table is executed, there should be greater use made of the possibilities of the presence in the UK of politicians and scientists from the GDR. Support was offered by Chatham House and the EEC. There was interest in particular in informal meetings with experts as well as lectures by distinguished representatives of the GDR.

In this connection, Roper repeated his already-stated interest in the carrying out of a meeting for the fortieth anniversary of the GDR in Chatham House. Interest in the GDR as well as in German–German relations had grown. Gorbachev's visit to the FRG had aroused great interest in the UK. Roper also pointed to the meeting on the fortieth anniversary of the [West German] Basic Law in Chatham House. In connection with Chatham House, it was concerned right from the beginning to offer both German states if it could a chance to present their own balance sheets, future and development. Roper suggested having a GDR day at Chatham House in November. The working title could be 'Forty years of the GDR – results, possibilities, problems and further development'. It would be desirable to have a lecture from a GDR politician as well as a conference to include politicians, scientists, the military, journalists, representatives of culture. It would also be possible to have a meeting on security policy. He pointed to his extremely positive impression of his talks in Ebenhausen with representatives of the Military Academy F. Engels. The contacts between the NVA and the Bundeswehr as well as the 'Saarbrücken' talks had strengthened the interest in such talks.

3. I advise testing Roper's suggestions in a positive way. It would offer the possibility of executing an exceptionally effective measure in support of foreign information gathering, strengthening our contact to leading British scientific institutions and to develop contacts in the security policy and military spheres. It would also meet WEU General Secretary van Eekelen's expressed wish for contact. At the same time it would be a successful measure of countering FRG's attempts to portray itself in the UK as the single representative of Germans.

As we can readily appreciate from the above, top secret, memo, Roper's suggestions appeared to make the East Germans' Christmas come early that year. He was now proposing to use Chatham House as the venue for what the East Germans would see as an extremely prestigious way of 'celebrating' the fortieth anniversary of the GDR and plainly snubbing Britain's West German allies (who were nevertheless certainly no less anxious to please the GDR than was Roper) at the same time. He was also offering a conference which the East Germans believed 'would strengthen their contact to leading British scientific institutions' and people 'in the security policy and military sphere'.

Would the propaganda event that Lord Roper was proposing have helped undermine the reputation of the GDR Politburo, or loosened the hold of Communism on East Germany? Would it have enhanced the standing of the East German dissidents? These, we should recall, were Sir Geoffrey Howe's 1985 policy aims. It is not hard to answer these questions for the Roper event would plainly have both bolstered the Politburo and promoted the GDR's image in the UK – the opposite of what Britain truly wanted.

While it is perfectly true that Roper's idea of offering the East Germans a much desired propaganda platform in London may have been a sweetener to get them to accept his idea of security policy meetings which van Eekelen, for the Western European Union, also appeared to like, Roper's linking them with the idea of marking forty years of East German Communism was clearly not best placed to appeal to those East Germans in the GDR who were struggling vainly for their human and civil rights. Yet these were the people who were the intended beneficiaries of the changes in British foreign policy after 1985.

But very much more dangerous was Roper's plan for a conference to bring East Germans together with members of the scientific, security and military communities in the UK. What is startling is not that the East Germans should have rushed to accept this generous offer, but that Roper should have made it in the first place. The second half of the 1980s show Lord Roper drawing, like a moth to a light, ever closer to the Stasi which was increasingly – and alarmingly – getting what it wanted from its *Kewa* against him. In dealing face to face with Jörg Döring (whom he never even knew by name) he was eyeballing the best military intelligence officer the East Germans had in London. Roper had deliberately placed himself in harm's way, and was offering the Stasi precisely the openings they wanted for their own unwholesome purposes. As the Stasi files show, his suggestion was highly appealing because – as Mitdank said – 'it would offer the possibility of executing an exceptionally effective measure in support of foreign information gathering'. Roper, in the eyes of the Stasi, was once again helping them to gain secret intelligence. For the second time (the first involved inviting East Germans to Chatham House in 1988) it was he, rather than they, who had seized the initiative.

Sir James Eberle says today that he knew nothing at all about any of these particular planned Chatham House bridges to East Germany, a country in which he had no real interest. He did support

Chatham House's greater involvement in Soviet and East European affairs, but relations with the East Germans were left, he says, entirely to John Roper. When it was put to him that they were intended to lead to meetings which could include East German intelligence officers, Sir James said, without hesitation, that, had he known it at the time, he would have regarded this as 'completely unacceptable' and at once informed the MI5 officer with whom he chatted informally. Were such meetings, he was asked, consistent with his own view of Chatham House's goals? His blunt response was 'absolutely not – it was not our job to speak to intelligence officers'. Sir James's forthright response clearly confirmed the Stasi's own opinion on his loyalty to Britain.

We may wonder, too, whether Lord Roper informed the Foreign Office about this particular initiative. He says that he remembered telephoning them to tell them about it, but he did not need their permission to proceed because he was 'not their agent on this venture', and the purpose of his call was probably 'just to get some money from them'.[43]

By now, however, he was doing the Stasi favours which far exceeded those provided by the round tables. It would require only one further Stasi twist to force history to put an entirely different interpretation on Roper's bridge-building to the East German intelligence community. It was fortunate for everyone in Britain, including Lord Roper and his British team (all of whom were located in the very sites targeted by Wolf and Mielke in directive after directive), that within five months Mitdank and his cronies had all disappeared.

Lord Roper has said about this evidence that he does indeed accept that he may well have been a 'source' for the Stasi (in the English sense that information might have or would have ended up with them) bearing in mind his view that anything he may have said during his meetings with the East Germans was 'of no security interest whatsoever'. He says he had no access to any British secrets. In a long, and generously given interview, he stated that he realised he knew many things, from the ins and outs of British left-of-centre politics to British strategic policy, which would naturally have been of interest to the Stasi. However, he could not recall contact with any East German, whether diplomat or journalist, before 1985, and although he could see that there were items in the SIRA material which had links to Chatham House, and that he himself had worked at Chatham House, he had not started there as an actual employee until 1983 – some time after the East Germans had started to pick up information from that route. He argues today that the significance of much of the Stasi's intelligence should be discounted.

When asked about his subsequent contacts with East Germans, Lord Roper was quite happy to confirm that they had been several in number and always pleasant in character. On one occasion, an East German, whose name (many years later) he could no longer recall, had said he would like to meet William (Lord) Rodgers (one of the 'Gang of Four' who had broken away from the Labour Party to form the SDP) and his wife Sylvia, who had been born in Poland. Roper had been happy to arrange for them all to have dinner together.[44] After each round table, he would make a 'courtesy call' on the East German ambassador, and he believes that he may have attended 'two East German Embassy receptions a year'. He particularly enjoyed the annual Christmas party there. Meetings with East Germans outside the embassy were 'minimal' – perhaps once or twice a year.

Lord Roper agreed to examine a list of names of East Germans, and identify any he could recall, albeit ten years later. He recognised Lindner's name at once, but not, of course, as a Stasi officer. He was surprised that H. H. Kasper had been listed as an attaché, with diplomatic status, since he had believed him to be a full-time academic. He was, Lord Roper said, now a journalist in eastern Berlin who had, rather curiously, 'bumped into' him quite recently. He certainly recalled the name 'Schneidratus' ('now he rings a bell – he attended a round table – it is such a remarkable name that one does not forget it,' Lord Roper said). He could recall a 'Dr Rudering' but there was no one with this name although a Dr Rudolph was listed.

These, Lord Roper said, were the only names he could recall. Asked whether he ever met a man called 'Linser', he replied that this 'said something' – perhaps he had met him at a party. Linser, of course, was, like Schneidratus and Döring, a military intelligence officer. However, he had died in October 1984 and since Lord Roper says that his contacts with the East German Embassy began only after 1985, it is possible that he confused his name with that of Lindner. When asked whether he could remember meeting Lindner's successor, Joachim Mitdank, he replied that he did remember the name, but had certainly never met him. When it was pointed out to him that, according to the Stasi files, a meeting – indeed a significant one – had taken place, Lord Roper remembered that he had attended a 'farewell party' for him although he could not at first recall what had been said so many years ago. He did then remember that his security proposal to the East Germans was designed to match one made by some West Germans.

When it was explained to Lord Roper that there were grounds for thinking the Stasi might have been trying to set him up as a source in the Stasi sense (he had, after all, accepted that he knew things they might like to learn), he replied he had had a good understanding of the Stasi. As far as the round tables were concerned, he accepts that such meetings gave the East Germans an opportunity to meet influential people such as himself. That was their purpose. He was fully aware of the fact that some people, such as the American foreign policy hardliner Richard Perle, believed they were giving 'sustenance to the enemy'. At the same time, he was not surprised to learn that some of those to whom he had spoken in London – Döring/'Harke' – had been a military intelligence officer. It was interesting that he could not recall Döring's name: it is just possible that in dealing with Lord Roper (but – incomprehensibly – not Hyde-Price), Döring may have become 'Dr Rudering'.

Lord Roper has said clearly that, to the best of his knowledge, he had no contact with any East German in London before the mid-1980s. The name Uher meant absolutely nothing to him. The East German journalist Oschmann (who has never mentioned any connection with Roper and had returned to East Berlin by 1985) was, however, known to Roper as a guest at one or two round tables. If Lord Roper was being worked on (*abgeschöpft*, 'squeezed dry', was a common Stasi term) he will obviously have known the person involved, whether he was 'Eckhart' himself or a go-between. He adds that he accepts he knew 'a lot about British defence policy but military intelligence officers are interested in technical matters (about which I know relatively little although I was well-briefed in the 1970s)'. In fact, as we have seen, the Stasi's military intelligence officers were also concerned with military and strategic policy and the British peace movement. In any case, Roper points out that he had left the Defence Committee in 1980 and says that what he knew was out of date and no longer secret.

Our difficulty with all of this is that we know from the Stasi files that it was always the HVA who decided what sort of intelligence was of use to them. If they found it useful in their terms, it served their purpose even if from a British perspective the information seemed harmless. An enemy is helped when he is given what he wants, and not necessarily when he is given what one might assume he wants.

The Stasi files show that by 1987 Roper had indeed become their source (in the English sense) and a 'person of trust' in Stasi terms, and that by 1988 we are right to regard him as an agent of influence. At the moment, these represent the sum total of the documents on these matters in the Stasi Archives, but, because of changes in German law, any new discoveries will no longer be open to research.

But the Roper puzzle contains even more than this. As we have seen, we have hard evidence that the Stasi brushed up against Lord Roper, to their advantage, in 1986. But what if they had done so much earlier?

Let us return for a moment to the question of 'Eckhart' and Chatham House. As we have seen, someone passed Eberle's name to the Stasi and possibly his passports as well. We have also seen that there was overwhelming circumstantial evidence that 'Eckhart' did not derive his intelligence from open or private Chatham House sessions but from some consultant's 'take' on the issues examined there (as well as other ones which had nothing to do with Chatham House). That 'take' included the views of the SDP's leaders and security and defence issues.[45] We must remember, too, that what 'Eckhart' sent back to East Berlin was centrally assessed as secret intelligence by one of the best intelligence services in the world. We know, too, that from 1983 until 1987 the East German Embassy had stopped paying its membership dues to Chatham House, and came to the conclusion that something happened in 1983 to cause the Stasi to want to distance East Germany from Chatham House, and that this had to do with a person whose views they had been picking up, and not the institution itself. By 1987 that decision had to be reversed. In 1983, we proposed, they needed to avoid any suggestion that Chatham House was of particular interest to them. In 1987 they were presented with a most advantageous offer of collaboration with Chatham House – and a perfectly legitimate reason for having contact with it. Indeed, the offer would have been impossible to take up without membership of Chatham House.

So what *had* happened in 1983? One thing that happened was that Lord Roper became a senior staff member of Chatham House. Another was that Wolf decreed that HVA resources should be focused on a few influential sources. If Lord Roper had been in some way used by 'Eckhart' before 1983 (and we have seen that from 1981 Chatham House topics were subject to analysis from someone whom 'Eckhart' was able, directly or indirectly, to consult), that would be a strong reason why, in order to maintain what was now an increasingly important connection with him, the 'Centre' would have immediately ordered the embassy to withdraw from Chatham House and break off all institutional contact.

This behaviour on the part of the Stasi may strike us as being counter-intuitive. To have a source inside Chatham House, and to be a member of it at the same time, might seem a convenient way of working on, or with, that source, and of explaining any East German interest in him, or her. In the Stasi's eyes, however, the rules of conspiracy demanded that any operational interest in a person required there to be no visible East German connection to him or her.[46] Without one, they reasoned, there was no need to suspect a covert connection. From the Stasi's viewpoint, it was always rather to prevent a question about this even being raised than to have to wrestle with a possible answer to it. Not to be a member of Chatham House implied, 'No East German interest here.' To be a member would always imply, 'Some interest – why?'

But by 1987, Lord Roper was proposing an institutional and therefore official link between Chatham House and the IPW, the

Stasi front. This was something from which the Stasi could obtain huge benefit, but first the East German Embassy had to demonstrate that it had become engaged once again with Chatham House. In 1987 the advantages of membership on balance outweighed the security risks (which had by no means vanished). The scales now tipped the other way. Not to be associated with Chatham House under these new circumstances would inevitably trigger the question, 'No interest in it – why not?' Being members again, however, would elicit the comment, 'Interested again? Jolly good'. Avoiding the 'why not' question made perfect sense now. Indeed, Döring himself began to go to the meetings at which Hyde-Price recalls coming across him.

The evidence that Lord Roper was a Stasi target long before 1987 is indeed overwhelming. Careful study and cross-referencing of the Stasi files leads us to what is certainly one possible conclusion. It is that by 1986 Lord Roper was *already* being tapped by the Stasi as their source. The fact that HA II checked him out in 1987 might well indicate that at this time the HVA had already decided to see if he might become a formal co-opted worker. This would mean that he, rather than Döring, had been the co-opted worker who was being tested for contact with MI5. While Lord Roper accepts that it is possible he was being set up as a Stasi source, he makes it absolutely plain that he knows of no way in which this could ever have been brought to fruition. On the basis of the available evidence in the Stasi files, it seems plausible to hold that the targeting may well have begun as early as his first visit to East Germany in 1957, or possibly during visits in the 1970s.

Lord Roper today fully accepts that there is considerable and remarkable congruence between his expertise and the subject matter of many of 'Eckhart's' reports and he can offer no explanation for this – the Chatham House reports, British thoughts on NATO's out-of-area contingents, the arms industry, arms control, the foreign policy of the SDP, the views of SDP leaders, David Owen's role as foreign policy spokesman of the SDP, Labour's attitude towards the Falklands war, the SDP's attitude towards the Falklands war and so on.[47] There is the Eberle passport conundrum but also the question of how the Stasi knew that none of the round table members had any role in British counter-intelligence. As we have seen, Lord Roper states that he did believe that British intelligence were watching over the round tables. Had the Stasi known everything that Roper knew, it might be deduced that it would have concluded its original assessment had been wrong, that the round tables *were* UK intelligence operations, and it ought to move away from them sharply. That the Stasi got at the truth may mean it had a way of double-checking Roper's opinions. Yet it could also indicate that Roper was indulging in wishful thinking.

In Lord Roper we have perhaps yet another example of someone who was 'victim' *and* 'source' for East German intelligence. Roper was certainly not 'Eckhart' the individual, but there are grounds for supposing he was one of the 'Eckharts' *behind* 'Eckhart'. Roper, demonstrably a Stasi target by April 1986, is a perfect fit for the Stasi's source inside Chatham House – or at least one of them if it had two – and he is the only person whose background matches the profile outlined in the files. None of the other major figures at Chatham House generates as many hits as he does. Oddly enough, Roper also meets the Wolf criteria of being close to those with power, but having little himself. Wolf has written: 'We would never have approached a minister with the clumsy request to become formal sources. But as long as he was chatting away with old friends and colleagues who reported to us, we did not need to.'[48]

Today it seems hard to doubt that there are important lessons to be learned from the Stasi's astonishing and – many would say – outrageous efforts by both Britons in high places and by the institutions located there. The Stasi's targeting of Roper was clearly an East German intelligence success. It is also certainly possible that ever since the early 1980s the HVA had been able to profit from his views. He cannot explain how this may have taken place. By 1989, however, Lord Roper was undoubtedly ready to extend to the East Germans, whom he says he knew included members of the Stasi and those reporting to it, a hot hand of friendship, thanks to his projects, the purposes of which were, to the East Germans, of huge benefit and entirely straightforward. He was to be a conduit which would propel their key people – Stasi people – deep into the heart of the British establishment and into defence and security circles. His good name would be attached to their enterprises, and would only help to improve the image of East Germany in the UK to their advantage.

As we have seen, this had been an East German goal ever since the regime was set up in 1949. For the reality of the appalling police state, men like Lord Roper would substitute an image of a Communist regime with whom Britain could happily do business. Human rights abuses were to be forgotten when it came to academic exchanges with Chatham House and defence and security openings to Britain.

Some of those in Britain who played into the Stasi's hands were, in Lenin's phrase, simply 'useful idiots'. It would be wrong to describe Roper as anything other than brilliant. He was not ignorant about the risks he was running, but he believed he could manage them. Yet we should recall that it was not any policy of good relations with the East Germans, still less the Stasi, that caused the Berlin Wall to collapse. If this had been Roper's ambition, the projects he was developing were self-defeating. Indeed, the reverse is the case. If German Communism collapsed because of a change in Soviet policy, the enterprises that Lord Roper and others supported begin to appear as ways of appeasing and therefore sustaining the East Germans, not assisting in getting rid of them.

As someone unlikely ever to gain the high government office to which he once seemed destined, the idea of being a leading figure in détente policy towards the GDR may have been attractive. He, like many others, could not know that German Communism was to disappear with such unseemly haste. Had it not done so, he would have been rightly lauded as Britain's chief link to the East German regime. For his part, he is adamant that he did nothing unwittingly, and that Britain gained far more from his work than the East Germans.

If we are taken with the notion that in some way Roper's expertise was tapped by the Stasi before 1986, it must be said at once that the Stasi files do not show how it did so without Roper's knowledge. It is possible that some go-between, trusted by both the Stasi and Roper, was the channel between them. Yet although the Stasi was very good, it did not possess magical powers. If Roper cannot recall a middleman, we may wonder whether one ever existed. If Roper himself had perhaps been more candid than was wise in his dealings with the Stasi prior to 1987, he himself states he cannot think when – or how – this could have happened. Some may believe it is remarkable that at no time in the 1980s did he in person give MI5 or MI6 even a whiff of his intentions, let alone check with them whether his ideas were safe. The Security Service is highly approachable, and understands fully the need for confidentiality. Lord Roper's plain response is that this was not necessary since he believed British intelligence knew about his round table activities and kept a watching brief on them. Certainly, in the world of secrets, stranger things do happen. If he chose not to tell the FCO or MI5 about his 1989 plan, as he himself declares, this may have been because, like others in the world of diplomacy and academe, he feared their 'heavy hand' would put the kibosh on him. While he may have deduced that only he and the Stasi knew about his personal commitment to improved relationships with East Germany, he might reasonably respond that it was not his fault if he was being 'left out in the cold' by MI5. A fully alert Security Service open to the tactics used by the officers at 34 Belgrave Square, could – and should – have ensured that someone as prominent as Roper was kept well away from people who might do him damage. That being so, the Stasi's success was our failure.

# 14

# The Stasi's British Assets

The Stasi files often make dense and difficult reading, yet they provide a unique record of the different ways in which a hostile intelligence service can operate, gaining facts to support its goals and sowing discord among its enemies. This chapter uses the files to expose both the Stasi's methods and its British sources exploited by the East Germans to score its many espionage successes. One constant Stasi preoccupation was the search for possible recruits, of whom a few, if they were lucky, might be close to the centre of British political power. One such example was Ron Hayward, the subject of close Stasi scrutiny when he visited East Berlin and Dresden in March 1975. At the time, Hayward was General Secretary of the Labour Party.[1] He was almost certainly completely unaware of the Stasi's interest in him, which in any case proved quite misplaced.

The Stasi was evidently intrigued by this stalwart 'old' Labour character. Revealing its own mindset more than his, its first comment was a criticism of his 'modest' grasp of Marxist theory. But it relished his praise for the GDR. The Communists, he opined, 'had built up the country, and created a new type of human being there'. He noted the 'pulsating life in Dresden' and how well dressed the people there were. At the same time (thankfully) he said he did not think that the methods used in the GDR would work in Britain. He told the East Germans he did not wish to waste time 'discussing ideological differences' but preferred to concentrate on the issues that 'united Labour and the SED' which, he said, were peace and disarmament. The Stasi was pleased about this and also about the fact that he said he had a lot of power. He would visit the Prime Minister, Harold Wilson, every Tuesday and he had permission to speak publicly about his differences with him. Indeed, he claimed that Wilson wanted to increase his power and the power of the Labour Party in the governing of Britain. Yet the Stasi discovered there was little chance of getting him on side. Although it recorded two possible Achilles heels – women and alcohol – neither could be exploited. 'He likes chatting to women and is a heavy drinker,' the Stasi noted, 'but his wife, Phyllis, exerts a strong influence on him and he can clearly consume vast amounts of beer, cognac, champagne and whisky with no ill effect.' He was quickly forgotten.

The Stasi files, it is worth emphasising, do not merely contain a record of those who were being sized up or who, in one way, or another, assisted it. They also reveal the innocence of individuals often falsely accused of treachery. Hidden among the six million Stasi dossiers is one which finally solves one of Britain's major political mysteries, namely the allegation that Harold Wilson, leader of the Labour Party after 1962 and Prime Minister twice (from 1964 to 1970, and then again from 1974 to 1976) was a Communist mole.[2] Although the subject of this particular dossier is Rudy Sternberg, a close friend of Wilson's, its most astonishing revelation concerns Wilson himself. He is still regarded as Britain's most secretive Prime Minister, and, despite several biographies and autobiographies, his attitude towards Communism and his dealings with a number of businessmen who had strong links with Eastern Europe – men such as the publisher Robert Maxwell and Sternberg himself – remain enigmatic to say the least. During Wilson's second term, in 1975, he was badly wounded by a whispering campaign against him, initiated from within British intelligence and led by Peter Wright in MI5. It spread rapidly throughout the British media, was widely believed on the principle that there is 'no smoke without fire', and may have contributed to Wilson's surprise resignation in 1976.[3]

Its substance was that Wilson was a Soviet 'asset', and very possibly an agent. The charges focused on his past as a committed left winger, the means by which he had become leader of the Labour Party, on his vociferous opposition to West German rearmament in the 1950s, and his support for the recognition of Communist East Germany at a time when the United States and the Federal Republic of Germany opposed it, and, above all, the fact that ever since 1951 he had surrounded himself with a circle of foreign-born Jewish friends whose loyalty to Britain was said to be suspect. When Wilson became Prime Minister, this circle, it was claimed, became a 'Communist cell in Downing Street'. An alleged key member of this 'cell' was Rudy Sternberg. MI5 officers pointed out – perfectly correctly – that Sternberg was a frequent traveller to the GDR, whose visits increased dramatically after Wilson became Prime Minister. In 1964 he visited it twice, in 1965 eight times, fourteen times in 1966, twenty-three times in 1967 and twenty-two times in 1968. Would a mere businessman, they asked, have been able to gain the trust of East European Communists to this extent? Or was Sternberg steering Wilson, using his business as a cover to report directly to East Berlin and Moscow? Sternberg was knighted in Wilson's 1970s retirement honours list; earlier attempts by Wilson to honour him were allegedly stalled by MI5 who claimed he was a security risk. In 1975 he was elevated to the peerage as Lord Plurenden. He died in 1978.

In fact, the Stasi files show that Sternberg was most certainly not a Communist agent of any description and what the Stasi recorded about him throughout the 1960s also proves conclusively that neither Wilson, nor anyone in his well-known circle, had any links or connections to a Communist intelligence agency. Not only was Sternberg himself entirely in the clear but it was, in fact, the other way round. Both the KGB and the Stasi strongly suspected Sternberg of being an MI6 agent, as their in-depth investigations to which Czech intelligence also contributed make clear. On one occasion, his dossier relates, Sternberg noticed Stasi agents trying to photograph him covertly in a West Berlin street. He caused a major commotion, involving bystanders, and forced the agents to break cover and run. The Stasi also minuted notes of repeated contact with what it said was the MI6 station in West Berlin and one of its agents there with whom Sternberg was very friendly.

Given Sternberg's close association with Wilson, this dossier also disposes of the suggestion that the Labour leader was a secret Communist. For if this had been true, and since Sternberg was firmly believed to be working for MI6, Wilson would have been instructed to distance himself immediately from Sternberg. That this never happened shows there was no link whatsoever between Wilson and any Soviet bloc intelligence and his 'Communist cell' was a figment of Wright's fevered imagination.

Even where information did pass from Britons to the Stasi, it is vital to note that targets and sources were frequently not opposites but part of the same continuum of corrosive conspiracy that marked the Stasi way of spying. Nowhere is the fluidity of the categories of 'victim' and 'perpetrator' more clearly visible than in the case of those British citizens who acted as 'sources' (in the English sense) for the HVA's intelligence on the peace movement.

Bruce Kent was one prominent example of a victim who was also regarded by the Stasi as a palpable asset, and one to be cosseted. The files show that the East German leadership and the Stasi 'Centre' went to some lengths to remain on good terms with Kent even though he was clearly not popular with sections of the East German clergy. A Stasi report, dated 15 February 1985, minutes that 'a visit [to the GDR] by Bruce Kent is not wanted by GDR Protestant Church leaders. However, Comrade Manfred Feist, Head of Foreign Information of the Central Committee of the SED, orders that Kent is not to be told of the real reason why his visit should be put off, but simply that there is not enough time to arrange it.[4]

What this shows is that the Stasi and the SED, at the highest levels, did not want to fall out with Bruce Kent. Although it was decided to accept the judgement of the East German Church on this occasion, it was best, the East Germans reasoned, not to force the issue or risk alienating Kent. Why did the Stasi regard Kent as an asset? As early as November 1981, it had noted his robust attack on Josef Luns, the secretary general of NATO, who had claimed that CND was funded by the Soviet Union. Kent said that this was a 'lie'.[5] Two further reports on Kent, who was given the codename 'Pact', show that he continued to pursue a line the Stasi regarded as helpful to them.[6]

One dated 8 April 1985 informed the Stasi that Kent had been heard saying that he was interested in contacting East German dissidents. Now this was bad news from its point of view. Kent was a significant British public figure, and the Stasi did not want him getting close to its dissidents. But on 24 June 1985 one of the Stasi's London spies reported that Kent had declared that 'CND would never pass a policy proposal which condemned the Soviet Union'. This suited the East Germans well. And then Kent decided to visit 34 Belgrave Square, bringing even better news. He wanted to make an official visit to the East German (state-run) Peace Council (implying thereby that CND continued to recognise this Soviet front) and that he wished to visit Dresden to commemorate the fortieth anniversary of the RAF and USAF bombings of the city, which he wished forthrightly to condemn. Kent did, however, raise two further matters which incommoded the East Germans. He asked why they had not returned the Greenpeace balloon which they had confiscated, and he also wondered why two prominent CND supporters, John Sandford and Lynne Jones, had been refused visas for the GDR in 1984. Kent was told only that the Peace Council would be delighted to receive him.

A further report dated 20 July 1988 gave an account of Bruce Kent's 'One World Walk'. Kienberg had been alerted to Bruce Kent's plan to walk, in support of world peace, from Warsaw to Brussels, and reported that he wished to 'walk' through East Germany. Kienberg decided at once that, 'because of the political significance of this project' from the Stasi viewpoint, Kent was to be allowed in. Secretly, Kienberg gave the order that Kent was to be trailed for his entire visit by the Stasi and that all dissidents he might otherwise encounter were to be detained, so as not to cause trouble. Bugging his phone there revealed to the Stasi that he had spoken to various members of the British media 'praising the peace policy of the GDR' and adding that he had been given a 'wonderful reception' by the East Germans who were swamping him (Kent had no idea they were all members of the Stasi). To the huge amusement of the officers watching him (as their remarks on his file show), the 'walk' had actually been conducted in a Renault Espace people-carrier.

Bruce Kent has confirmed that he was 'useful to the East Germans'. He visited the GDR no more than three or four times. It had been the Stasi who prevented him from actually walking in the GDR – they feared he might become a 'pied piper', and insisted he used the van. Kent says that he knew the Peace Council was 'GDR government approved' but was perfectly content to have dealings with it. He did not wish to dilute CND's message by involving it with the dissident movement, although he did speak up for conscientious objectors (who he knew were badly treated). Kent also says he was aware that the GDR 'locked its people up' and agrees it was a 'difficult line to tread' – today he is glad the Soviet empire has gone but insists there had been 'better ways to achieve this than with an arms race'.[7]

What Kent meant to the Stasi was summed up in his desire to deal with the Communist-front East German Peace Council, and his refusal to allow CND to support human rights activists apart from conscientious objectors. Bruce Kent was, then, clearly a *victim* of the Stasi's spy system: he was spied upon. But he was also a useful source of information (because he talked to East German officials about the peace movement matters that concerned him). There is, however, no evidence he was aware that some of the East Germans to whom he spoke were Stasi officers. He was also, in the eyes of the Stasi, an asset who not only wanted to work with the GDR Peace Council but had praised publicly what he termed the 'peace policy of East Germany'. The GDR, it will be recalled, did not simply regard it as legitimate to imprison its own peace campaigners as it saw fit, but its militaristic public stance, which can hardly have escaped Bruce Kent, made his lauding of its 'peace policy' hugely advantageous to the goals of the East German state.

Another example of Stasi spying on the British peace movement emerges from the record of a tip from a Stasi END source. It states that: 'The appeal "from Berlin and Prague" in fact comes from London but only a few people know this. Lynne Jones is watched by the Hungarian security service; an active END member with links to an East German Protestant priest in Wera. Roger Williamson has visited GDR, supports END and lives at Forest Gate, London.'

Towards the end of March 1985, then, the Stasi learned that the 'Berlin' and 'Prague Appeals' were allegedly written in London, doubtless with the assistance of E. P. Thompson, who could then use the arguments presented therein to support his own case.[8] A minute added in 1986 by a Stasi officer said that, 'The source of this information is by 1986 on our instructions no longer taking an active part in END but has contact to those who do. Sheila and Graham Taylor are Communists but decent. Dan Smith is anti-Soviet, so the source has heard.'

Over and above the significance of these comments to the East Germans, this note gives us some key information about this particular spy inside END. As we shall see below, this clue points us firmly towards an individual called Irene Fick, a British trade union official and CPGB member. Her story is discussed below.

The Stasi files are littered with END documents, many marked 'confidential'. Not only do we have to ask ourselves who had access to the END material which was given to the Stasi, but we also have to ask how it came into the Stasi hands. As we have seen, 'Hans Reichert', a Stasi spy, was also Gerhard Lindner, the East German ambassador from 1984 to 1989. He was a major collector of intelligence on the UK peace movement, supplied among others by his sources within it. From the Stasi's point of view, a clear distinction could be drawn between his work as a spy and any work he may have carried out as an East German diplomat. From the point of view of his British contacts, however, it might be said that they could not possibly know whether what they were saying to him was being said in his persona of 'Hans Reichert' or as Gerhard Lindner. They might argue that their dealings with him rested on a view that he was the East German ambassador and that any information they passed on was given on this legal basis.

There are, however, two problems with such an argument. The first is that many of those who spoke to the East Germans (and all those named below) have said that they accepted that intelligence officers would in one way or another be the recipients of the information they were providing. The second is that the *sort* of information that was being requested will inevitably have made it clear to the donor that the information itself served the purposes of secret intelligence and not normal diplomatic discourse. In his secret 'discussions' with CND and END sources, Lindner was not after their take on the broad sweep of British policy, understanding its details and how they affected those promoting it. Rather, what he plainly wanted was information that was exploitable: the latest shifts of position within the British peace movement, whose stock was rising, whose was falling, what their relationship to their colleagues was like and what they felt about specific policy lines in which the Stasi was taking an interest. If we look at the *sort* of information they were being asked to supply, only a complete fool could fail to understand that this would be used to maim and wound those the Stasi regarded as their enemies and that had nothing to do with diplomacy.

A further example of someone who was both victim and source is provided by the case of Barbara Einhorn. She was a victim but was also used not just as a source but as a weapon in order to destroy a discrete group of East German dissidents by being forced, inadvertently, to provide 'proof' that they were 'treacherously' in league with Westerners who wished to undermine East Germany.

## The Einhorn Story

On or around 11 October 1983 the Stasi's London agents discovered that an END–GDR Women's Group contact to the East German dissidents called Barbara Einhorn (a Brighton academic with research and family ties to the GDR) would be travelling to meet them during the period 1–11 December 1983, at which time information would be passed to her about the dissidents' activities.[9] On 14 November 1983 Markus Wolf prepared his junior colleagues in Department XX for action). To catch Einhorn receiving information from Poppe and Bohley would provide the smoking-gun evidence the Stasi needed to destroy them, and it was agreed on 2 December to make the necessary moves. It would also help undermine END since catching Einhorn would demonstrate that the Stasi knew everything there was to know about END's secret plans. It would make the point that END's actions were endangering the very people whom it was intended they should support. It is clear from the Stasi files that two British sources (in the East German sense, one working for the HVA and one for HVA III) were aware of this (the latter was clearly run from 34 Belgrave Square, although the former could have been an 'illegal' in London or an HVA source operating in East Berlin).

Einhorn, by now in East Berlin, was arrested as she tried to cross the border back to West Berlin. She was transferred (at midnight) to Hohenschönhausen, the Stasi jail and interrogation and torture centre in Berlin. At her third interrogation she gave the Stasi the statement it required. It had already confiscated the material she had collected from the dissidents, as well as her diary. She was charged with crimes against the State, under paragraph 99 of the legal code, carrying a sentence of two to twelve years and Poppe and Bohley were duly arrested.

Einhorn was released after several days, partly because she was of more use to the Stasi back in London and, it seems, also because of the efforts of Canon Paul Oestreicher. It is by no means implausible that her incarceration and interrogation was a life-defining event for Dr Einhorn, not least because she knows herself to have been betrayed to the Stasi by one of her English END colleagues.[10] What is more, END was badly demoralised by her arrest because it indicated that the Stasi now knew everything about its organisation and its aim. While this assumption was correct, the knowledge had not come from the Stasi's questioning of Einhorn, but from its own subversion of END. The Stasi had known all about Einhorn before her arrest.

Not surprisingly, Poppe and Bohley were also dangerously demoralised. Their arrest, Poppe said in 1998, had been 'a concrete result of Barbara Einhorn's activities'.[11] What the dissidents had wanted, she insisted, were 'public declarations of support' – such as those made by E. P. Thompson. They certainly did not want 'publicity' which would reveal their private and secret deliberations. This point is an important, if obvious, statement to which we must return. It was one thing to publicise their plight were they to be arrested; quite another if their names and activities were to be disclosed to the Stasi by its spies within END and then used as a pretext for arresting them.

Barbara Einhorn was an asset to the Stasi twice over. First, because through her enthusiasm for contacts with the East German dissident movement she had inadvertently given the Stasi a chance to lock up Bohley and Poppe, intimidate them and discredit them in the eyes of fellow East Germans by demonstrating that they were the agents of the West. Second, however, and more bizarrely, she was an asset because she remained convinced that it might be possible to do some sort of a deal with the East Germans, believing like some others that a quiet word with them might encourage them to stop behaving like 'real, existing' Communists. As she herself accepts today, she wanted to believe in the potential of East German Communism to deliver a better state, despite the evidence of human rights abuses – abuses of which she knew not only from her academic researches but from her personal experience.[12]

Remarkably, a Stasi minute on her noted on 24 February 1986 that 'Einhorn personally is not an enemy of the GDR'.[13] A previous Stasi report on Einhorn, dated 6 November 1985 – that is, two years *after* her appalling experiences at the hands of the East German secret police – said that 'Hans Reichert' had heard her speak well about East Germany as well as having a subsequent confidential discussion with her. Her attitudes, he said, 'were positive and credible' and she used 'well-schooled (*geschulten*) arguments on disarmament issues'. He continued: 'her attitudes were very positive in our sense (*ihre Haltungen waren in unserem Sinne sehr positiv*). This was confirmed in our subsequent personal conversation. She offered no provocation, nor raised any questions about "the independents" . . . the Delegation of the [GDR] Peace Council believed she was totally trustworthy (*einhellig vertrauenswürdig*).' The report concluded that Lindner/'Reichert' was convinced that 'she must genuinely have corrected her previous position or consistently have pursued the goal of winning [our] trust (*Nach Meinung der Quelle muss sie tatsächlich ihre früheren Haltung korrigiert haben, oder konsequent das Ziel der Vertrauensgwinnung verfolgt [haben]*)'.

A month later, however, Einhorn was causing the Stasi a headache again: she had wanted to be included in a CND delegation to East Germany, at 'END's instigation', which meant granting her a visa. On 6 December 1985 Lindner/'Reichert' wrote to Feist for his reaction. The East German position was plain, he said. Einhorn knew she had been released for 'humanitarian' reasons but had not kept her side of the bargain, and had continued to undertake actions against the GDR by defaming the very Peace Council she wanted to visit.

But there was a twist. Although the Stasi did not want Einhorn, it did want the CND delegation to visit its Peace Council. If CND decided to make an issue out of it, Feist said it would have to reconsider. CND did make an issue out of it: on 7 February Lindner told Feist that 'in a private letter' Oestreicher had begged him to include Einhorn. The East German ambassador had also learned that CND were compiling a dossier to prove that Einhorn was not anti-GDR. Paul John of CND wrote to him on 22 January 1985 to say that Einhorn could have used her detention by the GDR as an excuse to 'discredit' it but had refused to do so, apart from writing one letter to the *Guardian*. At some stage, an accusation was made that the GDR was trying to interfere in the internal affairs of CND, to which Feist responded in a note to General Kienberg on 18 February 1986 that it was CND who were trying to interfere in East German affairs. In the end, CND agreed to postpone their visit to East Germany and in return the East German Peace Council agreed to visit the UK and see Einhorn there. The delegation turned up in Coventry in 1987. The GDR, in short, had not budged. Einhorn had been cynically used by the Stasi to demonstrate precisely who was to be portrayed in the public eye as calling the shots.

A report made by a different source inside East Germany two years later, however, talked about her 'negative role', although it conceded that 'negative comments about East Germany had been balanced by similar ones about Britain'.

A report on 11 April 1988 gives a final Stasi view of Einhorn and her relations with her 1983 dissident contacts, Bärbel Bohley, Werner Fischer and Vera Wollenberger. It was said that 'Einhorn and Oestreicher are very cross with them for not keeping their side of the deal. David Childs is a '*Scharfmacher*' ['twister'] who supports END's solidarity with negative-hostile forces in the GDR. Oestreicher, on the other hand, believes in sensitivity and thoughtfulness.'

This intelligence would have delighted the Stasi: Oestreicher and Einhorn, who were supposed to be the dissidents' strongest friends in Britain, can be seen to have fallen out with them. Oestreicher, according to the Stasi spy, is 'thoughtful and sensitive' – a man with whom it could do business.

In an interview, generously given, Barbara Einhorn explored her complicated and often ambiguous relationship with the East Germans. She explained that she was one of the large group of people who worked on the GDR and were 'critically sympathetic' of it. She did not like West Germany and 'the Cold War arguments'. She stated that she knew 'everything there was to know, except the extent of the Stasi'. She believed in the 1980s that the 'GDR was shooting itself in the foot' but did not believe what she regarded as 'horror stories' about human rights abuses. Becoming a member of END in 1981, she first met women dissidents in East Germany in 1982 and, thanks to an assignation made by Irene Fick, she had arranged a further meeting in the autumn of 1983. She believed that the Stasi thought she was more important than she really was – this was why she was not granted a visa to visit the GDR until 1990. The Stasi did succeed in wrecking the END–GDR group because it fell apart and the END Women's Group also dissolved. This was due to 'mistrust, fear and corrosion'. The Stasi wanted, she says, to know who was leading the END–GDR group so that it could 'cut them off'.

Despite her experience at Hohenschönhausen, she says that she continued to have meetings with East Germans 'off site', as she put it, after 1983. She met Lindner, for example, but only once, she claims: 'he was new, but a hopeless bureaucrat'. 'We called him *Betonkopf*, or concrete head,' she recalls. She also had contact with Jörg Döring, whom she regarded as the first embassy official she had come across with whom it was possible to have a 'real dialogue'. He had been informal, adaptable to British ways, and keen on a real political exchange. Döring had also visited her friends the Zutschi's in Putney in 1988. At a meeting between Döring, Bohley and possibly Vera Wollenberger, it seemed, she said, as if a 'real dialogue' between the dissidents and the East German Embassy official had finally been established. It was, Einhorn said, 'like being at Wimbledon' watching the arguments being batted to and fro. She also met H. H. Kasper at meetings arranged by Peter Jarman. She had met Kasper, who was an embassy official but also a Stasi spy, on several occasions, including meetings arranged by Peter Jarman, at the time the Europe secretary of the British and International Quakers. His wife, Roswitha, had been East German. Today, Jarman is listed by the Quakers as a specialist in conflict resolution. They met at William Goodenough House, a Quaker establishment in Mecklenburgh Square in London. She went on to meet Döring more and more: he attended a peace demonstration in Hyde Park and at the end of 1989 he invited her to his flat where he showed her a film of the fall of the Wall in Berlin. All the END members were invited to his flat, she added, and there she met Ulrike Birkner-Kettenacker, the first post-Communist East German ambassador. It was only subsequently, Einhorn attests, that she found out that Döring was a first secretary who had duties concerned with surveillance on the Royal Navy.

Here, on the one hand, is a living British testimonial to the wickedness of the Stasi, from a true victim. On the other we find someone who did not simply maintain sympathy for the GDR but who ought to have known she continued to put herself and her comrades in harm's way by meeting with Lindner and Döring – both of them men who were highly skilled secret intelligence professionals. As far as the latter was concerned, Barbara Einhorn even went so far as to introduce him to the Poppe–Bohley–Wollenberger circle in 1988. Today Barbara Einhorn believes she was 'naive' about the East German political leaders.

## The Sandford Story

John Sandford, the Reading University expert on German literature, had a book on the independent peace movement in the GDR published by END in 1983.[14] On the one hand it spoke about the desire of the dissidents to see peace policies and human rights prevail in East Germany. On the other, however, Sandford made it clear that he regarded the GDR in a positive light, and that within its existing system the demands of the dissidents could be accommodated.

The Berlin Wall, we learn, was an 'anti-Fascist protection wall' and 'celebrated in the GDR as a major contribution to détente'. Sandford claimed that 'on the international level the Berlin Wall helped [. . .] to solve [sic] one of the great outstanding problems of the Cold War years', conceding, it is true, that it did this in a 'singularly brutal fashion'. Sandford adds that 'many in the West assumed that the erection of the Wall would lead to sullen resentment and possible rebellion in the East. In the event August 1961 turned out to be a major turning point not only in the history of the GDR, but in East–West relations in general. Resentment there undoubtedly was, but more important was a new determination among East Germans to "make a go of it" in their own country . . . The economy picked up, giving the GDR the highest standard of living in Eastern Europe, and Western visitors began noticing a growing willingness on the part of East Germans to identify with "their" GDR, to take pride in its achievements and to defend it indignantly against the arrogant West German paternalism.' He talked about the GDR's relative openness to the West which he opined was a 'distinctive feature' about the country compared with other Soviet bloc states, a highly curious comment since he was, from 1984 on, himself banned from visiting it, despite the fact that he was never its enemy. Sandford goes on, even more bizarrely, that a 'very high degree of contact with Westerners' was possible and that moreover it was 'contact which can take place within the privacy of the home'.

Westerners were not to be put off by the alleged existence of a one-party state, Sandford affirmed. He conceded that 'it is not possible to vote for the party of one's choice in elections as happens in the West', but added a positive reason which made it all sound perfectly all right: 'as the parties cooperate rather than compete, that would not make sense. Instead, voters are presented with a common electoral programme drawn up jointly by the political parties and the mass organisations.'[15]

There was, he stated, every reason to believe that liberalism could flourish within the GDR system because it was already guaranteed in the Constitution ('it is in this context that one has to view the civil rights guaranteed to citizens of the GDR by the country's

Constitution. Those that an autonomous peace movement might want to take its stand on – freedom of expression, freedom of assembly, freedom of association – are all there. Thus article 27, on freedom of opinion, states [this exists]').[16]

A neutral reader might suppose that Sandford's position was that those who sought to 'turn swords into ploughshares' were not confronting an immovable police state but knocking at an open door – the reverse of E. P. Thompson's line which was that the successful demand for civil rights would undermine Communist totalitarianism. What was critical about people like Sandford, even within END, was that they wanted to sustain the Communist state and not overthrow it.

Sandford hove into the Stasi's peace files on 27 July 1983 when a report on him suggested that he was in touch with the International Committee of the British Church Council and was responsible for Church contacts between the UK and the GDR. A minute to this effect was recorded in the diary of HA XX, entry number 2691. Then, on 6 December 1983, a Stasi spy stated that he was a 'suspected' (vermutlich) British secret service contact. His name cropped up on numerous occasions after this, although there was never any further suggestion that he had anything to do with British intelligence. Not only would the Stasi have dropped him like a hot potato had this initial suspicion been substantiated, but we know from Sandford himself that no such link existed.[17]

Sandford had joined the East German group of END in the summer of 1980, answering an open invitation from E. P. Thompson which had been published in the *Guardian*. He was yet another self-appointed and self-styled supporter of the East German dissident movement. The END–GDR group met once a month, 'a close group of friends who even went to the seaside together'.

From time to time, he says today, he believed he was under surveillance but he did not know by whom: on one occasion a letter to him from Mary Kaldor had been opened. However, he insists, he would not have been worried if the Stasi was watching him. He states that he does not believe that END meetings, at which East German dissidents were named and discussed, could have endangered them. Discretion, he suggests, was therefore not required. The group, he says, would meet in Putney at the house of Mr and

Mrs Zutschi – the same couple who entertained Barbara Einhorn and Kasper. He did not think this group had been penetrated by the Stasi at the time, and, he insists, knowing that it had been does not worry him today. The dissidents, he claims, 'wanted publicity' and END, in publicising the existence of dissidents, was doing what they wished. Sandford says that nothing END did could have 'conceivably deserved the interest of the Stasi'.

At the same time, Sandford says that he regards the Stasi's END spy or spies as being guilty of a 'betrayal of trust', a 'moral betrayal', even though he insists no practical harm could have been done. He could recall that from time to time Dr H. H. Kasper turned up at END meetings and they all assumed that he was connected in some way with East German intelligence. However, he says, when Kasper was in the room they did not 'chat about people, there were things you simply wouldn't say'. Sandford adds, for the record, that in all his dealings with the East Germans, the Stasi had never tried to recruit him because he was 'too clearly on the wrong side'.

Interestingly, Paul Oestreicher is adamant that East Germans were not formally invited to any END meetings, although it is possible that very rarely one or the other might have attended as someone's guest. The point matters because it was a tenet of Stasi spycraft to show no formal interest in any intelligence target since this could lead to questions being asked about their motives which would be highly perilous. If Kasper (or any other East German) did attend a particular meeting, we may be sure that their real spying and subversion was conducted at private, and from their point of view, secret meetings. Indeed, Sandford did recall that Peter Jarman had organised private meetings with Kasper. It was true that he and other members of the group had 'sympathy' for the aims of the GDR (he mentioned Irene Fick in particular) but, he adds, that was equally true for the dissidents themselves. They did not wish to be conspiratorial ('we had a philosophy of not having secrets') but nor did they intend the Stasi to be informed through spying.

On 17 November 1984, according to a report made for the Stasi, at a meeting attended by END members listed as Peter Findley, Irene Fick, Gwynne Edwards, Barbara Einhorn, Jan Williams, Ingrid Gilbert, John Theobold and Sandford himself, he had

informed his friends of a meeting he had had with Kasper on 8
November 1984 which 'confidentially', Kasper had assured him,
'was not taking place as far as the outside world was concerned'. He
apologised to Sandford for the fact that the East German government
were preventing him from visiting the GDR; he had, Sandford told
his friends, assured him that this was not because the book he had
published in 1983 had been 'factually incorrect' but merely 'one-
sided'. The GDR, Kasper claimed, accepted that 'END was a fact of
life' and wanted dialogue with it.

According to the report Sandford assured Kasper that every END
member had a professional interest in East Germany and 'all were
sympathetic' to it. The dissidents, Sandford said, were 'not anti-
GDR' either. Kasper replied that it was not up to the embassy to
decide who might or might not visit East Germany but a matter for
GDR security. Sandford said he assumed 'security' had all their
names and addresses. Kasper had replied that only Barbara Einhorn
was in a special category because she alone had broken East
German law. She had been released from prison as a 'gesture of
goodwill' to END. Finally, Kasper said, he would like Sandford to
arrange a meeting with Mary Kaldor.

Then, according to the Stasi files, John Sandford announced –
one would imagine to everyone's surprise – that he wanted a full
examination of what the Stasi's translation called 'the motives and
interests' of the END–GDR group. He claimed that most of his academic colleagues in Britain were 'too far to the left' thanks to their
personal contacts with GDR citizens (though it was not clear what
this phrase actually meant – that they were too sympathetic to the
East German state, or that they were too sympathetic to the dissidents and wanted to undermine the GDR). At any rate, Sandford
persuaded all his colleagues to give an account of their fundamental attitude to East Germany.

Sandford explained to his colleagues that his circumstances were
clearly different: he came from a working-class family with special
sympathy for the USSR. He had become interested in East Germany
through his work with West German experts. Because of his knowledge of German he had joined END. His position was, he said,
'complex and difficult. He was committed to Socialism but had to

distance himself from concrete things that were not acceptable, e.g. aspects of the GDR's totalitarian policy, the suppression of human rights, the lack of liberty and democratic rights.'[18]

When Sandford's remarks, made in an interview in November 1998, are set against the records of END meetings obtained by the Stasi's END spies, there appear to be a number of curious contradictions or points of confusion. In 1998 Sandford suggested that there was nothing in END that 'deserved the interest of the Stasi' and that nothing that was said there could conceivably have harmed the dissidents. We have seen that in the case of the Einhorn trap this was patently not the case.

In 1998 Sandford accepted the END–GDR group had been penetrated by the Stasi but insists this did not matter: the Stasi used secrecy, END did not. This penetration, however, was regarded by him as a 'moral betrayal' because END did not want the Stasi to get its information about END in this way, even if Sandford believed that the information itself was of no value. He insisted that END had taken no precautions against being spied upon yet, at the same time, had said END members were 'careful' not to 'talk about people' when Kasper was present. Sandford accepted the record of the Stasi files which stated that, on at least one occasion, Peter Jarman had organised a secret 'off-site' meeting between him (Sandford) and Kasper. It is true that Sandford told some of his colleagues in END about this meeting (including the END spy because this, too, was reported back to the Stasi).

The question, of course, is why have these private meetings? From the East German viewpoint, as we have seen, there was a conspiratorial reason for them. From END's point of view, however, we may ask why it was not enough for them to present the East Germans with their policy at an open meeting. Why private meetings, particularly those which might include intelligence officers? Sandford's argument is that such meetings were held to oblige the dissidents who wanted 'publicity'. If END's purpose was to give publicity to the protests of the East German dissidents, then telling the East German 'diplomats' about them in private was doubly idiotic: they knew about them anyway, and the publicity the dissidents wanted was in the British and Western media, not at 34 Belgrave

Square or some sordid off-site get-together. There is, for whatever reason, not a single document in the Stasi files which reports any complaint made privately by Sandford about human rights abuses in the GDR. The only requests are those to grant Einhorn and Sandford visas and to take note of their basic sympathy towards the GDR.

Sandford says the END group 'had no secrets'. Yet at the same time the files do report the fact that as a group END members discussed matters which it knew at the time would be of intelligence interest to the East Germans (and they clearly *were* of interest) and were, for this reason, not disclosed when an East German was present.

Why does Sandford not accept that secrets were being disclosed? Does he imply that he did not regard them as secrets? Ironically, when END talked about the dissidents' activities in the absence of Kasper (but in the presence of whoever was the END spy) the END group was still unwittingly giving away secrets. In reality, END recognised that, although it may not have had 'secrets' of its 'own', it was certainly a repository of the secrets of the dissidents. It had advance warning of their plans, and platforms and full lists of the personnel involved in their struggle both in the GDR and in the UK. The Einhorn story proves the point.

We may wonder, too, what was said at the private meetings between Sandford, Kasper and possibly Jarman, the records of which have been destroyed by the HVA. What might Kasper have wanted to know from Sandford and Jarman that he was not getting to hear from his END source? Did he want information from them, or did he want to pass information on to them? Was it possible that Sandford was both 'hostile-negative' (Stasi speak for 'supporting the dissidents') and an East German source (in the English sense)? The information was clearly confidential and fell outside of what an ordinary diplomat might expect to be told. If Sandford were not passing on confidential material to Kasper, why were private meetings in a neutral place necessary, especially as Sandford says Kasper attended END meetings? It can only have been to learn things that were not said at the public events. Unfortunately, Professor Sandford is, quite properly, not prepared to answer these questions.

Yet the fact remains that here we have not only contradictions, not just evidence of sustained Stasi penetration of END, but also of at least one meeting with Kasper and two END members, Sandford and Jarman, one of whom – Sandford – has stated quite openly that he knew Kasper was connected with East German intelligence. Furthermore, at this meeting Sandford had assured Kasper that he was personally 'sympathetic' to the GDR. Why, if not to assure him that he was on Kasper's side? But Kasper's side was not the side of the dissidents.

Once more, a victim was also a perpetrator.

## The Oestreicher Story

Canon Paul Oestreicher of Coventry Cathedral was one of the most prominent British Stasi victims and sources. On the one hand he was a man with a distinguished record in the human rights field who maintained links to the British Foreign Office, the Soviet Embassy (where he dealt with Oleg Gordievsky but in his KGB role, of course, with whom he had become quite friendly) and leading East German dissidents. On the other he supported the ideals of Communism and, as the Stasi files show, not only took great pains to stay in with the East German regime but gave its officers useful information and some real propaganda help. He, too, was an example of someone who was a source and an asset, but also a target and a victim.[19]

A report dated 22 November 1980 was based on an interview with him conducted by a Stasi officer. He had suggested to the officer that he had resigned from his post as general secretary of the British section of Amnesty International 'because it had brought him special difficulties in his work in the Socialist States, especially the GDR'. He had also emphasised his role as a founding member of the Recognition Committee of the GDR in the UK. According to this file, Oestreicher had told the East Germans that he believed 'there was a danger that Poland would once again become anti-Communist; it was the weakest link in the chain of Socialist States. Everything was helping the democratic movement and the destabilisation of Poland.' The East Germans doubtless assumed this meant that he was fundamentally opposed to Solidarity in Poland and this, combined with his other opinions, indicated that he might be useful to the Stasi.

Another report concerning Oestreicher, dated 14 June 1982, described a visit to East Germany during which he had made a number of speeches. He had told his audience about an American friend who had been imprisoned for three years for opposing the Vietnam war. 'Communism,' he had declared, 'has, as its end purpose, a society without a state. This makes sense and is the view of the Church.' Four days later he was said to have delivered another attack on the British government, speaking of its 'social injustice as seen in the arbitrary and brutal treatment meted out by the police, the use of state power against the socially weak, and black people.' He had spoken of his 'energetic fight against NATO's high-gear rearmament, and against the politics and the person of Margaret Thatcher', adding, the report continued, the sentiments that 'he could not despise her: that was for God to do'.

In November 1984, on a further visit to East Berlin, he had made several remarks equally helpful to the GDR regime which the Stasi had also recorded. He appeared to recognise the East German Peace Council.[20] He had told them that Bruce Kent was proposing to resign as general secretary of CND and Joan Ruddock as president, and that this had led to a 'fear that with these changes in office the weight of realistic people in the CND will further decline'. He warned them specifically about the danger of what he called 'Thompson's circle', who he said would 'be able to increase their influence, and determine CND's policy'. He added that they could be assured that CND would always 'in the first instance act against NATO and its policy of high armament', despite any 'attacks from the UK government and its supporters'. At the same time, Oestreicher advised the East Germans that time seemed to be running out for the straightforward line taken by CND. Increasingly, he alleged, 'CND was being accused of one-sided criticism of NATO, especially of the USA, and failing to protest against the counter-measures taken by the Socialist States'. All this was precisely the sort of intelligence the Stasi found so useful.

In many ways, then, Oestreicher's obvious interest in projecting himself as a true friend of the GDR offered many advantages to the regime. His links to the Church hierarchy in the UK, his connections with the BBC and with Amnesty International, as well as his 'progressive views' on the Thatcher government and its policies, indicated that he was a partner worth having. Always distrustful of everyone, however, the Stasi pointed out that its man or woman spying on Oestreicher had concluded that his 'political attitude' was 'contradictory'. Despite holding a number of views of which the East Germans approved, he also chose to emphasise his commitment to 'Amnesty International' and, most dangerously, he had told various groups of East Germans that 'Christians should get even closer together in order to possess even better tactical means for making demands on the state'.

The Stasi said it had evidence that in May 1985 Oestreicher had made contact with East German dissidents, including Bohley and Poppe, and that he confirmed their belief that 'civil and basic rights were not guaranteed in the GDR'. In October 1982 he had met Eppelmann, the leading GDR civil rights campaigner. He was thought to be encouraging him and his followers to form a broadly based popular movement 'to make demands on the state'. After a meeting in 1986, the East Germans noted that this interview with Oestreicher had ended on a most positive note: unlike at the 'previous meeting of May 1984', he had not this time handed the East Germans a list of 'peace activists allegedly in prison in the GDR' and he had categorically promised that CND would continue to cooperate with the Peace Council and support 'further exchanges' with it.

Yet despite this, as late as 6 May 1988 the HVA reported that 'so far Oestreicher's visits have not been hostile-negative', a surprising comment in light of the fact that for at least four years Oestreicher had been talking to the dissidents. Either the Stasi believed that in meeting the dissidents he was not actually helping them, or Wolf's men had failed to understand Oestreicher's particular take on East Germany.

Explaining his position in August 2001, the by now Canon Emeritus Dr Oestreicher has said he was both a source for the Stasi (his codename was 'Kranz' – German for cross, or wreath) and their victim.[21] In 1956, while on a family visit to the GDR, he had been arrested, handed over to the KGB and interrogated for three days, under suspicion of being a West German spy. He was then expelled from the GDR. Yet despite this awful experience, even today he insists that 'at its root Communism is a good idea, fundamentally right' but that it had been 'corrupted, rather as the Church had been'. He had, however, he says, been more critical of Communism than some of his good friends such as Sandford and Einhorn.[22] He added that every East German had been obliged to make compromises with Communism – even those running it – because most of them hated the country.

Asked whether he had ever been aware that East Germans were being locked up for their political beliefs, he replied 'of course'. He had been one of the founders of Amnesty International. But, he adds, 'the Stasi did not operate a Gulag system'. He had, he said, been 'an enthusiastic member of CND and then of END which was much more of a human rights organisation and one the Communists hated'. At one stage, the Stasi had up to eight people tracking him.

As to the Stasi spies who reported on him throughout the 1980s, his view was that they had betrayed him. One, in particular, he said had 'lied to me' ('betrayal by a friend is a nasty thing'); the others were employees of the state, and obviously 'pro-regime people'. He knew that there were things in his files (some of which had been destroyed, some of which he had seen) that could only have come from English spies who must have been END members. What is more, given the sustained spying on him, it must have been someone who had been in END for a number of years. That ruled certain people out. But Oestreicher was convinced they were not his close friends. He confirmed that these spies were not East German diplomats – East Germans, he said (contradicting what Sandford has said) were never invited to END meetings, at any rate as regular members. Today, Oestreicher insists, he has no interest in finding out who spied on him.

Oestreicher stated his main contacts at 34 Belgrave Square had been Oswald Schneidratus (who by chance he had recently met near Friedrichstrasse railway station in East Berlin) and was now selling insurance, and Jörg Döring, now working in Düsseldorf. Today Oestreicher says that in his dealings with the East Germans he never told the East Germans any of the secrets he held.

# The Fick Story

Irene Fick, listed as a national trade union official working for the Broadcasting, Entertainment and Cinematograph Union, was someone with a strong track record of social concern for equality issues as well as an interest in the children of Holocaust victims. According to the Stasi files – and her own testimony – Irene Fick was a person trusted by the East Germans in London.[23] Her name and allusions to her crop up at various places in a two-year period, beginning on 30 March 1984. At this point she is described as 'a person of significance' to the East Germans. This implies that she had already passed information to them before this date.

Interestingly, there is a very full report on END and the Einhorn case, dated 23 January 1984, for whom the source is given. It is 'Source: XV/45555/83'. From the garage list discussed in Chapter 10, we know that this code number refers to the agent code-named 'Freundin'. From the SIRA files, also discussed above (Chapter 10), we know that 'Freundin' supplied at least ten pieces of secret intelligence that made it into the Archive, some of which were passed on by the HVA, and some by the secret military intelligence unit (who were ordered to gain information about the strategic thinking of the British peace movement). Furthermore, 'Freundin's' period as a 'source' lasted from 1984 until 1986, when it stopped (her last report on END was dated 1 December 1985), precisely the period during which Irene Fick was involved with END. Was Fick therefore 'Freundin'? It is an intriguing question and an important one. If Fick were indeed 'Freundin' it would show that a SIRA source could be British (which might then shed light on the identity of 'Eckhart'). It would also show that formal contracts were not always required when someone was minded to assist the East Germans.

It is perfectly true that the Stasi files show that, from time to time, doubts were raised about Fick's reliability from the East German point of view. Lindner/'Hans Reichert', who did know her well, believed there were question marks against her name. Yet we know that the Stasi was always suspicious of anyone with whom it had contact. It is possible, too, that those who queried Fick's behaviour did not realise that beneath the surface Fick was deeply enmeshed in the Stasi net.

It will be recalled that the report of 23 January 1984, described in Chapter 11, had passed on details of a highly confidential and extremely heated END meeting held on 8 January 1984. At this meeting, Oestreicher had all but accused Einhorn of betraying the East German dissidents. The Stasi must have been delighted to read this. Their source added that a decision had been reached that in future only verbal information should be taken from the dissidents and, in the case of an arrest by the East German police, END members were instructed to stay silent at all costs and to make contact with the British Embassy in East Berlin immediately. The same meeting also heard that the links between an END figure in West Berlin and the dissidents had proved successful (the name of the individual was on the report but it had been blacked out) and that Poppe had told them she had spoken to an American (once again he was named but this was subsequently blacked out too) about a dissident from Jena named Jahn.

There was, perhaps, a certain irony in the fact that, according to the Stasi files, Oestreicher was furious with Einhorn but nonetheless blissfully unaware that in his own way he was doing every bit as much damage to the dissidents in London as Einhorn had in East Berlin by speaking about things which, unbeknownst to him, were being reported directly back to the Stasi. Even more ironic was the fact that Oestreicher himself had contact with East Germans, although, as he says, he would not have made these sort of disclosures to them.

To return to Irene Fick, we see that in a minute dated 30 April 1984 she was said to be of 'special importance' in the UK–GDR Friendship Association, although it was not clear whether this referred to her importance to the East Germans or to the Association. Both were true. Then, however, on 1 April 1985, a report compiled in East Berlin stated that Fick, who had helped arrange British university visits to the GDR since 1981, had now become 'not transparent' and was 'complicated'. She refused to reveal her political attitude to the GDR but it was thought, the report stated, that she had a 'British' attitude to it, not least because of her friendship with Sheila Taylor, a London member of the CPGB and the Friendship Society, 'whose anti-Communist view was well known'.

Fick, the report concluded, was unreliable and handed over papers for British exchange participants 'too late' (hardly a hanging offence, it is safe to say). She was also said to be interested in meeting East German dissidents. The very next day, 2 April 1985, the Stasi decided to tell Fick that this would be seen as an 'unfriendly act' and that she should be questioned about her contacts. 'Hans Reichert', it was suggested, should pay Fick a visit in London and quiz her about the strategy and tactics of END. HA VIII was ordered to keep tabs on her.

On 17 November 1984 Fick's name appears on a list of those present at a private END meeting and on 29 April 1985 Lindner/'Hans Reichert' had a 'confidential discussion' with her.[24] In this context, we may recall that a piece of Stasi intelligence from 1986 on END, mentioned below, states that it comes from a 'source' (the German word is used) who had been 'instructed' (again, the word is significant) to stay away from END the year before, that is some time in 1985. It is worth recalling that Markus Wolf writes, referring to Stasi agents in the British peace movement: 'in a number of cases we did approach likely targets [in it]; if they agreed to work with us, we recommended that they quit active involvement in the disarmament campaign'.[25] The Stasi wanted them there, but they were not to become too prominent; if doubts about them surfaced, they were to be discarded altogether. If, however, they were to be made inactive for a period, then Stasi purposes would be realised by someone other than the target in question. Perhaps Fick's pro-GDR stance was causing too many questions to be asked. Sandford, we recall, said that her sympathies were evident.

The report of 29 April says that 'Hans Reichert' interviewed Fick. She was, it said, open about the activities of the Friendship Society but closed up at once when asked about END. This was presumably because she had been told to stay away from it. She said she had nothing to do with END, although a year earlier she had been active but would now have nothing more to do with them. But, the report continued, her understanding of END ideas was such that it cast doubts on the idea that her work with it had finished. E. P. Thompson, she said, was happy to include Friendship Society people in END activities because he knew so little about the GDR. He was chiefly keen on links with the CSSR and USSR, not, she thought, with the GDR. 'Hans Reichert' believed that Fick was seeking to minimise the influence of END. Fick believed CND and END could work with the Friendship Society but, the report concluded, 'Reichert' told her 'politely but fairly unmistakeably that such work on the basis of END ideology would not be in accord with the facts of life in a Socialist country'.

At some stage after this report was compiled, that is, *after* 29 April 1985, a further, undated, note in pencil has been attached which records that Fick 'has been told' by the writer 'to stay away from END meetings in the future'. This note is accompanied by another handwritten note, written by Lindner/'Hans Reichert'. The handwriting is different from Lindner's: he was not the person who instructed her to remove herself from END for the time being.

In a different run of Stasi papers, there is a note dated 16 May 1985 concerning 'information of interest' which Fick is said to have provided to the East German Embassy. About nine months later, in February 1986, there is what seems to be a final note on information 'of interest' on END which she is alleged to have provided for the East Germans. The documents show that Fick was not asked to stay away from END until well into the second half of 1985.

These detailed facts, of course, link 'Freundin's' last piece of SIRA intelligence, dated 1 December 1985, with Fick's final conversation with Lindner and one of his HVA colleagues.

Interviewed on 22 October 2001, Irene Fick readily confirmed that the meetings outlined in the Stasi files had taken place. She accepted that she had been a source for the East Germans and today understands this means the Stasi, although she adds that she 'never signed any contract' with anyone. She agreed that she was an entirely 'self-appointed supporter' of the dissidents. She said that meetings with the East Germans took place at the East German Embassy and at private meetings in the house of a mutual, unnamed friend in Putney.[26] She explained that she had been a member of the CPGB and expresses surprise about the extent of the reporting on her in the Stasi files, and possibly by her, although she always told 'the truth'. She says that she talked informally to East Germans about a 'variety of things, including British politics'. But she insists that she possessed no secrets about anything.

Since the late 1960s Fick had a loose association with the GDR but it began properly when she joined the Friendship Society around 1975 and remained until 1989. She became a committee member in charge of organising the summer courses for students, the somewhat unfortunately named 'Intercourse programme' (the East Germans were keen on labelling and always refused to change the name). She was a frequent visitor to the GDR. Her politics, she accepts, were on the 'far left'.

Irene Fick says that she visited 34 Belgrave Square from time to time on social occasions and that sometimes friends would entertain her in the presence of the East German ambassador. She could not recall his name. She expressed no surprise at being invited to meet him and was always entirely open with him. She recalled disliking one particular diplomat, whom she found 'judgemental, like a school teacher'. Einhorn, she recalls, who was a cousin, was on far more friendly terms with the embassy officials.

It did not occur to Fick that Lindner might have had a second identity as a Stasi intelligence officer, but she had always accepted that what she told the East Germans would be reported 'further'. She believes that this is what diplomats were paid to do. This means that today she does not feel betrayed in any way, although she is surprised that some of the things she said were regarded as secret intelligence. She would, she says, give her opinion on things in the normal run of conversation. If the Stasi found her reliable, it was because she was always completely truthful with them. Generally, she reports, she had dealings with two individuals, of whom one 'may' have been Lindner, and the other Oswald Schneidratus. She knew that other END people were in the habit of speaking to Schneidratus, in particular John Theobold. She had never met Peter Jarman. The last time she visited 34 Belgrave Square had been on the fortieth anniversary of the creation of the GDR.

Although she was a source – seen from the Stasi perspective – she had no contract; if they took her remarks seriously, she regards them now as 'incredibly lazy'. She was never offered any money by the East Germans but she says she was given cash by individuals who used her house as lodgings when visiting London. On one occasion she says she benefited from a free trip to Berlin. She accepts that she wrote 'letters to people' about 'various matters', but never wrote any reports. She believes that she may quite inadvertently have passed on information about Barbara Einhorn's ill-fated trip to Berlin.

When asked to explain why, if END conducted itself in such an open manner, people like Einhorn, Sandford and Oestreicher might say they felt 'betrayed', she replied that the END group consisted of about twelve people. Their meetings were not secret but nor were they public either. The purpose of the meetings was to discuss their interest in a particular country. They were all, she says, experts. In this case they discussed the women's and peace movements. They all wanted to help the unofficial women's peace movement. They believed they were helping dissidents. It was, she says, important to convince the East Germans that END was not hostile towards it. They knew that intellectuals in East Germany wanted 'Socialism with a human face'. Asked if it was not putting the dissidents at risk to tell a man like Schneidratus about them, she replied, 'This was a risk you took; we had no idea what the dissidents in Berlin thought. These decisions were taken in London.'

END, she said, did not want to see the GDR destroyed. They believed it had potential. 'What we had to do,' she said, 'was convince Schneidratus that we were on his side.' Irene Fick was then asked whether she had agreed to stop going to END meetings. 'It could be true,' she replied, 'but I would not have taken any notice: I did what I wanted.' She says she was not aware that the GDR was a police state and did not think that her diplomatic contacts might themselves be spies. 'We knew it was not paradise,' she says, but she did not feel restricted when visiting. Did she know they took political prisoners? 'Yes,' she replies, 'but we would not have known who were the political ones and who were the ones who were ordinary criminals.' When asked if she thought taking prisoners was part of the system, she replied, 'no – possibly we were naive'. She says, 'We felt we had a role to play in directing the GDR away from its hardline course by engaging with them. We wanted to help the dissidents but first we needed to create a situation where this might be possible. We believed Communism was reformable. We wanted to bridge the gap. Today we know that this had not been possible.'

Irene Fick denies that she was the source of information which suggested that Sheila Taylor might be an MI5 contact. She was a close friend and they believed an English END member 'had informed against her' (this malicious tale had prevented her from getting a visa to the GDR).

To date, no one from MI5 has ever interviewed Irene Fick or any of the other individuals mentioned here about their experiences of – and with – the Stasi.

# 15

# Recruiting British Penetration Agents

The Stasi's pursuit of new British agents, sources, contacts and persons of trust was not merely undertaken within the British Isles. Another prime source of British recruits lay in East Germany itself. Each year a small number of British universities sent students, chiefly (but not always) of German language and literature, to *East* German rather than West German universities. Humboldt University in East Berlin was one favoured location. Another was Karl-Marx-University at Leipzig, well situated about two hundred kilometres to the south-west of Berlin, with Erfurt, Dresden and Karl-Marx-Stadt about one hundred kilometres away.

Young British people, sufficiently interested in East Germany to want to come and study there, were a blatant and unmissable target. In going to the GDR they were likely to have made a clear and conscious decision to study in Communist East Germany rather than in liberal West Germany. This might mean simply that they were interested in seeing what a Communist regime was like – as was the case with Mark Brayne – but it might also be an indication of political sympathy which the Stasi might be able to develop. As young adults crossing the Iron Curtain and confronting unfamiliar surroundings, they may well have experienced some excitement. They may have read John le Carré or Len Deighton and, one might hope, *Animal Farm* and *1984* as well. Far from home, in a different world, perhaps glamorous to their East German fellow students, they will not have found it hard to indulge in sexual liaisons and all the other pursuits of the young. Here, too, lay a possible opening for the Stasi.

Recruiting a young British student in East Germany (the Stasi expression was 'winning them over', or *Gewinnung*) might also provide the Stasi with the best chance available to them of securing the biggest 'humint' prize of all: a long-term penetration agent. In the 1930s the Soviets had come to realise that winning over to Communism bright young students at the major British universities could eventually produce a crop of first-division spies as these students became professionals and began their long career marches through the institutions they had joined. The Stasi saw that their visiting undergraduates might one day enter the upper reaches of the British state.

The Stasi files show that the East Germans were more than ready to devote considerable time, cost and energy to the recruitment of likely long-term penetration agents from among the British students in East Germany. We know most about their efforts in Leipzig. One reason for this is that Leipzig was the designated Stasi centre for running Western agents, perhaps because of the possibilities that the university there provided. And because its files were archived in Leipzig rather than Berlin, the HVA's efforts at destroying them were less successful than in Berlin. Even so, there is clear evidence of destruction. Despite this, fragments reveal the successful recruitment of a British long-term penetration agent code-named 'Jaguar', who signed a contract with the Stasi on 14 May 1986 run by a Stasi 'co-opted worker', Ralf-Jürgen Böhme, with a strong track record as a successful spymaster.[1] We know that 'Jaguar' lived in a small town near Oxford.[2] There is also mention of another successful British spy code-named 'Lissy'. But this is all we know about these three at present.

After 1985, but before 1989, a Stasi recruiter also visited Leeds and Bradford. He debriefed his controllers in a tape-recorded interview which has survived.[3] It shows that 'Anthony', a student at Leeds University, regarded by fellow students as a role model, had taken a strong interest in Arab affairs and – critically – was to visit Syria for three months to learn Arabic. What will have made Stasi mouths water even more was that he had expressed a strong interest in studying in East Germany. No one knows what became of 'Anthony', but it shows how carefully the Stasi plied their trade. This recruiter also urged the Stasi to look at a certain Peter Lancaster, a man in his fifties teaching at Bradford University. He was, it was claimed, an enthusiastic member of the UK–GDR Friendship Society and keen to travel in the GDR; critical of the treatment of the GDR in the British press, he said he was anxious to promote a 'more realistic picture'. Leeds and Bradford (each of which had a Peace Studies department) were places in which the Stasi had more than a passing interest.

Files on recruited agents consisted of several parts. The three main ones contained, first, the agent's personal folder, second, a record on the agent compiled by his or her controller, and the third was the file produced by the senior officers who ran the controller. From time to time these files would be reviewed by a commanding officer. Once again, we can discern a very careful process of evaluation and analysis: what the agent said was analysed by the agent's controller; what the controller wrote was analysed usually by two senior Stasi officers and often by a third. Throughout an agent's career with the Stasi, regular secret meetings – 'Treffs' – were arranged, often at monthly intervals, sometimes just once or twice a year. Material would be conveyed in the lining of coats, or in 'containers', briefcases with false bottoms which could sometimes be detonated. As agents progressed, they would be taught how to use secret means of communications (invisible writing using a *Geheimschreiber*, or secret writer, or short-wave burst radio transmissions). 'Treffs', always inherently risky, became less vital once other forms of communication had been established. Frequently, information gained from other controllers about the agent was checked against the reports filed by the main controller. In this way, the Stasi believed they could be sure that what ended up in the records of the senior officers was an accurate account of the facts, unvarnished by any ambitions or overkeenness on the part of those who might be thought to have a vested interest in making out that intelligence gains were either more substantial than they really were, or trying to palm off information which had merely been copied from open sources as secret intelligence.

A clear pattern of recruitment existed: observation, approach, vetting, then an oblique introduction to the work of security, some form of tasking and then the revelation that the tasker was a Stasi officer. If things went smoothly, recruitment would follow and a series of ever more challenging duties would be put to the spy.

The British students were sent to Leipzig by a number of universities including Edinburgh, Heriot-Watt and Leeds. Leipzig had a reputation as an international university in an 'international' city (Leipzig had been home to an international trade fair long before the GDR was born).

Complete espionage files exist in the case of two fully-fledged British Stasi agents in the English sense (IMs in the German) – 'Armin' (Robin Pearson) and 'Diana' (Fiona Houlding), AIM 1825/91 and AIM 2127/91 respectively. The reference numbers are themselves interesting because they suggest that, in between the recruitment of the former in 1978 and the latter in 1988, some 302 additional foreign spies had signed up to the Stasi. Both Pearson and Houlding were intended to be long-term penetration agents. Their files show that – in the eyes of their recruiters – they demonstrated great political sympathy for the East German way of life, but also that they were systematically manipulated, deceived and lied to over long periods by the very officers they put themselves out to serve and in whom they had complete trust.[4] The files of both agents show that they, like almost everyone else the Stasi touched, were victims as well as perpetrators.

Both were young, arguably put in harm's way by careless tutors who came close to procuring recruits for the Stasi. Some of those who sent them to Leipzig, like the Scottish academic Karin McPherson, were themselves sympathetic to East Germany, and hardly well placed to warn their students to be careful. The files show that the East German authorities preferred students who were politically 'clean' (from their viewpoint) or even well disposed to East Germany. Dr McPherson, for example, clearly knew, as the files show, that she herself needed to demonstrate her 'cleanness' were she to continue to send students to the GDR – and to continue to be allowed to pursue her own research.[5]

The record shows the Stasi knew that when they were seeking to recruit a long-term agent they would have to play a very long game. The files demonstrate the Stasi accepted that, although links might be constructed during the students' period in Leipzig, once they returned to the UK great efforts would have to be made to keep them on side. The Stasi also understood well that the sort of person who made a good long-term agent was also likely to have certain personality traits (to be a loner, self-sufficient or adventurous) which might make them more or less reliable at certain times in their lives, because such traits might also make an individual awkward or lacking in self-confidence and lead them either to change sides or abandon their cause. Successful long-term spies would have to be prepared to cheat and lie, in some cases for a lifetime; this was difficult for most people, given the temptations of alcohol and careless philandering that were likely to be open to them along the way. Recruitment was formally associated with a signed agreement to work for the Stasi; in the real world, however, collecting the sort of intelligence the East Germans wanted required continual encouragement. Spies were nurtured and cherished, in the bad times – when intelligence was thin on the ground – as well as the good.

In the case of 'Armin' – Robin Pearson – the files reveal that his career began very well from the Stasi's point of view; it then wobbled before grinding to a complete halt which lasted from May 1983 until December 1985, when he was successfully reactivated. Curiously, his work for the Stasi became much more intense, and professionally thorough at the precise moment that the GDR's fortunes began to deteriorate. His last known recorded contact with them came in April 1989, cancelling a 'Treff' in Amsterdam. In the view of MI5 (who had known absolutely nothing about him) Pearson was a serious spy who did some damage to British security interests and represented a serious potential threat.[6]

The Stasi files show that Robin Pearson, who was born in Belfast, was a little bit older than many students partly because, to improve his German, he had been advised to spend six months working for the big German chemical company, BASF. He graduated in 1979 and was offered a research post at Leeds. In 1982 he went to London to work and conduct further research at Phoenix Assurance. From 1984 until 1987 he had a temporary post at Hull University and then spent a year at York University. In 1988 he returned to a lecturership at Hull.

In his third year, 1977–8, he was encouraged to go to Leipzig through the good offices of Dr Karin McPherson. Of McPherson, the Stasi said, 'she is a progressive scholar, closely linked to us'. Pearson had been 'chosen' at the beginning of 1978 because the Stasi's Leipzig University talent spotters, 'Gerd' (Bernhard Kartheus) and 'Max' (Peter Kunz), regarded him as 'operationally the most suited member of a group of English students'. He was noticed at once: his German was 'perfect' and his French also very good. He came over a sporty, persistent and hard-working man. He and another student were then selected for further processing, but the second student fell by the wayside: he was apparently uncooperative. This first report on both was dated 29 October 1977. The Stasi was getting to work quickly.

At each stage of the recruitment process, and – at this stage – unbeknownst to Pearson, 'Gerd' followed the orders provided by his senior officers, who are identified in the files. They were Lieutenant Jörg Hirschfeld (whom Pearson knew as Jörg Hilpert, of the Ministry for State Security – note the Stasi once again using a cover-name similar to the officer's real name), Major Helfried Schlinsog (known to Pearson as Dr Schlinder, also of the Ministry), Major Manfred Bols, Major Brüning (known as Claus), Lieutenant Siegfried Hausotte, Major Fritz Neuhaus, Heinz-Peter Berger and Karl-Heinz Troller. The files show that the first two had been involved in the Pearson case since December 1977, the third since January 1978, the fourth since September 1978, the fifth since November 1977 when his operational activities in the UK began, and that he was controlled by the final three after February/October 1988.

At the beginning of 1978, 'Gerd' was ordered to strike up a friendship with Pearson. The first attempt was made on 28 January 1978, when he discovered that he was a keen fencer. Pearson also told him that he would like to research for a doctorate in history at Leipzig (and would contact the GDR–UK Friendship Society to see how they might help). This suggested that Pearson was keen on a sport which could be played internationally (providing easy opportunities for speaking with him out of MI5's earshot), and that he wanted further contact with the GDR (which could be manipulated).

'Gerd' returned to Pearson three days later, suggesting that, together with other students, they go away on a weekend excursion some ten days later. Here Pearson revealed his interest in travel and his career plan to work for an 'international institution'. The Stasi were beginning to drool. 'Gerd' then went off to the Soviet Union and did not see Pearson for some time. Meanwhile, the Stasi had set another agent on to him, code-named 'Max', who also befriended him. One day Pearson complained to Max that his girlfriend had suddenly said she no longer wished to see him, perhaps, he thought, because her father disapproved of her going out with an Englishman.

What Pearson could not know – but 'Max' was soon to find out – was that the girl's father was a general in the National People's Army. The Stasi had realised this friendship threatened their plans to turn Pearson into their spy. Any link between Pearson and an East German girl whose father was a senior officer would immediately, they reasoned, come to the attention of MI5. The relationship therefore had to be terminated but without telling Pearson the real reason. The girl's father was ordered to forbid his daughter from seeing Pearson. It was not surprising that Pearson found this hard to fathom – he still had no idea he was being converted into a Stasi agent – but he did offer to consider taking out East German citizenship in order to pursue this interest – again, an important plus about him for the East Germans.

On returning from the Soviet Union, 'Gerd' was worried by what he found. The problem with the girlfriend had changed Pearson's view of the GDR and 'represented a break with his idealistic conception of our system'. He was also fed up with the lack of fencing facilities offered in Leipzig. But he soon changed his mind: 'Gerd' reported he had later turned up wearing 'the blue shirt of the Free German Youth'. He was 'childishly pleased to be the first Scot to bear the symbolic colours of our youth organisation; as he went away he whistled "Sacco and Vanzetti" loudly; any FDJ functionary would have been delighted'. 'Max' confirmed that Pearson seemed to be altogether more cheerful. Major Schlinsog decided to extend Pearson's visa until the beginning of July.

On 27 April 1978, the Stasi drew up an 'operational plan' for 'working on' Pearson. He was to be asked to provide inside information, in a 'conspiratorial way', about the various British universities which sent their students to Leipzig to see if any of them were pursuing covert aims. Pearson was to be told that this was work required by the international department of Karl-Marx-University. This would allow the Stasi, in the future, to indicate to him that because the department reported to the Ministry for State Security, he had in effect already begun to work for them. Pearson agreed. This was a decisive moment in Pearson's spying career. Knowing 'Gerd' worked in security but not, at this stage, for the Stasi, Pearson passed on confidential information to them about his fellow students. One of them, Pearson reported, was particularly worth looking at closely: this was Graham Watson (later to become a leading Liberal Democrat MEP), a student at Heriot-Watt but deputy secretary of the Young Scottish Liberals. He gave about thirty other pieces of information to 'Gerd' relating to things that he did and did not know about other students and lecturers. On 14 June he was told that, on his return to Edinburgh, the Stasi wished him to execute further tasks, including information on who there was using 'the human rights question' to cause trouble for the GDR. He was told not to mention this to anyone. Once again, Pearson agreed, adding that he knew Dr McPherson had a tough time because of her political beliefs.

'Gerd' and Pearson then went off to Prague from 8 until 11 June 1978, the first of what would be many trips undertaken together. On 17 July, 'Gerd' noted that Pearson fully accepted his future task would be 'collecting information to provide insights into the motives, the course and the purpose of the UK's policy of contacts with the GDR'. Specifically, he was told to investigate Professors Prais, Paton and Salmon, Andrew Hollis at Salford, Michael Humble at St Andrews, Michael Holman at Leeds, Subiotto at Birmingham, a Dr Tate at the New University of Ulster, Dr Tomaner at Aberdeen, a Professor Stone, Dr Barbara Einhorn, Dr Mitchell at Stirling, and Dr Jürgen Thomanek at Aberdeen. In addition he was to list all students and lecturers he knew of with links to East Germany. But Pearson had also made it clear that he was willing to undertake any additional, as yet unspecified, 'special tasks' that might arise. He accepted that his work for them was to be 'long-term'. He was to return to East Germany that Christmas with the first fruits of his espionage (where he would be told that 'behind' 'Gerd' stood the 'security department at Leipzig University').

What the Stasi did not tell him at this point was that their priority for him was that he should pursue Eastern European studies in Britain. Nor did they tell him that they intended to offer him 'financial support' (another important means of binding him to them). Their final secret was that they wished him to alter his career plans to suit them. The Stasi realised that research in Leipzig would not suit their purpose since it might deny him a post at GCHQ, the MoD, UNESCO, the European Commission or NATO – all of which locations they had cherry-picked for him.

Pearson would leave Leipzig once and for all on 25 August 1978, following a boating holiday with 'Gerd'. He was told that any letters he wrote to 'Gerd' from Edinburgh should be kept personal and simple, warned to keep his mouth shut – and given DM 500 'for expenses'. 'Gerd' minuted at this stage that he did not believe Pearson was an MI5 or MI6 contact, not least because it was the Stasi who had approached Pearson and had maintained the initiative throughout. Every step they had taken had been a 'genuine surprise'. His superiors agreed: Pearson was absolutely 'clean' as far as they could tell.

On 15 December 1978 Pearson returned to East Berlin and presented the results of his work. 'Gerd' and Schlinsog were delighted. It is not hard to see why. Pearson gave them confidential information about Professor Prais, Christa Wolf's visit to Edinburgh, Birmingham and Swansea, of Ian Wallace, then at Dundee. He reported that Karin McPherson had told her colleagues that she opposed the invitation to Jurek Becker, a GDR writer, because it could damage her relations to the GDR. The Stasi report noted that Pearson was now 'able to prove he could work for us and fully understands the implication of bringing information to us'. 'Gerd' noted 'he was impatient and expectant about our evaluation of his work. His pleasure at our recognition of it was unrestrained. He said on many occasions how sorry he was not to have produced more, and told me of the energy and methods he would use for the next stage.'

Pearson also provided details about current Scottish students at Leipzig, pointing out that one of them would take up a post as translator for the European Commission in Brussels which suggested, he said, that study in Leipzig was seen as a security problem. He described senior staff in the European and Peace Studies institutes at Bradford University, and a link he said the director had with Moscow University. On 2 January 1979, prior to Pearson's return to Edinburgh, a further 'Treff' took place. Schlinsog was there, as planned, as a 'member of the university's security department' and a further commission was given before an additional DM 500 was handed over.

At the next 'Treff' in June 1979 in Leipzig, Pearson was told that, in future, he would be working not just for the university but for the Ministry for State Security. He agreed to this. Pearson now relayed more information: he had come across two students from Salford University – Jean Cameron and Phil Mannion – who had contacts with East Germans. A man named Clive Gray, a Briton living in Hamburg, was said to be 'very left-wing', with a grandmother who was a noted member of the CPGB. He reported on Jurek Becker (who had visited on 2 March, despite McPherson's objection). He told them about Prais, Paton, Sara Salmon, Hollis ('very pro-GDR, the only person in Salford really interested in it'), Einhorn ('because of her attitude and politics, excluded from ever getting a permanent university job in Britain'), and that Karin McPherson had insisted that German language instructors from the GDR be recognised as equally employable as those from West Germany, Austria or Switzerland.

Once again, the Stasi were delighted. While they understood that he was still 'too young to understand the full dimensions of our work', this did not worry them ('this is not insoluble').

Pearson next informed the Stasi about his plans to move to Leeds University and work with Professor Beresford. The Stasi said they would see if he might be able to secure a post in West Germany but secretly they were very pleased with the choice of Leeds, prompting Schlinsog to comment: 'There are many people there in whom we take an interest'. It was decided that the next 'Treff' should be in Scotland and the Stasi decided that 'Gerd' and Pearson should then go on holiday together. This time he was given DM 1,000.

The next stage had been reached. Pearson was now working for both the university and the Ministry for State Security. He had made it clear that he was ready to do this work and that his motives for doing so were political. He understood that his relationship with the Stasi – as he now knew them to be – was long-term.

In October 1979 the first moves were started formally to confirm Pearson's recruitment. For the time being, there were to be standard 'Treffs' in Leeds (every first Tuesday of the month, at eight in the morning at the Town Hall, by the left lion at the entrance steps) and other meetings all over Europe connected with his fencing engagements.

On 25 January 1980 a 'Treff' took place in Paris, at which Pearson passed over what was regarded as useful intelligence, handed on to MfS A IX. He had details of who at Leeds was getting research money, told them that Professor Brian Hook had been to visit Margaret Thatcher at 10 Downing Street and, worst of all, named a student who had graduated in 1975 and was now working at the MoD, another one about to be appointed a translator in the European Commission, and a further fellow student who would be taking up a post at NATO. He also supplied information about the work of Amnesty International in Leeds. Pearson said he wished to visit Leipzig again. 'Gerd' said that this might be possible but they would have to be very careful. He was instructed not to contact any girl there and to ignore the East Germans who were visiting Leeds.

The next meeting took place in March 1980 at the Hotel Emke in Budapest. Pearson was told his work was valuable: an issue he had raised had been taken up with the British Foreign Office and a student he had recommended had been offered a place at Leipzig. He was encouraged to apply for a post with NATO but he was reluctant to do so. The next meeting was scheduled for July 1980 in Varna in Bulgaria, to be preceded by instruction in Berlin. For the first time, Pearson was to use his fictional passport, issued under the name of Robert Behlert, and to present himself as an East German while he was in Bulgaria. The Varna 'Treff' was a success. Pearson was totally convincing as Behlert, even to Germans. His career worries were evident, however, and it had occurred to him that a move into Chinese studies might make sense. Beresford, he thought, might help him get a post in the Foreign Office. He handed over information on various individuals – including the Russian girlfriend of a fellow student, a link with the British Embassy in East Berlin, an MoD translator, someone currently being vetted by the MoD – and he also supplied an internal university document (of little intrinsic value but proof he could get hold of such things).

Further 'Treffs' took place in Copenhagen and in Amsterdam that October, where Pearson provided more information on previous lines. He said that his Chinese was coming on well and 'Gerd' advised him to ingratiate himself with Professor Beresford, who might be a lonely bachelor; a Christmas present, he said, was always a good tactic in such situations. At another in Vienna, Pearson was given DM 1,000 again, and in December 1980 a 'Treff' took place in Scotland, taking in Edinburgh, Inverness, Loch Ness and the Isle of Skye. As it was his birthday, 'Gerd' would bring him a gift from the 'Centre'.

In 1981, there were 'Treffs' in Antwerp, Paris and the Soviet Union, where he was to be shown Second World War memorials, in order to understand Soviet attitudes better, and to meet KGB members. Further meetings took place at which Pearson always delivered material, sometimes extensive, sometimes not. But the Stasi were delighted with him. Pearson was now to be trained in spying on a particular individual (they suggested he chose a fellow student), to collect material on Polish studies at Leeds, and to find out if the department there had any links to Solidarity. He was also told to recruit a student working on Chinese studies and to consider, once again, a career with NATO, for the EEC, in Paris or West Germany. At the very least, he ought to be persuaded to target the MoD in London. In March 1981 Pearson handed over two full reports. Both were passed to the 'Centre'. He described the efforts to promote links with China made by Brian Hook, Sidney Dugdale, Peter Lawrenson and David Birchall at Leeds. Hook himself, Pearson judged, was a key figure in this. Furthermore, someone else thought his work was important because his department, and the one dealing with Eastern Europe, had been, so Pearson claimed, exempt from the more general educational cuts imposed by the Thatcher government. He also described the work of several other Leeds academics – D. N. Collins, R. Davis and J. D. Morrison among them – adding that Professor Zygmunt Baumann from the Department of Sociology was also active in this area.

Pearson suggested that the central figure was Holman, who had studied German and Slav languages at Oxford in 1960. In 1961 he had been made a member of the 'national committee for the civil service' and in 1962 chairman of the Oxford regional group of international civil servants. From September 1962 until August 1963 he had studied German at Leipzig. He was responsible for student exchanges with Eastern Europe and had travelled widely. Pearson believed him to be a 'marked anti-Communist' and he suspected he might have connections to British Intelligence. Baumann, he said, had worked in Israel and was 'an influential figure in Polish affairs who had worked together with the Institute of Strategic Studies'. In February 1981 Baumann had briefed fellow researchers on Solidarity and also had contacts with an Oxford academic working on this at St Antony's College who had discussed alleged CIA involvement with Solidarity.

Further 'Treffs' were planned for Antwerp, Berlin, Manchester and Lucerne. Then, in November 1981, Pearson cancelled the next meeting, promising to visit Berlin the following April. The Stasi were concerned but he turned up and was duly given DM 1,000. In June he met 'Gerd' in Denmark and supplied information 'on the NUS President' and a visiting East German professor. He was given DM 500 and an expensive camera (which, as the Stasi receipt showed, cost DM 850). In August 1982, Pearson was provided with a new secret writer and instructions on how to use it and write in code. He was also given training in short-wave burst radio transmission. He showed 'complete understanding' of the technology involved. At the beginning of December 1982, 'Gerd' was to fly to London to check out the suitability of Pearson's flat for short-wave burst radio transmissions, and, if it worked, to pass over the codes to be used. Pearson seemed pleased with all of this and said he would be prepared to work as an intelligence agent for Cuba or some other Soviet bloc state.

Then, in May 1983, Pearson wrote to break off contact. The Stasi were seriously worried that they had lost him. It was decided to offer him an invitation he would not be able to refuse: they actually created an occasion in Leipzig to which he was to be invited by 'Max', or Peter Kunz, who ran Pearson's beloved haunt, the Moritzbastei, with all expenses paid.[7] Given that everything the Stasi did was vile, wicked and cynical, Kunz's letter was not exceptional.

Dear Robin,

To the fifth anniversary of the opening of the youth and student centre 'Moritzbastei' we want to invite above all the activists of the building phase. Since you belong to those foreign students who were an active part of the building-up of the place and helped with its internal profile, and since your essay on it has made you the chronicler of our work, we hereby invite you heartily to visit us for the celebration on 08.02.85.

Ample care will be taken of you for your stay here. For many of your friends it would be a great pleasure to see you again.

With friendly greetings

Peter Kunz

But Pearson did not respond. Then, out of the blue, on 13 November 1985, 'Gerd' received a letter from the Department of Economic History at Hull. It indicated that Pearson wished to make contact again, but it was not clear why.

'It has been a long time since we last wrote to each other . . .' Pearson said that he had been made a temporary lecturer at Hull. He explained that at the beginning of the year he had been invited to visit Leipzig and the Moritzbastei but 'unfortunately' could not make it. However, he now had sufficient cash 'to have a small holiday in the Erzgebirge [in East Germany]. I will arrange everything with Berolina Travel.'

Significantly, Pearson concluded his letter with the recognised code, *'Anker runter . . .'* (anchors away). This told 'Gerd' that he wished to make operational contact with him. The Stasi were pleased. 'Gerd' was instructed to give him DM 1,000 and to take him skiing to Cranzahl, a place he had enjoyed in the past. But to no apparent advantage, however: Pearson told 'Gerd' he wished to 'freeze' his relationship with the Stasi but not to break it off entirely. In April 1987 Pearson reported that he had secured a post at York University – but would visit 'Gerd' in August, and would start work again. He began this letter with the agreed code *'Anker hoch'* (anchors up). He offered information on David Irving (a visiting speaker at Brentwood School in Essex, where Pearson had been teaching). He also agreed to find out more about the current crop of Heriot-Watt students.

Clearly the next 'Treff' would be a make or break event. When Pearson turned up on 23 August, the Stasi were shocked – they noted he was 'in a state of physical and psychological exhaustion'. But he had come with an offer. He would start operating again and was ready to recruit for them at York University. He also offered his flat there as a safe house for other 'illegals'. Finally, he agreed to adopt a 'false flag' identity: to pose as a West German intelligence officer and recruit both British and visiting German students to the university. The Stasi were delighted. What 'Gerd' did not know – just as Pearson was unaware that Schlinsog and Hirschfeld knew – was that for some time Pearson had been maintaining a relationship with an East German girl. At the same time, his failure to get a proper job had demoralised him and he had written that he believed he did not have it in him to become a full-time intelligence officer ('I am not the person you want,' he had insisted).

If this seemed grim, that was not how the Stasi saw it: they admired his skill in handling the girl and believed that he retained a 'lust for adventure'. Basically, he was still their man. What was more, MI5 were clearly totally unaware of his existence. There were still possibilities here after all.

On 27 November 1987 Brüning and Hirschfeld gave him a new task. They had received information from an agent called 'Peter' (they did not, of course, reveal his name – he was probably an East German lecturer at Ealing College) about a Polish woman – Joanna Kalinowska – living in Cumberland Road, north Acton. Kalinowska's son-in-law was said to be working for the Ministry of Defence as an explosives expert. 'Peter' held the view that Joanna would be a useful spy for the East Germans both because of her son-in-law,

Toni (who was given a codename, 'Dom'), and because of her friends in the émigré Polish community in London. Her daughter, Barbara, was a civil servant. There was, however, a problem. Madame Kalinowska was anything but a Communist – she admired Margaret Thatcher, thought Stalin was as bad as Hitler, that the Communists had ruined the Polish economy and that Neil Kinnock was the most dangerous man in Britain. 'Peter', not surprisingly, said there was no chance of recruiting her to the East German cause. However, she might agree to work for British intelligence: a 'false flag' approach to her might just do the trick.

From 3 to 10 May 1988, 'Gerd' visited Pearson in London to put the job to him. In three meetings with Pearson – at the Westminster Abbey bookshop and at Victoria and King's Cross stations – he found Pearson alert and professional, addressing him by his agreed cover-name 'Dieter' throughout. Pearson agreed to execute the operation – indeed, he was 'very happy' with it and promised to gain entry (by 'legal' means) to the household, and see what he could discover and do. He added that he had the chance of a post at the LSE, at Hull or one in the West Indies. Taking instructions from Leipzig, 'Gerd' pushed him towards the LSE – 'best for us, from an operational standpoint', as Schlinsog commented. But Hull would suit them almost as well.

A 'Treff' was arranged in Berlin for 3–9 September 1988 to review his progress. When Pearson turned up in Berlin he gave them all another shock. He was livid because, having managed to make contact with Mme Kalinowska, the first thing he had learned from her was that she had previously been visited by someone allegedly 'from Heidelberg in West Germany, researching the similarities between Churchill and Bismarck'. Pearson told the Stasi that he had guessed at once that this person (who was 'Peter') must be an intelligence agent as the topic of his research was too simplistic to be real. 'Gerd' lied, telling him this was complete nonsense ('this person has nothing to do with us'). Pearson calmed down. He then described his work on Mme Kalinowska, getting confirmation of the MoD posting of her son-in-law. He had read her telephone and address books, and had seen that Toni had lectured in the USA (in Washington and Nevada). He had discovered that Toni had now completed his work for the MoD and was therefore at liberty to travel to Poland.

The next 'Treff' was to take place on 7 December 1988 at the William Wilberforce Museum in Hull. All in all, he had returned with a vengeance to his work for the Stasi, exhibiting a new confidence and tenacity. On 11 November 1988, Pearson wrote, as arranged, to set up the 'Treff' and, intriguingly, to propose a student exchange between Hull and the GDR.

Anchors up!

Greetings from Hull. I have received your letter and am enclosing the sheets you asked for in this. As you certainly know, Hull has one of the most famous provincial theatres in the UK. I hope the material will be of use. The term is flying by without my being able to pause. I have taken many chores within the Dept. Such as registration of graduate students, member of the committee for research development and coordination, and I have to plan my lectures and seminars. All of this is fun but I need more time for my own research. I am busy until 1800 every day. I say that's it for the day – but work sometimes at home as well.

One of my tasks will be to build up foreign relations in the University which have been somewhat neglected by us recently. We would be delighted to have a link or a student exchange with universities in the GDR. It would, of course, also be a plus for me if I could organise something like this. I know that you are no longer at the KMU but in case you know people, either in Berlin, or Leipzig or anywhere, who would be interested in this sort of thing, please do write to me. Our teaching and research interests extend across a wide field . . . Please think about this. We could perhaps really do something for East–West relations. Must go now. Fencing still beckons. Many greetings . . . Anchors away . . .

Just as Karin McPherson had put Pearson in harm's way a decade earlier, he was now planning to do the same for his own students at Hull. This shows not only that – at a fairly late stage in the game as far as the GDR was concerned – Pearson still regarded helping it as a priority. It also shows, of course, that he had not been in any way upset by his contact with the Stasi. Far from it; he now wished to give others the 'benefits' that he had enjoyed himself.

At the Hull 'Treff', 'Gerd' told him of the Stasi's interest in the support that the dissidents in Poland and elsewhere were getting from Britons and British institutions. 'Gerd' said they would take up his suggestion regarding a link between staff at Hull University and an East German university. Pearson was given, and accepted, the phone number of a cover for further contact. Pearson also gave 'Gerd' information about Hull University and its leading lights. In Amsterdam on 24 February, Pearson gave more information about the Poles in London. The Stasi were once more delighted with his progress and, paradoxically, thrilled that he had correctly suspected 'Peter'. It was good tradecraft. A further meeting was fixed for Amsterdam in April, but this one was not to be. On 2 April 1989 Pearson sent 'Gerd' his last letter as a Stasi spy:

> Anchors up
>
> Holiday, I'm at home, in a few weeks I have to go to the north again. I am not pleased about this. I had hoped to have a holiday at the end of April but can't manage it – job interviews, permanent posts finally. I will perhaps [underlined] be able to visit at the end of May but I cannot make any firm plans now as next term will be busy. Must go. Gorbachev is visiting London on Friday and the Library will be closed. You can see how politics interrupts science!

Politics may not actually have interrupted science, but they had plainly interrupted spying. Pearson was clever enough to see that the writing was on the wall – and that Wall would come down.

He went on to make a substantial reputation for himself at Hull University, with no one any the wiser about his Stasi past. He was unmasked publicly only in 1999 when, as a result of my early research on the Stasi files, the evidence entered the public domain. There is evidence that he was interviewed a year or so before this by MI5.

The Stasi admired Pearson not only for the information he provided but for demonstrating a rugged personal toughness – at times even with them. For example, he had kept quiet about the fact that he had formed a personal friendship with a Leipzig girl which the Stasi believed had been ended at their behest. This deceit impressed them hugely. Similarly, like all Stasi spies, he was also spied upon during his career; unlike most of them, he realised that this might be going on and expressed his displeasure. Equally, under quite different circumstances, when he was confronted with evidence of his spying by BBC Television, he remained cool and dispassionate, immediately seeking to fend off further questions by suggesting that he had signed the Official Secrets Act (not, in theory, implausible), thereby implying that he was a double agent who had been working for the Stasi. He did have a contract of secrecy, but with the East Germans, not the Crown.[8]

Pearson's duties for the Stasi were core ones. Asking him to discover who was doing what at Leeds University might have seemed little more than a simple exercise in espionage for a beginner, but what Leeds academics thought about, and how they might be involved with, the changes that were beginning to overwhelm the Soviet bloc states, in particular Poland, and the Soviet Union itself, did concern the Stasi deeply. Those Pearson named were put at risk. The possible links with the British intelligence community were another area of real interest, as was Leeds's exchange programme with the People's Republic of China. At the very end of his career in spying, Pearson returned to working on collecting information on the Polish community in London, investigating in particular a link which tied it directly to the Ministry of Defence and a Polish explosives expert working there. Here, too, people were put at grave risk.

The Stasi files on the second British penetration agent, 'Diana', or Fiona Houlding, provide a very similar pattern of approach, entrapment and escalating pressure. In view of the fact that Houlding was not recruited until 1987, the files on her are far slimmer than on Pearson. But in their own way they are every bit as depressing, both in terms of the cynical and odious way in which the Stasi behaved and in Houlding's response to them. Hirschfeld (now promoted to captain) and Schlinsog had overall charge of the operation.

Unlike Pearson, Holding had already graduated and was working as a language teacher in Leipzig when, at the age of twenty-five, she agreed to work for the Stasi. After Ilkley Grammar School, she went up to Heriot-Watt University to read German, spending a semester at Leipzig in 1984–5 before returning in 1986. A Stasi spy, 'Sender' (real name Heinz Hentschel, also known as 'Richard'), had written a report on Houlding and a fellow student, Alistair Mossman (from Edinburgh University). She was said by this talent spotter to be 'the more mature of the two' and clearly politically 'alert'. She was hard-working, a committed member of the Labour Party and Anti-Nazi League and was a strong supporter of the British peace movement. They noticed that she was lonely – and they saw their chance to strike. Hirschfeld wrote: 'She is the type of woman who craves understanding. Her sympathy towards the GDR is remarkable for an English person but it is linked to concrete individuals. She is very sensitive and reacts badly to certain phrases, generalisation and ultimata. She will need understanding during the process of winning her over.'

In November 1986 a Stasi agent, 'Schnitter' (real name Ralf-Jürgen Böhme, also known as Ralf Bönisch), was instructed to approach her.[9] (On 8 February 1989 he would be personally presented with a medal by Mielke for the 'Diana' operation.) Interestingly, Böhme had three identities. In addition to Bönisch, he had passports under the name of Thomas Jeschke, born in Colditz but with a West German passport, and Volker Hartnig, also born in Colditz on the same day, 15 January 1955. These multiple identities indicate that 'Schnitter' had important duties beyond the borders of the GDR.

In 1986, he was working for the ADN news agency as a journalist on the *Sächsischer Tageblatt*. He was keen to get permission to become a foreign correspondent. This made him an excellent control for a British student, and his senior officers ordered him to conduct an interview with Houlding for the paper. Flattered at his attention (and having no idea that it was not genuine) she allowed him to draw closer to her. He asked her to help him with his English and they went to concerts given by the famous Leipziger Gewandhaus orchestra; he had introduced her to his wife and family and, perhaps most odiously of all, he had initiated a sexual relationship with her. He told his senior officers in September 1987 that he counted on their 'moral support' when this had been achieved, a comment they adorned with various exclamation marks. He was told to tell her that she had become the 'most important thing in his life' and that he was impressed by her 'critical eye for politics'. This particular meeting took place, appropriately enough, in Auerbach's Cellar, the very place where Goethe's Faust had encountered Mephistopheles at what was said to be a five-hour wine-drinking session. The repugnant 'Schnitter' explained his 'family position' but insisted that this did not prevent him 'revealing his sudden affection for her'.

He then went on to explain that certain British students at Leipzig were working directly or indirectly for British intelligence and the British National Front. There were links, he would tell her, with West German Fascist groups. It would help 'Schnitter's' own work, he went on, were she to help him with research. She could do this both in Leipzig and later on, when she left to work – as was her plan – either in Britain or West Germany (she had to leave East Germany by 31 August 1988 at the latest). Houlding supplied the necessary information with obvious gusto. She accused a fellow Heriot-Watt student of being a member of the National Front – a very damaging accusation. She alleged that 'Lindsey and Chris' were hostile to the GDR. She offered to tell the Stasi about a meeting with a British diplomat in Berlin. She was also trained in covert photography techniques. She was told that 'Schnitter' would be meeting a contact with the neo-Nazis and needed a snapshot of him. She readily agreed.

In July 1987, the Stasi invited her to visit Prague. They had decided to play on her anxieties about the neo-Nazi movement by taking her to the Jewish Museum, where children's drawings from Theresienstadt concentration camp were being exhibited. What the Stasi did not tell her (and what she could not possibly have known) was that the Stasi itself was actively supporting, and in some cases actually manufacturing, the West German neo-Nazi movement: it served the East Germans extremely well to be able to claim that neo-Nazism was on the rise again in the Federal Republic, 'proving' that Fascism and West German capitalism went hand in hand.

Houlding now began to accept money from the Stasi, signing a receipt for DM 900 on 8 February 1989. On 23 June 1988 she made her first overt contact with the Stasi, fully aware of who they were. She agreed to work for them once she had returned to Britain (she had won a place at Manchester University) and accepted a two-year plan that had been worked out for her. She was given DM 500. A week later, on 30 June, she met Hirschfeld together with 'Schnitter' for the second time at the Falstaff restaurant. She was told the purpose of the meal was to 'thank them both for their work' and 'to stress that their decision to involve the Party and the Ministry for State Security was good, right and important'. Houlding replied that she was pleased to help 'Schnitter' in his work and to support 'the interests of the GDR'. She agreed to maintain contact once in Manchester and accepted a proposal for a 'Treff' in East Germany at Christmas or New Year 1988–9. Finally, she agreed to work on David Irving (whose telephone number she was intriguingly given) and report on right-wing students at Manchester. On 28 July she was invited to the Milano, her favourite restaurant in Leipzig, to seal the deal. She was then presented with a picture as a token of the GDR's esteem. The picture was a 'small peaceful landscape, in oils'.

In this way, Houlding had slowly been drawn towards under-standing that the work she was doing was for the East German Ministry for State Security. According to her file, she was formally recruited by 10 November 1988, given the code number XV 5395/88 and the codename 'Diana'. The controlling officer min-uted: 'She will give the results of her research to the Ministry for State Security and is therefore, in a certain way, aware that she is working against her system (Thatcher, the Conservatives, neo-Nazis) in a conspiratorial, secret way, using an alibi to do so.'

A report dated 14 November 1988 noted that, at the end of June 1988, she, Hirschfeld and 'Schnitter' had met and agreed that she would carry on working as before on her return to Britain. She men-tioned that she was also thinking of a post in the European Commission in Brussels, to which she already had an entrée, or of working in West Berlin where 'Schnitter' could continue to visit her. Hirschfeld's superior minuted 'good work – a good operation' on her file.

On 9 January 1989, the Stasi worked out a longer-term plan for Houlding, now back in Britain. She was to continue with her work on neo-Fascists in Europe, focusing on Irving and the Frenchman

Jean-Marie Le Pen, and to be asked to look at their activities in the European Parliament. She was to be encouraged to seek employment in Brussels. Here, the officer noted, she might get an interesting job and they 'a faithful ally in an institution from which intelligence can be gained for the security policy interests of the GDR'.

Houlding agreed readily to all this. But the next 'Treff' planned for 26 March 1989 never took place. On 6 April 1989, 'Schnitter' succeeded in contacting a friend of hers. Despite his letters to her ('My dearest Fi – are you still amongst the living? I simply cannot imagine that we will not see each other again') she had not replied. Her friend, too, had heard nothing. Houlding had gone cold.

The lives of Pearson and Houlding – both perfectly ordinary British citizens – were effectively ruined by the Stasi in ways neither of them could ever have imagined. Even today they are probably still unaware of the extent to which their work for the Stasi will damage them in the future, both in terms of their careers (both hold publicly accountable appointments) and privately. It is true that both were committed to 'Socialism' and were knowingly and willingly Stasi spies, and that 'Armin' in particular did serious damage to the groups on which he spied as well as to his colleagues and friends in various British universities. But it is also true that they were manipulated and misled with total viciousness and brazen mendacity by a secret police who served a state which had absolutely no respect for the lawfulness or the need to protect basic human rights. In this way, then, 'Diana' and 'Armin', and many like them, were also victims of the SED state.

Fiona Houlding – by now a respected school teacher in London who was also unmasked in 1999 as a result of my early research on the Stasi files – wrote an article in the *Guardian* in which she claimed that she was not a traitor and that the evidence against her was 'laughable'.[10] The evidence is not as serious as it is in Pearson's case, but it is certainly no laughing matter. She knowingly worked for a police state whose record on human rights – the very thing she claimed to revere – was appalling. She had spied on her fellow students and on her British teachers; it was only the imminent collapse of the GDR which brought her work for the Stasi to an abrupt end. She donated her fee from the *Guardian* to Amnesty International, an organisation the Stasi sought to penetrate, because it had done more than any other to point the West towards the abuses which were taking place every day in the GDR. To donate cash to it at that stage might be said by some to have added insult to injury.

These people, along with 'Jaguar' and 'Lissy' and their colleagues, were not, as Oleg Gordievsky has insisted, simply 'useful idiots'.[11] They put countless people at risk from a vicious and highly efficient secret police. Whether their targets were students, dons or civil servants, whether in Leipzig, Edinburgh, at Heriot-Watt, York, Hull or Leeds, all were spied upon, all harmed in one way or another. By acting in this way, the Stasi's British assets did not simply wound their unknowing targets (some of whom, had the plans worked as intended, would themselves have been recruited), they betrayed an open society to a closed one, doing damage to the national interest of a state which stood foursquare for the liberal values and human rights the Stasi had always sought to destroy.

# Conclusion

The history of the Stasi's operations against the UK is a genuine cause for alarm to anyone concerned with how we protect our liberal institutions and our democratic way of life from individuals, groups and hostile states which choose to do us harm. Espionage and subversion is a complex form of political activity which many prefer to ignore altogether even when 'fanatics armed with power' (as Elie Wiesel described modern terrorism) force us to stand up and take note. Dissent is, of course, a vital activity in any free democracy and dissenters must be enabled to influence public opinion – in the open. Those who seek to manipulate it covertly, whether working for themselves or for hostile powers, are another matter altogether. Where they are a serious danger to Britain's democratic way of life, it is right that the Security Service should monitor what they do, and ensure to the best of its ability that we are protected from them. Exercising secret influence, of course, as well as spying, is what the Stasi wanted their British sources to do. Even so, it has not always been easy in this book to characterise properly those in Britain who helped the Stasi to become one of the best intelligence services in the world, and not merely for legal reasons. Were the Stasi's British sources spies? How significant was what they did? Indeed, how significant was the role that intelligence played in sustaining German Communism – given that in the autumn and winter of 1989–90 it began to disintegrate, its security and intelligence service plainly incapable of keeping it alive.

We will return to this second point at the end of this chapter (where the limitations of intelligence are made crystal clear). We should begin, however, with the problem of definition. We have seen that in Britain the Stasi plainly had a number of paid agents operating deep under cover. With certainty we know only what their codenames were. We may surmise, however, that at least some of them were recruited from a far broader band of British sources. The Stasi files indicate that a considerable number of Britons assisted the Stasi and that some of them were certainly their paid agents. The fact of cash handed over cannot be explained away. But even when individuals took East German gold, it cannot be automatically concluded that all such Britons were damaging Britain or acting disloyally – although ethically they can be charged with assisting a regime which locked up its own people for trying to exercise civil rights. From the Stasi's point of view, however, these Britons were certainly regarded as intelligence assets, whether they slaked the Stasi thirst for confidential knowledge or helped steer British institutions on their behalf.

Of course, not everyone who supported East Germany and its so-called ideals was a Stasi source. As we have seen, those whom the Stasi chose to trust were not always those who trusted the GDR. To be a fan of the 'Workers' and Peasants' State' was not synonymous with being a source. Where co-operation was offered and accepted, however, all fell neatly into Wolf's 'grey area'. From the viewpoint of the Britons inhabiting it, they had clearly helped East Germany knowingly, although some apparently believed (without any supporting evidence) that, by working with the East German authorities, the GDR leopard might change one or two of its nastier spots. Some of them were Communists, some were not. But all of them, without exception, were perfectly aware that the GDR was a German police state with an appalling record on human rights abuses (outlined at the beginning of this book) and yet none of them was deterred by this from co-operating with the East Germans.

We must forget that, despite the grandeur of Belgrave Square, the embassy cocktail parties, the chatter about 'culture' and 'the benefits of mutual understanding', the GDR never ceased to regard Britain as an 'enemy', ideologically and politically, and that, although its

British friends may have discounted this fact, it, too, was not a secret. For the whole of the 1980s, East Germany was waging war against Britain – an *intelligence* war – fought with spies and disruptive action and not with missiles or tanks, but a war nonetheless. It was, furthermore, a war the Germans won, one they were helped to win by their British assets. That the GDR collapsed chiefly because of changes taking place inside the Soviet Union, over which it had no control, should not be allowed to conceal its intelligence victory over Britain.

The roles played by the Stasi's British sources stemmed from their possession of inside ('internal') information about individuals and issues which were of major concern to the Stasi. Each of them, in their own way, was a genuinely significant repository of the secrets of others. It was this that inevitably attracted the Stasi to them and, we can safely say, their expertise here that attracted – for one reason or another – the Britons to the Stasi. There was a real community of interest between them, whether or not it revolved around cash or intellectual sympathy firmly grounded on the basis that the Britons knew things that the Stasi wanted to know.

Those who were their formal agents were (and are), of course, as culpable as the Stasi officers who ran them. As to the persons of trust, and the assorted other sources, it was, at best, utter folly for them to draw so close to the East Germans. Each of them failed to realise that highly trained Stasi intelligence officers were bound to be effective intelligence gatherers, past masters in drawing from them by one means or another the information East Berlin demanded.

The question will, of course, be begged whether sources like these, who tell us that they were not 'agents' in the East German sense, should nevertheless be classified as 'spies', working for the GDR and against the UK simply because this is what the Stasi files allege. Sadly, in the cases of Irene Fick and Vic Allen, like those who were fully primed agents, there can be no question about what they did.

This book does not, however, make any such blanket allegation against individual sources. We need to emphasise that, on the basis of existing evidence, it would be premature to do so. As we have seen throughout this book, the strength of the Stasi lay in part in the fluid but conspiratorial way in which their intelligence gathering was executed. Where the term 'spy' relies on a rigid and classic definition of espionage, it becomes difficult meaningfully to affix it to every single one of the Stasi's helpers. Were its sense to be adapted to their changed and more amorphous ways of intelligence gathering, it might – paradoxically – cause us to call all of them spies, which would be equally imprecise. About the *informal* Stasi sources in Britain we may safely say that they were content to pass information to the Stasi, but with no real strings attached. To make things even more complex, some of these people accept fully that they were sources (in the English sense) – indeed, they volunteer the information – but claim either that they were doing this for higher motives (providing dissidents with publicity, and showing the Stasi that Westerners were interested in them) or because they were part of a personal, or a Foreign Office, plan to undermine Communism.

For some sources, such claims may have some merit – given that we live in a world that is full of risk, which frequently requires diplomats and others in official life to chance their arms – but they need to be tested on a case by case basis, and this book has done just that. The Stasi was, of course, aware of the possibility that some of its sources might be working for British counter-intelligence – although, according to the files, the merest hint of this was sufficient immediately to deter the Stasi from any further contact with them. All the evidence we have suggests that none of the Stasi's known sources was working in any way for British counter-intelligence. Lord Roper was one of the most important agents of influence and he, along with Paul Oestreicher, was probably the most celebrated of the Stasi's UK sources. But they have categorically denied, on several occasions, that they had any formal contact with British intelligence and seem genuinely outraged at the suggestion which someone, initially, floated in Stasi circles. Many of those named as Stasi informants in Britain appear today to be open, engaging, if intense and serious people, who will be deeply wounded by any criticism or any doubts expressed about their loyalty to Britain today (though perhaps less wounded if reference is made to 'Thatcher's Britain' of the 1980s). As for Lord Roper, he firmly believes that he was enacting British policy and that in doing so British intelligence authorised and kept an eye upon his own contact with the East Germans (although, as we have seen, the evidence contradicts him on this latter point).

The Stasi files indicate that where sources disclosed secret or sensitive information about third parties, they were clearly guilty of betraying the trust that had been placed in them by these people. In this sense, everyone included in these files who is recorded as having knowingly passed information or documents to the Stasi is, *in the eyes of the Stasi*, their 'spy', whatever their motives. Where sources were members of CND or END, for example, they will dispute that they 'assisted' the Stasi (though they do not deny speaking to it, confirming the evidence of the files in this regard). This book has described their arguments with the greatest of care. These individuals will point out that since they supported END, and END's fine leaders, Thompson, Kaldor and Coates, gave succour to the East German dissidents' movement, they cannot be accused of helping the Stasi. They will add that they themselves were spied on by the Stasi (as if this implied automatically that they were enemies of the GDR). These things may be perfectly true. But, tantalisingly for the British sources, this cannot be the complete story.

For one thing, END's GDR work disintegrated in the mid-1980s thanks to Stasi machinations which, for the time being at any rate, brought the immediate END problem to a close. For another, however, given the allegations contained in the Stasi files, it is inevitable that historians will ask whether confidential contacts by many Britons with the Stasi were wise and what, precisely, these individuals truly thought would be achieved by them. Could secret words, spoken softly to the Stasi, be a serious means of changing the repressive tactics of German Communism? It might be said that to believe this would be to believe anything. We should never forget that in their intelligence work the Stasi always had specific and carefully focused outcomes in mind. Sources had specific roles, never general ones.

In this sense, Roper and Oestreicher are part of the same fundamental problem. The winners in all the exchanges recorded in the Stasi files were the East Germans. It really did not assist British policy, which was to seek to undermine Communist control over the states of Eastern Europe, by upholding the GDR's political claims and bringing its intelligence officers into contact with British institutions and people in whom they had an interest. Nor did it help the British goal by trying to cajole the East Germans into being less repressive. That the GDR collapsed (for reasons which had nothing at all to do with their British operations) does not exculpate those who may today claim they did their bit to make this happen, when in fact they were doing the precise reverse. What is more, many of those who were fellow-travellers did not want German Communism to go under. The matters of which they informed the East Germans were not, it may seem, matters of life and death. But those who fell foul of the Stasi in the GDR could suffer very badly for this, and some did lose their lives as a result of doing so. The UK sources were not able to judge from the safety of the UK, what use the Stasi might make of information passed to them, however innocuous it might have seemed to the sources themselves.

There *is* an argument – one which should be put – that by wishing to sustain Communism, the root of the political ills and human rights abuses in the GDR (the reason, after all, why it was a totalitarian state) and knowingly offering information to the Stasi, whether directly or indirectly, these sources were, without doubt, regarded by the Stasi as being 'spies' or intelligence assets. To state this is not to make some crude indictment that anyone who supported the 'ideals' of Communism from afar shares the same level of guilt as the Stasi officers within the GDR who used terror and violence on the ground in order to uphold Communist rule. Without going into legal detail, the latter were criminals in the eyes of the various UN resolutions which the GDR had signed up to and almost certainly in the strict letter of the admittedly meaningless East German constitutions.[1] The former may share some moral responsibility for what went on inside the GDR, but it is in a different category and reduced by their physical distance from East Germany (even if this does not expunge it altogether).

The GDR in the 1980s was not the Third Reich, nor was it Stalin's Russia. But it *was* a hardline Communist state, one which had played a key role in the suppression of the Prague Spring of

1968, not to mention a host of other offences against civilised standards. In its governance, it was by no means dissimilar from the Third Reich before 1938. It did not persecute Jews but it did persecute and terrorise its political opponents with a secret police force, the Stasi. What would we think about Britons who before 1938 had helped the Gestapo to be more effective? What would we say about Britons who had helped the Stalinist NKVD conduct itself with greater success? Many people today might think that anyone with expert knowledge of East Germany would have wanted to contribute to its extinction rather than its survival. As Paul Oestreicher wryly observed, it was just as well for all the East Germans' British helpers that East Germany did collapse, enabling them now to emphasise the support they say they gave to the dissidents before 1990. Had the GDR not fallen, he accepts, their activities as sources would have been regarded by the Stasi as measures helping the regime to survive.

The fact is that the history of these informal Stasi sources illuminates a very complex and fluid aspect of contemporary espionage. By dovetailing the contradictory categories of 'victim' and 'perpetrator', the Stasi had successfully reframed the context in which intelligence gathering could take place. Acquiring diplomatic recognition, a seat in the UN and an embassy in Belgrave Square were necessary prerequisites whose significance is hard to exaggerate. Recognition not only provided a relatively safe physical base for espionage but provided a diplomatic setting which permitted the East Germans in London to play down their fundamental hatred of Western ways. These inputs into their tradecraft refined their spying and made it far easier for the Stasi to extract the information they wanted. The proviso, of course, was that their British sources were motivated by a fundamental sympathy for what they wrongly regarded as the ideals of East German Communism. It was this that allowed them to be manipulated. No great imagination is required to see that the Stasi's practices chimed not merely with those described by Arthur Koestler and John le Carré but also with those used by the Nazis in many European and American states prior to the outbreak of the Second World War.

So it is that the Stasi's British sources serve as a grim warning from history. All of them should be identified, not just because some of them may now be working for the KGB's successor, the SVR (who will have a full list of their names), or for certain Arab or Latin American states with whom the East Germans had a long history of close association.[2] Other countries which have a fanatical faith in the power of conspiracy, which is what held the Stasi together at all times, and other 'sub-national' groups of fanatics, who today regard the West as their enemies, are operating in the same way as the Stasi did in the 1980s, busy exploiting the 'grey' area for all it is worth. Those vulnerable to being targeted need to understand how it is done.

Should some, any – all – of those who agreed to become sources for the Stasi have been prosecuted for espionage? Would they have been found guilty? Certainly, under the old 1911 Official Secrets Act (the OSA), widely condemned because its sweep was so broad, most would have stood a real chance of prosecution.

Today, things are rather different. Section 5 of the Official Secrets Act 1989 makes it an offence for a person (who need not be a Crown servant) to make an unauthorised disclosure of official information protected under sections 1–4 of the Act *where the information has come into his possession as a result of an unlawful disclosure by a Crown servant or Government contractor* and where the person believes this disclosure to be damaging. The person making it must be a British citizen. Where the material is compiled from non-classified sources, no offence takes place. For an offence to occur, the information must be likely to damage the work of the security and intelligence services, the armed forces, international relations or crime.

Bizarrely – and to some, outrageously – working for a hostile intelligence agency is, therefore, of itself not an offence under the OSA.[3] The East Germans were surely right to see it as a law designed more to attack the Peter Wrights of the world than to constrain those ready to help secret services who regarded this country as their enemy. In the aftermath of 9/11 can it be doubted that the Act must be amended?

If what the Stasi spies did was treachery, could they be prosecuted for treason? The Treason Act of 1351 (which makes it illegal to 'levy war against the King in his realm, or be adherent to the

King's enemies in his realm, giving to them aid and comfort'), or the 1842 Treason Act, which adds only the offence of encouraging an enemy to invade the Queen's realm, rely on a definition of 'enemy' to mean a state with which the UK is at war.

The Cold War was not a war within the meaning of the 1351 or 1842 Acts. Thus, although the Stasi undoubtedly considered the UK their 'enemy', the GDR was not formally the UK's enemy.

Once again, this means that under British law it is perfectly lawful for British citizens to work for a foreign intelligence agency which regards Britain as hostile but is not at war with us. It seems likely that the lawmakers who drew up the 1989 OSA made a serious error here, as well, not least because a British agent of a foreign intelligence agency may gain access to secret information without its having come into his possession as a result of an unlawful disclosure, whether by simple trickery, or simply keeping his or her eyes wide open.

In his remarkable 'farewell' speech to East Germany after the Wall began to crumble, Mielke demonstrated in public, for the last time, that he had not lost one iota of his fanaticism: 'We, the Stasi,' he shrieked, 'are the sons and daughters of the working class, and always represent their interests. That is our most important duty. Our first task was to discover everything that might endanger peace; second, we worked to strengthen Socialist society. Comrades [shout from the chamber: 'we're not all Communists here'] – but I love you all, all of you. We have been criticised for shortcomings for which we were not responsible. We told everyone about the doctors and teachers who were fleeing. We tried to work according to the constitution and the laws.'[4]

The GDR was collapsing even as he spoke. But were he and his 'Ministry' to blame? On one level, clearly yes: the East German citizens had, by autumn 1989, plainly had more than enough of the secret police. But on another level, it was less clear-cut. Nineteen eighty-nine was indeed a Stasi failure but far more of a subconscious than a conscious one. It stemmed from a flaw in their mindset – but not their tradecraft – and it was one which neither of the two Erichs (Honecker and Mielke), who ran the GDR, had been able to predict.

There was one country upon which the Stasi did not spy, and yet it was certainly the most important single country in the world as far as East Germany was concerned. It was the country which had always held the GDR's future in its hands, and about which the Stasi – in theory – needed to know more than any other country. That country was the Soviet Union. A document contained in the Stasi files, and described below, proves the importance of intelligence to policy makers. In this particular case, however, it also flags its shortcomings. Because the Stasi did not spy on its 'friends', the East German leadership failed, in the critical days of November 1989, to realise that the Russians were actually lying to them. Despite their protestations of support, the Soviets had already signed East Germany's death warrant. What they now said was no longer what they truly thought. The price of ignorance became a catastrophe for German Communism.

On 17 November 1989, eight days after the Berlin Wall was opened, the East German leadership received a top secret 'blitz', teleprinted from their man in Moscow, the East German ambassador to the Soviet Union.[5] He said that he had just had a meeting with the Soviet foreign minister Eduard Shevardnadze and had been assured that the Soviet Union was determined at all costs to secure the continued existence of East Germany as a sovereign state, that it would promote the further development of 'Socialism' there and that German Communism would never be allowed to go under. In his view, the problems facing the GDR were domestic in origin, even if 'massive' interference from outside, in the form of a West German political campaign against 'Socialism' and vast amounts of cash, were fanning the flames. He said he promised the East Germans that the Soviet Union had warned West Germany to avoid turning up the heat. Both Gorbachev and Shevardnadze, the East Germans were told, thought Helmut Kohl was a 'cynical hypocrite' but they did see hope for the regime – in the figure of Margaret Thatcher. They thought she was the only person who could call Kohl to heel ('Great Britain,' the Soviets said, 'is becoming an ever stronger supporter of the status quo in Europe'). The Soviet foreign minister suggested inviting her to East Germany. While the Americans were less keen on halting the collapse of the GDR, support for it from

Thatcher would, they reckoned, at least 'flash an amber light, rather than a green one, at Helmut Kohl'.

Was Shevardnadze deliberately misleading the East Germans, or trying to be nice to them? (He also said that 'an island could not survive in a sea of change', which implied that, one way or another, Honecker's and Mielke's brand of Communism was in trouble, although East Germany itself could be rescued by going the Soviet way.) We do not know and nor did the East Germans. They were obliged to decipher his remarks without the help of secret information and made no progress. At the end of 1989, at their most critical time, they were paralysed by ignorance – the one thing their massive intelligence service had been designed to prevent. The Stasi had failed, and in a big way. This does not prove that intelligence cannot produce results, merely that the Stasi failed to identify the terminal source of danger.

East Germany fell, and with it fell its chilling secret police. Yet we should not conclude from this catastrophic failure of intelligence that prior to 1989 in general, and in 34 Belgrave Square, London in particular, the Stasi's record was a poor one. That, unfortunately, would be far from the truth.

# APPENDICES

# Appendix 1

# The Stasi's Own Lists of Their Targets in the UK and the USA

All were organisations deemed part of the intelligence communities of the respective states, or those directly or indirectly regarded as sources of support for Soviet bloc dissident movements as well as those rated as neo-Nazi. The following list has never previously been published.[1]

*UK*
Amnesty International
Brigade 88 (a neo-Nazi group)
British Frontier Service Organisation
British Service Security Organisation
British Movement (a neo-Nazi group)
British National Front
Campaign for Nuclear Disarmament
Defence Intelligence Staff
European Nuclear Disarmament
Foreign and Commonwealth Office
Foreign Office Intelligence Department (FOID)
General Staff Intelligence
GCHQ Cheltenham
Index on Censorship
International PEN Club
International Institute for Strategic Studies

IRA
Keston College
League of St George
Leo Baeck Institute
Liaison Committee/Bertrand Russell Foundation
Naval Intelligence Defence/NID
Official Committee on Security/OCS
Overseas Economic Intelligence Committee
Security Service/MI5
Viking Youth (neo-Nazi)

*USA*
Agape (US/Italy)
Agency for National Security Planning
Air Force Intelligence
Air Force Office of Assistant Chief of Staff
Air Force Office of Security Police
Air Intelligence Service
Alpha 66
American Association for the Advancement of Slavic Studies
   (Stanford University)
American Institute of Problems of European Unity
American Society for the Study of the GDR
Aspen Institute
Board for International Broadcasting
Brookings Institution
Bureau for Intelligence and Research (FBI)
Center for International and Strategic Studies
CIA
Counter Intelligence Corps
Defense Intelligence Agency
Defense Investigative Service
Deputy Chief of Staff Intelligence
Document Center Berlin
Electronic and Security Command
Hoover Institution
Hudson Institute

Institute for East–West Security Studies
Intelligence Oversight Board/Foreign Intelligence Board
Manson-Branded
National Council of Churches
Naval Intelligence Service/NIS
Naval Investigative Service
Naval Security Group
NSC Special Coordination Committee
Office of Intelligence Support
Office of Special Investigations/OSÍ
Operation and Research Detachment
President's Foreign Intelligence Board
Radio Free Europe/Radio Liberty
Treasury Department Intelligence
US Force Security/USAFSS
US Army Institute for Advanced Russian Studies
Watch Tower Bible and Tract Society

*Arab organisations*
AI – Istinbarat Al-Askanya, Iraq
Al Muhabarat Al-Aman, Iraq
Arab Organisation of 15 May
Fatima Action
Ibrahim

# Appendix 2

# Mielke's Directives in Espionage and Subversion

The Stasi's operations in Britain were developed according to a series of detailed directives issued by Erich Mielke; they demonstrate the ever increasing and almost hysterical emphasis that the Stasi laid on secret intelligence work in the 1980s. The first one in the archives is dated February 1979.[2]

1. To gain timely and reliable intelligence on the aims, the agents, the means and the methods of the Enemy. To investigate them and forestall any surprises in military, scientific and technological fields.
2. To uncover and destroy hostile bases and agents in the GDR.
3. To gain precise knowledge of the most important enemy centres [the Stasi's definition of its targets is given below], on the potential strength of the enemy; to undertake offensive measures against hostile centres and hostile forces in the operational area [that is, the West].
4. To make the foreign legations of the GDR secure.
5. Within the operational area, the service units of the intelligence service are to be especially concerned with the USA, the FRG, the other NATO states and Westberlin [the East German term for West Berlin].
6. Intelligence is to be gained on: hostile plans, aims, agents, means and methods, connections, facts, the contents necessary for the

execution of active measures, hostile centres and objects, operationally interesting individuals, the working methods of hostile agencies.

In July 1983, Mielke issued a second directive, ordering that renewed effort be put into all operations in the West and that intelligence gathering be even more focused than it had been previously. He reiterated a point he had first made in a 1974 directive – that when it came to secret intelligence, the Stasi wanted *quality* rather than *quantity*, which probably means that his officers had been doing the reverse – providing lots of intelligence but of limited quality.

Ever since October 1982, Department XV of the Leipzig HVA District Office had been given overall responsibility for operations in the West. Markus Wolf issued precise instructions for all his officers and agents working there: he did not require vast numbers of individuals to be milling around in the USA, Britain and France but rather to have people who could gain access to those areas 'where, if questions of war and peace exist, they are able to provide us with the decisive information about this'. Wolf added that he had a need for 'comprehensive information on the personalities' in the target areas so that the HVA might 'compile dossiers'. His deputy added that there was a strong imperative on them to 'create and use *Quellen* in the West' and that universities might be a useful place to start. If possible, the HVA should also seek to penetrate the security and intelligence services of the West.

On 21 May 1986 Erich Mielke issued a further directive for the Stasi, to cover the period from 1986 until 1989. The Ministry for State Security, so he instructed its members, 'has as its goal to provide the maximum support to the Party and State leadership'. They were ordered to co-operate with all forces for peace, 'to further develop brotherly relations with the Soviet Union, to take active measures against the imperialist forces, to guard against any surprise actions by the enemy, to support the GDR government in its struggle against the Federal Republic, and to uncover and render harmless the strategic plans of the imperialist nations against the Socialist States'.

Mielke's directive went on to demand 'intelligence from all operational units on the plans, aims and proposed measures of the USA

administration, intelligence on and assessment of the military policies of the main imperialist states in NATO (the USA, the FRG, the
UK and France); intelligence about ideas on strengthening NATO's
offensive strategy, including the "Air–land battle strategy, the
decapitation strike concept and horizontal escalation" '. He needed
'internal assessments from within imperialist circles concerning the
readiness for war of the armed forces and populations of these
states, and their evaluation of the same questions concerning the
Socialist States'.

Precise intelligence was required about the concrete plans and
measures surrounding SDI, secret work on rocket technology and
biological warfare, the 'Eureka' project [the European technology
programme] and the European Defence Initiative. All members of
the service were to act decisively against the weakening and desta-
bilising of the Socialist States by those who sought to meddle in their
internal affairs or by exploiting problems arising in these states or
forcing the human rights issue.

Mielke then proceeded to order 'increased use' of the operational
basis of their activities by instructing their agents to work harder on
'the personalities' in the states in the operational areas, securing
new positions in the enemy's space using the full resources of the
HVA and the various Department XVs of the areas of East Germany;
to exploit as a resource all foreign visitors to the GDR; to step up the
drive to find reliable agents (IMs) in the operational areas; to gain a
systematic and comprehensive listing of all ministry links in the
operational areas in respect of economics, sciences, including the
social sciences, the arts, culture and sport in order to exploit them
for 'operational purposes'.

Mielke wanted a stronger collection of 'dossiers on operationally
relevant people', greater use of IMs with special links to hostile
intelligence services and a comprehensive who's who of Western
intelligence. He said that operational work in the political arena was
to be conducted 'more offensively' and that the 'centres of hostile
activity' were now to be penetrated more deeply in order to supply
intelligence 'even earlier' than at present. In addition, greater attention was to be paid to the hostile plans and links that Western
intelligence had to the GDR.

The Stasi were instructed to 'disinform, disorientate, make insecure and subvert' all hostile forces wherever they were uncovered and where possible given a steer to serve GDR interests. The search for suitable IMs in the operational area was to continue with a special focus on the following categories: military and civilian members of NATO bodies in West Germany, Belgium, Great Britain, France, the USA and the European Community in Brussels. Americans working in Europe were to be targeted, as were all foreigners in the GDR, in particular visiting dignitaries, especially where they were party or organisational functionaries or members of Parliaments.

East German intelligence officers were asked to compile information on all operationally interesting people proposing to visit the GDR, all members of intelligence services and their agents encountered working against the Socialist States. An emphasis was to be placed on covering travel writers and students, particularly those studying law and economics, and all translators where these students were not members of left-wing organisations. Finally, all secretaries in official positions were to be targeted where possible.

This was the plan for 1986. We will see that in great measure, albeit with varying amounts of success, the Stasi managed to realise Mielke's aims. What proved to be the final plan was drawn up for 1989. Dated 6 December 1988, it looks very similar to the above document but it adds that 'a new quality was now required in the fight against the secret services of the USA, West Germany, Great Britain and France' who are increasingly trying to destabilise the GDR and construct an 'oppositional movement in it steered from the outside'.

# Appendix 3

# Names of Accredited GDR Diplomats

It is important to emphasise that many of those listed below were not Stasi spies.

| April 1980 | April 1981 | April 1982 | June 1983 | June/July 1984 |
| --- | --- | --- | --- | --- |
| Karl-Heinz Kern | Martin Bierbach | Martin Bierbach | Martin Bierbach | Gerhard Lindner |
| Heinz Knobbe | Heinz Knobbe | Heinz Knobbe | Heinz Knobbe | Gerhard Liebig |
| Arndt Schönherr | Arndt Schönherr | Arndt Schönherr | Arndt Schönherr | Erich Schwager |
| Manfred Käbel | Manfred Käbel | Manfred Käbel | Karlheinz Bauer | Karlheinz Bauer |
| Lutz Buschendorf | Lutz Buschendorf | Lutz Buschendorf | Hans Zabel | Hans Zabel |
| Karl Steiner | Karl Steiner | | Georg Menzel | Georg Menzel |
| Hans-Jürgen Brückner | Hans- Jürgen Brückner | Hans-Jürgen Brückner | Hans-Jürgen Brückner | Arnold Andres |
| Willi Lange | Willi Lange | Willi Lange | Bernd Schuster | Bernd Schuster |
| Bernd Wesser | | | Günter Siebert | Günter Siebert |
| Peter Escher | Peter Escher | Peter Escher | Oswald Schneidratus | Oswald Schneidratus |
| Roland Haufe | Klaus Herrmann | | Hans-Hendrik Kasper | Hans-Hendrik Kasper |
| Klaus Krupke | Klaus Krupke | Klaus Krupke | Klaus Krupke | |
| Bernhard Koch | Bernhard Koch | Bernhard Koch | | |
| Franz Beyer | Heinrich Lutzke | Heinrich Lutzke | Heinrich Lutzke | Heinrich Lutzke |
| Klaus Hörnig | Klaus Hörnig | Hartmut Linser | Hartmut Linser | Hartmut Linser |
| Siegfried Lafeldt | Siegfried Lafeldt | Siegfried Lafeldt | Edgar Uher | Edgar Uher |
| | Edgar Uher | Edgar Uher | Eva-Maria Uher | Eva-Maria Uher |
| | Christian Pech | Dietrich Grossmann | Dietrich Grossmann | Dietrich Grossmann |

| June 1985 | June 1986 | June 1987 | June 1988 | June 1989 |
|---|---|---|---|---|
| Gerhard Lindner | Gerhard Lindner | Gerhard Lindner | Gerhard Lindner | Joachim Mitdank |
| Gerhard Liebig | Heino Bock | Heino Bock | Heino Bock | Siegfried Reichel |
| Erich Schwager | Erich Schwager | Erich Schwager | Herbert Vorpahl | Herbert Vorpahl |
| Herbert Vorpahl | Herbert Vorpahl | Herbert Vorpahl | Alfred Schaller | Alfred Schaller |
| Heiner Kluge | Heiner Kluge | Heiner Kluge | Klaus Pfenning | Klaus Pfenning |
| Georg Menzel | Hans Georg Riegg | Hans-Georg Riegg | Hans-Georg Riegg | Hans-Georg Riegg |
| Arnold Andres | Manfred Rudolph | Manfred Rudolph | Heiner Kluge | Heiner Kluge |
| Bernd Schuster | Bernd Schuster | Rüdiger Wilhelm | Hans-Werner Koop | Gerhard Sander |
| Günter Siebert | Günter Siebert | Alfred Schaller | Manfred Rudolph | Manfred Rudolph |
| Oswald Schneidratus | Oswald Schneidratus | Oswald Schneidratus | Jörg Döring | Jörg Döring |
| Hans-Hendrik Kasper | Hans-Hendrik Kasper | Lili Bock | Ulrich Kempf | Michael Juhran |
| Ulrich Kempf | Ulrich Kempf | | Rüdiger Wilhelm | Rüdiger Wilhelm |
| Dieter Unger | Hans-Werner Koop | Hans-Werner Koop | Lili Bock | |
| Stefan Wetzel | Stefan Wetzel | | Friedbert Krebs | |
| Alfred Schröder | Wilhelm Koch | Wilhelm Koch | Gunter Voigtländer | Gunter Voigtländer |
| Edgar Uher | Edgar Uher | Bernd Huhn | Bernd Huhn | Bernd Huhn |
| Eva-Maria Uher | Eva-Maria Uher | | Wolfram Jork | Wolfram Jork |
| Dietrich Grossmann | Friedbert Krebs | Friedbert Krebs | Wilhelm Koch | Rainer Hesse |

There were a further sixteen or so members of the ancillary staff –
clerks, economic advisers and administrative officers; all of them
changed every three years.

# Appendix 4

## Speakers at Chatham House During the 1980s

They included: Maurice Couve de Murville, the former French Prime Minister; Roy Jenkins, the President of the European Commission, then head of the new SDP (a guest more than once); Abba Eban, the Foreign Minister of Israel; Christopher Mallaby, ambassador in Bonn and Paris, one of Britain's most influential foreign policy experts; Lord Soames; Geoffrey Pattie MP (the Defence Minister for the RAF); David Howell MP (then Secretary of State for Energy); Sir Anthony Parsons (then the UK's Permanent Representative to the United Nations); Lawrence Eagleburger (at that time US Assistant Secretary of State for European Affairs); Eugene Rostow (then Director of the US Arms Control Agency); Douglas Hurd (variously Minister of State at the Foreign Office and Foreign Secretary); Hans-Jochen Vogel, the leader of the German Social Democratic Party, the SPD; Dr Boutros Boutros-Ghali (at the time Egyptian Minister of Foreign Affairs); Vice-President George Bush; Francis Pym (then British Foreign Secretary); Volker Rühe (leading German Christian Democrat, subsequently General Secretary of the CDU and Defence Minister under Kohl); Denis Healey; Denis McShane; Pauline Neville-Jones (another of the brightest sparks in the British Foreign Office); Dr Jonathan Mirsky; Richard von Weizsäcker (then Governing Mayor of Berlin); Sir Reg Hibbert; Lord Shackleton; Dr David Owen (former British Foreign Secretary and at the time, leader of the Parliamentary Committee of the SDP); Sir

Clive Rose (an ex-ambassador to NATO and senior defence expert); Michael Foot MP, then leader of the Labour Party; Jacques Chirac; Geoffrey Howe; Kurt Biedenkopf (another leading German politician, and opponent of Herr Kohl); Dr Joseph Luns, then Secretary General of NATO; HRH Princess Anne; Johannes Rau (then leader of the SPD and today President of Germany); Shimon Peres (the Israeli Socialist leader); Mark Tully; Malcolm Rifkind MP; Dr Beryl Sprinkel of the World Bank; Professor Michael Kaser (a noted expert on Communism); General Sir Hugh Beach; Paul Warnke; Michael Heseltine MP (then Defence Minister); François Mitterrand (then President of France); Lynda Chalker MP; Rauf Denktash; Professors Archie Brown and Alex Pravda (both acclaimed experts on Communism, the former listened to by Margaret Thatcher); Admiral Sir James Eberle; Patrick Jenkin MP; Sir Nicholas Henderson; Timothy Garton Ash, the Oxford specialist on Eastern Europe; Chris Patten MP (a Government Minister and later Chairman of the Conservative Party and European Commissioner); Edward Heath MP; Sir Percy Cradock (a foreign affairs adviser to the Prime Minister); the Rev. Michael Bourdeaux (principal of Keston College, which had numerous secret links to Church dissidents in the Soviet Union and elsewhere in Eastern Europe); Sir Curtis Keeble (then HM Ambassador to the Soviet Union); Peter Riddell (the influential journalist); Lord Chalfont; Malcolm Fraser (then Prime Minister of Australia); David Steel (then leader of the Liberal Party); Lord Young of Graffham (a Government Minister and confidant of Mrs Thatcher); Wolfgang Schäuble (the leading German Christian Democrat); Admiral of the Fleet, Lord Lewin; Field Marshall Lord Carver; President Ronald Reagan; and Mikhail Gorbachev.[3]

# Appendix 5

# The Stasi's Operations in Britain: The SIRA Material

## The Espionage of the HVA

This material gives precise details of every significant HVA operation in the UK. So far the data has been confined to the 1980s. SIRA XII (Evaluation) and SIRA IX (Secret Foreign Intelligence) are the most important data banks. To date, SIRA XII has been decoded for the years 1969–87; SIRA IX has been decoded for 1988 and 1989 only.

The SIRA archive, it should be emphasised, supplies the code-names of the 'source', or *Quelle*, and the material gathered displays special areas of interest.

*1981*
16.02.81, 'Brücke', 17.02.81, 'Current Internal Political Situation in the UK – Margaret Thatcher'/28.02.81, 'Eckhart', 25.03.81, 'UK FCO and Poland – Social Causes of Unrest'/28.02.81, 'Eckhart', 06.04.81, RIIA Study: NATO Financial Policy on Poland/17.03.81, 'Jäger', 18.03.81, 'British Attitudes Towards the Proposals of the CPSU'/10.04.81, 'Jäger', 14.04.81, 'Planned Conference on the GDR in the UK'/15.03.81, 'Dreher', 02.04.81, 'British Industry'/30.04.81, 'Eckhart', 21.05.81, Speech by Former Ambassador to Saudi Arabia on Middle East after Reagan's Victory/12.06.81, 'Brücke', 19.06.81, 'Meeting of the Central Committee of the CPGB

on 11.06.81'/08.08.81, 'Granit', 12.08.81, 'Forces in the Labour Party'/11.08.81, 'Rat', 12.08.81, Document, 'Labour Party Executive View on Withdrawal from the EEC'/12.08.81, 'Dreher', 14.08.81, 'The Attitude of the UK Government to Trade with the GDR'/14.08.81, 'Eckhart', 18.08.81, 'Anthony Hore, Richard Portes, Yves Laulan: British Institute for International Relations and Economic Relations Between the West and East of Europe'/18.08.81, 'Eckhart', 10.09.81, Conference, Commercial Relations Between Eastern and Western Europe/18.08.81, 'Eckhart', 16.10.81, UK Foreign Office Minister on Nigeria Conference/20.09.81, 'Dreher', 26.09.81, Document, 'British Attitude to Intra-German Trade'/24.09.81, 'Eckhart', 26.09.81, Document, 'British Ideas on the Creation of NATO Contingents for Operations Outside Europe'/15.10.81, 'Eckhart', 20.10.81, Document, 'Chatham House on Armaments Industry'/15.10.81, 'Eckhart', 20.10.81, Document, 'Chatham House Study'/20.10.81, 'Eckhart', 11.11.81, RIIA Study on Arms Control in Europe/ 27.11.81, 'Eckhart', 01.12.81, Document, 'The Evaluation of the International Position of Chatham House'/09.12.81, 'Holz', 11.12.81, Document, 'Internal Evaluation of the British National Committee for Economic Development on Industrial Policy in Europe'/14.11.81, 'Eckhart', 30.12.81, SSES Report on Origins of East German National Identity Since 1971/01.12.81, 'Eckhart', 17.12.81, RIIA Assessment on Development of International Situation/01.12.81, 'Eckhart', 17.12.81, Symposium, Arab Research Centre, London.

*1982*
08.01.82, 'Direktor', 08.02.82, The Opinion of the Foreign Office Member Jenkins, Previously a Member of the British Embassy in the GDR on Current Political Problems/28.01.82, 'Eckhart', 29.01.82, 'The Foreign Policy of the SDP'/15.04.82, 'Holz', 06.04.82, 'Thatcher, Pym, Hurd, Onslow and Cockfield; on the Impact of the Falklands Conflict'/06.04.82, 'Eckhart', Reliability B, 12.04.82, 'Labour Attitudes to the Falklands Conflict'/20.04.82, 'Eckhart', 28.04.82, Document, 'A British Evaluation of the Falklands War'/16.04.82, 'Eckhart', 18.05.82, 'A Conservative View

of the Falklands Conflict'/28.04.82, 'Helfried', 28.04.82, 'Anti-GDR Attitudes in the UK; on Frank Allaun'/11.05.82, 'Eckhart', 14.07.82, 'Power and Violence in East Germany: the SED'/13.05.82, 'Eckhart', 14.05.82, 'The Corn Weapon'/14.05.82, 'Eckhart', 14.07.82, 'European Contribution to NATO'/19.05.82, 'Eckhart', 10.08.82, 'UK–China Technical Cooperation'/21.07.82, 'Eckhart', 23.07.82, 'UK Defence Policy After the Falklands War'/28.07.82, 'Eckhart', 29.07.82, 'The SDP's Evaluation of the Internal and External Effects of the Falklands War'/30.09.82, 'Doktor', 01.10.82, 'The SDP Leadership's Views on UK Political Situation'/10.10.82, 'Dreher', 20.10.82, 'The View of the UK Government on Kohl's Government'/08.10.82, 'Eckhart', 17.11.82 'UK Policy on China'/11.10.82, 'Eckhart', 13.10.82, 'The View of the Foreign Policy Committee of the Labour Party on the Creation of a CDU/CSU/FDP Government in the Federal Republic of Germany'/17.11.82, 'Helfried', 18.12.82, 'A British View of the Election of Andropov'/23.11.82, 'Erich', 26.11.82, Document, 'British Planning in the Event of a Nuclear War'/24.11.82, 'Gregor', 27.11.82, 'The Conservative Party and East–West Relations'/ 27.11.82, 'Eckhart', 29.11.82, 'Dr David Owen as Foreign Policy Spokesman of the SDP'/01.12.82, 'Eckhart', 04.04.83, Third Conference Gulf Cooperation Council: Conclusions/07.12.82, 'Erich', 09.12.82, 'CND'/21.12.82, 'Doktor', 11.02.83, 'David Owen: an Internal Evaluation of the Current Political Situation by the Leadership of the SDP'/21.12.82, 'Doktor', 11.02.83, 'SDP Leadership Views on Current Political Situation'/21.12.82, 'Eckhart', 02.03.83, 'Trident Programme'.

*1983*

01.01.83, 'Eckhart', 06.06.83, Report, 'UK Committee for Peace and Security in Europe'/01.01.83, Fröbel, 27.07.83, 'British Maps'/07.01.83, 'Erich', 01.01.83, 'CND and Westberlin'/13.01.83, 'Doktor', 19.01.83, 'The Position of the British Government on the Geneva Talks'/25.02.83, 'Eckhart', 29.03.83, 'Burden Sharing in NATO – Problems'/01.03.83, 'Kunze', 07.03.83, 'Edward Leigh, Julian Lewis, Rolihan, Karpel, Coates, Allerton'/02.03.83, 'Eckhart', 12.03.83, 'Foot, Shore, Kinnock and Healey'/10.03.83,

'Eckhart', 18.03.83, 'The Trotskyists in the UK'/26.03.83, 'Kunze', 05.04.83, 'END'/01.04.83, 'Eckhart', 28.04.83, 'An Evaluation of the Leadership of the SDP and the Forthcoming Elections'/ 01.04.83, 'Eckhart', 12.05.83, 'UK Position on Preparation of Williamsburg Summit'/01.04.83, 'Eckhart', 30.05.83, 'Current Questions of UK Peace Movement re Second Konvent. Westberlin'/03.04.83, 'Eckhart', 07.04.83, 'The UK Position Towards the Williamsburg Summit'/01.05.83, 'Haussler', 11.05.83, 'Naval Armaments'/20.05.83, 'Kunze', 03.06.83, 'The British Church Council's View of Activities in the GDR'/13.06.83, 'Erich', 20.06.83, 'The Representatives of CND'/20.07.83, 'Dreher', 26.07.83, 'UK Civil Defence'/20.07.83, 'Kunze', 29.07.83, 'The UK Peace Movement'/15.09.83, 'Eckhart', 22.09.83, 'Nuclear Weapons in the UK and France'/01.10.83, 'Eckhart', 01.11.83, 'Current Situation of CPGB'/20.11.83, 'Eckhart', 28.11.83, 'British Foreign and Military Policy'/01.12.83, 'Kunze', 12.12.83, 'The Dissent in Mrs Thatcher's Cabinet'.

*1984*
01.01.84, 'Kunze', 20.01.84, 'The Institute for Strategic Studies and East–West Relations'/01.01.84, 'Eckhart', 05.03.84, 'South Africa'/01.01.84, 'Fröbel', 30.01.84, 'East–West Trade'/03.01.84, Eckhart, 07.02.84, 'Planned Manoeuvres of British Navy'/13.01.84, 'Gerald', The Farewell Meeting of FRG Ambassador Dr Ruhfuss with Defence Minister Heseltine/01.02.84, 'Eckhart', 23.02.84, Document, 'UK View on FRG–GDR Relations'/02.02.84, 'Kunze', 16.02.84, 'NATO'/20.02.84, 'Wald', 27.02.84, 'UK Policy in Eastern Europe'/28.02.84, 'Eckhart', 09.03.84, 'CPGB'/01.03.84, 'Eckhart', 09.04.84, 'Mozambique Contract'/24.03.84, 'Kunze', 27.03.84, Document, 'English Defence'/01.05.84, 'Eckhart', 12.07.84, 'South African President's Visit to UK'/10.05.84, 'Kunze', 18.05.84, 'The Use of the British Armaments Industry for Civilian Purposes'/10.05.84, 'Lehrer', 18.05.84, Document, 'The CPGB'/01.06.84, 'Freundin', 12.07.84, Document, 'END'/01.11.84, 'Kunze', 08.12.84, 'The Planned Activities of the British Peace Movement CND in December 1984'/07.11.84, 'Freundin', 13.11.84, Document, 'Einhorn, Childs and Williams'/26.11.84, 'Eckhart',

12.12.84, 'The Position of Leading British Military Figures on Waging Nuclear War'/10.12.84, 'Freundin', 21.12.84, Document, 'Hella Pick and END'.

*1985*

01.01.85, 'Wien', 01.10.85, 'The Evaluation of the Labour Party and Mrs Thatcher's Policy'/01.01.85, 'Eckhart', 29.01.85, 'CPGB'/01.01.85, 'Kunze', 06.02.85, 'Sheila Taylor, John Sandford, E.P. Thompson, Barbara Einhorn'; Detailed Data on the Establishment, Goals and Work of END/01.01.85, 'Freundin', 26.02.85, 'Perspectives on GDR Peace Activities'/01.01.85, 'Wien', 18.02.85, 'UK Nuclear Weapons Systems'/20.02.85, 'Johann', 01.07.85, Document, 'UK–GDR Relations'/01.03.85, 'Eckhart', 15.03.85, 'The German Foreign Office's Influence on Geoffrey Howe'/01.04.85, 'Eckhart', 24.05.85, Document, 'The British Defence White Book'/01.04.85, 'Eckhart', 12.06.85, 'The Sacharov Hearing'/26.04.85, 'Freundin', 20.05.85, 'END and Travel'/01.05.85, 'Eckhart', 16.05.85, Document, 'The CPGB'/01.05.85, 'Eckhart', 06.06.85, Conference, UK Chamber of Commerce/06.06.85, 'Eckhart', 25.06.85, Document, 'SDI'/01.07.85, 'Eckhart', 24.07.85, Document, 'CPGB'/01.07.85, 'Kraft', 20.08.85, Report on Speech of Mozambique Foreign Minister at Wilton Park/11.07.85, 'Freundin', 10.08.85, 'The DDR Group in END'/08.08.85, 'Kraft', 20.08.85, Document, 'A UK View of Eureka'/29.08.85, 'Kunze', 10.09.85, 'The SDP's View of SDI'/17.10.85, 'Genf', 28.10.85, 'UK Policy Towards the Soviet Disarmament Plans'/01.11.85, 'Kraft', 10.01.86, 'UK Peace Movement and GDR'/01.11.85, 'Berg', Document, 20.11.85, 'A British View of the Development of the GDR'/01.11.85, 'Eckhart', 27.11.85, Reactions to Reagan–Gorbachev Summit – UK Views of US Ambassadors Female Circle in London/11.12.85, 'Kraft', 16.01.86, 'UK–Albanian Relations'.

*1986*

14.01.86, 'Berg', 10.02.86, 'The Oil Price'/28.01.86, 'Birke', 10.02.86, 'The Resignation of Michael Heseltine'/01.02.86, 'Eckhart', 11.03.86, 'UK View on SED Congress'/01.03.86, 'Berg', 19.03.86, 'The Economic Policy of the British Government'/26.03.86,

'Kraft', 16.04.86, Document, 'UK Views on SDI Research'/01.04.86, 'Eckhart', 06.05.86, UK Participants GDR Round Table 28–29.04.86/ 23.04.86, 'Eckhart', 20.05.85, 'The GDR Round Table: On Childs, Moreton, Roper, Pearce, Neville-Jones'/29.05.86, 'Kraft', 10.07.86, Document, 'The British Defence White Book 1986'/01.07.86, 'Eckhart', 08.08.86, 'UK View of Paris END Convention'/09.07.86, 'Eckhart', 01.06.86, UK Labour Party Study Group to SED Congress/28.07.86, 'Kraft', 18.09.86, Document, 'Research Work on SDI Project'/01.10.86, 'Kraft', 11.11.86, 'UK Assessment of World Peace Congress'/01.10.86, 'Kraft', 21.10.86, 'The Conservatives' and Labour Party's Election Plans'/17.10.86, 'Kraft', 05.11.86, Document, 'UK Assessment of SDI Programme'/01.11.86, 'Wald', 26.11.86, 'British–American Relations and their Input into Domestic Politics in the UK'/20.11.86, 'Kraft', 12.12.86, 'Development of END'/21.11.86, 'Kraft', 08.01.87, Document, 'US Military Structure and Staff'/01.12.86, 'Kraft', 20.01.87, Document, 'Third END Convention, Coventry'.

*1987*
01.01.87, 'Rat', 20.01.87, 'Relations Between the EEC and the Socialist States'/13.01.87, 'Kraft', 02.02.87, Document, 'Structure of UK Armed Forces'/01.02.87, 'Kraft', 23.02.87, 'Berlin's 750th Anniversary'/01.03.87, 'Pepp', 14.04.87, 'Information from Leading Economic Circles on the Leipzig Fair'/11.03.87, 'Kraft', 14.04.87, Document, 'UK Views on SDI Research'/06.03.87, 'Kraft', 20.04.87, 'UK Position on US Position on ABM Treaty'/10.04.87, 'Kraft', 04.05.87, 'Amnesty International'/10.04.87, 'Kraft', 23.04.87, Document, 'END Convention, Coventry'/16.04.87, 'Kraft', 12.05.87, Document, 'Developments in the CPGB'/ 14.05.87, 'Kraft', 17.06.87, Document, 'The Defence White Book'/02.07.87, 'Mark', 02.10.87, Document, 'The EP Socialist Groups' Views on the Socialist States'/29.07.87, 'Kraft', 29.07.87, Document, 'Development of Nuclear Weapons'.

# Incomplete SIRA Listings

24.03.87, 'Stern'/13.01.87, 'Johann', 'An Evaluation of the Development of the GDR from a British Viewpoint'/15.01.87, 'Johann', 'The British Attitude Towards the 750th Anniversary of Berlin'/20.01.87, 'Johann', 'Thatcher's Goals for her USSR Visit'/'Kraft', 'Defence Policy of the Labour Party; British Attitudes on the US View on the ABM Treaty'/17.03.87, 'Johann', 'Western Reaction to the Soviet ABM Disarmament Plans'/06.04.87, 'Diskont', 'An Evaluation by the Midland Bank on the Economic Situation in Bulgaria'/14.05.87, 'Kraft', 'A British Position on Soviet Disarmament Plans and Preparations for Elections in the UK'/14.05.87, 'Kraft', 'The Defence Policy of the Labour Party'/14.05.87, 'Kraft', 'The Labour Party Executive's Views of the Elections'/03.07.87, 'Kraft', 'Conclusions of Political Circles to the UK Elections'/04.08.87, 'Kraft', 'The Shadow Cabinet of the Labour Party'/02.01.87, 'Johann', 'Perspectives of USA/USSR Relations in the View of US Ambassador in Germany, Richard Burt'/16.06.87, 'Kraft', 'UK–GDR Relations'/15.07.87, 'Kraft', 'The Election Results in the UK'/17.08.87, 'Kraft, 'The Labour Shadow Cabinet'.

# Acknowledgements

Many people helped me with this book. First and foremost, however, my thanks are due to Frank Zwicker, archivist at the Stasi Archives, and Dr Rüdiger Stang. Both of them exceeded the call of duty in delving into the archives at my request, retrieving fragments of files and spending many hours explaining how the Stasi worked, confirming what the files revealed and what they concealed. Dr Bernhard Wilhelm of Berlin is also owed special thanks since he first encouraged me in 1987, before anyone could know its archives would become available, to take a research interest in the Stasi. David Rose of the *Observer* was another huge source of encouragement, as were his fellow journalists Ian Cobain of *The Times* and Steve Doughty of the *Daily Mail*. My work with them shows how fruitful it can be for academics to work with journalists. Bill Hamilton, my agent, was a model of what one might hope an agent would be: careful, constructive and shrewd. Andrew Gordon, my editor, agreed to take me on at an early stage, and repeatedly gave me excellent advice. My biggest debt, however, is to Linda, my wife. Without the support of each and every one of these people, it would have been impossible to write this book. Needless to say, however, the views expressed in it are entirely my own.

Substantial help, in the form of advice and interviews (with dates where they fed into my narrative), came from the following, to whom I am very grateful indeed, especially, perhaps, those I was obliged to confront with unpleasant facts from the Stasi files: six unnamed members of the Security Service, the Secret Intelligence Service, the CIA and the FBI; members of the Oxford Intelligence Seminar, 2001 and 2002; members of the York Anglo-German Society, of which I have the honour to be President; Christopher Andrew; Bert Becker; Oliver Berlau (interview, 15 October 1998); Sir John Birch (15 May 2001); David Blow (30 September 1998); Nicky Bolster; Sir Rodric Braithwaite; Mark Brayne (31 August 2001); Sir Nigel Broomfield (October 1998); a Friend of Chatham House (22 March 2002 and subsequently); David Childs (30 September 1998); Cornelius Creutzfeldt; Oldrich Czerny; Richard Davy (29 December 2000); Bob Dixon (on several occasions, 2000–2002); Mike Dennis (24 November 1998); Klaus Eichner (31 May 1994); Barbara Einhorn (4 December 1998); Erhard Eppler; Timothy Everard (27 August 1998); Irene Fick (22 October 2001, 17 January 2002); Mike Fröhnel; Oleg Gordievsky (22 September 1998); Sarah Hann; Karl-Günther von Hase (12 January 2002); Michael Herman; Marianne Howarth; Lynne Jones (16 September 1998); Bruce Kent; Thomas Kielinger; Timothy Kirkhope MEP; Manfred Kittlaus (on several occasions, 1994–8); Richard Klein; Dr Hubertus Knabe (29 February 2002); Hermann Kreutzer; James Lamond; Sir Stephen Lander and unnamed colleagues (3 March, 16 October and 22 December 2000 and 1 July 2002); John le Carré; Dr Julian Lewis MP; Christian Leitz; Jim McAdams (29 April 2002); John Milfull; Pauline Neville-Jones; Bill Newton-Smith; Canon Paul Oestreicher (23 August 2001); Ulrike Poppe (15 September 1998); Lord Roper (22 June 2001); John Sandford (17 November 1998); David Stafford; Roger Scruton (27 October 1998); Harald Strunz; Günter Töpfer; Hans Völkner (31 May 1994); Jonathan Wright; Ian Wallace; William Wallace; Dr Philip Walters (22 October 1998); Bernd Zufelde (25 August 1998).

## Documents Used

This book relies on the following documents held in the Stasi Archive in Berlin: SIRA Teildatenbank 12 1579 Res 201 DB 12 SE

8221268; MfS ZAIG 6300c; MfS HVA 154; MfS ZAIG 2140; MfS ZAIG 7494; MfS HVA IX CE; MfS HVA 58; MfS HVA 100; MfS HVA 169; MfS HVA 57; MfS HVA 386; MfS Rechtsstelle 1061; MfS – Abt Finanzen 1579; MfS – Abt Finanzen 1653; MfS HA XXII 19022; DN 'Clarus' – Rost Dieter I, II; MfS – AIOBE 16603191; MfS HA XX AKG II; MfS HA XX AKG 188; MfS HA XX AKG K/2955/88; MfS HA XXII 19156; MfS HA XXII 6065/1; MfS HA XXII 6083/13; MfS HA XXII 19156; MfS HA XXII 17219 (Rote Brigaden, IRA, CCC); MfS HA XXII 19022 Operation 'Feldwebel'; MfS HA XX 518; MfS HA I 1641; MfS HA II 15605 Eberle, James Henry Fuller; MfS HA II 15610; MfS HA II 21648; MfS Allg P 7969/73 Sternberg; MfS 17203/91 'Louis' XVIII 554/87; MfS HA XVIII 11260; MfS Abt X 837; MfS HA XX/ZMA 20585 Bd 1, 2, 6, 7, 8; MfS ZAIG 6300C; MfS HA II 15610 Roper, John Francis Hodges; MfS HA II 21648; MfS AP 17203/91; MfS HA I 1639; MfS HA I 1641; MfS HAI 1643; MfS HA I 1644; MfS HA I 1647; MfS AP 5614/86 Bd 1 and 2; MfS – AIOBE 16799/91 'Waldner' Bd 1 and 2; MfS HA XX 3225; Leipzig KSII 2688/91; Leipzig AIM 1825/91 Bd 1, 2, 3 'Armin'; Leipzig AIM 2127/91 Bd 1 and 2 'Diana'; Leipzig AIM 2008/91 Bd 1 and 2; HA XXII/Ka/294 (tape); MfS HA XX AKG/II 109; MfS HA XX/AKG/II 108; MfS HVA 58; MfS HA XX14 5699.

# Notes

## Note to Chronology

1. Margaret Thatcher, *The Downing Street Years*. See in particular pp. 866–72.

## Notes to Introduction

1. See Christopher Andrew and D. Dilks, *The Missing Dimension*. The editors of this groundbreaking book write: 'Secret intelligence has been described by one distinguished diplomat [Sir Alexander Cadogan] as the "missing dimension of most of diplomatic history". The same dimension is also absent from most political and much military history. Academic historians have frequently tended either to ignore intelligence altogether, or to treat it as of little importance . . . Historians have a . . . tendency to pay too much attention to the evidence which survives, and to make too little allowance for what does not. Intelligence has become a "missing dimension" first and foremost because its written records are so difficult to come by', pp. 1–2.
2. According to Jens Gieseke, at the end of October 1989 the Ministry consisted of 91,015 members of whom 71,233 held the rank equivalent of officer, 2,232 were officers for special duties (OibEs), 143 so-called anonymous members, 185 civilian employees, 13,073 soldiers on secondment and 2,301 on other duties. Jens Gieseke, *Mielke-Konzern: die Geschichte der Stasi 1945–1990*, Stuttgart: DVA (2001), p. 70.
3. Karl Wilhelm Fricke, *Die DDR-Staatssicherheit*, p. 8.

4. Hubertus Knabe, *West-Arbeit des MfS*, p. 61.

5. R. F. Gellately, *The Gestapo and German Society*. Arguably the Gestapo's grip was hugely strengthened by those many ordinary Nazis who happily collaborated with it.

6. Compare Konrad Jarausch, 'A Double Burden', in Jörn Leonhard and Lothar Funk (eds), *Ten Years of German Unification*, pp. 98–111.

7. Equivalent ratios in the Czech Republic were 1:867 and in Poland 1:1,574. Gieseke, loc. cit.

8. Interviews with Dr Rüdiger Stang and Frank Zwicker (Stasi Archive, Berlin) and Dr Hubertus Knabe (Hohenschönhausen Memorial Site), 28–29 February 2002, Berlin. See also Gesamtdeutsches Institut/ Bundesanstalt für gesamtdeutsche Aufgaben, *Dokumentation zum Staatssicherheitsdienst der ehemaligen DDR in 6 Teilen*. Volume 1 contains numerous post-1990 reports on these matters.

9. Knabe, *West-Arbeit des MfS*, p. 150.

10. See Mielke's various directives, and Wolf, pp. 205 ff., 286, where the USA is called the 'main enemy'. Markus Wolf with Anne McElvoy, *Man Without a Face*, pp. xi ff.

11. Wolf, p. 196, writes that he failed to criticise loudly and early enough the 'workings' of a judicial system so closely allied to the state. Knabe, *West-Arbeit des MfS*, p. 33, is one of several writers to expose Wolf's special pleading on this issue.

12. *Official Report (Hansard)*, 21 October 1999, vol. 336, c 555.

13. Information from a CIA source, London, June–December 2001.

14. *MI5: The Security Service*, 3rd edn, introduction by Sir Stephen Lander. We should not forget that it is only since 1989 that the UK authorities formally admitted the very existence of MI5 and MI6; MI5 has provided a broad and non-specific account of its activities on three occasions since then. Today it is considerably easier to write accurately about what the Stasi did than about what MI5 did during the same period – see *MI5: The Security Service*. The first edition was published in 1993, the second in 1996.

15. Stella Rimington, *Open Secret* (2nd edn), pp. 140–1.

16. Ibid., pp. 139–40.

17. Information provided by the House of Commons Library Research Service to Dr Julian Lewis MP, 30 November 2000.

18. Confidential comment by a former British counter-intelligence chief, 26 April 2001.

19. See David Gill, 'Breaking New Ground' in Leonhard and Funk (eds), *Ten Years of German Unification*, pp. 139–49.

20. From 1949 to 1992 103,823 people were investigated by the (West) German authorities for complicity in Nazi human rights abuses. Of these some 6 per cent were convicted, of whom 85 per cent were convicted of minor crimes only. This means that only five out of every 1,000 people suspected of Nazi crimes was punished (with seven out of every 1,000 investigated). See Anthony Glees, *Reinventing Germany*, p. 31; and A. James McAdams, *Judging the Past*. McAdams argues that, on the whole, the Federal Republic has not repeated earlier mistakes and not done a bad job in addressing the Communist past. His important case, however, relies on the very small number of trials of political and military leaders, and ordinary soldiers who had shot East Germans seeking refuge in the West: Stasi abusers do not come into his equation except where they were forced to resign from their jobs.

21. Thanks are due to the Bishop of Oxford, Richard Harries, for sourcing this quote, which is also used in the film *Air Force One*.

22. Several interviews with Dr Rüdiger Stang, Frank Zwicker and Dr Hubertus Knabe, 1998–2002.

23. McAdams, *Judging the Past*, p. 69.

24. Ibid., pp. 85–6.

## Notes to Chapter 1

1. Interview with Siegfried Rataizick, *Der Tagesspiegel*, 15 May 2002.

2. *Der Stacheldraht*, May 2002, p. 10.

3. *Introducing the GDR* (Dresden: Verlag Zeit im Bild, 1997).

4. This was a point continually made: another official GDR publication, *The GDR Review*, trumpeted the apparent fact that in 1981 99.86 per cent of 'valid votes' were cast for National Front candidates and that the East German leaders, Honecker and Stoph, deserved to be lauded as 'proven public figures who enjoy the confidence of the population'. *GDR Review*, 8/81.

5. See Anthony Glees, *Reinventing Germany*, p. 218, and Gesamtdeutsches Institut/Bundesanstalt für gesamtdeutsche Aufgaben, *Dokumentation zum Staatssicherheitsdienst der ehemaligen DDR in 6 Teilen*, vol. 5.

6. *GDR Review*, 8/81.

7. Ibid., 2/82.

8. Jonathan Steele, *Socialism With a German Face*, pp. 4, 5, 12, 75.

9. Klaus von Beyme (ed.), *Policymaking in the GDR*: 'There is the watch regiment of the Ministry of State Security (more than 5,000 men) whose task it is to protect government buildings and institutions', p. 174.

10. Hermann Weber, *Die DDR*, p. 105.

11. Klaus-Dieter Muller, ' "Jeder kriminelle Morder is mir lieber . . ." Haftbedingungen für politische Haftlinge in der SBZ und der DDR und ihre Veranderungen von 1945–89', p. 10.

12. *Introducing the GDR*, pp. 37–76.

13. Ibid., p. 64.

14. Ibid., p. 11.

15. Ibid., p. 13.

16. Ibid., p. 21.

17. Ibid., p. 45.

18. There are interesting distinctions and parallels to be drawn here with the Third Reich, which made not the slightest pretence at respecting human rights. Indeed, whereas the GDR produced more than one written constitution, the Third Reich produced none (the Weimar Constitution of 1919 was never formally abrogated). Yet in both states, the regime's disregard for the rule of its own law served the same ends: to terrorise and intimidate the German subjects of those regimes. This point was made in 1981 by Timothy Garton Ash, *Und Willst Du Nicht*, p. 23. He speaks of '*kalkulierte Abschreckungsmittel*'. He points out that *Neues Deutschland* published the text of the 1975 Helsinki Final Act which spoke of the aim of 'free movement and contact' on the Continent. See also Michael Klopfer and Gerhard Michael, *Das Stasi unterlagen Gesetz und die Pressefreiheit*.

19. Garton Ash, *Und Willst Du Nicht*, p. 177.

20. See Die Gedenkstätte für die Opfer politischer Gewalt et al., *Die Vergangenheit lässt uns los . . . Haftbedingungen politischer Gefangener in der SBZ/DDR und deren gesundheitliche Folgen* (1997), pp. 15, 129–43.

21. See Ludwig A. Rehlinger, *Freikauf*.

22. Weber, *Die DDR*, p. 105 (my emphasis).

23. See, for example, Lex Hornsby (ed.), *Profile of East Germany*; Arthur M. Hanhardt, *The German Democratic Republic*; and John P. Hoover, *East Germany*.

24. Childs, in Hornsby, *Profile*, pp. 18, 22–5.

25. Charles S. Maier, *Dissolution*, pp. xi, 82 ff.

26. Ibid., p. 94.

27. Karl Wilhelm Fricke, *Die DDR-Staatssicherheit*; *Politischer Stafvollzug in der DDR*; and his *Opposition und Widerstand in der DDR*. Weber, *Die DDR*, p. 159, praises Fricke and testifies to the uniqueness of his work in all studies of East Germany. Even so Weber devotes only one paragraph in his entire book to the activities of the MfS, and only ten pages to the general subject of 'opposition and persecution' in which there is only one vague reference taken from Fricke to the effect that there had been 4,000 political prisoners in the GDR.

28. Weber, *Die DDR*, loc. cit.

29. *Amnesty International UK* Country Reports after 1975, and publications after 1962, held at Westminster Reference Library.

30. Norman Naimark, 'To Know Everything', p. 1.

31. See *Materialien der Enquete-Kommission 'Aufarbeitung von Geschichte und Folgen des SED Diktaturs in Deutschland'*, 30 vols (Baden-Baden: Nomos Verlag, 1995); 18 vols paperback edn (Frankfurt am Main: Suhrkamp Verlag, 1995).

32. See Markus Wolf with Anne McElvoy, *Man Without a Face*, pp. xi ff.

33. Joachim Gauck et al., *Die Stasi-Akten*, pp. 69–72. Gauck writes: 'The question of who controlled whom was never asked because state apparatus, party apparatus and security apparatus were all melted into a closely fitting union.'

34. Naimark, 'To Know Everything', p. 2.

35. *Die Vergangenheit*, pp. 13, 15, 24. Information from Manfred Kittlaus, Head of ZERV, Berlin Police, Ministerialdirektor a. D. Hermann Kreutzer, Dr Bernhard Wilhelm, Berlin, May 1997.

36. HELP e V Hilfsorganisation für die Opfer politische Gewalt in Europa, Selbstdarstellung, Dokumentation, Information. Ein Help Report 1999, p. 55.

37. See, for example, David Rose and Anthony Glees, *Observer*, 10 August 1997, and 4 July 1994. Also Gerhard Finn and Karl Wilhelm Fricke, *Politischer Strafvollzug in der DDR*; Gerhard Finn, *Sachsenhausen 1936–1950*.

38. Interview with Frau Margret Bechler, 17 June 1997. See also her book, *Warten auf Antwort*.

39. Interviews published with David Rose in the *Observer*, 4 July 1994 and 10 August 1997. See also Anthony Glees, 'Social Transformation Studies and Human Rights Abuses in East Germany after 1945', in *German Politics*, vol. 7, no. 3, pp. 165–89.

40. A. James McAdams, *Judging the Past*, p. 14.

41. See Anthony Glees and David Rose, *Observer*, 10 August 1997.

42. Falco Werkentin, 'Zur Dimension politischer Inhaftierungen 1949–89', in Die Gedenkstätte für die Opfer politischer Gewalt et al., *Die Vergangenheit*, p. 77.

43. Written information from Hermann Kreutzer, Berlin, 28 February 1998 (Kurt–Schumacher–Kreis document: prepared for the Federal government, published at the Angeburger Allee 41, 14055 Berlin); *Guardian*, 7 August 2001.

44. *Die Vergangenheit*, pp. 78, 129–43.

45. Werkentin, *Die Vergangenheit*, pp. 136, 137.

46. Information from Hermann Kreutzer, himself imprisoned in Bautzen, 11 June 1996, interviewed in Berlin. Kreutzer alleges that at least 170,000 individuals were arrested by the 'M-Apparats', German Communist agents of the Russians, from 1945 to 1947, of whom he, a Social Democrat from Thuringia, was but one. Some 60–70,000 died of starvation and typhoid. Kreutzer claims that many of those who were arrested were considered to constitute political or potential political opposition to Communism, as he was himself.

47. *Die Vergangenheit*, pp. 153–9, detailing the testimony of Albert Wesemeyer, arrested in 1948 for Social Democratic activity (making contact with Schumacher, for example) in Erfurt. He had been in prison for four years during the Third Reich. See also Dieter Rieke (ed.), *Sozialdemokraten als Opfer im Kampf gegen die rote Diktatur: Arbeitsmaterialien zur politischen Bildung* (Bonn: Friedrich Ebert Foundation, 1994). He states that from 1948 to 1950 some 200,000 Social Democrats were persecuted, or forced to flee. Five thousand were imprisoned, of whom four hundred died (p. 6).

48. Thanks are due to the British Council, the *Observer* and, more recently, BBC TV Current Affairs, for funding research on these accounts in Germany from 1994 to 1998. Interviews were conducted with Dr Bernhard Wilhelm, Ministerialdirektor i. R. Hermann Kreutzer, Heinz Gerull, Mike Fröhnel, Frau Dr R. Camphausen, E. O. Hellwig-Wilson, Jörg Drieselmann, Rainer Lippmann, Harald Strunz, Günter Töpfer MdA, Polizeidirektor Manfred Kittlaus (head of ZERV), Margret Bechler (Wedel). Also Klaus Eichner and Hans Völkner, formerly of the MfS.

49. See Sigurd Binski (ed.), *Zwischen Waldheim und Workuta*, with an introduction by Karl Wilhelm Fricke.

50. See Bechler, *Warten auf Antwort*.

51. Ibid., pp. 20, 61–3. David Childs and Richard Popplewell note in

*The Stasi*, p. 96, 'The 1968 GDR constitution was not as liberal as that of 1949 but it had the usual clauses safeguarding freedoms of speech, assembly and association (arts 27, 28, 29) and freedom of conscience and belief was upheld in art. 20 whilst the secrecy of post and telephone was "guaranteed" under art. 31.'

52. See Werkentin, Die Gedenkstätte für die Opfer politischer Gewalt et al., *Die Vergangenheit*.

53. Compare Richard Bessel, 'Police of a New Type: Police and Society in East Germany after 1945', in *German History*, vol. 10, no. 3, 1992, pp. 290–301. He writes: 'Having to live a lie ... may have induced people [in East Germany] all the more to repress their own politically dangerous feelings and identify with the Socialist order which [the police] outwardly represented.'

54. See Jeffrey Herf, *Divided Memory*, in particular the account of the persecution of the so-called 'Cosmopolitan opposition' in East Germany after 1949.

55. McAdams, *Judging the Past*, pp. 9, 26.

56. Gesamtdeutsches Institut/Bundesanstalt für gesamtdeutsche Aufgaben, *Dokumentation zum Staatssicherheitsdienst der ehemaligen DDR in 6 Teilen*; see vol. 1, pp. 91–3.

57. Evidence provided by Peter-Michael Diestel, the first post-revolutionary Minister of the Interior, charged with dismantling the Stasi in 1990. It has to be said that Diestel's reputation suffered when it transpired that he bought a Stasi property for his own use at a knockdown price, for which he was acquitted in 1998, and then, in 2001, found guilty and fined. Wolf Biermann famously called him 'a piece of dog shit', referring to allegations of collaboration with the Stasi made against various people, including the unimpeachable Joachim Gauck. When Diestel threatened to sue, Biermann withdrew the charge, offering the slur of 'federal shit' (*Bundesscheisse*) in its place. Diestel seemed content. There is, however, absolutely no reason to believe that the evidence his office provided on the size of the Stasi in 1989 was inaccurate, and Diestel's figures have never been challenged: see Gesamtdeutsches Institut/Bundesanstalt für gesamtdeutsche Aufgaben, *Dokumentation*, vol. 1, pp. 58, 85–90.

58. Ibid., vol. 3, p. 37.

59. Ibid., vol. 1, pp. 85–90.

## Notes to Chapter 2

1. See Chapter 3 by Klaus Larres, in Klaus Larres with Elizabeth Meehan (eds), *Uneasy Allies*; also Klaus Larres, 'Britain and the GDR in the 1960s: The Politics of Recognition by Stealth', in Jeremy Noakes et al., *Britain and Germany in Europe* – the 'stealth' in the sub-title refers to what the author claims was *de facto* prior to *de iure* recognition and has nothing to do with covert operations.

2. See Bert Becker, *Die DDR*.

3. Information from Bob Dixon, Foreign Office Research Department, 23 October 2001.

4. See Henning Hoff, 'Largely the Prisoners of Dr Adenauer's Policy: Grossbritannien und die DDR 1949–73', in Ulrich Pfeil (ed.), *Die DDR und der Westen: Transnationale Beziehungen 1949–89*, and Marianne Howarth, 'Die Westpolitik der DDR zwischen internationaler Aufwertung und ideologischer Offensive (1966–1989)', in Ulrich Pfeil (ed.), *Die DDR und der Westen*.

5. E.g. in one file (MfS Abteilung X 837), Mielke can be seen being asked for his view on UN Conventions and how they would affect the GDR's security in 1973. In another (MfS Abteilung X 1121) the Stasi was asked in November 1978 whether it had any objections to a proposed UK–GDR treaty on legal assistance. Mielke told the Minister of Justice that he had none, and the treaty was duly promulgated. In MfS Rechtsstelle 888, Mielke is asked to comment on a 1985 request from Tony Ford that the Stasi should not interfere in any way at all with visitors to the reading room in the British Embassy in East Berlin. His response, if there was one, is not extant. In May 1984 Mielke was asked to note that, in accordance with his wishes, the creation of a Federal German cultural centre in the GDR had not been included in the final agreement of a cultural treaty.

6. Joachim Gauck et al., *Die Stasi-Akten*, p. 72.

7. Ibid., p. 73.

8. A. James McAdams, *Judging the Past*, p. 61.

9. Marianne Howarth, 'Britain and East Germany: The Politics of Non-recognition', p. 287.

10. *Werwarwer in der DDR. Ein biographisches Lexicon* (Berlin: Ch. Links, 2000).

11. Interview, 15 May 2002.

12. Ruth Werner, *Sonja's Report* (Berlin: Verlag Neues Leben, 1977).

13. Howarth, 'Britain and East Germany', p. 126.
14. See Anthony Glees, *Exile Politics During the Second World War*.
15. See Chapter 10.
16. See Larres, in Noakes, *Britain and Germany in Europe*, p. 205.
17. Quoted in Christopher Andrew and Oleg Gordievsky, *KGB: The Inside Story*, p. 289.
18. Norman Naimark, *The Russians in Germany*, pp. 21–4. See also Norman Naimark and Leonid Gibianskii, *The Establishment of Communist Regimes in Eastern Europe*.
19. Top Secret FO 371 55587.
20. David Childs and Richard Popplewell, *The Stasi*, p. 34.
21. John and Ann Tusa, *The Berlin Blockade*, p. 59. See Norman Naimark, 'To Know Everything', pp. 2–3. See also his standard work on broader history of this period, *The Russians in Germany*, and also Naimark and Gibianskii, *The Establishment of Communist Regimes in Eastern Europe*. See also Childs and Popplewell, *The Stasi*, pp. 38 ff., and Christopher Andrew and Oleg Gordievsky, *KGB*, p. 289.
22. Naimark, 'To Know Everything', p. 14.
23. Naimark, *The Russians in Germany*, p. 378.
24. Günther Wagenlehner, *Die russischen Bemühungen um die Rehabilitierung*.

## Notes to Chapter 3

1. FO 371 76617 11 October 1949.
2. Marianne Howarth, 'Britain and East Germany', p. 15.
3. See Anthony Glees, *Reinventing Germany*, pp. 125, 154.
4. See Dennis L. Bark and David R. Gress, *A History of West Germany*, 1st edn, pp. 374, 468, 479, 509. For the abandonment of the Hallstein Doctrine see Glees, *Reinventing Germany*, p. 154, and Bark and Gress, *A History of West Germany* 2nd edn, pp. 182, 305, 323. See also Rolf Steiniger (ed.), 'Die britische Deutschland – und Besatzungspolitik 1945–49' (Paderborn, 1985), p. 67.
5. See Marianne Howarth, 'Die Westpolitik der DDR zwischen internationaler Aufwertung und ideologischer Offensive (1966–1989)', in Ulrich Pfeil (ed.), *Die DDR und der Westen*. Once recognition had been achieved, the overt diplomatic relationship between the two states was marked by a distinct lack of interest on the part of the GDR in engaging with the UK.

6. Howarth, 'Britain and East Germany', pp. 184–6.

7. Ibid., p. 180.

8. This is the view of Howarth, ibid., p. 144. She points out that several of the MPs who lobbied for the GDR discovered their interest in trading with it only after they themselves had been indoctrinated into the financial advantages for them as individuals which would flow from their lobbying work.

9. A Parliamentary Question produced an account of trade with East Germany from 1965 to 1971:

| | 1965 | 1966 | 1967 | 1968 | 1969 | 1970 | 1971 |
|---|---|---|---|---|---|---|---|
| UK exports | 8.3 | 16.4 | 17.1 | 12.5 | 12.8 | 17.0 | 17.3 |
| UK imports | 12.1 | 13.5 | 12.1 | 17.6 | 14.6 | 16.1 | 19.6 |

*Hansard*, vol. 837, 1971–2, cols 487/8.

10. Bert Becker, *Die DDR*, p. 179.

11. Chapman Pincher, *Their Trade is Treachery*, p. 237.

12. Christopher Andrew and Oleg Gordievsky, *KGB*, pp. 432–5.

13. Interview with Marianne Howarth, 15 August 2001. Howarth, 'Britain and East Germany', pp. 141–4.

14. Ibid., pp. 161 ff.

15. Ibid., p. 162.

16. Ibid., pp. 164, 178.

17. Ibid., p. 86.

18. Ibid., p. 237. The previous year Emrys Hughes MP had written in similar vein, 'I can claim to have seen only a small cross section of the prison population but what I saw, and I went where I insisted, did not support the allegation of starvation. I have been a prisoner myself in half a dozen British gaols and have also been a visiting magistrate in Glasgow, and have an idea of what to look for and I cannot say that this prison was any worse than Barlinnie or Wormwood Scrubs or any other British prison.' Quoted in Howarth, p. 224.

19. Ibid., p. 211. Professor Howarth herself, who first visited the GDR in 1970 on a foreign language 'Intercourse programme', was invited to the GDR in 1979 and found it 'a terrible place', to which she never returned. Interview 15 August 2001.

20. Howarth, 'Britain and East Germany', p. 252.

21. John Peet published the *Democratic German Report*. Some 15,000 copies were sent to the UK, to MPs and teachers. It was wound up in 1975 but had had a modest success. Becker, *Die DDR*, p. 258.

22. Hayes and Drayson are both listed on the F16 register of HVA contacts and agents – information from Frank Zwicker, 28 January 2002.

23. Childs wrote that the 'great majority of East Germans' who chose to 'go West' did so to gain better living standards and that 'in practice they needed no permission or passport to go' – which was a quaint way of describing the process by which the refugees had to risk their lives by fleeing from a police state. The building of the Berlin Wall is alluded to – briefly – as 'the crisis of 1961'.

24. Marianne Howarth shows how the argument used by Mikardo was recycled by the (Conservative but anti-West German) *Daily Express* on 15 March 1961: '. . . astonishing catalogue of missed opportunities in East Germany. Our trade with that country is just a tiny £4 mill a year. Why? Because the government heeds Dr Adenauer, who tells Britain not to trade with "wicked Communists" in East Germany. Does he obey the advice he hands out to others? Not likely. With their competitors out of the way, the West Germans are doing a roaring trade with the East worth £100 mill a year . . . There is only one way to deal with these wily West Germans. To sell as much as we can to East Germany . . .'. Quoted in Howarth, 'Britain and East Germany', p. 166.

25. Quoted in Becker, *Die DDR*, p. 225.

26. Roger Boyes, *The Times*, 14 August 2000.

27. Marianne Howarth recalls that Malcolm Arnold and Beattie Plummer changed their minds and left the committee. Interview 27 July 2001.

28. Becker, *Die DDR*, p. 296.

29. Purporting to be an 'independent' view of German affairs, Peet in fact almost always peddled the Politburo's line with nauseating sycophancy. He was not, however, as has sometimes been alleged, strictly speaking a Stasi spy, having been signed up by the KGB during the Spanish Civil War. His usefulness was in any case limited, since his defection and subsequent tirades had made it only too clear whose side he was on. See David Caute, *Fellow Travellers: A Postscript to the Enlightenment* (London: Weidenfeld & Nicolson 1973), pp. 281–2.

30. Information from Frank Zwicker, Stasi Archive, 28 January 2002.

31. See pp. 316–17

32. Interview with Marianne Howarth, 15 August 2001.

33. Quoted in Becker, *Die DDR*, p. 265.

34. See Glees, *Reinventing Germany*, pp. 169–95, from which the following account of the progress of Ostpolitik is taken.
35. Alistair Horne, *Macmillan 1957–68* (London: Macmillan, 1991), pp. 313, 363, 507 ff.
36. Glees, *Reinventing Germany*, p. 187.
37. See Timothy Garton Ash, *In Europe's Name*, pp. 263, 260–67. He writes: 'From the mid-1970s the United States saw the positive meaning and dynamic potential of Helsinki above all in its provisions for human rights. For the Federal Republic of Germany [. . .] this lay in its provisions for cooperation and human contacts.'

## Notes to Chapter 4

1. Information from Norbert Meyer, German Embassy.
2. Information from J.S., 24 April 2002.
3. Sir Percy Cradock, for example, Margaret Thatcher's intelligence adviser, puts it like this: 'Intelligence successes are usually unsung. They are usually the things that do not happen – the terrorist attempt that fails, the piece of international negotiation smoothly concluded; the thoughts of aggression that become second thoughts.' Percy Cradock, *In Pursuit of British Interests*. See also Percy Cradock, *Know Your Enemy*, London, pp. 42 ff. Another former senior civil servant, Sir Michael Quinlan, has written in the same vein: 'Much intelligence effort is directed towards insurance against events whose probability, importance and cost cannot themselves be measured. The most measurable things about intelligence are usually to be found in its failures.' Quoted in Harold Shukman (ed.), *Agents for Change*, p. 68.
4. See Peter Wright, *Spycatcher*.
5. See Chapter 8. Ed Vulliamy, *Guardian*, 9 July 1986, and MfS HAI 1639.
6. Stella Rimington, *Open Secret*.
7. An excellent thumbnail account of these issues is given in Richard Sahwa, *The Rise and Fall of the Soviet Union, 1917–1991*.
8. See www.oss.net/Papers/white/TexasReflections.
9. S. Payne Best, *The Venlo Incident*. Payne Best was one of the officers involved; both he and his colleague Stevens were held in various concentration camps during the war and denied pensions because of the information they had given to the Germans.
10. This was a point stressed by a former Italian intelligence chief at a

major conference on intelligence held at St Antony's College, Oxford, in October 1999.

11. Information from J.S., 24 April 2002.
12. MfS HVA 83 1977.
13. Christopher Andrew and Oleg Gordievsky, *KGB*, p. 487.
14. Ibid., p. 488.
15. Markus Wolf with Anne McElvoy, *Man Without a Face*, p. 244.
16. Ibid., p. 243.
17. Andrew and Gordievsky, *KGB*, p. 491.
18. Ibid., pp. 490–496.
19. Cradock, *In Pursuit of British Interests*, pp. 42 ff.
20. There is no record of 'C' in MI6 doing this except in Ian Fleming's fiction. Wolf, *Man Without a Face*, p. 101.
21. HMSO, *The Security Service*.
22. Wolf, *Man Without a Face*, p. 206.
23. In this respect, Stasi espionage in Britain seems different from the more structured approach which seems to have been followed in the Federal Republic.
24. There is much evidence to suggest that the organisation of espionage by the HVA was different in the UK (and presumably in the USA and France) from that in the Federal Republic or East Germany itself where the categories seem to have been less fluid. IMs, who were first termed GIs (*geheieme Informanten*, or secret informants), were invariably signed up as such. The files do not provide a conclusive view on a nomenclature and it is something about which former Stasi officers remain silent. See Joachim Gauck et al., *Die Stasi-Akten*, p. 58.
25. Pearson and Houlding are good examples of 'illegals'.
26. See MfS HAI 1641, Chapter 8, below.
27. See MfS HAI 1649 and Knabe, *Die Unterwanderte Republik*, p. 345.
28. Wolf notes: 'even within the closest confines of the Ministry we always referred to our agents and even the "legal" residents in our embassies by their codenames, lest their real identities leak, thus putting them at even greater risk'. Quoted in Wolf, *Man Without a Face*, p. 101.
29. See Chapter 15, below. Robin Pearson's controller noted that he had been disquieted by the trial of the Schulzes.
30. Tina Krone et al., *Wenn Wir Unsere Akten Lesen*, p. 94.
31. Gesamtdeutsches Institut/Bundesanstalt für gesamtdeutsche Aufgaben, *Dokumentation zum Staatssicherheitsdienst der ehemaligen DDR in 6 Teilen Teil*, vol. 1.
32. Krone et al., *Wenn Wir Unsere Akten Lesen*, p. 87.

33. U.N.T.S. Nos 7310–12, vol. 500, pp. 95–239, Vienna Convention on Diplomatic Relations and Optional Protocols Done at Vienna, on 18 April 1961.

34. Sir Michael Quinlan, quoted in Shukman (ed.), *Agents for Change*, pp. 61–3.

35. MfS ZAIG Nr 7494:

> 20 June 1980
> 30 copies
> Ministerrat der DDR
> Ministerium für Staatssicherheit
> Der Minister
> Order no 9/80
>
> Concerning co-operation by the service units of the MfS in political and technical operations in the foreign legations of the GDR in the operational area.
>
> The increased number of foreign legations has placed an increased security task on the MfS to safeguard the objects and their personnel. In order to maximise the use of the possibilities available to the legations by the MfS and in order to address the ever more complex conditions in the field, it is vital that operations be concentrated on the main tasks and be organised with precision.
>
> These important and increasingly significant tasks make high demands on conspiracy, on the selection and preparation of personnel and measures for operations. It demands a high quality of effective leadership in political operational work and high quality in the cooperation with the HVA and with other units of the MfS.
>
> In order to solve these problems, I order that:
>
> 1. The HVA assume responsibility for all political and technical operations in our foreign legations;
>
> 2. My Deputy, and the head of the HVA, is required to demonstrate that he has developed measures to set up the necessary order and structural pre-conditions to
>
> – secure the legation against hostile actions
> – exploit the possibilities of the legation to solve the tasks imposed by the MfS
> – establish operational means of communication.
>
> 3. All decisions on the use, tasking, nature and extent of technical means in the operational area are to be taken by my Deputy, the head of the HVA. He will receive the technical support necessary from the MfS on the basis of my orders.

4. A unit in the HVA, Department VIII, is to execute operational technical measures. The head of Cadres and Schooling is to arrange the necessary permanent posts.

5. The responsible service units of the MfS will develop the necessary operational technical means.

Mielke

Armeegeneral

36. At a conference on intelligence held at St Antony's College, Oxford, October 1999. He makes the point that Stalin, for example, was much more concerned about murdering Trotsky than working out how to protect the Soviet Union from Hitler. Politburo member Suslov was woken by the KGB so that he could be told a Russian dissident had just won the Nobel Prize. He notes, too, in passing that Communist intelligence services were invariably more interested in 'humint' than Western ones and were also almost pathologically suspicious of their own spies.

37. Cradock, *Know Your Enemy,* p. 150.

38. Rimington, *Open Secret*, p. 139.

39. Nor was it clear to the very senior figure who told me about this in 2000. That MI5 seem to have had only very limited success in discovering what the Stasi was doing in the UK is a view confirmed by four meetings with the Security Service, 2000–2002.

40. Letter from John le Carré, 18 February 2002.

41. See H. Knabe, *West-Arbeit des MfS.*

42. See Karl Wilhelm Fricke, *Die Staatssicherheitsdienst.* Fricke was the first author to point to the Stasi's work against the West, pp. 173–6, but does not mention its work in the UK.

## Notes to Chapter 5

1. Interview with K.-G. von Hase, 12 January 2002.

2. Interview with Bob Dixon, 29 October 2001.

3. London Lists supplied by the FCO Research Department.

4. Interview with Klaus Eichner, Berlin, 31 May 1994.

5. 'We graded Britain as only a Category 2 country as far as our intelligence interest was concerned. It was handled by the Department which handled France and Sweden. We did manage to infiltrate several people through the West German [sic] consular Department in Edinburgh where the vetting procedure was more lax than in London

but very few of these illegals remained in Britain because our government preferred to maintain good relations with London, especially given the effects of superpower politics on our dealings with America. One of our targets was Amnesty International. Mielke deemed it a subversive organisation and would dearly have loved to infiltrate it in order to discover the source of information from the Soviet Union and Eastern Europe. We never succeeded. Another reason why we did not bother much to spy on Britain (apart from the usual intelligence gathering by the foreign intelligence resident [sic] inside East Germany's London embassy) was that we had another source in Bonn. For about a decade starting in the middle of the 1970s a political counsellor in the West German Foreign Ministry, Dr Hagen Blau, gave us access to all the intelligence the West Germans had on Britain and was one of the best sources in the West German foreign service.' Quoted in Markus Wolf with Anne McElvoy, *Man Without a Face*, p. 290.

6. We know this thanks to the archival research of Dr Hubertus Knabe, formerly at the Stasi Archive. See Hubertus Knabe, *West-Arbeit des MfS*, in particular pp. 19, 147 and 120–164.

7. In 1953 Wolf had taken over foreign intelligence; it became the HVA in 1956 and reorganised in 1959 to consist of four departments, two dealing with West Germany, one with the 'political centres of the imperialist powers in West Germany' and one with NATO powers. Knabe, *West-Arbeit des MfS*, p. 9.

8. Knabe, *West-Arbeit des MfS*, p. 112; he mentions HVA Department XV at Leipzig only in passing on p. 114. The failure by the HVA in Leipzig to destroy all their files led to the discovery of at least two British Stasi agents, Robin Pearson and Fiona Houlding. IM Akte AIM 1825/91 (Robin Pearson, or 'Armin') and AIM 2127/91 (Fiona Houlding, or 'Diana').

9. Karl Wilhelm Fricke, *Die Staatssicherheitsdienst*, pp. 52 ff, 186–90. See also Knabe, *West-Arbeit des MfS*, p. 98.

10. Gesamtdeutsches Institut/Bundesanstalt für gesamtdeutsche Aufgaben, *Dokumentation zum Staatssicherheitdienst der ehemaligen DDR in 6 Teilen*, vol. 4, pp. 42 ff.

11. See Chapter 9.

12. Knabe, *West-Arbeit des MfS*, p. 102.

13. Ibid., p. 19.

14. Ibid., pp. 150–52.

15. Ibid., pp. 75–8.

16. Ibid., pp. 88–97. In March 1972 Mielke had ordered the further strengthening of the Stasi's work against the West and it supported the work of the KGB 'Databank for Facts About the Enemy' established in Moscow at this time; by 1989 data on 188,343 Western individuals existed.

17. See various files on Pearson, including IM Akte AIM 1825/91.

18. Knabe, *West-Arbeit des MfS*, pp. 96–7.

19. Ibid., p. 100.

20. Ibid., p. 147.

21. Ibid., pp. 110, 208– 3, 221.

22. After 1983 HA III was made responsible for electronic and signals intelligence – 'Sigint' – under General Horst Männchen with a staff of more than 2,000 technical officers. The Federal Republic was thoroughly saturated by GDR listening devices with ten large aerials listening in to West German signals traffic. Their codenames were 'Kormora', 'Lupine', 'Urian', 'Horizont' and 'Kondor', which monitored north-west German and British signals; 'Blitz', 'Radar' and 'Rubin', which monitored Frankfurt and southern Germany and thus American signals; and 'Topaz', which listened in to signals traffic in the Munich area, including, most importantly, the BND's wireless traffic to and from its headquarters at Pullach. In addition to these devices, the Stasi operated 'Echo', which undertook satellite surveillance; it had three stations listening to West Berlin signals traffic ('QU3', 'QU1' and 'QU4') and four 'support stations' in Dortmund, Düsseldorf, Cologne ('1B') and Bonn ('1A'). Situated in the GDR trade mission, consulate and the Office of the Representative of GDR in Bonn in the Königsallee, these outstations were able to listen in to a variety of signals in the capital of the Federal Republic as well as to monitor mobile phone traffic. Additional outstations were established in the GDR embassies in Vienna ('2') and Brussels ('3'). In *Man Without a Face*, p. 147, Wolf identifies the Cadiz station as codename 'Ice Sea' (*Eismeer*). There is clear evidence that some form of highly sophisticated listening devices was installed in the London embassy. See MfS HAI 1647.

23. It is interesting to compare this list with the much shorter one provided by Hubertus Knabe in *West-Arbeit des MfS*, pp. 518 ff. (*Zielobjekte der HVA – alphabetische Liste* BstU Ast Gera BV Gera/Abt XV 0187 21–39): Amnesty International, CND, DIS (Defence Intelligence Staff), END, the 'highschool'/University of European Economics at Oxford, the Foreign and Commonwealth

Office, GCHQ Cheltenham, the Intelligence Corps, the Institute for Strategic Studies, the Joint Intelligence Committee, Keston College, the London League for Human Rights, the London Signals Intelligence Board, PSIS (Permanent Secretary Commonwealth Intelligence Service), the (Bertrand) Russell Peace Foundation, Special Branch at New Scotland Yard, the Socialist International, the Secret Intelligence Service (MI6), the Security Service (MI5).

A document in the Stasi files contains a list of Stasi targets identified as 'undertaking subversive acts' against East Germany and which therefore 'represent a risk to the interests of the GDR and other Socialist states' but were either not 'imperialist secret services' or 'criminal organisations dealing in human beings' (GVS MfS 0008–4/85): Amnesty International; END; Greenpeace; International Institute for Strategic Studies; IRA; Keston College; PEN club 'Writers in Prison'; League for Human Rights, London; RAND Corporation (USA); Arab Organisations: Abu Mohamed Group; Abu Nidal Group; Muslim Brotherhood.

24. Joachim Gauck et al., *Die Stasi-Akten*, p. 61.
25. Gesamtdeutsches Institut/Bundesanstalt für gesamtdeutsche Aufgaben, *Dokumentation*, vol. 1, p. 109.
26. Ibid., vol. 4, pp. 65–8.

## Notes to Chapter 6

1. Gesamtdeutsches Institut/Bundesanstalt für gesamtdeutsche Aufgaben, *Dokumentation zum Staatssicherheitdienst der ehemaligen DDR in 6 Teilen*, vol. 3, p. 35.
2. Interview with Police Director Manfred Kittlaus, Berlin, 30 May 1994.
3. Interview with *Die Welt*, 4 March 1990, in Gesamtdeutsches Institut/Bundesanstalt für gesamtdeutsche Aufgaben, *Dokumentation*, vol. 3, pp. 35–8.
4. Compare Doug McEachin's comments – see Chapter 8, note 8.
5. Wolf wrote: 'The only way Robotron could even hope to keep pace with America and Japan was by acquiring Western knowledge and software forbidden us under the embargo'. Quoted in Markus Wolf, with Anne McElvoy, *Man Without a Face*, p. 182.
6. See Wolf, *Man Without a Face*, p. 268.
7. Gesamtdeutsches Institut/Bundesanstalt für gesamtdeutsche Aufgaben, *Dokumentation*, vol. 4, pp. 42–9.
8. Margaret Thatcher, *The Downing Street Years*, p. 452.

## Notes to Chapter 8

1. MfS HA I 1644, October 1988.
2. Stella Rimington, *Open Secret*, p. 140.
3. MfS HA I 1639 and MfS HA I 1647.
4. Interview with Oleg Gordievsky, 22 September 1998.
5. MfS 15905/60.
6. We cannot say that MI5 had no knowledge of any of these people (although none has ever been charged or publicly identified and neutralised) [interviews at Thames House 2000–2002]. It seems reasonable to assume, once more, that what MI5 did not know was the extent of military spying, and that, prior to this research, they had no idea of the names of the officers involved. What is more, there is no evidence in the files to indicate that the military intelligence unit suffered seriously as a result of any knowledge that MI5 may have had. Indeed, the opposite is patently the case: the 'Centre' was pleased with what the military spies had achieved.
7. We should recall that 50 per cent of Stasi intelligence went to the KGB. See Knabe, *West-Arbeit des MfS*, p. 150. It is true that in 1983 the deputy ambassador, Heinz Knobbe, was identified by an East German Embassy defector, Mitschka (and not by MI5) as 'the HVA resident' in London and asked to leave (he was gone by June 1984). But he was not a military spy (and his forced departure was not reflected in the unit's reports). Curiously, however, in April 1984, a cutting from the 'London *Mail*' was added to the military intelligence files (MfS HA I 1643). It reported Mitschka's defection three years before and his claim, which had just been passed to the media, that Heinz Knobbe was 'one of the highest spy chiefs of the Eastern bloc'. The paper quoted the Foreign Office as saying 'we know all about this report'. The Stasi was not too worried: the strict conspiracy which it employed at all times was designed to reduce the fallout from discovery or defection as much as possible. The 'Centre' knew Mitschka could have only a very limited understanding of anything of any consequence to the work of the residency. What this item did suggest – which was doubtless why it was kept – was that it might indicate that MI5 were increasingly going to be on the prowl and that other East Germans might shortly follow Knobbe on the plane back to East Berlin's Schönefeld airport.

   Bizarrely, Knobbe's expulsion did not lead to any further overt MI5 activity against the East Germans. The arrest on 23 August

1985 of two East German HVA agents, Sonja and Reinhardt Schulze, who were run by the HVA and were also not involved with military intelligence, was connected in the official British mind with the activities of the KGB (twenty-five of whose officers were expelled a few days after the arrest) but not the HVA. The Schulzes were found guilty on 8 July 1986, marking the first successful prosecution of *any* foreign spies by MI5 in twenty-five years (see Ed Vulliamy, *Guardian*, 9 July 1986). They had been picked up following the defection to East Germany of the West German counter-espionage chief, Hans-Joachim Tiedge. The *Guardian* was told that they were 'illegals' (which they were) spying for *the Russians* (which they were not). The Stasi files reveal that the Schulzes worked for the HVA although a military intelligence officer in London, Friedbert Krebs, was asked to watch over them while in jail. Canon Paul Oestreicher has stated that he visited them in prison. See also Markus Wolf with Anne McElvoy, *Man Without a Face*, p. 133.

8.   MfS HA I 1649.
9.   Wolf, *Man Without a Face*, p. 284.
10.  Under the recognition agreement of 1972–3, the East Germans were not permitted to have military attachés in London. Military attachés were postings entirely consistent with the Vienna Convention and were meant to supply information about their own armed forces and, where appropriate, liaise with the British defence community. In uniform, and therefore easily identifiable as military personnel, their risks to British security were slight. They would be known and recognised, and could be removed if they appeared to be getting too inquisitive. There were specific reasons why the GDR was excluded from this particular benefit of recognition which had to do with the peculiar status that Germany's division had on international relations and Britain's refusal to recognise the East German armed forces as independent armed forces (only after the Stockholm agreement of 1986 were East German armed forces officially recognised by the UK – information from Colonel Roy Giles CBE, 4 June 2001).
11.  MfS HA I 1639.
12.  Gesamtdeutsches Institut/Bundesanstalt für gesamtdeutsche Aufgaben, *Dokumentation zum staatssicherheitsdient der ehemaligen DDR in 6 Teilen*, vol. 1, pp. 91–3; vol. 4, pp. 65–8.
13.  MfS HA I 1641, Diary Entry Nr 039321/94Z.
14.  MfS HA I 1639.
15.  MfS AP 5614/86 Bd 1.

16. Nr 1250/82.
17. MfS AP 5614/86 Bd I with MfS 1647.
18. See Chapter 14.
19. MfS HA I 1639.
20. MfS HA I 1647 HVA IX/B.
21. MfS AP 5614/86 Bd 1.
22. Information from British military intelligence indicates that this meant the 'Navforchan', or NATO minesweeper and escort fleet for the Channel (interview with Colonel Roy Giles CBE, 4 June 2001). One British admiral was 'double-hatted' and commanded the Channel minesweeper and escort fleet. He would have been based in Northwood.
23. These matters can be helpfully explained by comparing this aspect of secret military intelligence gathering with the work done by 'Brixmis' (see Tony Geraghty, *Beyond the Front Line*; interview with Colonel Roy Giles CBE, 4 June 2001). Thanks to a 1944 agreement between Britain, the United States and the Soviet Union, the armies of the three states established liaison units. What this meant in the case of Britain was that the Russians trailed and tracked British armed forces in West Germany and the British trailed and tracked Soviet armed forces in East Germany. The British liaison mission, 'Brixmis', involved its officers in extremely dangerous work because the Stasi (nicknamed 'the narks' by the British soldiers, and led by a 'king nark' who drove a superior BMW obviously acquired in some way from the West) were given the duty of securing the Russian forces (an American officer had actually been shot dead while on one mission).

## Notes to Chapter 9

1. MfS AP 5614/86 Bd 1.
2. Christopher Dobson and Ronald Payne, *The Dictionary of Espionage*, p. 216: 'Howard Marks had worked for MI6 for a time at the suggestion of Norman McMillan who later joined the FO.' It is possible that McMillan may have been targeting Linser but formally this would have been difficult as his record in *Who's Who* indicates that he was either in Dhaka or Cairo at this time: McMillan, (Norman) Hamilton CMG OBE director of operations, CIEX Ltd. Joined diplomatic service in 1968, FCO 1960–70, 3rd sec. Vienna 1970–72, FCO 1972–77, 1st sec. Rome 1997–81, Dhaka 1981–4, Cairo 1984–6, Vienna 1989–93. CIEX Ltd.

3. Interview, 1 July 2002.
4. MfS HA I 1643.
5. MfS HA I 1639.
6. MfS HA I 1639.
7. MfS HA II 10213.
8. Prior to arriving in Belgrave Square, Döring had been required to attend a 'who's who' course, to learn about the security systems in his 'cover service' – the East German Foreign Ministry – to be indoctrinated into the work of the 'Centre' and attend counter-espionage training, appropriate for the London Embassy. In his own hand, on 11 March 1987, he wrote: 'I, Jörg Döring, commit myself freely to unofficial work with the Ministry for State Security. I am prepared to work to prevent attacks on the National People's Army and the GDR. I will maintain the strongest silence about my work with the Ministry, including with my relations and all of those with whom I shall work' (XVIII 554187). He added: 'I understand that my codewords for contact should all communications fail are as follows – question: Do you have the collected works of Aragon?, answer: There is no English edition.' He was also obliged to be trained in recognising MI5 activities and how to run operations. In this context, he was instructed that he should be prepared to be provoked by MI5, to be recruited by them, to be accused of various criminal acts and that his wife would be targeted by the British as well.
9. File no. 17203/91.
10. MfS 16603/91 and MfS 16799/91.
11. MfS HA I 1644.
12. MfS HA I 1639.
13. MfS HA I 1644.
14. Information from Canon Paul Oestreicher 23 August 2001:

### Military Spies in London

| Name | Rank | Role | Operative | Codename |
|------|------|------|-----------|----------|
| Wahner, Jürgen | Major | Legalist | 1970–73, 1977–9 | 'Hampel' |
| Escher, Peter | Hptmn | Legalist | 1977–81 | 'Hohlfeld' |
| Knott, Bernd | | | 1976–80 | 'Hoppe' |
| Linser, Hartmut | ? | | 1981–5 | 'Harald' (deceased) |
| Kreissig, Gerd | ? | | 1974–9 | 'Haupt' |

| Name | Rank | Role | Operative | Codename |
|------|------|------|-----------|----------|
| Schneidratus, Oswald | Hptm | | 1983–7 | 'Helios' |
| Wetzel, Stefan | | | 1985–7 | 'Hecht' |
| Krebs, Friedbert | | | 26 August 1985– | 'Hammer' |
| Döring, Jörg | | | October 1987– | 'Harke' |

## Notes to Chapter 10

1. Markus Wolf with Anne McElvoy, *Man Without a Face*, p. 330.
2. Ibid., p. 110.
3. Communication from M. Herman, December 2000.
4. Barely a fortnight after the completion of my research on Uher, and my conclusion as to his identity had been discussed with MI5, a story appeared in the *Washington Post*, whose reporter had, bizarrely perhaps, chanced upon Uher in Berlin. Uher took the opportunity readily to confirm that he had, in fact, been 'Eckhart'. His interviewer, Jim Hoagland, noted that he was 'courteous and engaging' and spoke 'uncommonly smooth English'. Uher insisted that he had gone along to Chatham House in the 1980s where he had 'read and listened to public and unclassified information', which was regarded as 'gold' in East Berlin. *Washington Post*, 18 July 2002.
5. Other material of interest is listed in Appendix 5.
6. We find this with several Leipzig outstation Stasi officers and spies: Jörg Hirschfeld used the cover-name 'Jörg Hilpert' and Helfried Schlinsog called himself 'Dr Schlinder'; the spy 'Schnitter', whose real name was Bönisch, also called himself 'Böhme'. Lt. Günter Pommer calls himself 'Sommer', Major Neuhaus was 'Neumann'. AIM 2008/91. Robin (Pearson) was 'Armin', Fiona (Houlding) was 'Diana'.
7. Where individuals worked on East Germany, for example, 'facts' about it, and the chance to visit it for research which could then be published and used for promotion or financial gain.
8. Wolf, pp. 123–9.
9. Ibid.
10. Intelligence officers' codenames were intended to be absolutely secure (it goes without saying that the Stasi never imagined that its archives would ever enter the public domain). Why differentiate between the two if they were the same? There would have been no advantage in security terms. Indeed, as we explore in Chapter 11,

*Quellen* and officers can have entirely different registration numbers. As the Stasi virtually always gave one registration number to one officer, two registration numbers indicate two different persons. However, sometimes one officer had more than one cover-name (though always the same registration number).

Frank Zwicker of the Stasi Archive says that the registration numbers are vital; it was extremely rare to ever have one changed and the vast majority of them were never changed. This was to ensure that, on the one hand, the rules of conspiracy would not be broken by recruitment (using the real or cover-name of the agent), while on the other, one department would know at once if a candidate was already of interest to another department. The first number was a Roman numeral, usually XV, for the HVA's secret intelligence agents, denoting that they had been recruited through the Leipzig Office, or IV, which designated Potsdam, chosen as the main location for the recruitment of agents for the Stasi's security activities. The next set of figures, separated by a slash, indicated the number of recruitments made (the first figures) and the year in which the recruitment took place (the second set). If a spy changed his or her area of activity inside the GDR, the Roman numerals could be altered (interview 8 April 2002).

11. 28 September 1990. In 1986 Honecker had ordered an extension in their duties, believing that Gorbachev's reforms might cause chaos. Order of 16 March 1986, no. 6/86. Gesamtdeutsches Institut/ Bundesanstalt für gesamtdeutsche Aufgaben, *Dokumentation zum Staatssicherheitsdienst der ehemaligen DDR in 6 Teilen*, vol. 2, p. 45.

12. Ian Cobain, Chief Reporter of *The Times*.

13. During Wolf's trial, Schröter exclaimed, 'It was a pleasure to have worked for you, Herr General.' Wolf, *Man Without a Face*, p. 338.

14. The *Sunday Times* quotes Sir Timothy Garden, former assistant chief of the Defence Staff, who states that the reports suggested the Stasi had gained access to important details of NATO plans for emergency deployments of its forces: 'Had we ever gone to war with the Warsaw Pact, it looks from these files that we would have been more vulnerable than we had hoped.' Alfred Spühler, a spy already convicted who worked for the BND in 1982, provided a secret British military assessment of Soviet air attack brigades. Spühler, who worked on a joint project with GCHQ, said: 'Virtually everything British intelligence gave to the West Germans landed shortly thereafter in the hands of the HVA'. *Sunday Times*, 26 November 2000.

15. Joachim Gauck et al., *Die Stasi-Akten*, p. 27.

16. Wolf, *Man Without a Face*, p. 115.
17. Tina Krone et al., *Wenn Wir Unsere Akten Lesen*, p. 95.
18. www.bstu.de/mfs/MfSorg/seiten/abtbcd.htm – the *Werwarwer* site.
19. Gesamtdeutsches Institut/Bundesanstalt für gesamtdeutsche Aufgaben, *Dokumentation*, vol. 3, p. 37.
20. *The Times*, 14 October 2000.
21. See www.mz-b.de/graphics/me.
22. Gesamtdeutsches Institut/Bundesanstalt für gesamtdeutsche Aufgaben, *Dokumentation*, vol. 1, pp. 91–3.
23. Ibid., vol. 4, pp. 24–9.
24. Ibid., vol. 1, pp. 109–14.
25. Ibid., vol. 4, pp. 24–9.
26. Ibid., vol. 4, pp. 65–8.

## Notes to Chapter 11

1. *Official Report (Hansard)*, 21 October 1999, vol. 336, c 555. Straw was, inadvertently, giving away more than outsiders knew at the time. Dr Julian Lewis MP had asked a parliamentary question about the Stasi's agents in the UK based on research undertaken by the author before August 2000. This had indicated the existence of perhaps twenty-five Stasi agents whose work was reflected in the existing documentary records; at that time, the results of a trawl through the HVA SIRA material were still awaited. They revealed the existence of a further hundred or so 'sources' – hence Straw's figure. MI5, however, had been aware of the SIRA material since earlier in 1999. See the debate on 'British Stasi Agents', *Official Report (Hansard)*, 21 December 1999, vol. 341, c 182. Straw also claimed these one hundred persons had been 'investigated', which appeared to mean 'identified'. In fact, none of those people identified in this book as sources has said they were interviewed by MI5.
2. MfS 11946/89 'Hans Reichert'.
3. Blau MfS X AP 1323/78, registered 31 December 1959, XV/6427/60/EH codename 'Merten'; see too Werner Grossmann in *Der Spiegel*, 5 February 2001. He stated that Blau was one of the three most important Stasi agents in the West German foreign office. He had been able to assure the East German leadership that the German Social Democratic government led by Willy Brandt was sincerely desirous of better relations with East Germany and that it had given up all thought of political unification at any time. Grossmann also claimed

that without Blau's intelligence the Politburo would never have signed the treaty with West Germany which 'normalised' relations between the two states. He says he was betrayed by his controller, Werner Roitzsch, in 1990. See too *The Times*, 18 August 1995.

4. Interview with K.-G. von Hase, 4 January 2002.
5. Linser was twenty-seven when he was sent to London, Döring twenty-seven when sent to Paris and thirty-one when he came to London; Schneidratus was thirty-three and Rost twenty-eight.
6. The recruitment of 'Diana' is just one example.
7. Markus Wolf with Anne McElvoy, *Man Without a Face*, p. 289.
8. Interviews at Thames House, 2000 and 2002.
9. Confidential interview, 26 April 2001. A recently retired senior British Council official has confirmed that although MI6 had tried to recruit him they had insisted that he first resign from the Council. Interview 28 October 2002.
10. Interview, 22 March 2002.
11. See p. 291.
12. Interview, Lord Roper, 22 June 2001.
13. See SIRA listings below, Appendix 5.
14. Communication from Chatham House, 24 April 2002.
15. MfS AP 5614/86 Bd 1.
16. We should recall a recent case, that of Raphael Bravo, a security guard at British Aerospace, who stole British and NATO defence secrets for the Russians, which led to his being jailed for eleven years on 1 February 2002; and that in 1962 Harry Houghton and Ethel Gee were given fifteen years for passing military secrets to the Russians. *Daily Telegraph*, 2 February 2002. A good agent can indeed be priceless, as Sheila Kerr reminds us, with reference to Donald Maclean in Anne Deighton (ed.), *Britain and the First Cold War*, pp. 71–87.

## Notes to Chapter 12

1. Joachim Gauck et al., *Die Stasi-Akten*, p. 27.
2. Markus Wolf with Anne McElvoy, *Man Without a Face*, p. 238.
3. A good history of the GDR dissident movement is provided by Christian Joppke, *East German Dissidents and the Revolution of 1989*. Interestingly, although END is mentioned in this text, CND is not. See too James McAdams, *East Germany and Détente*; Stefan Wolle, *Die heile Welt der Diktatur*; and Klaus Behnke and Jürgen Fuchs (eds), *Zersetzung der Seele*.

4. See Nancy Reagan with William Novak, *My Turn* (London: Weidenfeld & Nicolson, 1989).

5. Martin Westlake, *Kinnock: The Biography* (London: Little, Brown, 2001), p. 35.

6. Ibid., p. 374.

7. Kaldor repeatedly warned END members about spying. Unfortunately, the Stasi's END spies realised that she realised this! On 12 December 1984 she had written a report which included the statement: 'What was clearly unacceptable to the Soviet Peace Council was our support for the independent peace groups – something on which we cannot compromise. As long as we continue to support these groups they will interfere in our movement, i.e. encourage the Stalinists.' These words were passed on to the Stasi (MfS HA XX AKG II).

8. Stella Rimington, *Open Secret*, p. 140.

9. Hubertus Knabe, *West-Arbeit des MfS*, pp. 78, 180.

10. Interviewed by Tom Mangold on BBC TV, 9 June 1993.

11. The quotation comes from Irene Fick.

12. MfS 1643.

13. Interview with Barbara Einhorn, 4 December 1998.

14. See Chapter 8.

15. Ibid.

16. Wolf, *Man Without a Face*, pp. 242–3.

17. MfS HA XX AKG 109 Bd 1 contains a verbatim translation.

18. In issue February 1985, for example, a report was carried on a 'gala event' held in Sydney to mark the thirty-fifth anniversary of the birth of the GDR by the 'Australia–GDR Friendship Society'. The main speaker was John Milfull, a noted professor of German at the University of New South Wales (he was a vice-president of the Friendship Society). In his address Milfull said, 'the Socialist countries, with all their imperfections' – which he did specify – 'are in a very real sense the last bastion against a capitalist technology of destruction that has enslaved its masters . . . The GDR is a country which in itself exemplifies the strength of the weak in its rebuilding from the ruins and ashes of 1945.' Oddly, Gerhard Lindner ('Hans Reichert') had been the GDR ambassador in Australia. Through *The GDR Review* in August 1981 he had addressed the Friendship Society, declaring that the GDR was committed to 'peace, peace, peace', that 'peace was the most fundamental human right' and that there should be an 'end to the arms race'.

19. The Stasi were particularly worried about the role played by the BBC and Reuters in publicising the call for civil rights and peace

that they made. ZMA XX20585 Bd 6–8 6 December 1983. Interview with David Blow, 11 November 1998.

20. See for example S. Wolle, *Die heile Welt der Diktatur*; Behnke and Fuchs, *Zersetzung der Seele*.

21. Interview with Ulrike Poppe, Oxford, 14 September 1998.

22. As Eberhard Kuhrt had noted at the time, this shift had a 'system threatening potential'. E. Kuhrt, *Wider die Militisierung der Gesellschaft: Friedensbewegung und Kirche in der DDR* (Melle: Knoth Verlag, 1984), quoted in Christian Joppke, *East German Dissidents and the Revolution of 1989*, p 93.

23. Quoted in Joppke, *East German Dissidents and the Revolution of 1989*, p. 93.

24. Honecker had himself apparently (and a little unwisely) at one stage said that the dissidents 'had the great advantage that they exist in a state that pursues the same goals'. Quoted in Joppke, *East German Dissidents and the Revolution of 1989*, p. 89.

25. '*Die DDR ist ein starker in der Welt geachteter Staat des Friedens und des Sozialismus . . . Die DDR kampft für Frieden, Fortschritt und Sozialismus in der Welt*' ('The GDR is a strong state committed to peace and Socialism, respected throughout the world . . . it fights for peace, progress and Socialism throughout the world').

26. Thompson was 'enigmatic' because he was a deeper thinker than some of his polemical writings could indicate and not the unilateralist he is often believed to have been.

27. E. P. Thompson and Dan Smith (eds), *Protest and Survive*, pp. 9–62, 223–7.

28. ZMA XX20585 Bd 6–8 'END'. Joppke, *East German Dissidents and the Revolution of 1989*, p. 100, misunderstands the nature of END, which he mistakenly calls 'the European Conference for Nuclear Disarmament' and wrongly describes as 'the clearing house of Western peace movements'.

29. Source as above (my emphasis).

30. Source as above.

31. At the time, Sandford wrote (with admirable caution): '[. . .] the issue of civil liberties is implicit in much that the autonomous peace movement has said and done: only occasionally has it become an explicit and specific theme in its own right. Civil liberties . . . are inherent preconditions of any peace movement activity . . . At the same time, curtailment of civil liberties is scarcely conducive to an atmosphere in which peace may flourish if it leads to resentment,

disaffection, and tension within the population . . .' Sandford, *The Sword and the Ploughshare*, p. 44.

32. The 1968 GDR constitution was not as liberal as that of 1949 but it guaranteed freedoms of speech, assembly and association (Articles 27, 28, 29); freedom of conscience and belief was upheld in Article 20 while the secrecy of post and telephone was guaranteed under Article 31. David Childs and Richard Popplewell, *The Stasi*, p. 96.

33. See note 42 (below).

34. See the copious files, consisting of many thousands of pages, especially ZMA XX 20585 Bd 1–8, ZMA XX 20585 Bd 6–8, but also HA XX ZMA, MfS HAXX AKG 188 039321/947.

35. See Chapter 14.

36. Diary no. 1664/83.

37. ZMA XX 20585 Bd 4–8.

38. Information from a CIA source, June 2001.

39. ZMA XX 20585 Bd 7–8.

40. HVA III/A to XX/1 16 October 1985.

41. ZMA XX 20585.

42. Ibid., Bd 6–8.

43. Andrew and Gordievsky, pp. 541–2.

44. ZMA XX 20585 Bd 6–8.

45. Unpublished documentary evidence from Bernd Lippmann, Berlin, August 1996.

46. Unpublished documentary evidence supplied by Bernd Lippmann, Berlin, August 1996. See Behnke and Fuchs, *Zersetzung der Seele*, pp. 7–12, 27, 28–40 for further examples of *Zersetzung*, including the fate of Templin; and Joppke, *East German Dissidents and the Revolution of 1989*, pp. 112–14, who describes the attempted seduction of Ulrike Poppe by the Stasi in order to alienate her from her husband. He writes 'quite unique was the Stasi's attempt to steer and manipulate the direction and agenda of opposition groups'.

47. P. Cooke and N. Hubble, 'Die volkseigene Opposition? The Stasi and Alternative Culture in the GDR', in *German Politics*, vol. 6, no. 2, pp. 117–38.

48. Quoted frequently but see Joppke, *East German Dissidents and the Revolution of 1989*, p. 111.

49. ZMA 20585 Bd 6–8.

50. ZMA 20585 Bd 4–8.

51. Dr Jarman further states today that as the European secretary of 'Quaker Peace and Service' from 1982 to 1991, he was required to

maintain contacts with East German Communists in power including politicians and the state-run Peace Council as well as some of those they oppressed. He agrees that he may have met Lindner but only 'very briefly' and has 'no clear recollection of him'. Jarman accepts that he and his wife Roswitha invited 'GDR diplomats and their wives' to their home, visits which were reciprocated. What they discussed in these private meetings were, he insists, matters which were 'in the public domain'. He says that at the time he 'presumed at least one-third of them were from their security agencies and the rest would be expected to give intelligence to them'. As a member of the END liaison committee he suggested that END's 'hard line' of ignoring Communist peace committees should be 'softened'. As for the 'off-site meetings', he states that his wife was secretary of William Penn House, 'the venue for off-the-record meetings of East German diplomats'. Jarman recalled Kasper well as an official of the GDR Embassy in the mid-1980s who attended a single END-GDR group meeting. Jarman knew that Kasper had become a 'research worker' at a 'peace institute' in East Berlin. Together with Paul Oestreicher, Jarman also had contact with Oleg Gordievsky, and 'nearly came unstuck with him'. He was relieved to discover that he was a double agent.

52. MfS HA XX ZMA AKG II Nr 40354.
53. ZMA XX 20585 Bd 7–8.
54. ZMA XX 20585 Bd 2; all Allen's materials are filed under MfS HA XX AKG II.
55. ZMA XX 20585.
56. Letter from James Lamond, 26 February 2003.
57. Interview with David Blow, 11 November 1998; ZMA XX 20585 Bd 6–8, 7–8.
58. Interviews with Mark Brayne, 31 August 2001; Ian Wallace, 8 December 1998 and Jim McAdams, 29 April 2002; see also Anne McElvoy in the *Independent*, 20 September 1999.
59. MfS HA II 21648, MfS HA XX 3225.
60. McElvoy went on to translate Markus Wolf's autobiography into English. In her interesting book on East Germany, *The Saddled Cow*, she made a number of references to the Stasi and urged scholars not to probe too deeply into the Stasi files ('There are as many victims of the country's bureaucracy as there are of the Stasi's victims . . . the Stasi has been unanimously declared the scapegoat for the evils of the East German system . . . to dissect the workings of the

state security system, name the informers and look in horror at its methods will not help Germany . . . overexposure and overpromotion of this topic will result in people drowning in a sea of ghastly detail rather than gaining any useful perspective on the Stasi and its legacy'), p. 107.

61. McElvoy, *Independent*, 20 September 1999.
62. Interviewed by Michael Buerk on BBC Radio 4, 24 November 1998.

## Notes to Chapter 13

1. Hubertus Knabe, *West-Arbeit des MfS*, p. 82.
2. Quoted, ibid., p. 180.
3. Ibid.
4. See Chapter 8.
5. MfS 11946/89 'Hans Reichert'.
6. Letter from Lord Russell-Johnston, 28 February 2003.
7. Interview with Sir James Eberle GCB, 27 September 2002, and subsequent communications. MfS HA II 15605.
8. Bruce Kent, for example, was given the cover-name 'Pact'.
9. Interview with Sir John Birch, 15 May 2001.
10. HVA MfS /15996/60.
11. Confidential DD 1985/333 despatch, 5 September 1985. I was given permission to read and copy this document.
12. If Honecker had 'won' some 'independence' from the Russians it was only because they were becoming increasingly fed up with his hard-line Communist stonewalling which they thought endangered Gorbachev's reform programme.
13. Interview with Sir John Birch.
14. Interviews with Lord Roper, 10 May and 22 June 2001.
15. Information from Richard Davy, 29 January 2003.
16. This point is confirmed by Alan Brooke-Turner. Although he says that he accepted some of the Eastern European delegates might be security officers, he believed that if they were, it was only to keep an eye on their own people. In his eight years in charge of the round table exercises, he says, he never once had any contact with MI5, and would have expected M15 to have warned him if any of the East Germans were known to them as intelligence officers.
17. Markus Wolf with Anne McElvoy, *Man Without a Face*, p. 244.
18. Information from Lord Roper, 22 June 2001, and Richard Davy, 29 January 2003.

19. MfS HA II Nr 10213.
20. Interview with Richard Davy, 1 May 2001.
21. Stella Rimington, *Open Secret*, p. 140.
22. Communication, 4 May 2001.
23. Interview with Richard Davy, 29 December 2000.
24. Lord Roper, telephone conversation, 10 May 2001.
25. Numerous examples of such contacts may be found in the history of intelligence operations during the Second World War. See Anthony Glees, *The Secrets of the Service*.
26. It is by no means far-fetched to compare round table meetings at which the Stasi were present in the 1980s with ones conducted with the German Abwehr during the 'phoney war' period. It is true that even if the Stasi was 'at war' with Britain, Britain was not at war with the GDR but it was still unwise to have the Stasi present at round tables but British counter-intelligence absent. Glees, *The Secrets of the Service*, pp. 163–4.
27. Communication, 25 April 2001.
28. Communication from Sir R. Braithwaite, 5 April 2001.
29. Lord Roper also takes on board the force of the point that, had the Stasi files not revealed the existence of this policy, these contacts would not have been known about under the Public Records Act until 2015 at the earliest and possibly not until 2035, given the sensitive nature of the material they highlight.
30. Information received 1 July 2002.
31. Interview with Colonel Roy Giles, 4 June 2001.
32. MfS HA I 1644.
33. Interview with Lord Roper, 22 June 2001.
34. Interview with Adrian Hyde-Price, 11 October 2002.
35. Tina Krone et al., *Wenn Wir Unsere Akten Lesen*, p. 94.
36. MfS HA II 15610.
37. Interview with Frank Zwicker, Stasi Archive, 13 October 2002.
38. Ibid., see also Knabe, *West-Arbeit des MfS*, p. 194.
39. Interview with Frank Zwicker, Stasi Archive, 17 October 2002.
40. *Who's Who*, 1981.
41. E-mail from Sir James Eberle, 25 September 2002.
42. ZAIG MfS 6300C HVA Lagezentrum.
43. Alan Brooke-Turner, in charge of the round table exercise, has confirmed that he was never told of this follow-up plan. When asked whether he would have approved of it, had he known, he answered with some emphasis, 'No. We were not kitted out for this kind of thing,

we never worked with any serving army people, security officials or GDR ministry of defence civil servants.' Today Brooke-Turner finds it 'alarming and surprising' that the Stasi should have regarded the round tables as intelligence opportunities for recruiting or grooming Britons.

44. Information from Ian Cobain, 12 December 2000.

45. See the SIRA entries, Appendix 5.

46. Pearson, for example, was ordered to stay away from any group or event in Britain with an East German or Communist connection. Irene Fick was ordered to stay away from END, presumably because someone in it had suggested she was too close to the East German Embassy. Similarly, the East German Embassy stayed away from formal contact with END, as the private meetings with Sandford and Jarman showed.

47. Interview with Lord Roper, 22 June 2001.

48. Wolf, *Man Without a Face*, p. 115.

## Notes to Chapter 14

1. MfS HAPS DB Akte, 6 March 1975 (evaluation of Ron Hayward, general secretary of the Labour Party).

2. MfS Allg P 7969/73.

3. Pimlott has argued that doubts harboured against Sternberg by MI5 and MI6 officers may well have had some merit. Noting that he was 'viewed with distaste' by fellow businessmen and with 'suspicion' by diplomats, Pimlott accused Sternberg of being a 'public relations agent' for the East German regime (Pimlott, *Harold Wilson*, pp. 572, 693–723, 725). 'When Sternberg died in 1978 he was believed to have been under surveillance by both British and American intelligence – though whether he was a spy, a double agent, or neither remains unknown.' While Pimlott discounts the possibility that Wilson was a secret Communist, the friendship with Sternberg appears even here to leave a way open to link the former Prime Minister to individuals whose allegiance to the British way of life was in question.

4. MfS HA XX AKG 11, 15 February 1985.

5. ZMA XX 20585 Bd 6–8.

6. MfS AP31334/92 and ZMA XX 20585, vols 6–8.

7. Interview with Bruce Kent, 2 February 2003.

8. MfS HA XX AKG 109, Bd 1.

9. ZMA XX 20585 Bd 7–8, 25 November 1983, 5 January 1984.

Thanks are due to Barbara Einhorn for confirming the details in the Stasi report on her at an interview in Brighton on 4 December 1998.

10. Interview with Barbara Einhorn, 4 December 1998.

11. Interview with Ulrike Poppe, 14 September 1998. See also Gesamtdeutsches Institut/Bundesanstalt für gesamtdeutsche Aufgaben, *Dokumentation zum Staatssicherheitdienst der ehemaligen DDR in 6 Teilen*, vol. 3, p. 67.

12. Interview with Barbara Einhorn, 14 December 1998.

13. ZMA XX 20585 Bd 7–8.

14. John Sandford, *The Sword and the Ploughshare*, pp. 2–3.

15. Ibid., p. 11. This chimes with something a fellow academic had written forty years before about Stalin's Russia: 'A great number of the citizens of both Great Britain and the USSR think the other is not free . . . British subjects speak of GPU [KGB] surveillance, of the one-party system . . . Yet the Soviet electoral system is not a denial of parliamentary democracy . . . it is not a mere party dictatorship imposed from on top. It is an attempt to skip the stage of liberal democracy in politics and pass on to a society in which there shall be no deep conflicts of interests, no fundamental divergencies of opinion on political views.' K. E. Holme, *The Soviets and Ourselves*, p. 12. The author was the historian Christopher Hill, writing under the pseudonym of K. E. Holme (*Holm* is the Russian for hill) while working for the British Foreign Office.

16. Sandford, *The Sword and the Ploughshare*, p. 9.

17. Interview, 17 November 1998.

18. ZMA 20585, vols 6–8, vols 7–8.

19. MfS HA XX/ZMA 40354 039321/947.

20. Hauptabteilung XX/1, Berlin, 27 November 1984.

21. Interview with Canon Emeritus Dr Paul Oestreicher, 23 August 2001.

22. Telephone interview with Dr Oestreicher, 12 September 2001.

23. ZMA XX 20585 Bd 7–8. Interviews with Irene Fick, 22 October 2001 and 17 January 2002.

24. MfS 10888/92.

25. Markus Wolf with Anne McElvoy, *Man Without a Face*, p. 243.

26. It seems likely that this was the Zutschi household.

## Notes to Chapter 15

1. AIM 2008/91.

2. MfS 2668/91.

3. Tape MfS HA XXII/Ka/294.
4. This evidence was presented on BBC Television in September and October 1999. *IM Akten, Leipzig AIM*.
5. Dr McPherson told BBC Television in October 1999 that she was shocked to realise that she had unwittingly played a part in the Stasi's machinations. There is no record of any action having been taken against her.
6. Meetings with MI5 officer, 2000–2002.
7. 'Max's' file is AIM 1796/91.
8. Dr Pearson was disciplined by his employers, Hull University, allegedly on the grounds that he had deceived his students by not telling them he had been a spy. Sources close to MI5 have indicated that they believed there were grounds for proceedings against him under the Official Secrets Act, but the then Home Secretary, Jack Straw, did not share this view.
9. AIM 2008/91.
10. *Guardian*, 21 September 1999: 'I Am Not a Spy.'
11. *Sunday Telegraph*, 19 September 1999.

## Notes to Conclusion

1. See Corey Ross, *The East German Dictatorship*, pp. 191 ff., and A. James McAdams, *Judging the Past in Unified Germany*.
2. This was the SOUD system in the Moscow KGB Archives. See H. Knabe, *West-Arbeit des MfS*, pp. 109, 285.
3. This is the formal view of the House of Commons Library Research Service, 30 November 2000, expressed in a letter to Dr Julian Lewis MP.
4. Mielke's speech to the Volkskammer, 13 November – report dated 16 November 1989.
5. ZAIG MfS 6300c.

## Notes to Appendices

1. Letter to the author from Bernd Lippmann, April 2002 GVS 7/86 – ZAIG.
2. Hubertus Knabe, *West-Arbeit des MfS*, pp. 112, 147, 174, 449 ff., 485 ff.
3. Annual Reports of the Royal Institute of International Affairs, 1979 ff.

# Bibliography

Andrew, Christopher, and D. Dilks (eds), *The Missing Dimension: Government and Intelligence Communities in the Twentieth Century* (London: Macmillan, 1984)

——, and Oleg Gordievsky, *KGB: The Inside Story* (London: Hodder & Stoughton, 1990)

——, and Vasili Mitrokhin, *The Sword and the Shield: The Mitrokhin Archive and the Secret History of the KGB* (London: Allen Lane/The Penguin Press, 1999)

Arndt, Herbert et al., *Introducing the GDR* (Dresden: Verlag Zeit im Bild, 1971)

Bark, Dennis L., and David R. Gress, *A History of West Germany: From Shadow to Substance*, 1st edn (Oxford: Blackwell, 1989), 2nd edn (Oxford: Blackwell, 1993)

Bechler, Margret, *Warten auf Antwort: ein deutsches Schicksal* (Berlin: Ullstein, 1993)

Becker, Bert, *Die DDR und Grossbritannien 1945/49 bis 1973: Politische, wirtschaftliche und kulturelle Kontakte im Zeichen der Nichtanerkennungspolitik* (Bochum: Universitätsverlag Dr N. Brockmeyer, 1991)

Behnke, Klaus, and Jürgen Fuchs (eds), *Zersetzung der Seele: Psychologie und Psychiatrie in Dienste der Stasi* (Hamburg: Rottbuch Verlag, 1985)

Beyme, Klaus von (ed.), *Policymaking in the GDR* (Aldershot: Gower, 1984)

Binski, Sigurd (ed.), *Zwischen Waldheim und Workuta: Erlebnisse politis-cher Haftlinge 1945–1965* (Berlin: Westkreuz Druckerei, 1994)

Childs, David, and Richard Popplewell, *The Stasi: The East German Intelligence and Security Service* (London: Macmillan, 1996)

Colitt, Leslie, *Spymaster: The Exciting True Story of Markus Wolf* (London: Robson, 1996)

Cradock, Percy, *In Pursuit of British Interests* (London: John Murray, 1997)

——, *Know Your Enemy* (London: John Murray, 2002)

Deighton, Anne (ed.), *Britain and the First Cold War* (London: Macmillan, 1990)

Dobson, Christopher, and Ronald Payne, *The Dictionary of Espionage* (London: Collins, 1984)

Dörnberg, Stefan, *Die Geburt eines neuen Deutschland 1945–1949: die antifaschistisch-demokratische Umwälzung und die Entstehung der DDR* (Berlin: Rütten & Löning, 1959)

——, *Kurze Geschichte der DDR* (Berlin: Dietz Verlag, 1965)

Edwards, G. E., *GDR Society and Social Institutions* (London: Macmillan, 1985)

Eisenmann, Peter, and Gerhard Hirscher (eds), *Bilanz der zweiten deutschen Diktatur* (Munich: Von Hase & Köhler Verlag, 1993)

Finn, Gerhard, *Sachsenhausen 1936–1950: Geschichte eines Lagers* (Berlin: Westkreuz Verlag, 1988)

——, and Karl Wilhelm Fricke, *Politischer Strafvollzug in der DDR* (Cologne: Verlag Wissenschaft & Politik, 1981)

Flockton, C., and E. Kolinsky, *Recasting East Germany: Social Trans-formation After the GDR* (London: Frank Cass, 1999)

Fricke, Karl Wilhelm, *Die DDR-Staatssicherheit: Entwicklung, Strukturen, Aktionsfelder* (Cologne: Verlag Wissenschaft & Politik, 1982)

——, *Politischer Stafvollzug in der DDR* (Cologne: Verlag Wissenschaft & Politik, 1984)

——, *Opposition und Widerstand in der DDR. Ein Politischer Report* (Cologne: Verlag Wissenschaft & Politik, 1984)

——, *Die Staatssicherheitsdienst* (Cologne: Verlag Wissenshaft & Politik, 1989)

Fulbrook, Mary, *Anatomy of a Dictatorship: Inside the GDR, 1949–1989* (Oxford: OUP, 1995)

Garton Ash, Timothy, *In Europe's Name: Germany and the Divided Continent* (London: Jonathan Cape, 1993)

——, *The File: A Personal History* (London: HarperCollins, 1997)

——, *Und Willst Du Nicht Mein Bruder Sein* (Reinbek: Rowohlt, 1981)

Gauck, Joachim, with M. Steinhausen and H. Knabe, *Die Stasi-Akten* (Reinbek: Rowohlt, 1991)

Gellately, R. F., *The Gestapo: Enforcing Racial Policy 1935–45* (Oxford: OUP, 1990)

Geraghty, Tony, *Beyond the Front Line: The Official History of Britain's Secret Military Mission Behind the Iron Curtain, 1946–1990* (London: HarperCollins, 1996)

——, *Brixmis: The Untold Story of Britain's Most Daring Cold War Spy Mission* (London: HarperCollins, 1997)

Gesamtdeutsches Institut/Bundesanstalt für gesamtdeutsche Aufgaben, *Dokumentation zum Staatssicherheitsdienst der ehemaligen DDR in 6 Teilen* (Berlin, 1990)

Glees, Anthony, *Exile Politics During the Second World War* (Oxford: OUP, 1982)

——, *The Secrets of the Service: British Intelligence and Communist Subversion 1939–51* (London: Jonathan Cape, 1986)

——, *Reinventing Germany* (Oxford: Berg, 1996)

Hanhardt, Arthur M., *The German Democratic Republic* (Baltimore: Johns Hopkins Press, 1968)

Herf, Jeffrey, *Divided Memory: The Nazi Past in the Two Germanys* (Cambridge, MA: Harvard University Press, 1997)

HMSO, *The Security Service* (London: HMSO, 1993)

Hoff, Henning, 'Largely the Prisoners of Dr Adenauer's Policy', in Ulrich Pfeil (ed.), *Die DDR und der Westen: Transnationale Beziehungen 1949–1989* (Berlin: Links, 2001)

Holme, K. E. (pseud. Christopher Hill), *The Soviets and Ourselves: Two Commonwealths* (London: n.p., 1945)

Hoover, John P., *East Germany* (London: Sterling, 1977)

Hornsby, Lex (ed.), *Profile of East Germany* (London: Harrap, 1966)

Howarth, Marianne, 'Britain and East Germany: The Politics of Non-recognition' (M.Phil. thesis, University of Nottingham, 1977)

Joppke, Christian, *East German Dissidents and the Revolution of 1989: Social Movement in a Leninist Regime* (London: Macmillan, 1995)

Klopfer, Michael, and Gerhard Michael, *Das Stasi-unterlagen Gesetz und die Pressefreiheit: Verfassungsfragen des Gesetzes uber die Unterlagen des Staatssicherheitsdienstes der ehemaligen DDR* (Gottingen: Duncker & Humblot, 1993)

Knabe, Hubertus, *West-Arbeit des MfS: Das Zusammenspiel von 'Aufklärung' und 'Abwehr'* (Berlin: Links, 1999)

——, *Die Unterwanderte Republik* (Berlin: Propylaen, 2000)

Koestler, Arthur, *Darkness at Noon* (London: Macmillan, 1941)

Krisch, Henry, *German Politics Under Soviet Occupation* (New York: Columbia University Press, 1974)

Krone, Tina et al., *Wenn Wir Unsere Akten Lesen: Handbuch zum Umgang mit den Stasi-Akten* (Berlin: Basisdruck, 1997)

Larres, Klaus, in Klaus Larres with Elizabeth Meehan (eds), *Uneasy Allies: British German Relations and European Integration Since 1945* (Oxford: OUP, 2000)

le Carré, John, *The Spy Who Came in from the Cold* (London: Fontana 1962)

Leonhard, Jörn, and Lothar Funk (eds), *Ten Years of German Unification: Transfer, Transformation, Incorporation?* (Birmingham: University of Birmingham Press, 2002)

McAdams, A. James, *East Germany and Détente* (Cambridge: CUP, 1985)

——, *Judging the Past in Unified Germany* (Cambridge: CUP, 2001)

McElvoy, Anne, *The Saddled Cow: East Germany's Life and Legacy* (London: Faber & Faber, 1992)

Maier, C. S., *Dissolution: The Crisis of Communism and the End of East Germany* (Princeton: Princeton University Press, 1997)

Miller, Barbara, *Narratives of Guilt and Compliance in Unified Germany: Stasi Informers and their Impact on Society* (London: Routledge & Kegan Paul, 1995)

Muller, Klaus-Dieter, ' "Jeder kriminelle Morder is mir lieber . . ." Haftbedingungen für politische Haftlinge in der SBZ und der DDR und ihre Veranderungen von 1945–1989' in *'Die Vergangenheit lasst uns nicht los . . .' Haftbedingungen politischer Gefangener in der SBZ/DDR und deren gesundheitliche Folgen Erweiterte Berichte der gleichnamigen Fachtagung am 25.4.1997 in Hamburg für Arzte, Psychologen, Gutachter, Juristen der Sozialgerichtsbarkeit und Mitarbeiter der Landesversorgunsamter* (Berlin: Gedenkstatte für die Opfer politischer Gewalt Moritzplatz Magdeburg, Der Landesbeauftragte für die Unterlagen des Staatssicherheitsdienstes der ehemaligen DDR des Landes, n.d.)

Naimark, Norman, *The Russians in Germany: A History of the Soviet Zone of Occupation* (Cambridge, MA: Harvard University Press, 1995)

——, 'To Know Everything . . .': Building the East German State, 1945–49 (Working Paper No. 10, Cold War International History Project, The Woodrow Wilson Center, 1994)

——, and Leonid Gibianskii, *The Establishment of Communist Regimes in Eastern Europe, 1944–49* (Boulder, CO: Westview Press, 1997)

Noakes, Jeremy et al., *Britain and Germany in Europe, 1949–1990* (Oxford: OUP, 2002)

Payne Best, S., *The Venlo Incident* (London: Hutchinson, 1949)

Pfeil, Ulrich (ed.), *Die DDR und der Westen: Transnationale Beziehungen 1949–1989* (Berlin: Links, 2001)

Pimlott, Ben, *Harold Wilson* (London: HarperCollins, 1992)

Pincher, Chapman, *Their Trade is Treachery* (London: Sidgwick & Jackson, 1982)

Rehlinger, Ludwig A., *Freikauf. Die Geschaefte der DDR mit politisch Verfolgten 1963–1989* (Berlin: n.p., 1991)

Rimington, Stella, *Open Secret: The Autobiography of the Former Director-General of MI5*, 2nd edn (London: Arrow Books, 2001)

Ross, Corey, *The East German Dictatorship* (London: Edward Arnold, 2002)

Royal Institute of International Affairs, *Annual Reports* (1979 ff.)

Sa'adah, Anne, *Germany's Second Chance: Trust, Justice and Democratization* (Cambridge, MA: Harvard University Press, 1998)

Sahwa, Richard, *The Rise and Fall of the Soviet Union, 1917–1991* (London: Routledge & Kegan Paul, 1999)

Sandford, John, *The Sword and the Ploughshare: Autonomous Peace Initiatives in East Germany* (END Special Report, London: Merlin Press, 1983)

Shukman, Harold (ed.), *Agents for Change: Intelligence Services in the Twenty-First Century* (London: St Ermin's Press, 2000)

Sontheimer, Kurt, and Wilhelm Bleek, *The Government and Politics of East Germany* (London: Hutchinson, 1975)

Steele, Jonathan, *Socialism With a German Face: The State That Came in from the Cold* (London: Jonathan Cape, 1977)

Thatcher, Margaret, *The Downing Street Years* (London: HarperCollins, 1993)

Thompson, E. P., and Dan Smith (eds), *Protest and Survive* (London: Penguin, 1980)

Tusa, John, and Ann Tusa, *The Berlin Blockade* (London: Hodder & Stoughton, 1988)

Wagenlehner, Günther, *Die russischen Bemühungen um die Rehabilitierung der 1941–1956 verfolgten deutschen Staatsbürger* (Bonn: Friedrich Ebert Stiftung, 1999)

Weber, Hermann, *Von der SBZ zur DDR 1945–1968* (Hanover: Verlag für Literatur & Zeitgeschehen, 1966)

——, *Die DDR 1945–1986* (Munich: Oldenbourg, 1988)

——, *DDR: Grundriss der Geschichte* (Hanover: Fackeltraeger Verlag, 1991)

Wolf, Markus, with Anne McElvoy, *Man Without a Face: The Autobiography of Communism's Greatest Spymaster* (London: Jonathan Cape, 1997)

Wolle, Stefan, *Die heile Welt der Diktatur: Alltag und Herrschaft in der DDR 1971–89* (Berlin: Links, 1998)

Woods, R., *Opposition in the GDR Under Honecker, 1971–85: An Introduction and Documentation* (London: Macmillan, 1986)

Wright, Peter, *Spycatcher* (New York: Viking, 1987)

# Index